Social and Applied Aspects of Perceiving Faces

RESOURCES FOR ECOLOGICAL PSYCHOLOGY

A Series of Volumes Edited by:
Robert E. Shaw, William M. Mace, and Michael T. Turvey

REED/JONES • *Reasons for Realism: Selected Essays of James J. Gibson*

WARREN/SHAW • *Persistence and Change*

JOHNSTON/PIETREWICZ • *Issues in the Ecological Study of Learning*

KUGLER/TURVEY • *Information, Natural Law, and the Self-Assembly of Rhythmic Movement*

McCABE/BALZANO • *Event Cognition: An Ecological Perspective*

LOMBARDO • *The Reciprocity of Perceiver and Environment: The Evolution of James J. Gibson's Ecological Psychology*

ALLEY • *Social and Applied Aspects of Perceiving Faces*

Social and Applied Aspects of Perceiving Faces

Edited by
Thomas R. Alley
Clemson University

LEA LAWRENCE ERLBAUM ASSOCIATES, PUBLISHERS
1988 Hillsdale, New Jersey   Hove and London

Copyright © 1988 by Lawrence Erlbaum Associates, Inc.
All rights reserved. No part of this book may be reproduced in
any form, by photostat, microform, retrieval system, or any other
means, without the prior written permission of the publisher.

Lawrence Erlbaum Associates, Inc., Publishers
365 Broadway
Hillsdale, New Jersey 07642

Library of Congress Cataloging-in-Publication Data

Social and applied aspects of perceiving faces.

(Resources for ecological psychology)
Bibliography: p.
Includes indexes.
1. Face perception. 2. Face perception—Social aspects. I. Alley, Thomas R. II. Series.
BF242.S63 1988   302'.12   87-24611
ISBN 0-8058-0163-4

Printed in the United States of America
10 9 8 7 6 5 4 3 2 1

Resources for Ecological Psychology

Edited by
Robert E. Shaw, William M. Mace, and Michael Turvey

This series of volumes is dedicated to furthering the development of psychology as a branch of ecological science. In its broadest sense, ecology is a multidisciplinary approach to the study of living systems, their environments, and the reciprocity that has evolved between the two. Traditionally, ecological science emphasizes the study of the biological basis of *energy* transactions between animals and their physical environments across cellular, organismic, and population scales. Ecological psychology complements this traditional focus by emphasizing the study of *information* transactions between living systems and their environments, especially as they pertain to perceiving situations of significance to planning and execution of purposes activated in an environment.

The late James J. Gibson used the term *ecological psychology* to emphasize this animal-environment mutuality for the study of problems of perception. He believed that analyzing the environment to be perceived was just as much a part of the psychologist's task as analyzing animals themselves, and hence that the "physical" concepts applied to the environment and the "biological" and "psychological" concepts applied to organisms would have to be tailored to one another in a larger system of mutual constraint. His early interest in the applied problems of landing airplanes and driving automobiles led him to pioneer the study of the perceptual guidance of action.

The work of Nicolai Bernstein in biomechanics and physiology presents a complementary approach to problems of the coordination and control of movement. His work suggests that action, too, cannot be studied without reference to the environment, and that physical and biological concepts must be developed together. The coupling of Gibson's ideas with those of Bernstein forms a natural basis for looking at the traditional psychological topics of perceiving, acting, and knowing as activities of ecosystems rather than isolated animals.

The purpose of this series is to form a useful collection, a resource, for people who wish to learn about ecological psychology and for those who wish to contribute to its development. The series will include original research, collected papers, reports of conferences and symposia, theoretical monographs, technical handbooks, and works from the many disciplines relevant to ecological psychology.

Series Dedication

To James J. Gibson, whose pioneering work in ecological
psychology has opened new vistas in psychology and
related sciences, we respectfully dedicate this series.

Contents

	List of Contributors	xi
	Preface	xiii
	Foreword	xv
1	**Social and Applied Aspects of Face Perception: An Introduction**	1
	Thomas R. Alley	

    The Importance of Face Perception   *1*
    Studying Face Perception:
      The Problem of Presenting Faces   *2*
    Studying Face Perception:
      The Ecological Approach   *5*
    Information and Specification   *5*
    The Perception of Facial Growth
      and Aging   *6*

PART I
PERCEPTION OF GROWING FACES

2	**Natural Constraints, Scales of Analysis, and Information for the Perception of Growing Faces**	11
	Leonard S. Mark, Robert E. Shaw, and John B. Pittenger	

    The Ecological Approach to Event Perception   *13*

The Description of Craniofacial Growth 21
The Perception of Craniofacial Growth 30
Social Implications of the Ecological
   Approach to Perception 48

3 The Effects of Growth and Aging on Facial Aesthetics 51
Thomas R. Alley

Craniofacial Development and Perceived Cuteness 52
Age and Facial Attractiveness 55
Closing Remarks 61
Acknowledgment 62

4 The Impact of Age-Related Craniofacial Changes on Social Perception 63
Diane S. Berry and Leslie Zebrowitz-McArthur

Craniofacial Profile Shape 67
Vertical Placement: Forehead Size
   and Chin Size 71
Facial Shape 74
Eye Characteristics 75
Skin Qualities 76
Feature Length 77
Overall Facial Configuration 78
Summary and Conclusions 83
Acknowledgments 87

5 Facial Proportions, Perceived Age, and Caregiving 89
Viki McCabe

Introduction 89
Empirical Studies 90
Summary and Implications 94

PART II
PSYCHOSOCIAL ASPECTS OF NORMAL VARIATION IN FACIAL APPEARANCE

6 Determinants and Consequences of Facial Aesthetics   101
Thomas R. Alley and Katherine A. Hildebrandt

Overview   *101*
Facial Attractiveness   *102*
Facial Cuteness   *133*
Closing Remarks   *136*
Acknowledgment   *140*

7 The Perception of Facial Expression: Individual Regulation and Social Coordination   141
Ross Buck

Evolution and the Perception of Bodily and Social Information   *142*
Communication and Bioregulation   *149*
Face Perception and the Appraisal Process   *158*
Empathy: A New Perspective   *161*
Summary   *164*
Acknowledgments   *165*

8 Physiognomy and Social Perception   167
Thomas R. Alley

Introduction   *167*
Theory and Metatheory   *168*
Facial Features as a Guide to Character: The Issue of Validity   *171*
Reliability: Physiognomic Judgments as Facial Stereotypes   *173*
Concluding Remarks   *185*
Acknowledgment   *186*

PART III
PERCEIVING ABNORMAL FACES

9 Social Aspects of Dentofacial Anomalies   191
William C. Shaw

Introduction   *191*

Part One: The Origins of Facial Prejudice *192*
Part Two: Current Research *199*
Concluding Remarks *216*

10. The Role of Perception in Treatment of Impaired Facial Appearance 217
Judith E. Albino and Lisa A. Tedesco

Social Meanings of Facial Attractiveness and Disfigurement *218*
Evaluating the Aesthetic Impairment of Malocclusion *220*
Professional, Peer, and Self-Perceptions of Malocclusion *222*
Perceptions and Treatment Outcomes *232*
Developmental Influences *234*
Familial Influences *235*
A Final Comment *236*

References 239

Author Index 271

Subject Index 283

List of Contributors

JUDITH E. ALBINO, Professor, Department of Behavioral Sciences, State University of New York at Buffalo, Buffalo, NY 14214

THOMAS R. ALLEY, Assistant Professor, Department of Psychology, Clemson University, Clemson, SC 29634

DIANE S. BERRY, Assistant Professor, Department of Psychology, Southern Methodist University, Dallas, TX 75275

ROSS BUCK, Professor, Departments of Communication Sciences and Psychology, University of Connecticut, Storrs, CT 06268

KATHERINE A. HILDEBRANDT(-KARRAKER), Associate Professor, Department of Psychology, West Virginia University, Morgantown, WV 26506

LEONARD S. MARK, Associate Professor, Department of Psychology, Miami University, Oxford, OH 45056

LESLIE ZEBROWITZ-McARTHUR, Professor, Department of Psychology, Brandeis University, Waltham, MA 02254

VIKI McCABE, University of California at Los Angeles, Los Angeles, CA 90402

JOHN B. PITTENGER, Professor, Department of Psychology, University of Arkansas, Little Rock, AR 72204

ROBERT E. SHAW, Professor, Department of Psychology, University of Connecticut, Storrs, CT 06268

WILLIAM C. SHAW, Professor and Head, Department of Orthodontics, Turner Dental School, University of Manchester, England

LISA A. TEDESCO, Associate Professor, Department of Fixed Prosthodontics and Behavioral Sciences, School of Dental Medicine, State University of New York at Buffalo, Buffalo, NY 14214

Preface

The face is the source of vocal communication and most nonverbal communication, as well as an important source of information for individuals' identity, age, and sex. Hence, faces are often the center of attention when perceiving and evaluating others, and facial appearance is one of the chief factors influencing human social interactions. From this perspective, extensive analysis of perceiving faces seems warranted. The role of facial appearance in regulating or modifying social reactions and interactions is a major concern of this volume, but the perception of faces also constitutes a field of research in which many fundamental questions of perception can be addressed. For instance, understanding the perception of changes in facial expression, orientation, or age requires solutions to the problems of perceptual constancy and to the identification of events. Some basic theoretical issues are addressed in this volume but, as the title indicates, the book focuses on social and applied aspects of face perception.

An important motive for producing this volume is the unfortunate independence with which research and theory on face perception have been pursued across the disciplines of psychology, sociology, dental sciences, and plastic and reconstructive surgery. In contrast to much of the primary literature on face perception, this book is truly interdisciplinary. The contributors to this volume represent a variety of backgrounds, ranging from perceptual psychology to orthodontics. Consequently, they view face perception from varying perspectives and with somewhat different concerns. The contributors all share, however, an appreciation for the tremendous importance of face perception in determining how people, each with their own unique facial appearance and varying degrees of similarity to others, influence and are influenced by the world around them. We also share the basic ecological viewpoint that face perception cannot be understood without reference to the natural contexts in which it plays many important roles.

Although a wide range of topics and issues are addressed in this book, it is not intended to provide a comprehensive look at the research and theory concerning face perception. As a result, face recognition and some other topics do not receive the thorough discussion they deserve. Interested readers should know that there is an extensive literature, and much of it has been cited in this volume or reviewed in one of the other recent books on perceiving faces (see Davies, Ellis, & Shepherd, 1981; Ellis, Jeeves, Newcombe, & Young, 1986; Lucker, Ribbens, & McNamara, 1981).

On the other hand, the chapters in this book fill some notable gaps in the literature reviewing issues in face perception. These chapters have been split into three sections, although these partitions are somewhat arbitrary and clearly overlapping. The chapters in Part I focus on the age-related changes in facial appearance, and show that by studying them we can advance our understanding of both perception and social interaction. The psychosocial aspects of facial attractiveness, facial expression, and other "normal" variations are the subject of Part II. In Part III, the perception, evaluation, and treatment of facial anomalies become the focus of attention.

ACKNOWLEDGMENTS

A number of people provided advice, assistance, or support during the preparation of this book. Of these people, Len Mark deserves special thanks for his encouragement and help over the course of several years during which the book evolved into its present form. The editors of the series *Resources for Ecological Psychology*—Bob Shaw, Michael Turvey and, especially, Bill Mace—have my appreciation both for their confidence that this volume would make a valuable addition to the series, and for their encouragement and assistance during the preparation of this book. Of course, the chapter authors are to be thanked for agreeing to contribute to the book and for spending the time and effort required to produce high quality chapters. A postdoctoral fellowship from the National Institute of Dental Research (T32 DEO7047-07) provided financial support during the initial stages of preparing this book, including a significant portion of the work on chapters 3 and 6.

This volume is dedicated to my daughters Becky and Jennifer.

Thomas R. Alley

Foreword

The publication of this scholarly work on facial appearance and facial perception is more than a compendium of facial facts. It represents a new feature on the developing face of a body of significant scientific inquiry. In explanation, allow me a moment of personal and professional reminiscence.

Fifteen years ago one of my professors suggested that I include a measure of physical attractiveness as a key variable in my doctoral dissertation. I clearly recall my reluctance to pursue this matter that seemed to me destined for empirical disaster. I felt that I was already on shaky ground because I wished to conduct social psychological research to complete my degree requirements in clinical psychology. Besides, I had learned well our cultural cliches insisting that beauty is in the eye of the beholder (and therefore is unreliable), that people should not (and therefore do not) judge books by their covers, and that beauty is only skin deep (and therefore has no effect on the "real person" inside). Primarily to appease my mentor I headed for the library to locate whatever research might be published on the physical attractiveness variable. Although the studies I found were not voluminous, my skepticism weakened somewhat as I began to realize that the variable was not so homely as I had first assumed.

Subsequently, my dissertation's results further reinforced my attitude change and began my devotion to a continuing program of research on the "psychology of physical appearance." I have had the professional pleasure to investigate the influences of various aspects of physical appearance on human behavior in a range of situational contexts. I have witnessed a research literature grow from about 100 studies as we entered the 1970s to about 500 studies published by 1980 to well over 1,000 scientific investigations at the present time. Contrary to early "wisdom," the extant body of knowledge belies the simplicity of physical attractiveness, its unidimensionality in perception, its unidirectionality of psychosocial effects, its theoretical irrelevance, and its exclusive ownership by social psychology.

In this volume, Dr. Alley and his collaborators offer an insightful testimony to the state of our science on a prominent facet of the psychology of physical appearance. Historically, research on the physical attractiveness variable often has involved its manipulation by means of facial photographs consensually validated as globally "attractive" versus "unattractive." Although such research may be criticized for neglecting physical aesthetics below the neck, perhaps such an operational definition of attractiveness reflects researchers' conviction that the face is primary in the conveyance of attractiveness information. Their assumption is quite accurate. This fact does not invite us to ignore the systematic study of below-the-neck attributes, but underscores the importance of the comprehensive study of the face in its own right.

As the present volume attests, the problem is not so much one of facial focus but rather is the restriction of that focus to molar and static perceptions, ignoring the molecular and dynamic aspects of facial appearances and facial perceptions. In reality, we do not befriend, hire, date, elect, convict, marry, teach, or perform surgery upon a two-dimensional monochromatic facial photograph. So can we validly understand physical aesthetics from this stimulus representation by "Watch the birdie . . . Smile . . . Flash"? The answer is both no and yes. The faces move, express, react . . . communicate. The faces change with age. Faces possess precise structure and function that are at once universalistic and individualistic and are ecologically alive in their transactions with their ambient physical, social, intrapersonal, and temporal environments. The face is a whole, is its individual attributes, and is the proportionality and dynamic interaction of its anatomical attributes. And facial perception is indeed a significant ingredient in the interchange among people. This is the complexity of the collective photograph that is depicted by the contributors to this book.

We find here more than a compendium of correlation coefficients and F ratios. Certainly Dr. Alley and his colleagues show scholarly sensitivity to data, but their work balances basic scientific facts and the creativity of criticism in a manner that should enable us to move beyond our current conceptions and knowledge. The future of the scientific understanding derived from a psychology of physical appearance must avoid the parochial perspective and recognize, as these authors have, that fruitful inquiry must truly entail interdisciplinary interest and ownership. This enterprise does not belong to a narrow social psychology but also requires, as we can see, the contributions of perception, optical physics, biology, ethology, anthropology, sociobiology, neuropsychology, cognitive psychology, life-span developmental psychology, orthodontic dentistry, plastic and reconstructive surgery, and clinical psychology. One need only a moment's perusal of the lengthy bibliography of this book to appreciate its interdisciplinary accomplishment. The intra-disciplinary breadth is also impressive, as contributors draw upon perspectives that range from the classical (e.g., the Gibsons' valuable view of object perception) to the contemporary (e.g., the controversy on the primacy of cognition vs. affect). And the book's contents, rich in research findings and researchable ideas, are interwoven by an ecological perspective.

In recent years, we have seen an emergent emphasis of the application of social psychological knowledge to social problems and to the domain of clinical psychology. Dr. Alley and his contributors demonstrate well some of the applied implications of the study of the face. Perhaps reflecting our conscious cultural values and our unconscious discomforts, the psychology of physical appearance historically has attended more to the nature and nurture of beauty than to the opposite end of the continuum of physical aesthetics. However, one can argue that despite our label of the "what is beautiful is good" stereotype, the disadvantages of homeliness exceed the benefits of beauty (cf. Hatfield & Sprecher, 1986).

Accordingly, I must applaud the fact that the present work explores applications vis-á-vis facial anomaly. Whether congenital or traumatic, orofacial deformities or disfigurements are represented in the countenance of many children and adults. Although their experiences range from agony to adaptation, their lives incorporate the complex reality of their aesthetic differences and their frequent pursuit of surgical solutions. The authors juxtapose, and rightly so, our attempts to understand the normal and the anomalous in the study of facial appearance and facial perception. In breadth and depth, this is a volume of substantive and heuristic value to the behavioral science of physical appearance.

It is the common wonder of all men, how among so many millions of faces, there should be none alike.
—Sir Thomas Browne, Religio Medici II. ii.

Thomas F. Cash
Professor of Psychology
Old Dominion University

1 Social and Applied Aspects of Face Perception: An Introduction

Thomas R. Alley
Clemson University

I. The Importance of Face Perception
II. Studying Face Perception: The Problem of Presenting Faces
III. Studying Face Perception: The Ecological Approach
IV. Information and Specification
V. The Perception of Facial Growth and Aging

THE IMPORTANCE OF FACE PERCEPTION

How we are seen by ourselves and by others is tremendously important. Many aspects of physical appearance are potent, and often dominant, determinants of how we see, think, and feel about others. Of these numerous aspects of human physical appearance, facial appearance is probably the most important. The face is widely recognized as the most important area of our bodies in influencing and regulating our interactions with others (see Liggett, 1974; Macgregor, 1974), and with good reason. The face can reflect attitudes and intentions; it is the source of verbal communication and the chief bodily area associated with the expression of emotions and individual identity; and it plays an important, perhaps the most important, role in aesthetic judgments. The head and face also provide information about age and gender which, in turn, are major influences on social interaction. People readily make judgments about attractiveness and personality traits on the basis of even quite limited exposure to a face (or representation of a face). In short, the perception of others' faces is the chief component of social perception and usually exerts a major influence on social interactions. Of course, our facial appearance also influences how we think and feel about ourselves. Consequently facial appearance may affect an individual's behavior virtually any time others are present.

The social importance of facial appearance has made the elaboration or alteration of faces a common activity among humans. Nevertheless, the psychosocial impact of most techniques of changing facial appearance remains largely unexplored by science. This is quite unfortunate, for those who professionally alter facial appearance, particularly plastic surgeons and makeup artists, apparently have much to teach us about the important factors underlying many effects. One need only look at their results. For instance, in the outstanding book on facial makeup for the theater, Buchman (1971) created impressive alterations of age, facial size, and width as well as presenting principles underlying these and other types of change. Many of these principles, such as "the face can be made to appear larger by making some of the features appear smaller" (p. 69), should be subjected to empirical study.

Philosophers, medical practitioners, and others have studied and written about faces for centuries (see Liggett, 1974). Likewise, research on faces has been undertaken throughout the relatively short history of the behavioral sciences, but it is only recently that face perception has begun to emerge as a focus of attention and research activity (cf. Asendorpf, 1982; Goldstein, 1983). The great importance of facial appearance underlies much of this interest and activity. Yet, if faces were somehow considerably less important, we would continue to be fascinated by them. Our biological heritage apparently insures that human faces will be particularly good at attracting and holding our attention beginning at least by early infancy (Maurer, 1985). Furthermore, the uniqueness, prominence, and complexity of human faces make them endlessly fascinating.

STUDYING FACE PERCEPTION: THE PROBLEM OF PRESENTING FACES

Unfortunately, the very complexity of facial appearance that helps make faces so fascinating also makes it difficult to scientifically study face perception. In exploring the social and perceptual implications of variations in facial appearance, careful attention should be paid to the complex structural and dynamic characteristics of living faces. The psychological and social significance of specific facial features cannot be fully disclosed by studies of these features in isolation. (The term *feature* is used here and throughout this volume to refer to the eyes, nose, mouth, etc., as in common parlance, and not in any of the somewhat elusive ways it is often used in cognitive psychology.) Furthermore, variables such as the environmental context, co-occurring gestures and other behaviors certainly modify the effects of facial appearance.

On the other hand, present-day experimental methods require us to drastically reduce this multitude of variables in order to determine with any certainty the effects of specific facial characteristics. For this reason, among others, photographs and drawings have been used in most of the research on face perception. The relative ease and low cost of creating (or finding) photographic and schematic depictions of faces also encourage us to use such "stimuli".

Students of face perception must keep in mind that results obtained with these two-dimensional, static, and often monochromatic representations may not adequately generalize to real and, therefore, dynamic and three-dimensional faces seen in natural contexts. To begin, a distinction can be made between view-specific and face-specific information (Klatzky & Forest, 1984) or, similarly, between "pictorial details" and "structural features" (Bruce, 1982). View-specific (or "pictorial") information consists of the concrete information specific to the particular depiction that was viewed, such as the lighting. Face-specific components include abstract features that are invariant across changes in expression and orientation. These invariants are likely to be the prime support for the recognition of faces in natural contexts, whereas view-specific information may play a large role in standard laboratory tests of memory for facial photographs (cf. Bruce, 1982). This contrast, in turn, may invalidate the practice of generalizing from laboratory studies of face perception or recognition to more natural settings. In other words, the greater importance of view-specific information in many laboratory studies may lead to results that supply a distorted view of the processes involved in face perception under less artificial conditions. A case demonstrating this problem concerns age differences found in recognizing single photographs of faces (e.g., A.D. Smith & Winograd, 1978); these are eliminated when the to-be-remembered faces are presented in multiple views (Bartlett & Leslie, 1986). On the other hand, it seems clear that perception of a single picture of a face can be sufficient to allow the pick-up of information that remains invariant over changes in expression and orientation (e.g., Bruce, 1982; Patterson & Baddeley, 1977). Tasks that require viewers to assess global or configural properties of faces, such as rating facial attractiveness, may produce more reliance on face-specific information than do tasks like face recognition for which view-specific information can provide good support (Bruce, 1982).

The single views selected by psychologists for their research are most often frontal perspectives, whereas orthodontists and other dental–medical practitioners rely predominantly on lateral (anteroposterior) perspectives. The primary factors underlying this difference are, probably, (a) the psychologists' recognition of the importance of frontal views of faces in face-to-face interactions and in detecting facial expression, and (b) the clinicians' greater ability to alter anteroposterior facial relationships. Even though well-motivated, such differences in the facial perspective selected to support different research programs may produce what appear to be inconsistent results and incompatible conclusions. Police records and anthropometric studies require both frontal and lateral views because important characteristics often show up in one view but not in the other.

Photographs may be particularly poor instruments when used to study variables that inherently involve change, such as facial expression. A major problem with using a single static depiction of a face when studying facial events such as the expression of emotion is the fact that a static image can capture only one moment in the sequence of activities that constitute the complete facial event. Moreover, a photograph may not even capture the most significant or representative aspect of facial appearance under study. Nonetheless, research using photographs can reveal a great deal, even about things like facial expressions (e.g., Ekman & Friesen, 1975).

Photographs and drawings may also fail to capture all of the subtleties of facial appearance that are perceived in real faces. This problem is quite evident in the heavy use of poor and/or small photographs, often monochromatic, by psychologists as is usually the case when photographs are gathered from school yearbooks. A further concern is that the process of photography is not particularly conducive to naturalness. For instance, a posed facial expression may be quite atypical, as when a morose person puts on a "happy face."

Despite the heavy reliance on photographs and drawings it would be unfair and untrue to claim that we know little about perceiving faces but lots about perceiving pictures and drawings of them. Still, holes or distortions in the body of knowledge about face perception do surface from time to time when reactions to photographs or drawings fail to duplicate reactions to similar, but real faces. Let the reader beware.

The increasingly popular technique of presenting faces on videotape generally provides a more natural (i.e., ecologically valid) research technique than does showing photos or drawings of faces, but with videotapes of actual faces it is often difficult to identify the important variables that can produce the effects being investigated. The contrast between 'simple' schematic drawings and more complex videotapes highlights a common problem in perceptual research: In studying the perception of faces we must make a trade-off between ecological validity and stimulus control. That is, we must choose between presenting faces with all the richness and complexity required to reproduce natural conditions, on the one hand, or, on the other hand, representing faces with sufficient simplicity so that correlations and causal relations can be clarified. The mutual incompatibility of these goals means that some research on face perception should sacrifice control and clarity for naturalness and ecological validity while other research should forego naturalness to obtain the stimulus control necessary to make causal attributions. Fortunately, research on many issues involving face perception has included studies emphasizing both of these goals.

STUDYING FACE PERCEPTION: THE ECOLOGICAL APPROACH

All of the contributions to this book, to some degree, take an ecological perspective on face perception. Most importantly, this means that we are primarily interested in face perception as a process that affects the interrelations between humans and their natural environments, including social environments. Carefully controlled laboratory studies of representations of faces are typical of the work conducted and cited by most of the authors, but we remain highly sensitive to the dangers of generalizing from such studies to natural situations. Moreover, these experimental studies are performed primarily to address some problem or issue of real significance in natural settings.

In accord with an ecological viewpoint, many of the authors treat the adaptive significance of face perception and its effects as one of the central issues to be addressed. Thus, we often wonder why we see faces as we do, and why various facial characteristics produce the responses they do. We are not satisfied with simply compiling a list of perceptual phenomena. Hence, many reasons for variation in the affective responses to faces are mentioned in this book, but the explanations seen as most basic and generally receiving the greatest attention are those that trace affective responses to selective advantages during human evolution.

Another characteristic of an ecological approach to perception is apparent in the tendency to consider *what* information is available in faces before tackling the question of *how* we deal with or "process" this information. From this ecological perspective, the significance of perceiving faces that are, for example, upside down or portrayed in negative reversal film extends only so far as these phenomena bear on naturally occurring processes with some adaptive significance.

INFORMATION AND SPECIFICATION

From an ecological perspective facial appearance, even when portrayed by two-dimensional drawings or photographs, should influence psychosocial responses of others, for many physical attributes are specific to, or correlated with, certain behavioral tendencies or social affordances. Thus, the physical attributes that permit us to recognize the infancy of a young child specify certain limitations of this individual's behavioral competence. Likewise, it is logically possible and intuitively plausible that head size and mental capacity are slightly correlated such that perceived head size could provide a clue for mental capacity (see Chap. 8). In these two examples we see that physical attributes can provide information about others that can be either definite or probabilistic; that is, such information will have varying degrees of reliability. We should distinguish specification and the less reliable probabilistic information by restricting the use of "clues" or "cues" to probabilistic information, although nonecological perceptual psychologists (e.g., Rock, 1984) seldom make this distinction.

This distinction between specification and probabilistic information is not a simple dichotomy. Instead, the information that can be gleaned from facial appearance, like perceptual information in general, falls on a continuum from information that invariably specifies certain structural or functional characteristics to information that signifies certain structural or functional characteristics in a probabilistic manner ranging from near-specificity (high reliability) to so unreliable that the information is of no practical significance, and on to misinformation based on uncorrelated or inversely correlated links between facial characteristics and ascribed attributes. This range of informational specificity must be kept in mind to properly understand the psychosocial effects of facial appearance. The undeniably probabilistic information underlying many aspects of social perception contrasts with the typically highly specific information underlying the perception of basic properties of the physical environment like surface layout (see J.J. Gibson, 1979) as well as the perception of relative age in human faces (see Chap. 2). At the same time, only probabilistic information exists in faces for the perception of absolute age. Thus, "judgment" of relative age may occur through automatic purely perceptual processes, whereas judgment of absolute age (and other characteristics not specified in facial appearance) is more likely to stem from conscious, effortful and inferential processes (cf. Kassin & Baron, 1986). A perceptual system designed to function in a world of probabilistic events and information must sometimes operate as an "intuitive statistician" (Brunswik, 1956).

THE PERCEPTION OF FACIAL GROWTH AND AGING

I turn finally to some introductory remarks directed at the four chapters that compose Part I of this book. All four of these chapters focus on age-related changes in facial appearance; a topic of much significance. The head and face are important sources of information about growth and aging. The perception of age, in turn, is an important determinant of social interactions. Hence, age-related changes in facial appearance are, to some extent, specific to, or correlated with, certain behavioral tendencies or social affordances. Thus, the physical attributes that permit us to recognize the infancy of a young child *specify* certain limitations of this individual's knowledge and behavioral competence. Even young children realize that facial appearance changes as we grow and age, but these changes provide numerous puzzles for perceptual and social psychologists.

In the opening chapter, Bob Shaw and two of his former students provide a review of their important research program on the perception of craniofacial growth and aging. Prior to this review, the authors elucidate the influence of J.J. Gibson's work on their research program in particular, and on assumptions and theories in perceptual psychology in general. Most important here is the recognition of natural constraints on perception provided in natural environments. Tribute is also paid to the naturalist D'Arcy Thompson for his insights in *On Growth and Form* (1917/1942), a book thought to be among the finest in the annals of science (Gould, 1971). Thompson's classic book highlights the importance of considering scale of analysis and physical constraints for understanding morphogenesis. Proceeding from their discussion of the contributions of Thompson and Gibson to their own research, Mark, Shaw, and Pittenger are able to take what might be seen as a number of interesting but strange studies and show how they can be interwoven to form a remarkably coherent account of face perception. Moreover, as these authors take pains to show, important insights into social, applied, and theoretical aspects of face perception may be found in this research program.

The remaining three chapters all concern psychosocial aspects of growth and aging. Chapter 3 examines the aesthetic aspects of age-related changes in facial appearance, such as the effects of growth on facial cuteness and the impact of aging on facial attractiveness. The research reviewed in this chapter reveals that the simple notion that aging is detrimental to facial aesthetics, a message conveyed with remarkable frequency by the mass media, is not wholly substantiated by scientific study.

The following two chapters deal with the impact of age-related changes in facial appearance and perceived age on cognitive and behavioral responses of others. These two chapters are primarily concerned with ecologically significant social effects of the changes in craniofacial characteristics associated with human growth and development. An ethological perspective on these changes produces the expectation that they will have important social effects, for the recognition of maturational status is a basic and vital part of social perception. While much research remains to be done, the existing studies provide a sufficient basis for drawing some conclusions. For instance, the existing experimental studies support the ethological hypothesis that a youthful facial appearance tends to evoke a variety of favorable responses (see Chaps. 3, 4, and 5). Berry and Zebrowitz-McArthur review the social effects of facial aging, with a focus on the generally favorable consequences of relatively youthful facial characteristics. McCabe's short chapter looks the other way, arguing that facial characteristics that make children look older than their actual age can, and probably do, produce some detrimental effects. In all four of the chapters in the first section, most of the relevant research is very recent, reflecting a remarkable neglect of these topics by past researchers countered by a recent surge of interest and research activity.

I PERCEPTION OF GROWING FACES

2 Natural Constraints, Scales of Analysis, and Information for the Perception of Growing Faces

Leonard S. Mark
Miami University (Ohio)

Robert E. Shaw
University of Connecticut

John B. Pittenger
University of Arkansas at Little Rock

I. The Ecological Approach to Event Perception
   A. Natural Constraints on What
      There is to be Perceived
   B. The Importance of Craniofacial Growth:
      Social and Applied Concerns
   C. Events as the Primary Unit of Analysis
   D. Craniofacial Growth:
      A Slow Biological Event
II. The Description of Craniofacial Growth
   A. The Concept of a Geometric Transformation
   B. Transformations and the Description of Growth
      1. Transformations as descriptions of the effects of physical forces
   C. Scales of Analysis
   D. Finding a Growth Transformation
III. The Perception of Craniofacial Growth
   A. Defining the Class of Transformations Perceived as Growth
      1. Initial studies
      2. Shortcomings of the initial studies
      3. Studies on how growth can be distinguished from other styles of change
      4. Applying cardioidal strain to more realistic representations
   B. Abstractness of Information About Growth
      1. Delimiting the structures to which cardioidal strain produces growth
IV. Social Implications of the Ecological Approach to Perception

As psychologists studying human perception, we have frequently been asked why we are interested in the perception of growing faces. Each of us has been told many times during colloquia or informal presentations that although this growth research "sounds interesting, it isn't really psychology." Does research on the perception of craniofacial growth contribute to our understanding of fundamental problems in perception and cognition? After all, prior to the publication of Pittenger and Shaw's (1975a) study, there was no substantial literature or systematic psychological research on the subject. Moreover, the description of morphogenesis is usually viewed as the province of biology.

Many queries about our growth research reflect a second concern: one that pertains to some of the activities we have pursued during the course of our research. As part of our efforts to describe the perceptual information about growing faces and to validate a model of *craniofacial growth,* many activities have been performed that are not in the class of endeavors in which psychologists are typically engaged. These activities have included studying head-neck anatomy, clinical cephalometrics, radiology, and techniques for anthropometric measurement as well as learning orthodontic and surgical criteria for the evaluation of facial disorders, participating in a "growth seminar" in a School of Dentistry, and serving as members of a multidisciplinary clinical team concerned with the diagnosis, evaluation, treatment and management of craniofacial disorders. Our pursuit of these activities was driven primarily by an applied goal: developing a model of craniofacial growth that could enable surgeons and orthodontists to anticipate the effects of growth in their treatment of children with craniofacial disorders. Yet some of these endeavors eventually had a significant impact on the design of several perceptual studies that dealt primarily with fundamental issues in event perception (e.g., Mark, Shapiro, & Shaw, 1986; Mark & Todd, 1983, 1985; Mark, Todd, & Shaw, 1981).

Although the assigned mission of this chapter is to survey our 15 years of work on the perception of growing faces, we want to communicate more than what we did and learned about craniofacial growth. We also want to elucidate some of the reasons for our interest in this biological event—show how its study has contributed to our understanding of fundamental problems in perception and explore some of the tacit assumptions and applied concerns that have shaped the course our investigation.

To realize these objectives, we begin by examining two enterprises to which our project owes a substantial debt: James and Eleanor Gibson's ecological approach to perception (E.J. Gibson, 1969; J.J. Gibson, 1950, 1966, 1979) and D'Arcy Thompson's (1917/1942) approach to morphogenesis. The Gibsons have emphasized the importance of *natural constraints* on events as the basis of information for the perceiver about the world as well as about the perceiver's relationship to the world. D'Arcy Thompson's study of morphogenesis has demonstrated the importance of choosing the appropriate *scale of analysis* for examining the growth event. Moreover, his treatise helped us to identify the specific physical constraints that were responsible for the global remodeling of the craniofacial complex due to growth.

THE ECOLOGICAL APPROACH
TO EVENT PERCEPTION

The study of human perception has a long history in philosophy and psychology. With Kepler's (1611) discovery of the optics of image formation, one of the fundamental problems of perception emerged: The image on the retina was found to be neither a copy of the world nor an accurate depiction of our perceptual experience. Rather, it stands in poor correspondence to both. For example, the image is inherently two dimensional, yet we experience the world as three dimensional. Furthermore, any retinal image can be produced by an infinite number of scenes. This mismatch between the world and the resultant sensory stimulation poses a fundamental challenge for understanding why perceptual experience is usually such a good representation of the world. In order to limit the possible environmental scenes to which a given retinal image might correspond, *constraints* had to be introduced. Since Kepler, students of perception have appealed to internal epistemic (i.e., cognitive) processes as the source of the requisite constraints. While the origin of these epistemic processes, either inborn (nativism) or through experience (empiricism), has long been debated, their existence, indeed their necessity, has not been questioned until recently.

Natural Constraints
on What There Is To Be Perceived

In 1950 James Gibson introduced another source of constraints on the act of perception, namely the *terrestrial environment*. In doing so, he laid the foundation for an entirely different approach to perception.

Gibson observed that traditional perceptual theory has been directed toward understanding the perception of an object in otherwise *empty unstructured space* he termed this view the *air theory*. What was perceived (i.e., the environment and the events taking place in the environment) was neglected entirely. In contrast, Gibson sought to determine the consequences of taking the nature of the terrestrial environment into account. Regularities in the structure of the environment impose *constraints* on the pattern of light to the observer. This "ground theory" supposed that what was perceived was not empty space, *per se*, but the layout of surfaces yoked to the ground plane by gravity. Gibson demonstrated that while the optical projection of points floating in empty unstructured space was indeterminate with respect to their distance from point of observation, relations in the retinal image did correspond to the relative distance of landmarks in the environment, *assuming that those landmarks reside on the ground plane* (Fig. 2.1). And, Gibson has shown that a natural perspective provides information about whether an object is yoked to the ground plane. Object position, relative to the ground plane, is specified by the shadows cast by objects onto the ground plane. This observation challenged the traditional starting point from which fundamental problems and theories of perception have emerged.

Gibson had been led to appreciate the importance of the terrestrial environment partly as a result of the research that he had undertaken during the Second World War on training pilots to land aircraft (J.J. Gibson, 1947). Prior to that time, traditional perceptual theory assumed that perceived object size (i.e., size constancy) was maintained only at relatively short distances from the point of observation. As the object receded from the observer, its perceived size was believed to diminish, though not at the same rate as its image on the retina. The proposal that size constancy breaks down at some distance from the observer was necessary to account for the fact that at some far distance, the object ceased to be visible.

The Gibsons examined this assumption on a flat, evenly textured field. A wooden rod was placed at a variable distance from an observer, who was asked to estimate its size relative to a set of standards placed near the observer. These judgments were repeated for rods of different sizes at distances up to 784 yards. In contrast to the prediction of traditional perceptual theory, size constancy did not break down over the range of distances used in the experiment: Estimations of object height remained constant, even at the farthest distance, and size judgments were highly accurate at all distances. These findings posed two serious challenges for traditional perceptual theory: *First,* why didn't size constancy break down at the farther distances as

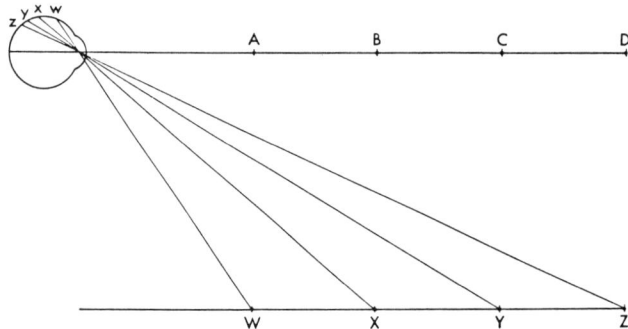

FIG. 2.1. Two formulations of the problem of distance perception. The "air theory of perception" (top) shows four points, A, B, C, D, in space that project to the same point on the retina. Since they have a common projection to the retina, there can be no information about distance given by any retinal projection. The "ground theory of perception" (bottom) shows four locations, W, X, Y, Z on a ground plane. These points are discriminable on the retina. The corresponding image represents a surface extending away from the observer. Note: From James J. Gibson: The Perception of the Visual World, p. 62. Copyright© 1959 by James J. Gibson, renewed 1977 by Houghton Mifflin Company. Used by permission.

2. PERCEPTION OF GROWING FACES   15

predicted? *Second,* how could the accuracy of observers' size estimations be explained in light of the supposed indeterminacy of the proximal stimulation?

The Gibsons' analysis of this situation revealed that the size and distance of the rods were *not* ambiguous if one took into account that the rods were planted on the ground. And, they argued, in the natural terrestrial environment, objects are yoked to the ground plane by gravity. Furthermore, that state of affairs is specified in the way shadows are attached to objects and cast onto the ground plane. (Objects are seen as floating "magically" in the air only under the most contrived circumstances. In such cases perceived size is more variable.) Given this "natural constraint" on the construction of the terrestrial environment, the Gibsons were able to identify a particular optical relationship between each rod and environment that was specific to the size of the rod and was preserved over distance. When a rod was seen to rise above the horizon, a ratio of the amounts of the rod extending above and below the horizon was maintained (invariant) over distance. This relationship was referred to as the *horizon–ratio invariant* (Fig 2.2). (A similar ratio was found to exist when the point of observation was such that the object did not extend above the horizon.) As a source of information about object size, the horizon-ratio invariant was based on two universal "facts of the aerial terrestrial environment": (a) objects rest on the ground plane, and (b) a horizon exists that relates an observer to the ground plane. From a generalization of this simple situation, James Gibson realized that the very nature of the terres-

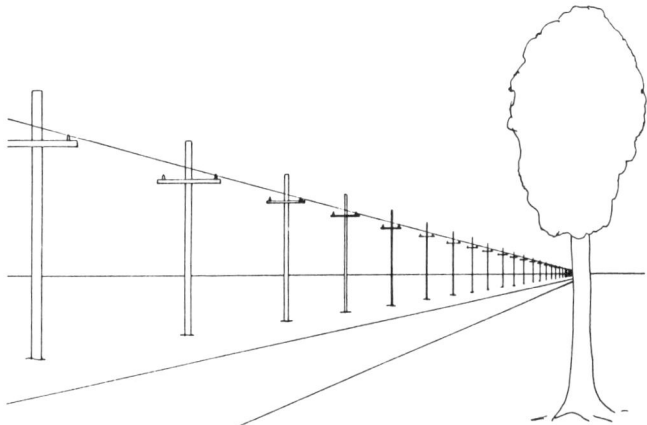

FIG. 2.2. The invariant horizon ratio for terrestrial objects. The telephone poles in this display are all cut by the horizon in the same ratio. The proportion differs for objects of different heights. The line where the horizon cuts the tree is just as high above the ground as the point of observation, that is, the height of the observer's eye. Hence, everyone can see his own eye-height on the standing objects of the terrain. Note: The Ecological Approach to Visual Perception (p. 165) by J.J. Gibson, 1979, p. 165. Houghton Mifflin Co. Reprinted by permission of the publisher.

trial environment could provide a source of constraints that might obviate the need for cognitive processes in perception.

As a psychologist in the functionalist tradition of American Pragmatism, Gibson was greatly concerned with the problem of *what* our perceptual systems have evolved to perceive. The evolutionary pressures on the human perceptual system must be rooted, at least in part, in the natural constraints (physical properties of surfaces and their layout) of the terrestrial environment. J.J. Gibson (1979, chapters 1-3) devoted considerable energy to identifying those events that are crucial to an animal's well-being. His survey of an animal's niche played an important role in delineating viable perceptual units of analysis. Gibson's pragmatic bent also led him to examine the utility of perception for providing information to control action. Perceiving and acting were seen as mutually supportive. Perception provides the animal with information about the environment for guiding action, which, in turn, provides the organism with new information about the environment.

From this ecological perspective, the study of perception began by delineating those natural constraints on the scene or event to be perceived as well as the importance of perception to the actor (J.J. Gibson, 1979). With those constraints in mind, the next task was to identify the relationships in the stimulus energy that are specific to properties of the layout and changes in layout of the environment. In short, Gibson began his study of perception by (to paraphrase Mace, 1977) asking what the head's inside of, rather than what goes on inside the head.

This strategy has important implications for dealing with a problem that is central to both studies of perception and social psychology: namely the basis for our belief in physical reality. In Asch's (1956) classic work on social conformity, virtually all of his subjects, regardless of whether they actually conformed to the judgments of the group, were extremely disturbed by the obvious discrepancy between their perception of the lengths of the lines and the group's. The situation proved so disturbing because it violated the basic assumption of each person that people share the same physical reality. What is the basis for this assumption?

Gibson's analysis of the optical information available, both at a glance and over time, as the observer moves around the world, demonstrates the basis for the consistency of the information provided by our senses. More importantly, the ecological survey of the natural constraints on the layout of the terrestrial/social environment establishes a lawful, physical basis for optical information that is specific to its source. It is precisely those lawful physical relations between observers and their environment that constitutes the basis of the shared "physical reality" that is crucial to our existence and well-being. The psychosocial consequences of perceived age level provide a useful illustration of these pragmatic concerns. In the next section, we briefly examine the psychosocial significance of the growth event.

The Importance of Craniofacial Growth: Social and Applied Concerns

Growth-related changes in craniofacial structure can have a significant effect on human action. Ethological studies suggest that perceived age is a significant factor in regulating the type and amount of behavior directed toward an individual. Age-variant characteristics like head shape have a vital bearing on various parental behaviors such as caregiving, warning, and protection (Alley, 1986). McCabe (chap. 5) examines some intriguing evidence that head shape may be a factor in at least some instances of child abuse. Age-related changes in the shape of the human head have other important consequences for human behavior (see Berry & Zebrowitz-McArthur, chap. 4).

Facial attractiveness (aesthetics) affects interpersonal relationships in numerous settings (Alley & Hildebrandt, chap. 6). Although the physiognomic enterprise ultimately failed to identify strong links between facial appearance and characteristics such as intelligence, personality, criminality, people do make such attributions about these characteristics of other people (see Alley, chap. 8). Changes in facial appearance, then, can be expected to have an important psychosocial impact on the individual. Since growth produces an extensive alteration of the entire head, it is likely to have some effect on facial aesthetics. In his review of the evidence to date, Alley (chap. 3) is skeptical that the nature of this impact is well understood. Nonetheless, he maintains that aging and perceived age level do affect facial attractiveness.

In light of the psychosocial importance of the human face, it is not surprising to discover that people attach great importance to their appearance. This is certainly evident in the ever increasing numbers of people who undergo various types of craniofacial treatment (e.g., plastic and maxillofacial surgery, orthodontics) primarily to improve their visage. These clinical enterprises make especially important contributions to the treatment of young children with serious craniofacial disorders. The technical capabilities of surgeons and orthodontists in treating even the most extensive disfigurements and deformities are truly remarkable. Yet until recently, there have been important limitations on the application of these treatment procedures to growing children. Unless practitioners are able to incorporate the effects of growth into their treatment plans, the immediate treatment outcome is likely to deteriorate as a result of normal, growth-related changes. Thus, "relapses" will necessitate further treatment and are often more difficult to treat than the original problem.

In the absence of a viable means for predicting the effect of growth on the immediate treatment outcome, many practitioners choose to begin treatment only after the child's growth is nearly complete. This decision has marked consequences for the psychological well-being of such children: They often have to go through childhood with a serious facial disfigurement. Too often, these children are subject to ridicule and experience difficulty in establishing strong interpersonal relations during childhood and adolescence (Shaw, chap. 9). Practitioners need a growth model that would allow them to anticipate the effects of growth in their treatment plan. Thus, another motivation for our study of craniofacial growth was to contribute to clinical efforts to develop a means for predicting the long-term effects of growth on treatment outcomes.

Events as the Primary Unit of Analysis

In the formative stage of his ecological approach to perception, J.J. Gibson (1950) adhered to the retinal image as a static projection of the world. Later on, he abandoned the retinal image in favor of the "ambient optic array" (J.J. Gibson, 1961, 1979), whereby properties of the environment were specified over time as the (observer's) point of observation moved through the environment.[1] Gibson observed that many classic demonstrations of inaccuracies of perception (e.g., those produced by the Ames Room) occurred only with a stationary, monocular vantage point. As soon as the observer moved, the ruse was revealed. Throughout the remainder of his career Gibson emphasized the importance of time and motion in the availability of information. He was able to show that many sources of information about the world and the observer's own movement through the environment were given, not in an instantaneous glance, but over time and multiple points of observation. To take but one example, consider the traditional pictorial depth cue of "interposition." This "cue" was widely acknowledged to be potentially misleading. However, when objects and/or the observer moved, the progressive hiding and/or revealing of one surface by another was specific to a particular configuration of surfaces (J.J. Gibson, Kaplan, Reynolds, & Wheeler, 1969; Kaplan, 1969).

Our investigation of craniofacial growth has attempted to develop Gibson's fundamental insights regarding the starting point for visual perception. Shaw (Pittenger & Shaw, 1975a; R.E. Shaw, McIntyre, & Mace, 1974; Shaw & Pittenger, 1977) viewed the *ambient optic array* as a reflection of the appropriate "unit of analysis" for describing the terrestrial environment. Gibson had demonstrated that many invariant relations between the environment

---

[1] In talking about the "ambient optic array," J.J. Gibson (1961, 1979) observed that the world structures (reflects) light to every potential point of observation in the transparent medium (air). This pattern of light surrounding any potential point of observation is specific to the layout and properties of surfaces in the environment, and, as such, is potentially informative about the world. The act of perceiving begins when a potential point of observation is actually occupied by the eye of an observer. By looking in a particular direction from a particular location, the observer samples the rich structure in the "optic array." Gibson further identified additional information about the environment for observers as they move their point of observation through the optic array, that is, as they move. Thus, for Gibson, the ambient optic array constitutes an informational basis for perception, one in which the challenge facing the perceiver is to detect information about the world, rather than construct a representation of the world from impoverished snippets. (See J.J. Gibson, 1979, chap. 5 for a detailed examination of the ambient optic array.)

and optical stimulation are revealed only over time. This encouraged Shaw to begin, not with static images, but with *events* involving a *structure undergoing a "style of change"* over time.[2]

To distinguish among the myriad of events typically encountered in natural environments, observers must detect both the *structure* (e.g., object) undergoing change and the particular *style of change* inherent in the event (e.g., rotating, bending, stretching, bouncing, running, walking, or growing). An object can undergo many different styles of change. A child, for example, can run, walk, bend, stretch, spin, smile, or grow. By the same token, many different objects can be seen to participate in a given event and, we postulate, undergo the same style of change: Records, tires, skaters, dancers, balls, pinwheels can all be seen as "spinning." With reference to "growth," a potentially infinite class of children can all be recognized as growing older. A basic problem in understanding the perception of an event is to determine how people are able to identify both the style of change and structure undergoing change.

Craniofacial Growth: A Slow Biological Event

Our investigation of craniofacial growth is fundamentally a study of event perception, which attempts to delineate the information for a complex biological change and for the structures that can be seen to undergo that style of change. As the human head grows from birth to early adulthood, it changes in both size and shape. An infant's head typically has a diminutive facial mask relative to its cranium. Within 2 years after birth, the facial mask starts to grow more rapidly than the cranium, thereby resulting in a marked change in facial proportions. The cranium typically approaches its adult size prior to the age of 10 years, whereas the face continues to grow well into early adulthood. Craniofacial growth, then, entails a salient style of change that can be recognized across a wide range of craniofacial structures.

An important objective in presenting this overview is to show how our work has contributed to a broader investigation of how human observers are

---

[2] In developing our conception of events as involving a structure undergoing a style of change, we acknowledge a significant debt to J.J. Gibson. Yet, at the same time, we note that Gibson did not use the phrase "style of change" to describe transformations in the world. In his writing he says only that:

> Continuous optical transformations can yield two kinds of perceptions at the same time, one of change and one of nonchange. The perspective transformation of a rectangle, for example was always perceived as something rotating and something rectangular. This suggests that the transformation, as such, is one of a kind of stimulus information for motion, and that the invariants under transformation are another type of stimulus information, for constant properties of the object. (J.J. Gibson, 1966b)

Although the framework for event analysis that was developed during the course of our growth research was inspired by Gibson's writings, it represents an elaboration and extension of his work.

able to recognize different styles of change. To date, there has been a considerable volume of research on the perception of *inanimate, nonbiological* events. Much of this work has focused on the analysis of *rigid* motions involving translations or rotations. However, many events involve *nonrigid, inanimate* motions, as bending and stretching. Other nonrigid events entail animate or biological styles of change, such as walking, running, and other forms of human movement, growth, facial expression and social interactions. (See Todd, 1982, for a list of relevant studies.)

Research on animate or biological events is of special significance to our concern with craniofacial growth. Inspired by the classic study of Michotte on causality, Heider and Simmel (1944) produced a now-classic 3-minute cartoon showing geometric figures (triangles and circles) acting out a complex social event involving such motives and emotions as aggression, courtship, fear, and frustration. A more recent impetus to studies of biological events derives from Johansson's (1973, 1975) patch+light demonstrations. These displays show spots of light in the dark attached to the joints of an otherwise invisible actor. In the absence of movement, these displays look like random dots: The human form to which they are attached is unrecognizable. However, when the actor starts to move, these point-light displays provide sufficient information for observers to distinguish not only the existence of a person, but the type of activity being performed (Johansson, 1973), the gender of the actor (Barclay, Cutting, & Kozlowski, 1978), the identity of the actor (Cutting & Kozlowski, 1977), the amount of force exerted by an actor in performing various activities such as lifting a box (Runeson & Frykholm, 1981), and even the intention of an actor to deceive the observer about the weight being lifted (Runeson & Frykholm, 1983).

In each of these studies of rigid or nonrigid styles of change, the event is specified by the relative motions of either one part of an object with respect to another or one object with respect to another. Growth, however, has a notable difference: It takes place over such long temporal periods that actual movement is too slow to be visible to the naked eye. The observer views only the *displacement* of craniofacial morphology, not the motion itself. This introduces a distinction between fast and slow events, a distinction that is orthogonal to the dichotomies of rigid and nonrigid or animate and inanimate events (R.E. Shaw & Pittenger, 1978). *Fast events* present observers with motion through which the style of change inherent to the event is defined. For *slow events*, like the displacement of the hour hand on a clock, blooming of flowers, and growth and evolution of biological forms, the motion is too slow to be noticed. The event, nonetheless, is perceived.

The distinction between slow and fast events raises an important question. Can the perceptual information for both types of events be described using the same principles or will additional cognitive processes (e.g., memory) be required to explain the apprehension of slow events? R.E. Shaw and Pittenger

(1978) and Warren and Shaw (1985) presented a detailed discussion of how slow and fast events can be understood within the same perceptual framework.

We now turn to our study of craniofacial growth. First, we explore the problems entailed in describing a complex biological event like craniofacial growth, and how the work of D'Arcy Thompson guided our efforts to identify both the natural constraints on the growth event and a geometric transformation that describes the global remodeling of the head due to growth. With that preparation we survey the contributions of perceptual research on craniofacial growth to our understanding of the fundamental problems in event perception identified previously.

THE DESCRIPTION OF CRANIOFACIAL GROWTH

From the ecological perspective, the study of any event—rigid or nonrigid, animate or inanimate, slow or fast—begins with a description of the event for the purpose of delineating the perceptual information specific to that class of events. The initial task in our investigation of craniofacial growth was, therefore, to develop a description of the global remodeling of the craniofacial complex entailed in this complex biological event. The requisite description had to capture those changes that were common to the myriad of structures that could be recognized as growing. Prior to confronting this challenge, we had to find an appropriate tool for describing craniofacial growth.

The Concept of a Geometric Transformation

The description of rigid styles of change is relatively straightforward, because formal descriptions of translations and rotations are well known and readily accessible. These formal descriptions are written in the language of *mathematical transformations*.[3] In mathematics these are functions that map the elements of a given nonempty set (domain) into or onto the elements of a second

---

[3] Although J.J. Gibson did discuss transformations extensively, he never gave an unqualified endorsement to our use of these mathematical entities to express the structural effects of change. He said they are not adequate to describe the information for event perception because only special cases of change are truly structure preserving. He did say, however, that it may be helpful, though insufficient, to examine mathematical transformations of the optic array. It is important to realize that our use of mathematical transformations is not to describe perturbations in the optic array. Rather, we are attempting to describe the pattern of craniofacial change associated with the growth event in the world. This invariant pattern of change is a product of the natural constraints on the growth event. To date, we have yet to examine the information about growth in the optic array.

nonempty set (range). To understand the notion of a transformation, imagine a two-dimensional object represented as a set of points—for example, a halftone photograph of the sort printed in the newspaper. The position of each point can be described using two coordinates. In some cases it is advantageous to use the standard Cartesian system, where X and Y represent distances from some reference point (the origin) on two perpendicular axes. In other cases, a polar coordinate system is more convenient. Again, two coordinates are also used: The distance of the point from the origin is denoted by R, while the angle or direction of the point from the origin is denoted by θ (Fig. 2.3). A geometric transformation provides a function for systematically altering the original coordinates of the object, thereby producing a new pair of coordinates for each point, (x', y') or (r', θ'), which are functionally related to the original coordinates $[x' = f(x), y' = f(y); \theta' = f(\theta), r' = f(r)]$.

Any system of equations relating the original and transformed coordinates can be interpreted in two ways. In one sense, these equations represent a change in the original coordinate system, such as when data are transformed from rectangular coordinates to polar coordinates (Fig. 2.3). Alternately, these equations represent a change in an object within a fixed coordinate system. The latter interpretation is easily demonstrated by considering the different ways in which a square object can be transformed (Fig. 2.4).

It is important to recognize two facts about spatial coordinate transformations: First, each transformation changes certain properties of the object to which it is applied, but leaves others unchanged; second, transformations differ with respect to those properties that they leave unchanged. To illustrate, consider a square that is rotated about a point within its perimeter. *Rotation* changes the location of every point on the square except the center of rotation. However, the square's metric shape (that is, the set of distances between pairs of corresponding or homologous points on the object) is unchanged. Rotation

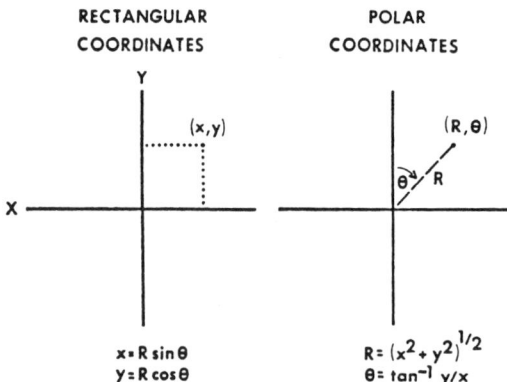

FIG. 2.3. An illustration of rectangular and polar coordinate systems along with equations for transforming coordinates between the two systems.

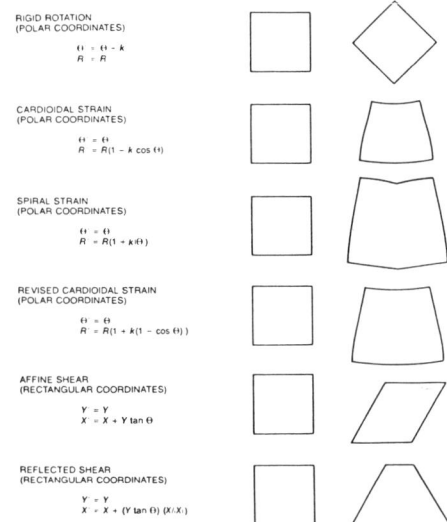

FIG. 2.4. The shape of an object can be altered within a fixed coordinate system by applying a variety of geometric transformations, six of which are listed by name and also represented in the form of the equations at the left. (The fixed coordinate system is given in parentheses.) The effects of the different transformations on a square are shown at right.

will produce just these effects on any planar figure. In the language of mathematics, the properties which do not change under a transformation are said to be "invariant" under it. Another transformation that preserves the square's metric shape is *translation*. Unlike rotation, however, translation changes the coordinates of every point on the object.

Now consider a similarity transformation, which results in a uniform expansion or contraction of an object. A similarity transformation changes the position of all points, with the exception of the center of expansion or contraction, as well as the distances between every pair of points. However, it preserves the proportions of the figure. Thus, if a square doubled in size, it is bigger, but the lengths of the sides of the new square remain equal to each other and the diagonal is still the length of one side times the square root of two. Unlike translation and rotation, a similarity transformation is said to be a nonrigid transformation, since the distances between all pairs of points are changed. The properties maintained under a similarity transformation are different from those left invariant under rotation or translation.

Each geometric transformation produces a mathematically distinct style of change that is independent of the particular object to which it is applied. Rotation, for example, entails the same style of change whether it is applied to a square, a triangle, or an ellipse; at the same time, rotation produces a distinct style of change. This property makes transformations especially useful tools for describing a salient style of change that can be perceived over a variety of objects. The abstract event of rotation can easily be recognized when it is applied to various objects including objects the observer has never seen before. In the next section of this chapter, we examine how these properties of mathematical transformations might enable psychologists to distinguish the information about perceptually salient styles of change, notably craniofacial growth.

Transformations and the Description of Growth

D'Arcy Thompson pioneered the use of geometric transformations in the study of morphogenesis. In his classic work, *On Growth and Form* (1917/1942), Thompson presented graphic representations of coordinate systems in which he had embedded a biological form. By transforming the coordinate system (carrying along the biological form with it), he was able to produce ontogenetic or phylogenetic relatives of the original object (Fig 2.5). These transformed coordinate systems provided a graphic depiction of the transformation associated with each morphogenetic event. Thompson's special insight and contribution lay in his *graphic* representation of a seemingly complex transformation of a biological form with a seemingly simpler object, such as a Cartesian grid. His drawings made it possible to "see" the abstract nature of the change, independently of the particular form undergoing change, thereby

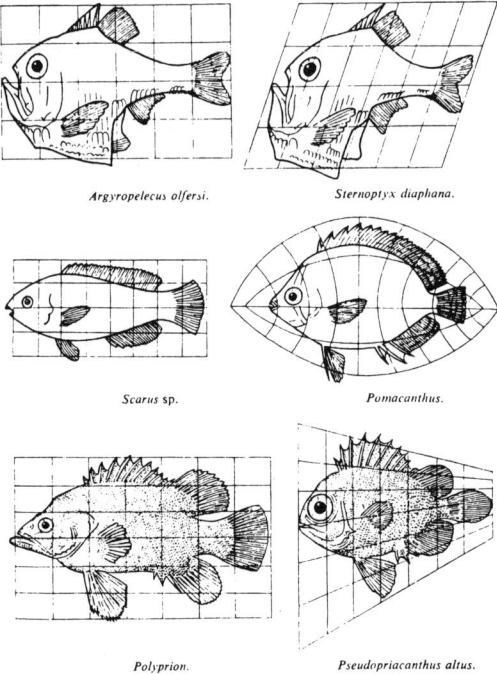

FIG. 2.5. Coordinate transformations from D'Arcy Thompson (D'Arcy Wentworth Thompson: On Growth and Form, p. 299. Copyright (c) 1944 by Cambridge University Press. Used by permission).

leading to an "intuitive" appreciation of invariant aspects of change in the growth or evolution of the species.

For our goal of describing the growth event, we were obliged to offer a formal description of the deformed grids. The development of viable mathematical transformations constitutes a formidable challenge in describing growth. From where do such candid descriptions derive? Again, D'Arcy Thompson's study of morphogensis provided valuable suggestions.

Transformations as Descriptions of the Effects of Physical Forces. Thompson contended that the geometric distortions associated with morphogenetic change are the result of physical forces in an animal's environment. According to a well-known principle, commonly referred to as Wolff's Law, *stress is a direct stimulus to growth*. A biological structure will remodel in accordance with the *amount* and *direction* of forces acting on that structure. For example, the weight-bearing bone of the lower leg, the tibia, grows so as to increase its cross-section in response to the weight that it must support. The fibula, in contrast, is a narrower bone, reflecting the lesser loads normally placed on it.

Thompson's method of coordinate transformations was developed to do more than describe changes in morphology through global geometric transformations. The resultant grids were intended to help identify the origin of biological forms in forces imposed by dynamic potentials, such as gravity and biomechanical stress. Thompson, in 1917, maintained that such forces act directly on organisms, shaping their changes to optimize resistance to stress. Although we now recognize that Thompson's proposed mechanism is in error, we should not reject completely the role of physical forces in shaping morphology (Gould, 1971; R.E. Shaw, Mark, Jenkins, & Mingolla, 1983). Rather, physical forces operate through natural selection; the genetically determined plan produces shape changes that are optimal with respect to the existing pattern of forces.

What D'Arcy Thompson appreciated was that any description of morphological change ought not to be a purely mathematical exercise, for geometric and kinematic descriptions of change cannot be evaluated without considering the forces responsible for the change. Specification of event dynamics is necessary in order to delimit the event in question and constrain the search for a kinematic description. To clarify this point, consider our interest in describing craniofacial growth. Our goal is to describe what is common to all growing individuals. The longitudinal data banks from which such descriptions are usually derived present students of growth with a serious problem that purely kinematic approaches cannot address. Changes reflected in longitudinal records for a given indivdual are the product of "more than just growth"; that is, the change in facial morphology is a product of both a style of change (growth) common to all individuals *and* various habits specific to an individual (e.g., changes produced by nonoptimal biomechanical forces such as thumb-sucking, nail-biting, and mouth-breathing, as well as diet, facial expressions, and other oral habits). Growth researchers who attempt to derive their descriptions from longitudinal records are confronted with the task of delimiting "pure" growth-related changes that are *invariant over all individuals* from those changes that are *specific to an individual*. All too often investigators fail to acknowledge this difficulty, let alone address the problem.

Thompson's work, then, has important implications for our efforts to describe craniofacial growth: The growth event must be delimited by identifying the *dynamic (physical) constraints common to all growing faces*. Curiously, this is the same point that we discussed in surveying the ecological approach to perception. James and Eleanor Gibson attached tremendous importance to the natural constraints on events and the layout of the terrestrial environment. The similarity between the Gibsons' and Thompson's respective enterprises does not end here. Both also recognized the importance of choosing a scale of analysis commensurate with their interests and goals.

Scales of Analysis

The description of events, like craniofacial growth, is an endeavor shared by many fields of scientific inquiry. It is rarely the case that descriptions developed by other disciplines can be transported directly to psychology. Events and the physical constraints on events can be studied at different *scales of analysis*, ranging from the quantum level through scales of far greater expanse than that of our terrestrial environment, such as employed in astrophysics. To be sure, there is no right or wrong scale for studying any event. Rather, the chosen spatial-temporal scale must be *appropriate to* or *commensurate with* the aims and concerns of the investigation, a point made by both the Gibsons and Thompson.

In his survey of the terrestrial environment and in his analysis of the physics required to describe how the material properties of surfaces structure light, J.J. Gibson (1961) contended that physics had to be *ecologized*. That is, specification of the information for an event utilized by a perceiver would entail delineating the material properties of the structure and the dynamic aspects of the change as they might relate to the ambient optic array. The problem was to discover how light is structured in a manner specific to the material properties of substances and the layout of surfaces, and in a manner useful to specific types of animals.

Similarly, much of D'Arcy Thompson's (1917/1942) treatise was predicated on the choice of a scale commensurate with the global morphological changes resulting from growth or evolution. In his analysis of the physical constraints on morphogenesis, Thompson was sensitive to the hazards of choosing a scale that was too molecular to account for the morphological change. He realized that analysis of forces affecting molecules or cells would be unable to illuminate the global morphologic transformation. Although Thompson did not discuss hereditary influences, we suspect he would have been skeptical that they could provide a wholly adequate explanation. Today, we know that the informational content of DNA is woefully inadequate to account for every detail in facial microstructure (Enlow, 1968; Moore & Lavelle, 1974). To summarize the essential point, both D'Arcy Thompson and J.J. Gibson were concerned with physical constraints that were both *global* and *universal*.

With respect to craniofacial growth, the head has to be viewed, not as a collection of chemicals, cells, or tissues, but as a complex, contoured, three-dimensional structure. Our objective was to identify those forces that affected the entire craniofacial structure and were applicable to all (normal) instances of this growth event. Modern biology usually works at the more "micro" scales of molecules, genes, cells, and tissues. (Unfortunately, the study of morphology, which proceeds at a "macro" scale akin to the requirements of Thompson's interest in morphogenesis and Gibson's ecological psychology, has been on the wane for several decades.) The challenge for the ecological psychologist was to develop a description of craniofacial growth at a scale appropriate to the human perceiver.

In this section, we have examined how mathematical transformations might enable us to describe various styles of change, including the global remodeling of the craniofacial complex due to growth. Consideration of scales of analysis at which the growth event is to be viewed and natural (physical) constraints common to all instances of growth have established limits on the search for a transformational description of craniofacial growth. The natural constraints on growth must be both *universal* and *global*. They must be universal, since they must be applicable to all heads that can be seen to grow. And they must be global, since they must apply to the remodeling of the entire craniofacial complex. It is this scale that seems commensurate with human perception. *What forces in the natural terrestrial environment satisfy these two conditions of acting on the head globally and universally?* There are few, if any, candidates other than gravity.

Finding a Growth Transformation

Earlier, we noted that Wolff's Law proposed that stress is a direct stimulus to growth. This means that a growing structure remodels in accordance with the amount and direction of stress acting on it. This principle was the basis for a hydrostatic analysis of the effects of gravity on a growing head. To simplify the analysis, Todd, Mark, Shaw, and Pittenger (1980) treated the human head as an idealized system: a fluid-filled, spherical water tank. What can be said about the distribution of pressure on the walls of the container? Four characteristics can be identified (Fig. 2.6): (a) the distribution of pressure is continuous throughout the container; (b) the direction of pressure is orthogonal to the wall of the container, radiating from the center of the sphere; (c) the pressure distribution is bilaterally symmetrical around the central vertical axis; and (d) the amount of pressure at any point is a function of the amount of fluid above it (i.e., the pressure increases from top to bottom).

Following Wolff's Law, what would happen if the tank were allowed to remodel (grow) in accordance with the direction and amount of pressure exerted by the fluid? (Assume for the purpose of this idealized analysis that additional fluid was being pumped into the tank to keep it filled.) This analysis produced the cardioidal strain transformation, which can be written in polar coordinates as: $\theta' = \theta$, $R' = R(1 + k(1 - \cos\theta))$, where k is a free parameter that increases over time. (See Fig. 2.7 for a depiction of the effects of this global geometric transformation when applied to a human head.)

Although the hydrostatic model is highly simplified and idealized, it has been extremely useful in helping us to appreciate the effects of a global and universal dynamic constraint, *gravity*, on the course of craniofacial growth. Todd and Mark (1981) have further shown that the resultant transformation makes highly accurate predictions of facial appearance when applied to hard tissue (bone) profiles (Fig. 2.8).

This hydrostatic model can be viewed as but one of a class of related growth models. Several years earlier, Robert Shaw had developed a similar "growth" transformation independently of this analysis of dynamic constraints on growth (Shaw et al., 1974). (We have come to refer to the transformation

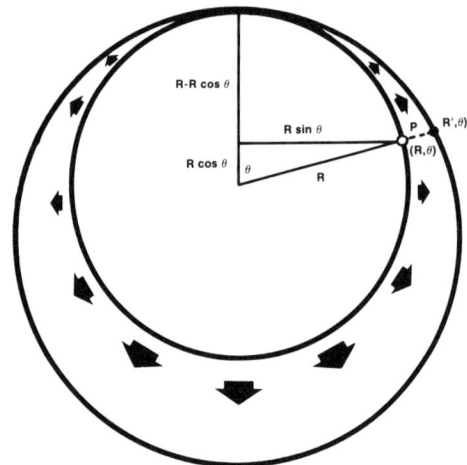

FIG. 2.6. The pressure distribution inside a fluid-filled sphere due to gravity. The inner circle represents a spherical tank filled with fluid. The pressure (P) at any point on the surface of the tank is always normal to the surface of the tank. From elementary hydrostatics, pressure can be expressed by the relation $P = k(R - R\cos\theta)$, where R is the radius of the sphere and k is a product of the density of the fluid and gravitational pressure. The distance (P) between any point on the surface of the tank (R,θ) and a point on the outer curve (R',θ), found by extending the radius through point (R,θ) to the outer curve, represents the pressure at point (R,θ). Thus, as angle θ increases, the pressure at point (R,θ) increases as the distance between (R,θ) and (R',θ) increases. If new material were laid down in accordance with this pressure gradient, the revised cardioidal strain transformation [$\theta' = \theta$, $R' = R(1 + k\{1 - \cos\theta\})$], would be observed.

2. PERCEPTION OF GROWING FACES   29

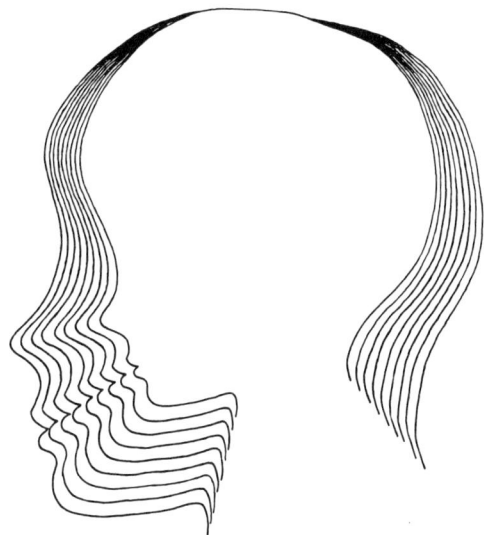

FIG. 2.7. Increasing amounts of the revised cardioidal strain transformation have been applied to the profile of a young child (innermost profile). Successive profiles appear older.

derived from the hydrostatic model as the "revised" cardioidal strain transformation.) Shaw's "growth" transformation (the cardioidal strain transformation depicted in Fig. 2.4) was intended to capture the effects of certain strain and radial patterns of change that D'Arcy Thompson had associated with growth. Although the effects of Shaw's original transformation were different from the transformation derived from the hydrostatic model in at least one aspect—Shaw's model did not produce an increase in head size—his nodal point-based

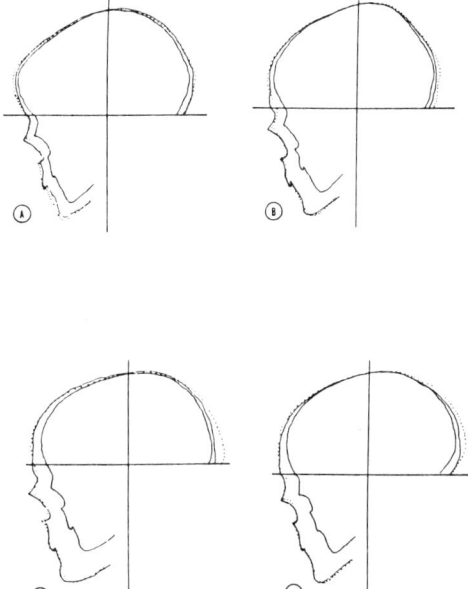

FIG. 2.8. Samples of growth predictions of 10 males and 10 females. The solid profile outlines show the younger (inner) and older (outer) profiles traced from lateral head films of a person's actual growth records. The dotted profile shows the growth prediction made by transforming the younger profile with the revised cardioidal strain transformation. A, Male, ages 5.9 and 13.9, 68.9%. B, Male, ages 6.3 and 19.0, 80.3%. C, Male, ages 4.3 and 18.6, 76.1%. D, Male, ages 5.1 and 17.0, 81.1%. Note: From "Issues Related to the Prediction of Craniofacial Growth" by J.T. Todd and L.S. Mark, 1981, *American Journal of Orthodontics, 242*, p. 74. Reprinted by permission.

cardioidal strain transformation shared the other essential geometric properties associated with the gravity-derived hydrostatic model.

While the similarity between the original cardioidal strain transformation and the later hydrostatic model might, at first, appear coincidental, this is not the case. Shaw's efforts to develop the cardioidal strain transformation were guided by the same constraints that eventually led to the development of the hydrostatic model and the revised cardioidal strain transformation. In fact, the similarity between the two transformations convinced us that what we were attempting to find was not a single "best" transformation, but a "class" of transformations that preserved certain geometric properties. Throughout the course of this project, assumptions entailed in the application of the relevant dynamic constraints on the growth event have led us to three such models of craniofacial growth: Shaw's original nodal point model (Pittenger & Shaw, 1975a; R.E. Shaw et al., 1974); a hydrostatic model (Todd et al., 1980; Todd & Mark, 1981); and finally a hydrodynamic model (R.E. Shaw et al., 1983). We now survey our investigation of the perceptual consequences of this class of transformations.

THE PERCEPTION OF CRANIOFACIAL GROWTH

Defining the Class of Transformations Perceived as Growth

Initial Studies. In their first investigation of craniofacial growth, Pittenger and Shaw (1975a) examined the relative importance of three characteristic patterns of growth—*strain, shear,* and *radial* growth (Thompson, 1917/1942)—which seemed applicable to the global remodeling of the human skull (R.E. Shaw et al., 1974). From Thompson's study of morphogenesis, Shaw devised two transformations depicting the strain and shear components: cardioidal strain and affine shear, respectively (see Fig. 2.4). (The radial component, by itself, could not be an appropriate model of growth, since it did not produce a remodeling of facial proportions. Cardioidal strain, however, incorporates a radial component, which D'Arcy Thompson, 1917/1942, had previously shown to be an aspect of growth.)

Various amounts of each transformation were applied to the profile of an 8-year-old child (Fig. 2.9, Profile 0/0). In all, 5 levels of shear were combined with 7 levels of strain, thereby producing the 35 profiles shown in Fig. 2.9. Three converging perceptual measures were employed. The first was designed to measure the effect of each transformation on perceived age by recording judgments of relative age. Observers were asked to make magnitude estimations of the age-level of each profile relative to the numerical rating that they had assigned a standard. Though both transformations affected the mag-

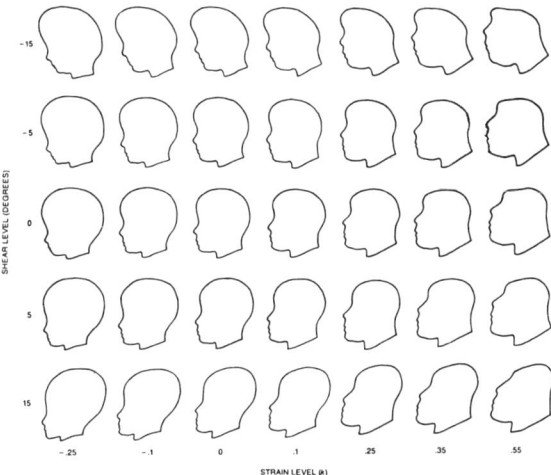

FIG. 2.9. Transformations of a facial profile by shear and cardioidal strain (untransformed profile is at shear = o, strain = 0). Note: From "Aging Faces as Viscal=Elastic Events" by J.B. Pittenger and R.E. Shaw, 1975, *Journal of Experimental Psychology: Human Perception and Performance, 5,* Expt. 1. Resprinted by permission.

nitude estimates of perceived age, cardioidal strain had a far more powerful and consistent effect than affine shear.

In their second experiment, Pittenger and Shaw used a paired comparison task to examine observers' sensitivity to small changes in the facial profile produced by cardioidal strain transformation. Observers were presented with pairs of profiles produced by differing amounts of the free parameter and asked to identify the "older" profile of each pair. The accuracy and reliability with which observers were able to perform this task was impressive, given the side-by-side arrangement of the profile pairs, and the extremely subtle differences between some of the profile pairs. R.E. Shaw and Pittenger (1977) later observed that, in light of the size of the projected images used in this experiment, observers were able to discriminate shape differences between adjacent profiles that were only a few times greater than the absolute limit determined for visual acuity in resolving spatially adjacent lines (Schlaer, 1937). Although this initial study did not examine observers' sensitivity with respect to age-related changes produced by the affine shear transformation, a later investigation found that observers were considerably more sensitive to small differences produced by cardioidal strain transformation than to comparable differences produced by affine shear (Mark & Todd, 1985).

These initial experiments provided valuable demonstrations of the relative importance to perception of the strain component over the shear component. This finding establishes an important constraint on the types of transformations that may prove to be viable descriptions of the growth event. In addition, observers were found to be extremely sensitive to the effects of the cardioidal strain transformation, both in terms of their ability to recognize differences in age level and to recognize individual identity in transformed profiles. At the very least, Pittenger and Shaw (1975a) had identified a psychologically interesting transformation, one worthy of additional study.

Shortcomings of the Initial Studies. With the benefit of hindsight, we can identify some methodological shortcomings of Pittenger and Shaw's original test of the cardioidal strain growth model as well as other problems that they were unable to address. Perhaps, the most significant problem was the lack of a baseline for comparing the perceived effects of this model to actual growth. Unfortunately, they did not have access to a longitudinal data bank required to construct such a standard. (Several years later, when Shaw came to the University of Connecticut, we discovered that records of one longitudinal study involving approximately 100 individuals were available at the University Health Center.) Such longitudinal records would have permitted them to equate the ranges of the free parameter used in producing the transformed profiles to the effects of actual growth.

Lacking these guidelines, extreme values of cardioidal strain changed the profile appearance well beyond the range associated with normal growth (see Fig. 2.9). Some of the younger profiles (i.e., high negative values of strain) were reminiscent of the "super-intelligent humanoids" depicted in science fiction movies, while many of the older profiles (i.e., high positive values of strain) appeared "Neanderthal-like." Thus, in addition to obtaining a longitudinal baseline against which to evaluate the perceptual consequences of the growth model, follow-up studies also had to restrict the range of the transformation to that produced by normal growth, thereby eliminating the nonhumanlike extremes.

Pittenger and Shaw might have also included a measure of the natural "salience" of the growth transformations, such as might be obtained from a free response task, in which observers viewed sequences of faces and were asked to label the event responsible for producing the observed change. This method would have permitted them to assess whether the age-related changes produced by the strain transformation could be detected spontaneously or whether they were noticed only when experimental instructions prompted the observers to attend to age. In the latter case, it would have been unlikely that the particular strain transformation used in the study would ultimately prove to be an adequate model of information about the growth event.

A frequently offered criticism of Pittenger and Shaw's initial study of the growth event is that they examined only two transformations: "How do you know there is not another transformation that would provide a better model of growth than cardioidal strain?" "There are an infinite number of mathematical transformations. How are you going to test them all?" With a little thought, it is not difficult to see that these criticisms are misguided. They are also unfair, for they establish a criterion that is never applied elsewhere: namely, to test *all possible* models. Because these criticisms are raised frequently, it behooves us to examine them.

To the critic who objects, "But how do you know that some other transformation wouldn't provide a better model of growth than cardioidal strain?", there is a relatively simple response: We do not know if the current model is the best possible model. In light of the vast number of untested candidates, we would not be surprised if a "better" model is found. The question, however, misses the essential thrust of this enterprise. Could this "better" model be *entirely* different from the one examined by Pittenger and Shaw? Given the observers' strong tendency to *perceive* the effects of cardioidal strain as growth, it is unlikely that a viable alternative could be identified that is entirely different from that original transformation. There are certain characteristics of the growth event that any viable candidate model of growth must depict. (As we demonstrate shortly, the hydrostatic model [Fig. 2.6] has permitted us to identify at least some of those characteristics that are shared among a class of transformations that are perceived as growth.)

What is perceived as growth should be related (i.e., similar) in some important way to the actual event. It stretches our commitment to realism to suggest that two transformations perceived as growth (and thus related to actual growth) are entirely unrelated to one another. What is really important about alternative growth models are not the differences among them, but the properties that are *shared* by such candidate transformations. We believe that other viable growth transformations can be found, but that they will share certain properties with the cardioidal strain transformation. These properties that are common to each member of the class of growth transformations constitute the perceptual information about this salient style of change. This observation points toward a potentially important contribution of research on growth to our understanding of a fundamental problem in event perception: How are observers able to distinguish different styles of change from one another?

Studies on How Growth can be Distinguished from Other Styles of Change

Until recently, there had been relatively little research on the specific properties of visual displays that make one style of change distinct from another. Because observers can recognize many styles of change in a variety of contexts, it is unlikely that the visual system handles each distinction as a separate problem. Event perception research needs to establish a unified framework for classifying the information by which perceivers are able to distinguish different styles of change from one another. An extension of Pittenger and Shaw's original study examined a geometric framework for distinguishing styles of change (Mark et al. 1981).

To this point, we have characterized transformations in terms of the pattern of change that they produce. For example, a translation moves every point the same distance in the same direction. A similarity transformation, which produces a uniform expansion or contraction of a form, moves each point out along a radial line from the origin.

Every transformation also preserves (leaves invariant) a unique set of properties in the transformed object. Translation, for example, leaves angles and lengths of lines unchanged; similarity also leaves angles invariant, but it changes the length of all lines, though it does maintain the proportions among them. The set of properties left invariant by a transformation thus serves as a second way to characterize the transformation. Of course, sets of transformations will share certain invariants. In the case of translation and similarity, both maintain angles and the proportions of lines.

These observations suggest an approach toward evaluating candidate growth transformations. It is most unlikely that our perceptual system has evolved so as to discriminate among all possible pairs of transformations or that all transformations have unique, perceptually salient (meaningful) consequences. It seems more reasonable to suppose that there will be classes of transformations defined by common invariants. Members of each class, while mathematically similar in some respects and different in others, will have "perceptually equivalent" effects; that is, they will produce the same style of change. In this view the style of change is established by the invariant characteristics of a class of transformations, rather than by a single, "best" transformation.

Delineation of the invariants associated with transformations provides a tool for selecting transformations for study in perceptual tests, and for specifying both the similarities among those transformations that are seen as growth and the differences between growth and nongrowth transformations. For a given event, a set of properties must be preserved for a particular style of change to be seen. If this framework provides a viable means for distinguishing the perceptual information specific to various styles of change, then it should be the case that: (a) transformations that maintain the same class of invariants should be seen as producing the same style of change; and (b) transformations that do not maintain the same class of invariants should not be seen as producing the same style of change. Mark et al.'s (1981) study of growth examined these predications.

Using Pittenger and Shaw's (1975a) initial findings and the global and universal constraints on the growth event that were established by the hydrostatic analysis of an idealized growing system (Fig. 2.6) which followed (Todd & Mark, 1981; Todd et al., 1980), Mark et al. (1981) distinguished three invariants that the cardioidal strain transformation preserved: (a) the angular coordinate of each point on the head, ($\theta'=\theta$); (b) bilateral symmetry across the vertical axis; and (c) the continuity of all contours and their directions of curvature. Each of these geometric invariants corresponds to one of the *dynamic* constraints on the remodeling of the idealized hydrostatic system analogous to a growing human head as discussed earlier. In contrast, affine shear, the transformation that, in earlier studies, had little effect on perceived age, preserved only one of these properties: continuity of the profile contour (cf. Fig. 2.4 and 2.6).

Mark et al.'s (1981) proposal for distinguishing styles of change leads to the following prediction: Only transformations that maintain all three of the invariants associated with the hydrostatic model and the resultant cardioidal strain transformation should be perceived as growth. To examine this proposal, two new transformations, illustrated in Fig. 2.4, were devised. The first, *spiral strain* preserved all three invariants and, thus, should be seen as growth about as often as cardioidal strain. The second, *reflected shear,* preserved only two of the three invariants and therefore, like affine shear, should not be seen as growth.

These predictions were tested using two experimental tasks. For each transformation a sequence of five facial profiles was produced by applying increasing amounts of the transformation to the profile of a 5-year-old male (Fig. 2.10). In the first task, observers labelled the event depicted in the sequence of facial profiles. In this "free response" task, observers were not instructed to look for growth in the series of faces. Thus, the frequency of spontaneous references to growth served as a measure of the perceptual salience of each transformation as a model of growth. The second task required observers to rate each sequence as to how much like growth it appeared; this provided a converging measure of each sequence's depiction of growth.

Mark et al. (1981) were also able to incorporate two baseline series. The first was a sequence of actual profiles taken from longitudinal records. This actual growth series (see Fig. 2.10) permitted us to compare observers' judg-

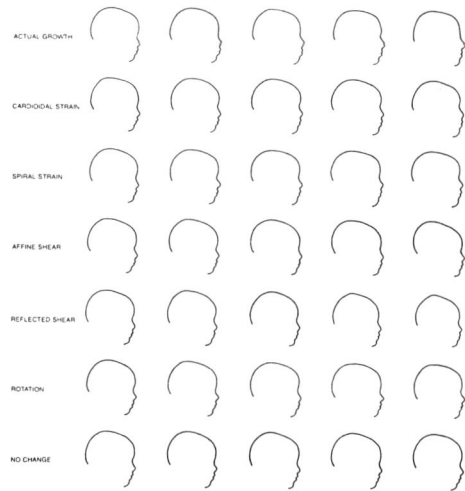

FIG. 2.10. Examples of profile sequences resulting from the four prospective growth transformations, actual growth and rotation. Note: From "Perception of Growth: A Geometric Analysis of How Different Styles of Change are Distinguished" by L.S. Mark, J.T. Todd, and R.E. Shaw, 1981, *Journal of Experimental Psychology: Human Perception and Performance, 7,* p. 859. Reprinted by permission.

ments of simulated growth to their judgments of the actual event. Although one transformation might be seen as more like growth than another, the better model might still not be judged as comparable to actual growth. The actual growth baseline established an upper limit on expectations for observers' performance on the experimental tasks. This baseline also equated the ranges of the various transformations to one another by finding the value of the free parameter that produced an equivalent amount of change in facial angle to that observed in the comparable profile in the actual growth sequence.

The second baseline series was used to determine the lower limit of expected performance. For this purpose, observers judged faces produced by a transformation that was not a reasonable candidate. Thus, a series of faces differing only in their degree of rotation from the upright position was used to establish this second baseline. As a rigid transformation, rotation cannot capture the nonrigid remodeling of facial proportions that characterizes growth.

The geometric framework for distinguishing different styles of change predicted that cardioidal strain and spiral strain would be seen as more like actual growth than affine shear, reflected shear, or rotation, because the latter do not preserve one or more of the three invariants. The results of both the free response and the growth rating tasks were consistent with these predictions (see Fig. 2.11). The categorical distinction between these two classes of transformations was further demonstrated by the finding that reflected shear, the transformation that preserved two invariants, was not seen as more like actual growth than affine shear, which preserved only one invariant.

In summary, Mark et al.'s (1981) study demonstrated that this class of transformations provides a naturally salient depiction of growth, when applied to the profile of a human head.

Before dismissing transformations that do not preserve all three "growth" invariants, it should be determined whether those transformations can produce changes that are perceived as growth under conditions where observers are

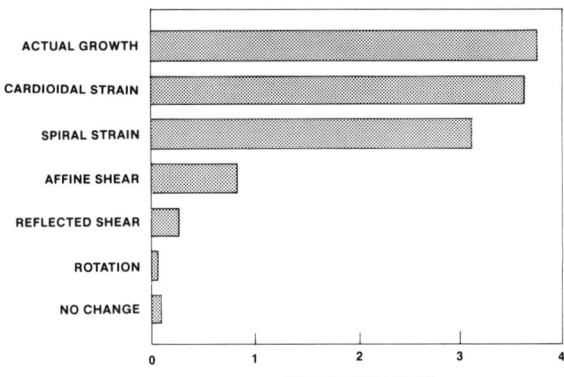

FIG. 2.11. Results of Mark et al.'s (1981) growth rating task. The mean growth scores for the cardioidal strain and spiral strain transformations were closest to that of the actual growth sequences. None of the other geometric transformations yielded a significantly greater score than that of the control sequence, "no change."

strongly urged to see the transformed profiles as being at different ages. The free response and rating tasks did *not* press observers to try to see each sequence as growth. Perhaps, the effects of the two shear transformations would be seen as growth if the response required participants to look more carefully for age-related differences. To test this possibility, a paired comparison task was used. In contrast to a free response procedure, observers are forced to choose which face of each pair looks older in the paired comparison task. Hence, this task more strongly encourages observers to attend to age-level differences.

Mark and Todd (1985) conducted such a paired comparison task using the profiles from Mark et al.'s (1981) study. For each pair of profiles, the "older" profile was taken as the one which had been produced by the larger value of the free parameter of the transformation. (The effects of each transformation had been equated to one another and actual growth by determining their effects on facial dimensions that are observed to change during growth.) The basic pattern of results conformed to the predictions: Ordinal age was judged more "accurately" for pairs of profiles produced by transformations that preserved the three growth invariants than the other transformations. In addition, performance on profiles produced by the cardioidal strain and spiral strain transformations was virtually indistinguishable from judgments made on the actual growth profiles. In contrast, pairs of profiles produced by the transformations that did not preserve the three growth invariants were not judged reliably above chance. Mark and Todd also demonstrated that the physical differences produced by the two classes of transformations were equally discriminable. Thus, differences in perceived age judgments could not be attributed to differences in discriminability.

The results of these experiments support the proposal that the styles of change produced by the two classes of transformations are perceived categorically. A question still remains, however, about the perceptual equivalence of the growth transformations and actual growth. Looking more closely at Mark et al.'s (1981, Exper. 1 and 3 findings), some of the sequences produced by the "growth" transformations were not judged as comparable to the actual growth sequences on which they were based. The informational basis for the lack of complete comparability lies in certain craniofacial changes that are not captured by the growth transformations.

When observers did not have a prior expectation that any of the sequences depicted growth, they were more likely either to label as growth or assign a high growth rating to at least two of the actual growth sequences than for sequences produced by the growth transformations. On debriefing, participants indicated that those two actual growth sequences depicted age-related characteristics that were not modeled by the "growth" transformations. These changes included the development of the frontal sinus (a bump just above the bridge of the nose that enlarges noticeably after puberty) and changes in the size and shape of the nose. Under these "unconstrained" viewing conditions, the additional cues apparently increased the likelihood that growth would be noticed on the, admittedly, impoverished profile silhouettes employed (Mark et al., 1981, Exper. 1). The findings of another experiment supported this interpretation: Under less demanding conditions, where observers were told beforehand of the experimenter's interest in the perception of growth, the growth ratings and number of free response "growth" labels for the growth transformations were comparable to those of the actual growth sequences (Exper. 2 and 3). In addition, the paired comparison experiment also failed to differentiate between the transformations and actual growth. This suggested that while profiles in the actual growth sequences were "contaminated" by the effects of certain idiosyncratic forces, perceptual judgments of actual growth sequences were based largely on the effects of the universal gravitational constraint modeled by the class of cardioidal growth transformations. These extraneous features in the actual growth sequences effectively made this study a more conservative test of the model, since the sequences produced by actual growth should have been more salient than the sequences produced by the growth transformations.

Applying Cardioidal Strain to More Realistic Representations

One reason why the facial characteristics that were present only in the actual growth sequences proved to be so important to observers' judgments was that the facial representations used in these experiments were highly impoverished profile silhouettes lacking internal detail. Two demonstrations showed that the cardioidal growth model can produce the appearance of growth when applied to more detailed representations of the human face (Mark & Todd, 1983). In the first, the cardioidal strain transformation was generalized to a three-dimensional data base. A 13-year-old girl was photographed using a special camera for gathering a three-dimensional data base. From that data base, a computer was able to carve a bust of the child. The original data base was then transformed using the three-dimensional cardioidal strain transformation and a new bust was generated from the transformed coordinates. We predicted that this bust would depict the child as she appeared at an *earlier* age (Fig. 2.12). Those people who knew the girl at roughly the time she first entered school agreed that the growth transformation had produced an excellent likeness of her, with the possible exception of some missing "baby fat." When asked to judge the relative age of the two busts, naive observers overwhelmingly (356 out of 360) saw the bust produced by the cardioidal strain transformation as younger than the original. Unfortunately, this demonstration proved to be a one time opportunity in light of the prohibitive cost of producing additional busts.

In the second demonstration, Mark and Todd (1983) employed a technique whereby a "photographic-quality" representation could be digitized on a computer and transformed to produce a comparable portrait of the individual as he

2. PERCEPTION OF GROWING FACES   39

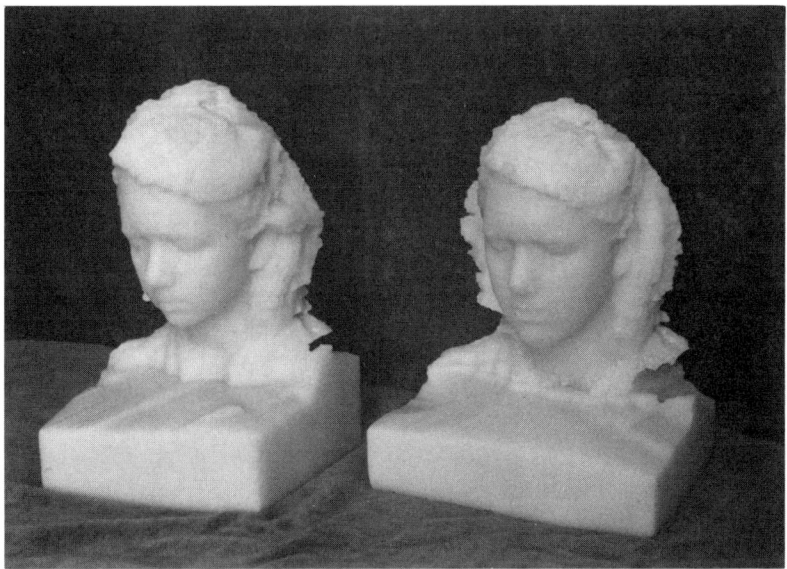

FIG. 2.12. The two, 3-dimensional busts used by Mark and Todd (1985). Right, the original bust of a girl, age 15 years, 1 month; left, the bust resulting from transformation of the original data structure by applying 3-dimensional cardioidal strain to make the head appear younger. Note: Figs. 2.12 and 2.13 [from Describing Geometric Information About Human Growth in Terms of Geometric Invariants" by L.S. Mark and J.T. Todd, 1985, *Perception and Psychophysics, 37,* p. 194. Reprinted by permission.

or she might appear at a later or earlier time. Figure 2.13 shows an example of the results of this procedure.

These demonstrations indicated that the growth transformations were applicable to more natural and realistic representations of faces.

To summarize, a series of studies have furnished evidence that information about craniofacial growth is specified by a class of transformations that preserve certain geometric characteristics of the head over the course of growth. From this work a geometric framework has emerged for describing the information about growth and, perhaps, other styles of change (cf. Todd, 1982). In each of the studies considered previously, the effects of a single transformation were perceived as growth over a number of different human heads. This finding shows that the perceptual information about the growth event must, indeed, be highly abstract; that is, it must be largely independent of the specific object undergoing change. In the next section, we consider just how abstract this information must be.

Abstractness of Information About Growth

As a mathematical formalism, a transformation can be applied to any structure. Thus, cardioidal strain could be applied to a drawing of any object, be it

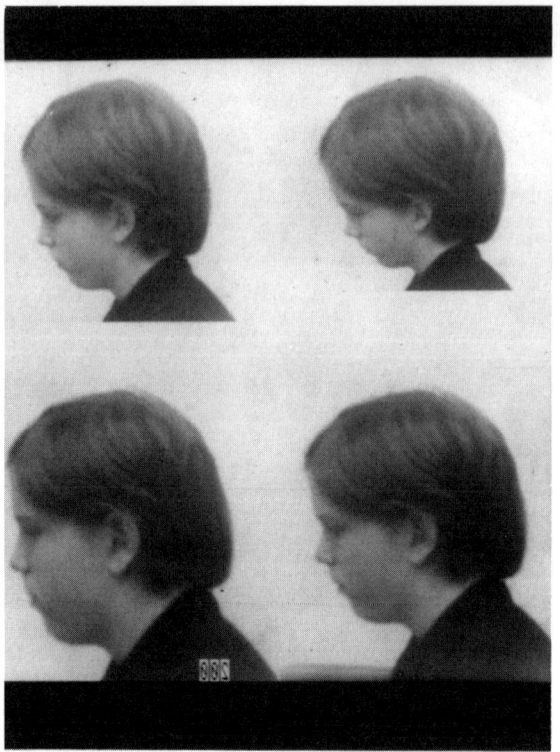

FIG. 2.13. A series of transformed photographs produced by applying cardioidal strain transformation to the actual photograph of a 12-year-old boy (lower right). The transformation producing the photographs on the upper row was intended to make the boy appear increasingly younger (left to right); the transformation producing the photograph at the lower left was intended to make the boy appear older. Note: From p.195.

a human face, an animal face, a flower, a rock, or even an abstract geometric form. However, we are concerned, not simply with transformations as mathematical formalisms *per se,* but with their use in characterizing the pattern of actual physical growth and in specifying the perceptual information for growth. We must then consider the problem of delineating the set of structures to which the growth transformation is physically and perceptually appropriate—at least as a growth transformation. From the standpoint of the physical event, all objects do not grow; and objects that do grow do not all do so in the same way. It seems likely that not every object transformed by cardioidal strain will be seen to grow.

The problem of specifying the range over which a transformation can be seen to produce a style of change, such as growth, is complex. First, it involves establishing the set of real objects for which the growth transformation is a physically accurate description of growth. Our hypothesis is that this set includes all normally growing heads. In light of the hydrostatic analysis (Fig. 2.6), heads of other mammals might well be expected to be members of the set. With respect to perception, we would predict that all objects for which the transformation is physically appropriate would be seen to grow. However, this set might be quite large. Cartoonists, for example, can make inanimate objects or imaginary animate objects take on the appearance of various ages. Thus, the information about a style of change like growth must be quite *abstract,* because a single globally applied transformation is applicable to a range of objects.

In this section we examine several studies that explore the domain of structures that can be seen to grow under our class of growth transformations. The outcome of the first set of studies emphasizes the diverse collection of objects that can be seen as growing under cardioidal strain. A second group of experiments begins to delimit the properties of objects that grow under these growth transformations.

An early study by Pittenger and Shaw (1975b) revealed that information about the age level of faces must be highly abstract. This work had been undertaken to assess observers' ability to judge age from facial photographs. The underlying rationale assumed that the transformation of facial structure produced by growth constitutes the primary information for age, and that information about age level exists throughout the craniofacial complex because of the global remodeling produced by growth. From yearbook photographs they constructed 15 longitudinal series with each set consisting of six photographs of a single person taken at roughly 1-year intervals between the ages of 12 and 19 (Grades 7 through 12). Cross-sectional series were also constructed from the longitudinal series; those sets consisted of photographs of six different individuals, one in each of the six grades. Observers were asked to make either ordinal or absolute age judgments for both the longitudinal and cross-sectional series.

Age judgments were quite accurate on both series. This result was consistent with the idea that age-level information was largely independent of the structural properties by which individuals were distinguished from one another. This does not mean that constancy of the underlying structure had no effect on age judgments. In fact, age estimates were slightly more accurate in the longitudinal condition than in the cross-sectional condition. However, a fixed identity was not required in order to make accurate ordinal age judgments.

By taking the longitudinal and cross-sectional series of photographs and masking out various parts of the photographs, Pittenger and Shaw were further able to demonstrate that age information is carried throughout the craniofacial complex. One mask blocked out all hair as well as the person's shoulders and neck, leaving the jaw untouched. This condition assessed the effects of hair and hair length on age judgments. A second mask blocked out all parts of the photograph except the eyes, eyebrows, nose, and mouth, thereby allowing them to assess information provided by the internal structure of the face independent of the outline of the craniofacial complex. The pattern of age judgments under the masked and unmasked conditions indicated that the presence or absence of either mask had surprisingly little effect on the overall ordinal relationships for either the absolute or ordinal age judgments. Observers, then, were able to utilize a variety of different facial areas for age information. The masks' effects were most noticeable on the absolute age judgments; people tended to overestimate the age of the masked photographs, with the degree of overestimation increasing with the amount of facial structure occluded by the mask.

In view of Pittenger and Shaw's (1975b) findings, it would be unreasonable as well as unparsimonious to suppose that growth information is specific to particular shapes of isolated features of an individual face at a given moment in time. Moreover, the information must be sufficiently general so as to apply across the facial features of all individuals during the period in which growth occurs. That is, it must be invariant across the range of faces that can be seen as growing. Two follow-up studies demonstrate the generality of the information specified by the growth transformations.

In an unpublished series of experiments, Mark replicated the paired comparison, free response, and growth-rating tasks discussed earlier using profiles of both sexes (the original study used only males) and different races (Black and Caucasian). The results of this replication showed that only the cardioidal strain and spiral strain transformations were perceived as growth over profiles of each race and sex. This evidence for a single pattern of morphological change across people of both sexes and different races is an important indication of the generality of the relationships captured by the class of growth transformations. To appreciate the significance of this result, one needs to understand that an important presupposition of traditional "normative" descriptions of craniofacial growth, derived from longitudinal data banks, is that any resulting description cannot be generalized from the population on which it was developed to other groups (e.g., from Caucasians to Blacks, males to females, etc.). Descriptions of growth, according to tradition, are highly limited in their generality, even to the point where one might hesitate to transfer a normative scheme developed in one geographic region to another region.

A second study (Pittenger, Shaw, & Mark, 1979) provides further insight concerning the generality and abstractness of the information specified by this class of growth transformations. Cardioidal strain and affine shear were applied to cartoon-like drawings of animal heads: the monkey, bird, dog shown in Fig. 2.14. Observers saw only the cardioidal strain transformation as having a significant monotonic effect on age, as indicated by their relative age judgments of the transformed animals.

2. PERCEPTION OF GROWING FACES   43

Two possible explanations for this finding were considered. First, people may try to explain the visual analogy between growth and cardioidal strain in terms of some "unconscious inference" derived from people's knowledge of animals and the styles of change to which they are normally subject. This "cognitive mediation" account assumed that any change is perceived with reference to the types of changes normally undergone by that object. An alternative interpretation attributed the effects of the cardioidal strain transformation to specific changes produced by the growth process itself. That is to say, the information specified by cardioidal strain was *invariant* in spite of the marked changes produced by growth, and was independent of all but a modicum of properties of the structure to which it was applied. This "invariance hypothesis" did not appeal to cognitive mediation in order to explain the generality òf the transformations across various animals.

To examine these contrasting proposals, the growth transformation was applied to an inanimate object, a Volkswagen "Beetle," which does not actually grow and for which no prior experience could have prepared observers to see the object as growing. The cognitive mediation account would require precisely such previous experience in order to recognize the object as growing under any transformation or set of conditions. Thus, evidence that observers can see a car as growing under cardioidal strain would damage the cognitive mediation account. The "invariance hypothesis" predicted that cardioidal strain would result in changes in age-level of the VW, assuming, of course that the VW satisfied the modicum of properties required to support the growth event.

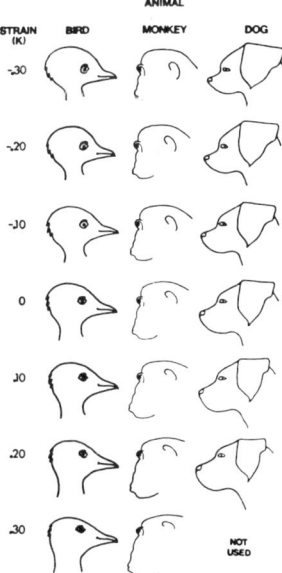

FIG. 2.14. Examples of the cartoon animals produced by applying cardioidal strain to the profiles shown at strain (k) equal to zero. Note: Figs. 2.14 and 2.15 from "Perceptual Information for The Age Level of Faces as a Higher Order Invariant of growth" by J.B. Pittenger, R.E. Shaw, and L.S. Mark, 1979, *Journal of Experimental Psychology: Human Perception and Performance, 5,* p. 482. Reprinted by permission.

Cardiodial strain and affine shear were applied to four different representations of the VW: front and side views, each view with and without cartooned in faces (Fig. 2.15). On a relative age judgment task, only the cardioidal strain transformation was perceived to have a consistent effect on the age of the VWs. The outcome, then, was inconsistent with the prediction of the cognitive mediation account. In accordance with the invariance hypothesis, observers seemed to be detecting highly abstract, "higher order" relationships independently of either the structure undergoing change or their experience in having seen that object grow previously.

But just how abstract was the information about growth? Can any structure be seen to undergo any style of change, or will only certain structures support a particular style of change?

Delimiting the Structures to Which Cardioidal Strain Produces Growth

Not all physical structures have the properties required to support every style of change. For instance, water and juice can flow, but paper and clothes will not. Paper and clothes, on the other hand, can be burned or cut, styles of change that are not supported by fluids, like water and juice. Similar restrictions are found with respect to the applicability of mathematical transformations that can be used for describing physical events. Recall that a *transformation* is a function that maps the elements of one nonempty set, called the "domain," into or onto the elements of another nonempty set, the "range." Just as physical events are defined only over a limited equivalence class, so

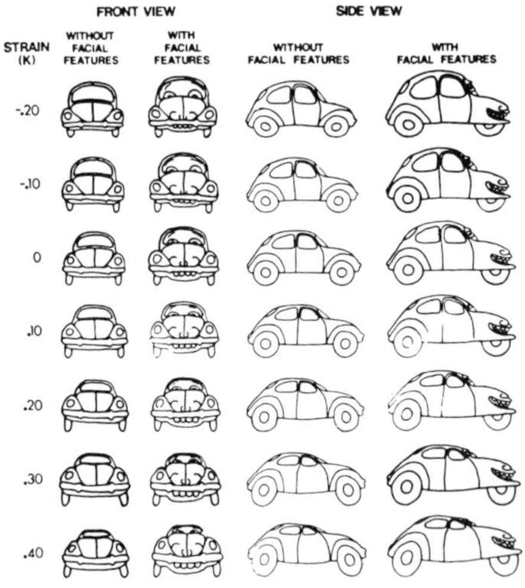

FIG. 2.15. Examples of the cartoon Volkswagens produced by applying cardioidal strain to the drawings at strain (k) equal to zero. p. 486.

mathematical transformations are defined over a restricted *domain*. (For example, the square root function is defined only over the domain of positive real numbers, unless one admits the use of imaginary numbers.)

These observations have important implications for efforts to describe perceptual information about events: Mathematical transformations should be seen as producing a particular style of change only over a restricted *domain of objects*. Although a transformation alters certain object properties, it must also preserve properties common to those structures that can support the style of change associated with that transformation. Just as physical events are limited in terms of the amount of change that naturally occurs (e.g., objects cannot stretch or bend indefinitely), so too a transformation may be seen as producing a style of change only within a limited range of change. Exceeding that range will produce the perception of a different style of change. For this reason, a complete description of a given style of change must delineate both the *range* of objects that are naturally produced by a given style of change and the *domain* of structures that can be subject to a particular transformation.

Although the findings of Pittenger et al. (1979) and Mark et al. (1981) have demonstrated the generality and abstractness of the information about growth provided by the cardioidal strain transformation, unpublished work by Pittenger and Shaw has shown that armchairs were not seen as growing older under cardioidal strain. Follow-up work by R.E. Shaw and Carello (1979) qualified this finding: Certain styles of armchairs and shoes could be seen as growing more consistently than other styles. This evidence provides an important challenge for research on event perception, namely, to delineate structural properties required to support the perception of a particular style of change.

Toward this goal, Mark et al. (1986) have begun to delineate the necessary structural properties of objects perceived to grow under the class of "growth" transformations. At the outset of their investigation, two object properties were of particular interest: the curvature of the object form and the deviation of the form from rectilinearity. These components contributed to what they intuitively thought of as the "biomorphicity" of an object. *Biomorphicity* literally means living shape or form, produced by processes such as growth or erosion. To that point, all objects seen as growing under the cardioidal strain transformation, including human and nonhuman heads, VWs, shoes, and armchairs, possessed a curved form, notable for the absence of straight lines and right angles. Naturally occurring biological forms are curved; the form of these curves has long fascinated biologists (Cook, 1911; Thompson, 1917/1942), architects (Stevens, 1974) and artists (Hogarth, 1965). Interestingly, when cartoonists attempt to animate objects, such as cars, tugboats or trains, they tend to curve straight lines and soften right angles. These observations are consistent with the proposal that biomorphicity is a necessary property in order for an object to be seen as growing under the class of growth transformations identified in previous work (Mark et al., 1981; Mark & Todd, 1985).

To evaluate the role of "biomorphicity," Mark et al. (1986) took a clearly nonbiomorphic face and transformed it in successive steps to make it look biomorphic. This was done by having an artist draw an inanimate, robot-like form (Fig. 2.16a) and progressively soften (curve) or "biomorphize" the form (Fig. 2.16b,c) into one that should be seen as growing (Fig. 2.16d). Although for these experiments the objects used were seen as "faces," "faceness" by itself is not a necessary structural property in order for an object to be seen as growing under cardioidal strain (R.E. Shaw & Carello, 1979). Faceness, however, is related to the applicability of cardioidal strain, because VWs with faces, when transformed with cardioidal strain, produce a stronger impression of growth than VWs without faces (Pittenger et al., 1979).

Three converging methods were used to examine the effects of growth (cardioidal strain) and nongrowth (affine shear and rotation) transformations on the continuum of profiles depicted in Fig. 2.16. Each procedure utilized series of five profiles (Fig. 2.17) produced by applying increasing amounts of each transformation to the four profiles comprising the biomorphic continuum.

A paired comparison procedure (Exper. 1) showed that observers' ability to discriminate the relative age levels of two profiles within a transformation series was a function of both the transformation used and the structure to which the transformation was applied (Fig. 2.18). That is, judgments of the "nonbiomorphic" robot profiles were equivalent for the growth and nongrowth transformations. However, as the profile became more biomorphic, the ordinal age judgments became more accurate for the pairs of profiles produced by the cardioidal strain (growth) transformation; in contrast, no such increase was observed for the nongrowth transformations. This interaction between transformation and structure was also found on a relative age judgment task (Exper. 2) and on an unpublished identity task, modeled after Pittenger and Shaw's (1975a) first and third experiments, respectively. An additional experiment demonstrated that the four profile series were comparable in their discriminability.

These data document an interaction between transformation and structure. As such, they constitute evidence for the importance of defining the domain

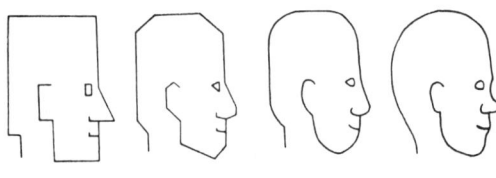

a   b   c   d

FIG. 2.16. The standard series of profiles employed by Mark et al. (1986). Profiles b, c, and d were created by applying successive amounts of a softening transformation to the robot profile, a . Note: Figs. 2.16, 2.17, and 2.18 from "Structural Support for the Perception of growth", by L.S. Mark, B.A. Shapiro, and R.E. Shaw, 1986, *Journal of Experimental Psychology: Human Perception and Performance, 12,* p. 152. Reprinted by permission.

2. PERCEPTION OF GROWING FACES   47

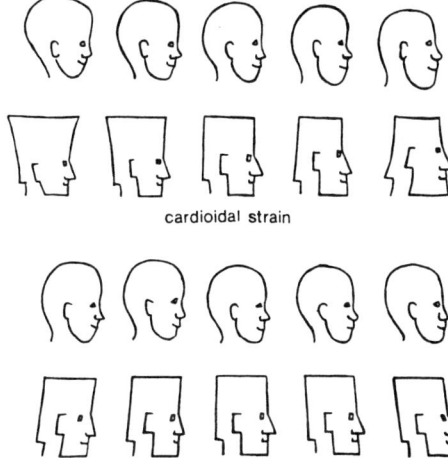

FIG. 2.17. An example of the stimulus sequences created by Mark et al. (1986, Exper.1). (Positive and negative values [+ or −10 degrees] of the cardioidal strain and affine shear transformations were applied to the robot and human profiles, Fig. 16, panels a and d.) p.153.

over which a particular style of change is defined. In addition, the characteristics of a structural continuum, which interacts with a class of transformations in producing a given style of change, are indicative of at least some of the defining structural properties required to support that style of change.

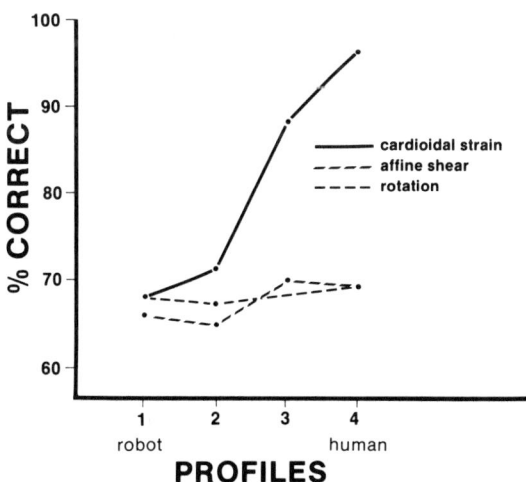

FIG. 2.18. The mean percentage of correct responses given by subjects is shown for the cardioidal strain, affine shear, and rotation transformations when applied to the continuum of heads depicted in Fig. 2.16. (From Mark et al., 1986, Experiment 1).

SOCIAL IMPLICATIONS OF THE ECOLOGICAL APPROACH TO PERCEPTION

This chapter has examined some influences on our investigation of the perception of craniofacial growth. Our plan of study was grounded on the Gibsons' ecological approach to perception: We began by examining the event itself in order to identify the natural constraints governing the global remodeling of the craniofacial complex. It was at this stage of our project that D'Arcy Thompson's treatise on morphogenesis provided numerous insights, which ultimately made it possible for us to develop a formal description of the perceptual information for craniofacial growth. The resultant perceptual research has demonstrated that the effects of a specific class of transformations were consistently perceived as growth over a broad range of craniofacial structures. It is important to emphasize that the properties of this class of growth transformations were specific to the natural, biomechanical constraints governing the growth event.

Looking at the outcome of this investigation as a whole, it becomes apparent that the ecological approach toward understanding perception addresses a seminal problem in the field of social psychology: An essential part of people's existence and well-being is the belief that they share the same physical reality. As Asch's (1956) work on social conformity has shown, it can be deeply disturbing to an individual when that belief is shaken. His experimental situation was so disturbing because it violated a basic premise of the subject's existence, namely, that people share the same physical reality.

The Gibsons' ecological approach to perception has shown that his belief in a shared reality rests, in part, on the *consistency* and *regularities* in sensory stimulation. Their ecological analysis of the available optical information, both at a glance and over time as the observer moves around the world, shows that the consistency of information provided by our senses rests on a solid foundation. For example, locomotion results in a pattern of optical flow specific to the direction of movement; parts of our visual field go out of view progressively in a manner specific to the environmental layout and the path of locomotion. In addition, the Gibsons have also observed that changes in observers' point and direction of observation—such as those that might result from movement of their eyes, head, or bodies—produce a change in the pattern of optical stimulation that is specific to their movement and the environmental layout.

Moreover, the ecological survey of the natural constraints on the layout of the terrestrial/social environment establishes a lawful, physical basis for optical information that is *specific to* its source. It is precisely this lawful, physical relationship between observers and their environment that lies at the heart of our collective belief in a shared "physical reality," a belief crucial to our existence and well-being. An ecological survey, then, addresses this fundamental social psychological problem, and the ecological approach to perception is, at heart, a social perspective on perception. It is directed toward identifying a lawful basis for the consistency of perceptual experience between and within individuals.

The investigation of craniofacial growth underscores the inherently social basis of the ecological approach to perception: Our objective was to identify the common basis on which observers perceive the same style of change across a myriad of different structures. The ecological approach further encouraged us to consider the adaptive significance of this growth event and its implications for various actions. (The remainder of this volume examines many of these implications.) Thus, several researchers have examined the adaptive significance of the perception of age level (see Berry & Zebrowitz-McArthur, chap. 4; and McCabe, chap. 5) for discussions of this and related issues. The psychosocial implications of those changes also motivated our concern with the application of this work to clinical treatment of children with craniofacial disorders. Our investigation of craniofacial growth, then, has turned out to be more than a study of perception. It has provided an example of how the specification of information about an event establishes a framework in which certain social psychological problems can be examined.

3 The Effects of Growth and Aging on Facial Aesthetics

Thomas R. Alley
Clemson University

I. Craniofacial Development and Perceived Cuteness
II. Age and Facial Attractiveness
   A. The Effect of Aging on Facial Attractiveness
   B. Longitudinal Stability of Facial Attractiveness
   C. Developmental Discontinuities and Sex Differences
III. Closing Remarks

Many diverse changes in craniofacial appearance characterize the transition from neonate to infant to child to adult. These changes include global remodeling of cephalic morphology as well as local changes in facial features such as changes in the relative and absolute size of the eyes (see chaps. 2 and 4). Compared to a mature adult, a baby's face has relatively large and wide-set eyes, dainty eyebrows, small jaws, a more concave profile, a small mouth with short lips, a relatively large and protuberant forehead, a low nasal bridge, a smallish pug nose, and smooth skin (see Enlow, 1982; Subtelny, 1959). Bilateral facial symmetry tends to decrease during the growth period and for some years thereafter (Sutton, 1968). Numerous other observable changes occur after the completion of the growth period, including loss of adipose tissue, qualitative and quantitative increases in wrinkles and bags, and changes in hair distribution and color (see Gonzalez-Ulloa & Flores, 1965; Guthrie, 1976). Also, ear and nose cartilage continue growing throughout life so that the nose becomes longer and broader, and ears (pinnae) increase in length with age (D.W. Smith, 1978).

Given such varied and pervasive changes, it seems reasonable to expect that age-related changes in facial appearance may have a significant impact on facial aesthetics. The mass media and many other segments of our culture would have us believe that aging has a negative impact on facial attractiveness, especially for women. This chapter presents a comprehensive review of this topic, focusing on the effects of growth on facial cuteness and on the stability of facial attractiveness from early childhood onward.

CRANIOFACIAL DEVELOPMENT AND PERCEIVED CUTENESS

Lorenz (1943) suggested that certain age-specific physical characteristics of infants—including their pudgy cheeks, relatively large heads, prominent and protruding foreheads, and large, low-set eyes—function as an "infant-schema" (*"Kindchenschema"*). According to Lorenz, perception of these characteristics by adults elicits a positive, affective response wherein the infantile objects are seen as cute, and parental caregiving is promoted. Lorenz relied on subjective experience, the products of the doll industry, and the dogs preferred as pets by elderly women to support his conjecture, but firmer evidence can be found in a number of experimental studies. Most of the small number of published studies on the effect of craniofacial characteristics on perceived cuteness have been concerned with the effects of various forms and configurations of facial features on cuteness, although some research has explored the effect of global changes in cephalic morphology. All of the latter and some of the studies on facial feature variation have been concerned with age-related changes.

Several of these studies used schematic line drawings to examine the effects of variation in one or more craniofacial characteristics on perceived cuteness. Others have used photographs to assess the impact of age-related changes in overall facial appearance on various judgments. Beginning with the latter, researchers using a variety of measures and photographs have reported that adults, and often younger individuals, prefer photographs of infants over matched photographs of adults (Berman, Goodman, Sloan, & Fernander, 1978; Fullard & Reiling, 1976; Goldberg, Blumberg, & Kriger, 1982). When shown slides of faces of 5-year-olds and adults (matched for size), infants prefer looking at babies to looking at the children's faces (Lewis & Brooks, 1974). Likewise, adults smile more in response to photographs of infants than photographs of adults (Hildebrandt & Fitzgerald, 1978, Exper. 2). Even infants as young as 4 months prefer looking at babies to looking at children or adults (McCall & Kennedy, 1980), which suggests that this visually guided favorable response to infants may be biologically based. Likewise, young adults, especially females, prefer young (2–5 years) children and peers (18–25 years) depicted in facial photographs over older (45–50 years) individuals (Beier, Izard, Smock, & Tougas, 1957). In one study (Bernick, 1966), children ranging in age from kindergarten through 12th grade were shown pictures from 11 categories, including babies. The verbally expressed preferences and the pupillary responses of both sexes were relatively high for the pictures of babies. Similarly, several other experiments using pupillometrics (reviewed in Hess, 1975) have found that photographs of babies are especially likely, at least in female viewers, to evoke pupil dilation, suggesting a rather specific elicitation of interest or a positive emotional response.

The existing studies on the effects of facial feature variations on perceived cuteness or attractiveness, although not designed to test Lorenz's conjecture, also provide some support for his ethological perspective on the effects of an infantile facial appearance. Two early studies of judgments of highly stylized and simplified line drawings of faces (Brunswik & Reiter, 1937; M.R. Samuels, 1939) found a positive correlation between favorable ratings of faces on a number of dimensions and forehead height. In a later study, Brooks and Hochberg (1960) varied eye height in a series of five line drawings. Their viewers tended to give higher cuteness ratings to profiles (but not full face drawings) with lower eye heights and (concomitantly) more prominent foreheads.

Hildebrandt and Fitzgerald (1979b) explored the relationship between facial feature measurements of 60 infants from 3 to 13 months of age and cuteness ratings of their photographs by 196 college students. They concluded that cute infants at all age levels tend to have babyish characteristics, including large foreheads, eyes and pupils, small features, and narrow faces below eye level. A recent pair of follow-up studies (Maier, Holmes, Slaymaker, & Reich, 1984) measured facial features in full-face photos of newborns with conceptional ages of 31–34 weeks, 35–37 weeks, and 40 weeks (full-term). By reversing some of the morphological changes characteristic of postnatal development, they found that full-term infants had proportionately wider, rounder faces with larger eyes located relatively lower in the face. These characteristics associated with postnatal babyishness and attractiveness were still found to be tied to positive responses in adult perceivers. Specifically, Maier et al. collected the responses of 147 adults to 3 composite drawings based on average facial feature measurements of faces in each age category (1 and 2 months premature and full-term). The younger preterm was seen as less cute and attractive than the older preterm which, in turn, was seen as less cute and attractive than the full-term infant. A positive relationship between conceptional age and favorable response held for all (11) other types of impression and expectation included in their questionnaire. The unfavorable responses to composite drawings of premature infants, particularly several items indicating lower willingness to interact with (e.g., take home, take care of) the preterms, suggest that the abnormal facial appearance of infants born prematurely may contribute to the high rate of parent–offspring disturbance among preterms (Friedrich & Boriskin, 1976; Klaus & Kennell, 1976, McCabe, this volume). This study also suggests that perceived age may be a less adequate index of facial cuteness than certain aspects of infantile facial morphology.

In potential opposition to the negative social effects of prematurity, labeling an unattractive neonate "premature" may favorably influence some responses of adults. Evidence for this comes from a study of attractive and unattractive full-term neonates depicted in facial photographs (Cloonan & Ottinger, 1987). These researchers found less positive behavioral inclination toward unattractive newborns when they were labeled *"full-term"* versus *"premature"*. Thus, adults may respond to facially unattractive neonates more favorably if their unattractiveness is seen as a temporary manifestation of prematurity rather than as a stable part of their appearance. In any case, future research should examine potential interactions between age-level information and facial aesthetics.

Like Maier et al. (1984), Hildebrandt and Fitzgerald (1979a) found a reversal within the period near birth of the generally negative correlation between facial cuteness and age. Using facial photographs to examine perceived cuteness over the period from 3 to 13 months, they found that cuteness was greatest at 9 (female infants) or 11 (males) months, being lower before and decreasing thereafter. Reduced cuteness of neonates compared to older infants may have contributed to adults' responses in a study in which a boy was rated as more cuddly at the ages of 6 months and 2 years than as a neonate (Alley & Baron, 1986).

Two studies have used line drawings to examine the effect of more global age-related variation in cephalic morphology on perceived cuteness. In both of these studies, some of the drawings used can be described as supranormal (infantile) stimuli. The first of these was conducted by a European ethologist (Huckstedt, 1965). She asked 250 persons ranging in age from 6 to 30 years to select the "more charming, sweeter, lovable, or cute" of pairs of cephalic profile drawing taken from one of three series. The drawings in these series varied in forehead height or curvature, or in the prominence of the cheeks. In summary, she found that all adults tended to prefer heads that were more infantile even when an exaggerated (supernormal) head shape was compared to a normally proportioned infant head, and even when the infant characteristics were found on another species (a donkey).

Huckstedt's main results, which were not entirely clear-cut due to a confounding of shape with size and amount of hair, have been confirmed in a study that was more carefully controlled and in which head shape was varied in a more biologically natural manner. For this study (Alley, 1981), a transformation that modeled the morphological changes in head shape during growth (see Todd et al., 1980; chap. 2, this volume) was applied to one frontal and two profile line drawings to create three series of human heads varying only in the babyishness of their overall shape. Young adults tended to order these from "youngest" to "oldest" (defined in terms of the growth transformation) when asked to rank them from most to least cute. Likewise, they tended to select the "younger" heads when asked to select the cuter individual in 20 pairs of profiles.

Overall, these results indicate that perceived cuteness tends to decrease sometime after 9 to 12 months of age, although the contribution of certain specific morphological characteristics (like global head shape) to perceived cuteness may decline from birth (or even earlier) onward. A note of caution needs to be inserted at this point: Not just any age-related physical characteristic, even if readily perceived, will alter perceived cuteness in such a way that cuteness decreases as aging occurs. For example, growth-produced changes in body proportions are not linearly associated with a decrement in perceived cuteness (Alley, 1983a) even though they provide sufficient information for accurate assessment of relative age (Alley, 1983b). Still, at least some aspects of the impact of age-related facial morphology on aesthetics seem to be consistent for the period from birth (at full-term) into adulthood. Moreover, infantile facial features may increase facial attractiveness in adults, especially females, due to their ties to the generally attractive and submissive immature age groups (cf. Berry & Zebrowitz-McArthur, this volume; and the following section) and to reproductive fitness (Buss, 1987).

AGE AND FACIAL ATTRACTIVENESS

Human perceivers are sensitive to age-related changes in facial appearance and can readily judge the relative age of different faces shown in photographs (Pittenger & Shaw, 1975b) or even schematic depictions of often subtle facial aging effects (see chaps. 2 and 4). Age, in turn, is correlated with reproductive status and affordances one might expect to be important influences on physical attractiveness (see Alley & Hildebrandt, this volume; Symons, 1979). Hence, there is good reason to suspect that facial aging will affect judgments of facial attractiveness (and other characteristics). If so, individuals displaying greater change in facial appearance due to aging are also likely to be affected by greater variation in their facial attractiveness.

The relationship between age and facial attractiveness mainly involves two separate issues. First, does aging have a negative impact on facial attractiveness? Is there evidence to support the commonplace assumption that the faces of most people, or at least most females, become less attractive as they age? Is there really a youthful standard of facial beauty? Second, how much stability is there in facial attractiveness? Does an exceptionally attractive infant usually become an exceptionally attractive child, adolescent, and adult? Is an ugly child doomed, barring treatment, to become an ugly adult? Unfortunately, there is not enough data with which to thoroughly evaluate these issues. Still, some research exists that at least suggests answers to these questions.

The Effect of Aging on Facial Attractiveness

The available evidence indicates that there is indeed a negative relationship between age and facial attractiveness, during certain developmental periods. To begin, note that facial attractiveness and cuteness are highly correlated (see Alley & Hildebrandt, this volume), and recall that the studies on facial cuteness previously reviewed indicate that perceived cuteness tends to decrease with age, at least after 9 to 12 months of age. In another suggestive study, Nowak (1977) found that facial photographs of adult women received higher attractiveness ratings when described as being 10 years older than they actually were (as opposed to conditions in which their actual age, no age, or an age 10 years younger than the actual age was given). This supports the common view that women who look young for their age are seen as more attractive, and suggests that increasing perceived age should lower perceived attractiveness. Nowak's raters did indeed see the youngest group of adult women targets as most attractive.

In a study based on personal interviews of over 2,000 American adults, interviewers' ratings of physical attractiveness seemed to reflect a negative correlation between age and attractiveness. Although the interviewers were asked to rate physical attractiveness as compared to others of the same sex and age, ratings of "striking" beauty or handsomeness were "quite heavily concentrated among respondents under 35, and the rest of the rating distribution tends to show steady deterioration of attractiveness with growing age" (Campbell, Converse, & Rodgers, 1976, p. 351). Of course, we cannot be sure that these results would hold for facial attractiveness alone, but other research suggests that they would.

Milord (1978) found that age was an important determinant of preference judgments for facial photographs of two age groups, with younger faces being preferred. Cash and Horton (1983) found a small but significant negative correlation between perceived age and physical attractiveness ratings of facial photographs of rhinoplasty patients. Some research aimed more directly at the effect of aging on facial atractiveness was conducted by Korthase and Trenholme (1982, 1983). They found a strong negative correlation ($r = -.91$) between perceived age and perceived physical attractiveness in the ratings of 18 monochromatic facial photographs of young, middle-aged, and older adults by children, adolescents, and adults. Likewise, Walsh and Locke (1980) reported that physical attractiveness ratings of monochrome photographs of young (20–30 years), middle-aged (40–50 years), and elderly (60–70 years) women show a consistent decline as the age-level of the target women increased. Although this study used waist-up rather than facial photographs, attractiveness of facial features (even when examined independent of perceived age) was determined to be a significant influence on these more general attractiveness ratings. Even male (but not female) preschoolers judge faces of elderly men and women to be less good-looking than faces of young adults (Downs & Walz, 1981).

A single study on facial attractiveness in elderly persons indicates that age and attractiveness are *not* related in old age. Johnson (1985) had 90 young and 90 elderly adults rate the attractiveness of facial photographs of 28 male and 28 female Whites age 60–93 years. Neither perceived nor actual age of the targets was correlated with rated attractiveness. Nonetheless, a follow-up study on the determinants of facial attractiveness ratings indicated that "attractive features are those often associated with youthfulness" and vice versa (Johnson, 1985, p. 160). Hence, biological age may be correlated with facial attractiveness in the elderly even if chronological age is not.

A finding of an earlier study (Cross & Cross, 1971) does not seem to be compatible with these other studies in that the attractiveness ratings of 17-year-olds' faces exceeded the ratings of 7-year-olds and adults. Perhaps, however, the decline in facial attractiveness does not begin until young adulthood. This view is consistent with these studies, as well as with a recent longitudinal study of facial attractiveness from early childhood to young adulthood (Alley, 1984); this study found no overall tendency for facial attractiveness to decrease (or increase) during this period. The mean rated facial attractiveness of male targets in the study, however, did decline significantly, but not precipitously ($r = -.31$), with age. Providing somewhat incompatible results, Maruyama and Miller (1981, Table V) reported negative correlations between physical attractiveness and grade in school for facial photographs of grade school children from all three ethnic groups included in their study. The photographs used in this study, however, were poorly standardized.

As all of us have observed, the effects of aging on facial attractiveness can vary greatly across individuals. Among the factors suggested to account for these individual differences is profile contour, with convex faces held to retain a youthful appearance longer than the concave or straight (Foster, 1973). This seems paradoxical in that profile convexity (soft tissue) increases during growth (Subtelny, 1959). Further research is needed to clarify the role of facial contour and numerous other facial characteristics in modifying facial aging effects. In any event, the existence of individual differences in the effects of facial aging limits the degree of stability in facial attractiveness (relative to age-cohorts) across time.

Additional work on the effects of variations in facial features reveals somewhat consistent effects of age-related changes on facial attractiveness, especially for males. Using Identi-Kit constructions (i.e., composites assembled using a standard police identification kit) of young adult faces varying in four facial characteristics, Keating (1985) found that mature traits (thick eyebrows, small eyes, thin lips, and square jaws) generally raised both male and female college students' ratings of the attractiveness (and dominance) of male faces. For female faces, on the other hand, mature traits sometimes raised (thin lips) and sometimes lowered (small eyes) attractiveness ratings, but often had no significant effect. As Keating (1985) suggested, perhaps facial features other than those she examined (excluding eye size) would reflect the predicted greater attractiveness of immature facial characteristics in females. One good candidate is skin texture, since "baby skin" seems to epitomize female skin beauty. Other good candidates can be gleaned from examination of common uses of facial cosmetics, for many cosmetic treatments promote a more youthful appearance (cf. Guthrie, 1976).

Longitudinal Stability of Facial Attractiveness

Until recently there were no published data concerning the stability of facial attractiveness. To date, the data remain notably incomplete, especially considering the tremendous weight this issue carries for both theoretical and applied problems (see chaps. 3, 4, and 5). For instance, the evaluation of the results of facial surgery or orthodontic treatment commonly assume that the facial attractiveness of patients would, without intervention, remain virtually invariant despite the passage of time. As others have noted (e.g. Berscheid & Walster, 1974; Langlois, 1986; Maruyama & Miller, 1981), the stability of physical attractiveness must be determined before one can assess the long-term effects of attractiveness on an individual's development: In order to exert maximum impact, perceived attractiveness must remain stable across both time and situations.

The available studies on the stability of facial attractiveness are all limited, some rather severely, in the generalizability of their findings. Together, however, they provide a rather consistent picture of significant, but low to moderate stability in facial attractiveness from childhood through late adulthood. They also indicate, to no one's surprise, that the similarity in attractiveness ratings of people's faces at different ages decreases as the intervening span of time increases.

In the only study of infants' faces, Langlois and Stephan (1981) examined the stability of facial attractiveness in early infancy by comparing the attractiveness rating of 35 infants photographed at 3 and 6 months of age. They found a moderate correlation ($r = .68$) indicating that facial attractiveness has considerable stability across this brief period.

Adams (1977) reported two "pilot" studies of physical attractiveness in which bodily and facial attractiveness were examined separately. In both studies, facial attractiveness was more stable than bodily attractiveness. Its greater stability and relative importance in determining overall physical attractiveness probably mean that facial attractiveness usually has more long-term impact on most individuals' psychosocial development than other aspects of physical attractiveness. One possible exception is obesity; it has consistently been found to have a highly negative impact on social reactions, even exceeding the negative impact of many physical disabilities and facial deformities (Richardson, Goodman, Hastorf, & Dornbusch, 1961). Still, obesity affects facial appearance, presumably lowering facial attractiveness.

Maruyama and Miller (1981) examined the correlations of attractiveness ratings for facial photographs of a mixed-race sample of 501 children originally photographed in kindergarten through sixth-grade and again 5 years later. They found significant correlations for all three racial groups (White = .34; Black = .38; Mexican-American = .40), both sexes (male = .34; female = .36), and 6 of the 7 grades included (r's for these ranged from .32 to .51). A nonsignificant correlation ($r = .17$) of facial attractiveness over the 5-year interval was found only for the relatively small sample ($n = 24$) of sixth graders. All of these correlations may have been artifactually lowered by poor standardization of the facial photos which varied in size, quality, distance of the child from the camera, facial expression, and color (some were monochromatic).

Two studies have focused on the stability of females' facial attractiveness. First, Livson (1979) found a correlation of .29 between the attractiveness of women rated at about 13 years and again about 25 years later. Second, Sussman, Mueser, Grau, and Yarnold (1983) collected males' ratings of facial (yearbook) photographs of 13 Caucasian girls taken during 1st, 4th, 7th, and 10th grades. The rather limited analysis performed on these data found some significant stability in facial attractiveness across age, as well as "a sizable changing component of physical attractiveness" (p. 1233). That is, the facial attractiveness ratings were significantly influenced by the identity of the stimulus person, but there was also a significant Stimulus Person × Grade interaction.

I have recently completed a more comprehensive study (Alley, 1984). In this study, ratings of 100 young adults were collected for each of 90 monochromatic standardized photographs selected from the First Zurich Longitudinal Study (1954–1980; Kinderspital Zurich). These 90 photos showed the faces of each of 9 male and 9 female targets at five different maturational levels: middle childhood ($M = 6.4$ years), shortly before the onset of puberty ($M = 11.6$), midpuberty ($M = 14.2$), immediately postpuberty ($M = 16.0$), and young adulthood ($M = 20.0$). Statistically significant, but low to moderate intercorrelations were found between ratings of facial attractiveness across the five age-levels ($Mdn = .214$). These correlations revealed a significant degree of stability in facial attractiveness during this period of development, particularly for the female targets. Nonetheless, a large amount of variation in the attractiveness ratings of photographs within most series remained, suggesting a significant, but not necessarily consistent or predictable, impact of aging on facial attractiveness. Follow-up studies are now pursuing questions concerning the causes or correlates of change and stability in facial attractiveness during this period.

Developmental Discontinuities and Sex Differences

One aspect of craniofacial development that probably imposes some discontinuity on facial attractiveness is dental development. The two critical periods in this respect are from about 6 months to 1.5 years of age when the anterior teeth emerge, and approximately 5 to 9 years when the anterior deciduous teeth fall out and are replaced by permanent teeth, with no significant sex differences in this process (Hagg & Taranger, 1985; Subtelny, 1959). Schour and Massler (1941, p. 1158), however, reported that girls "are generally ahead of boys in tooth eruption." Although it has not been adequately explored, it appears that facial attractiveness temporarily deteriorates during this period of mixed dentition; a stage sometimes referred to as the "ugly duckling stage." Not only are teeth missing during this period, but the new permanent dentition tends to remain spaced and poorly aligned for a while after eruption (Schour & Massler, 1941). Adams (1977) suggested that the loss of teeth may be partially responsible for the relatively low correlations of facial attractiveness ratings of second-grade girls and third-grade boys with photographs of these children in adjacent grades. The ecological perspective demands that we consider the potential impact of changing affordances due to dental development in addition to their effect on dentofacial appearance.

Sex differences almost surely exist in the effects of facial aging on physical attractiveness. There are sex differences in the common effects of aging on adults' facial appearance (Guthrie, 1976). Moreover, the mass media frequently express a double standard of aging in suggesting that men often improve as they age while women just get older (cf. Adams & Crossman, 1978; Freedman, 1986; Melamed, 1983). For instance, gray hair is often reported to make men look more "distinguished" while simply making women less attractive (Nowak, 1977).

There are other good reasons to expect aging to have the most negative impact on females' attractiveness besides the fact that we continually receive this message from the mass media and expressions of popular opinion. Females are inherently more childlike in many physical characteristics, including some facial characteristics, due to a sex difference in development whereby females tend to retain more "immature" features than males (Gould, 1977). Hence, for women the facial consequences of aging may make them less feminine appearing as the years pass, whereas men may tend to become more masculine appearing. In other words, youthful facial characteristics will naturally be seen as part of a feminine appearance, and being feminine is to some extent a requirement for being an attractive female (see chaps. 6; Freedman, 1986).

The stronger tie of female attractiveness and sex-typical facial appearance to youthful, or even infantile, physical characteristics (see chaps. 4 and 6; Freedman, 1986) may be partially responsible for the double standards by which facial aging effects are judged. Childlike qualities are often included among the characteristics that make women both feminine and attractive (see

Freedman, 1986; and the following discussion). In any case, the double standard of aging together with the greater importance of physical appearance for women create a gloomy forecast for the impact of facial aging on middle-aged and older women.

There is also a sociobiological argument that judgments of females' physical (e.g., facial) attractiveness have been shaped by evolutionary selection pressures on mate selection and, therefore, will favor youthful characteristics that generally signify a more suitable (e.g., fertile) mate (Buss, 1987; Symons, 1979). One main reason for a sex difference from this perspective is the relative importance of age as a determinant of females' reproductive capacity as compared to males. Moreover, during the period from young to middle adulthood when females' reproductive capacity generally declines, males' reproductive fitness may actually increase due to gains in power, status, knowledge and possessions. From this perspective we might expect that the female faces seen as most attractive by males would possess characteristics typical of women during and immediately preceding their optimal reproductive years; that is, from about 17 to 30 years of age (Symons, 1979). Females, on the other hand, should tend to see somewhat older male faces as most attractive.

Research supporting these hypotheses is sparse, but some exists. To begin, Secord, Dukes, and Bevan (1954), using monochrome facial photographs of adult White males, did find that people tend to see older males as more distinguished, responsible, refined, and conscientious. Also supporting this double standard of aging effects is a study in which elderly and college-aged subjects rated photographs of members of both sexes taken at three age-levels from young adulthood to over 60; the perceived attractiveness of women declined with age more than men (Deutsch, Clark, & Zalenski, 1983). Another study failed to find sex differences in facial attractiveness for middle-aged Whites (Berman, O'Nan, & Floyd, 1981), but this study was limited to 20 faces preselected to be of moderate attractiveness. Even so, all-male groups of raters still rated these women less attractive than the middle-aged men. The facial preferences of the mixed-sex raters in a study by Milord (1978, Experiment 1) displayed a Sex × Age interaction indicating a greater impact of facial aging for female faces: Faces of young females were most preferred and old females were least preferred, whereas both old and young males were between these two extremes and about equally preferred. Male preference judgments were discovered to be largely responsible for this preference ordering.

CLOSING REMARKS

The relationships between facial aesthetics and aging have been subject to far more discussion and conjecture than empirical research. Consequently, we still cannot evaluate even the basic and age-old claims that people, or at least adults, become less pleasing to look at as they age. Questions of why certain individuals remain stable in facial attractiveness despite aging while many others do not, and what morphological characteristics predispose individuals to varying degrees of change in attractiveness with age, remain almost completely unanswerable at present. Of course, everyone ages and, to varying degrees, displays their aging on their everchanging faces. The perceived age and attractiveness of faces are surely interrelated. Other chapters in this volume make it abundantly clear that both have widespread, numerous, and significant effects on social interactions and self-perception. Hence, it is time more perceptual and social psychologists turned their attention to this topic. In the following chapter, we see that this is already happening, particularly with regard to physiognomic effects of facial aging.

ACKNOWLEDGMENT

Thanks are due to Katherine Hildebrandt for her helpful comments on an earlier version of this chapter.

4 The Impact of Age-Related Craniofacial Changes on Social Perception

Diane S. Berry
Southern Methodist University

Leslie Zebrowitz-McArthur
Brandeis University

I. Introduction
II. Craniofacial Profile Shape
III. Vertical Placement: Forehead Size and Chin Size
IV. Facial Shape
V. Eye Characteristics
VI. Skin Qualities
VII. Feature Length
VIII. Overall Facial Configuration
IX. Summary and Conclusions

The countenance is the reflection of the soul.
—Cicero

Although most modern psychologists eschew the belief that character can be read from the face, this view has an ancient and distinguished history. It is found in the works of ancient philosophers, including Aristotle, who described at length the facial signs of strength and weakness, genius and stupidity, timidity and boldness. It is also found in the works of great writers, one notable example being Shakespeare, whose extensive use of physiognomic description attests to his conviction that the face reveals the inner person as well as his confidence that these correspondences would be understood by his readers.

The belief in facial cues to character seems to be quite widespread (see chap. 8). The reliance on physical appearance in descriptions of other people occurs at an early age (Livesley & Bromley, 1973), and although psychological descriptions do increase as a person matures, physical qualities continue to play a central role in our judgments of character. For instance, when Fiske and Cox (1979) asked people to describe another person, appearance was typically the first category of description employed. Moreover, the tendency to begin by describing the person in terms of appearance rather than other attributes occurred whether people were describing a familiar or an unfamiliar person and it was observed even when people had been instructed to describe the person so that someone else would know what it is like to be around him or her.

The prominent role of physical appearance in descriptions of others is paralleled by its role in attraction to others. Not only is there considerable evidence to indicate that people prefer to socialize with physically attractive members of the opposite sex (Berscheid & Walster, 1974), but it has been also found that people cite a variety of physical characteristics in addition to attractiveness as their reason for wanting to get to know a person. More specifically, Lyman, Hatlelid, and Macurdy (1981) found that when people gave reasons for wanting or not wanting to get to know someone whom they had seen engaging in a videotaped social interaction, they not only cited a variety of physical characteristics but these characteristics were better predictors of the desire to affiliate than were observed behaviors, inferred behaviors, or personality traits.

Further evidence for the impact of appearance on our impressions of others comes from research that has examined descriptions of people as a function of variations in their facial appearance. Kassin (1977) found that perceivers are more likely to ascribe stable personality traits to a person whose appearance is constant than to one whose appearance noticeably changes. Bowman (1979) found that perceivers were more apt to change their trait ascriptions to a person whose behavior changed if his facial appearance also changed than if it remained constant. Finally, Secord and his associates (Secord, Dukes, & Bevan, 1954; Secord & Muthard, 1955; Stritch & Secord, 1956) conducted a number of studies in which subjects were shown photographs of faces and asked to rate the facial features as well as their impressions of the personality traits of those pictured. The results revealed that people who were rated similarly on facial features were also rated similarly in personality. That is, people who physically resemble each other are perceived to have similar traits while those who look different from one another are perceived to have different traits (see chap. 8).

To summarize, it appears that our perception of people's character is strongly tied to their facial appearance. When asked to describe what someone is like, we begin by describing their appearance, and when asked why we want to get to know someone we cite aspects of their appearance. People who look alike are judged to be alike. When a person's appearance varies a lot, we do not perceive them as having stable personality characteristics. Furthermore, we more readily ascribe personality changes to people if their appearance has also changed.

Although it is clear that people's facial appearance influences our impressions of their psychological qualities, the question remains as to what facial characteristics communicate what psychological attributes. Secord tried to answer this question in his research, but he failed to identify clear correspondences between particular facial features and particular traits. Researchers studying the impact of variations in physical attractiveness on person perception have repeatedly demonstrated that attractive faces create positive perceptions on a variety of trait dimensions (see Alley & Hildebrandt, this volume). However, this work has not adequately identified which characteristics produce an attractive appearance, and thus which facial characteristics yield these perceptions. Other investigators have also failed to provide consistent and comprehensible generalizations, (see chap. 8 and McArthur, 1982, for reviews of the relevant literature.) A significant problem with past research is that it has essentially involved a shotgun approach to ascertaining what faces yield what impressions. A theoretical framework is needed to provide a plausible basis for the widespread belief that facial appearance and behavior are related as well as to provide specific hypotheses regarding what aspects of facial appearance influence our impressions of others.

The theoretical framework favored by early physiognomists was simple: People believe that facial appearance and behavior are related because facial appearance is an accurate indication of character (e.g., Lavater, 1783). Although this may in fact prove true for at least some face/behavior correspondences, most psychologists today are rightly skeptical of the notion that a facial feature like the length of a person's nose or the size of a person's eyes could really bear a direct relationship to his or her character. If we reject this view, the question then becomes "why do people *believe* that there are correspondences between facial appearance and character?"

One appealing explanation for such a belief is a self-fulfilling prophecy effect. Perhaps people with certain facial features behave in certain ways because others expect them to and, consequently, interact with them in a manner that elicits the expected behavior. Evidence for such an effect has been documented by Snyder, Tanke, and Berscheid (1977), who found that people expect physically attractive individuals to be more socially adept than unattractive people, and that social interactions with attractive versus unattractive people elicit the very behaviors that are expected. Although such self-fulfilling prophecy effects may occur, a crucial question remains: What is the origin of the expectancy that attractive people will be more sociable as well as other expectancies regarding the relationship between facial appearance and behavior?

McArthur and Baron (1983) have suggested an ecological approach to social perception that addresses this issue. First, they assume that person perception serves an adaptive purpose, inasmuch as our impressions of others' psychological attributes must guide our social interactions. Second, they propose that appearance-based expectancies will either be accurate or, if erroneous, will reflect the overgeneralization of expectancies that usually are adaptive. Finally, they suggest that the physical appearance variables that influence impressions are those that typically reveal psychological attributes whose detection is important either for the survival of the species or for the adaptive functioning of the individual. These assumptions provide some guidance regarding what types of attributes will be specified by facial characteristics, as well as the nature of the facial characteristics that will reveal these attributes.

Among those attributes whose detection is clearly essential for adaptive behavior are age-related behavioral affordances. Affordances are opportunities for acting or being acted upon that are provided by the environment (J.J. Gibson, 1979). Koffka (1935) captured this aspect of affordances more poetically: "Each thing says what it is—a fruit says 'eat me'; water says 'drink me'; thunder says 'fear me'; and woman says 'love me'" (p. 7). Age-related affordances are those opportunities for acting or being acted upon that vary with the age of the person with whom one might interact. Thus, for example, infants afford training, nurturing, and protecting. In Koffka's language, a baby says 'teach me' and 'cuddle me' and 'help me.' Mature individuals, on the other hand, are more apt to afford sexual pleasure, wisdom, or harm. Because the detection of age-related affordances such as these is clearly important for adaptive functioning, the ecological approach predicts that those facial characteristics that distinguish infants from more mature organisms will be sufficient to reveal them. The ecological approach further predicts that a strong attunement to facial information that identifies infants and their related affordances may be overgeneralized to adults who in some way resemble the young. This raises the question of what facial characteristics distinguish infants from mature adults.

Ethologists have identified a variety of facial characteristics that distinguish infants from adults. At the most global level, Lorenz (1943) noted that the infant has a large head in relation to the body, and Guthrie (1976) has noted that the infant's face is relatively hairless, smooth skinned and light-complexioned with fuller and pinker cheeks than the adult. Another general difference between the faces of infants and adults is the placement of the facial features. The vertical placement of features is lower in the infant face, yielding a relatively larger forehead and a shorter chin. The chin not only becomes longer with increasing age, but it also becomes more angular and more prominent, jutting forward rather than receding.

In addition to the foregoing age differences in the overall configuration of the face, distinguishing characteristics of individual features have also been identified by ethologists. The eyes of the infant are larger and the eyelashes are longer relative to the rest of the face. Young children have very fine eyebrows until puberty when longer, thicker brow hair develops, particularly among males. Also, since children typically look up at adults, raising their eyebrows, high eyebrows are another sign of youth (Guthrie, 1976). Other age differences related to the eyes include larger pupils in the infant and the young child than in the adult, and a greater tendency for the infant's iris and sclera to be blue. Differences in coloration are also found in the hair, which is more often blond in the young child. The mouth and nose of the infant can also be distinguished from their adult counterparts. "Children's lips are redder and proportionately larger than lips of adults . . . [and] the nose changes size and shape with age" (Guthrie, 1976, p. 106). More specifically, a baby's nose is typically small, wide, and concave with a sunken bridge; the adult's nose, particularly the male's, is proportionately larger, narrower, and convex in shape with a prominent bridge (Liggett, 1974).

While ethologists have identified the facial qualities that distinguish children from adults, the question of which of these characteristics communicate an individual's age to lay perceivers and which, if any, communicate an individual's behavioral affordances remains. It is expected that persons with childlike facial characteristics will be perceived as younger than those with more mature faces. It is also expected that those with a childlike appearance will be perceived as affording more warmth and cuddliness, more submission, less strength, less danger, less wisdom and more naivete than those with a mature appearance.

It should be noted that within the ecological approach these perceptions are assumed to reflect a direct response to a childlike facial appearance rather than a response mediated by labeling the person as *child* versus *adult*. Indeed, this is the explanation that this approach offers for the persistent belief that there are correspondences between adults' facial appearance and their character. To test this assumption, this chapter examines not only impressions of faces that vary in age, but also impressions of faces that vary in 'babyishness,' albeit not in chronological age. It is anticipated that impressions of people who vary in the maturity of their appearance will parallel perceptions of those who vary in actual maturity.

CRANIOFACIAL PROFILE SHAPE

Perpendicular foreheads . . . are certain signs of weakness, little understanding, little imagination. Retreating foreheads in general denote superiority of imagination and acuteness. (Lavater, 1783, pp. 381–382)

One important source of age information is the shape of the head when seen in profile. As an individual ages, the maturation of the facial structure combined with the influences of external forces such as gravity produce a distinctive remodeling of the cranium. One result of this change, as seen from a side view, involves a lessening of the predominance of the brain capsule with increasing age. Evidence that sufficient information for the identification of aging and growth is provided by this style of change has been supplied by research investigating the effects of the application of a growth-stimulating cardioidal strain transformation to standard profiles (cf. chap. 2). This transformation, which has been demonstrated to be an accurate approximation of real growth (Todd & Mark, 1981), is spontaneously perceived as such (Mark, Todd, & Shaw, 1981) and influences age estimates in a systematic manner (e.g., Pittenger & Shaw, 1975a). In addition, research has indicated that such age-related variations in cephalic shape systematically influence the perception of age-related affordances.

Alley (1983c) reports two experiments in which subjects were asked to identify the member of a stimulus pair that they would feel the most compelled to defend from a physical beating. In one study (Exper. 3) these stimulus pairs consisted of profiles derived from a series of frontal cephalic X-rays taken of a female child at 3, 57, 105, and 180 months. Subjects chose the younger of the pair as the most defense-provoking significantly more often than the older member. In another study (Exper. 1) subjects performed the same task with stimulus profiles in which shape was varied by applying various levels of cardioidal strain to a standard. Again subjects chose the younger (in terms of level of strain) profile as the most defense-providing. This indicates that information about a person's need for physical protection may be conveyed by age-variant profile shape cues. Moreover, these results were both powerful and consistent despite the subtle and abstract nature of the shape manipulations, suggesting that subjects were responding to the stimulus configuration itself rather than relying on a process of age-labeling to make their choices.

There is also evidence that profile shape may influence impressions of a stimulus person's affordances. McArthur (unpublished) presented seven profiles representing different levels of cardioidal strain to subjects one at a time in random order. Subjects were asked to rate each on a series of 7-point bipolar trait scales. After all seven profiles were rated on one dimension, they were presented again in a different random order and rated on the next dimension. After the profiles had been rated on all trait dimensions, they were presented one final time and subjects were asked to estimate the age of each profile. These procedures were adopted in order to weaken any carry-over effects of one trait rating of a profile onto another rating, and to reduce the likelihood that an explicit age label attached to each profile would influence the subjects' trait ratings. It should be noted that when the profiles are shown singly in a random order, the differences between those that are most similar in cardioidal strain are very subtle (see Fig. 4.1). Nevertheless, profile shape had a strong effect on subjects' impressions (see Table 4.1).

As the craniofacial profile decreased in maturity, the stimulus persons were perceived as increasing in dependency. More specifically, they were rated as decreasing in alertness, reliability, intelligence, and strength. Decreasing craniofacial profile maturity was also associated with increases in approachability; the more immature profiles were rated as less threatening, kinder, more

4. IMPACT OF CRANIOFACIAL CHANGES   69

FIG. 4.1. Stimulus profiles varying in cardioidal strain. (This transformation may be described in polar coordinates $\theta' = \theta$, $R' = R[1 + k(1 - \cos\theta)]$, where k is a constant representing the level of strain. From left to right, these profiles were produced by levels of strain (k) of $-.25$, $-.10$, 0, .25, .35, and .55, respectively. Note: From 'Aging Faces as Viscal-Elastic Events: Implications for a Theory of Nonrigid Shape Perception' by J.B. Pittenger and R.E. Shaw, 1975, *Journal of Experimental Psychology: Human Perception and Performance, 1,* p. 376. Copyright 1975 by the American Psychological Association, Inc. Reprinted by permission.

TABLE 4.1
Mean Ratings of Craniofacial Profiles Varying in Cardioidal Strain

	Level of Cardioidal Strain (k)							F	
	−.25	−.10	0	.10	.25	.35	.55	lin.	quad
Judged age	4.43	11.57	15.47	22.70	30.10	32.63	39.07	473.65	3.08
Affordances:									
Dependency									
Alert	3.40	4.50	5.10	5.57	4.10	3.23	2.90	12.35	54.75
Reliable	4.37	4.90	5.20	5.53	4.53	3.83	2.93	23.47	33.75
Intelligent	4.20	5.07	5.50	5.13	3.83	2.30	1.20	230.69	135.51
Strong	1.40	3.23	3.30	4.43	5.30	5.83	6.40	561.94	7.76
Approachability									
Nonthreatening	6.80	6.30	5.80	5.00	3.50	2.83	2.13	473.56	3.08
Kind	5.43	5.63	5.30	4.87	3.73	3.47	2.70	88.12	5.19
Flexible	5.20	4.63	4.90	4.76	3.13	3.46	2.70	55.54	1.86
Lovable	5.70	5.33	5.13	4.60	3.73	3.53	2.90	99.18	<1
Sexy	2.53	3.53	4.20	4.60	3.43	2.43	1.40	30.06	115.99

Note. All ratings were made on a seven point scale. $N = 30$ in each cell. Critical $F = 2.42$ for $p < .05$. While craniofacial growth is typically completed by age 20, the last two profiles in this series were judged to represent people in their 30s. Thus, it may be that these two levels of this version of the cardioidal strain provide information in addition to growth. Indeed, perceivers often called these two profiles "ape men." As such, the reader should be aware that ratings of the last two profiles may not really reflect age perceptions. *Note:* From "Perceiving character in faces: The impact of age-related craniofacial changes on social perception" by D. S. Berry and L. Z. McArthur, 1986, *Psychological Bulletin, 100,* p. 7. Copyright 1986 by the American Psychological Association, Inc. Reprinted by permission.

flexible, and more lovable than were older profiles. The only rating of approachability that decreased as profile maturity decreased was that of sexiness. Although the foregoing linear effects were highly significant, it should be noted that ratings of alertness, reliability, intelligence, and sexiness also showed strong quadratic trends, reflecting a curvilinear relationship with craniofacial maturity.

The impact of craniofacial profile shape on trait ratings in this study and on defense-provokingness in the studies by Alley suggest that adults' perceptions of a person's social affordances vary as a function of age-related physical information. Moreover, the direction of these effects is consistent with ecological hypotheses. It seems quite adaptive to perceive immature profiles as more dependent and approachable, but less sexy than mature ones. Such perceptions are fundamental to behavior geared toward protecting and nurturing, but not molesting, the young.

Research conducted by Montepare and McArthur (1982, 1986) has investigated the sensitivity of preschoolers to the age information available in the shape of the craniofacial profile. Varying levels of cardioidal strain were applied to a standard schematic profile to produce three age-variant stimuli that adults judged to represent a 4-, a 16-, and a 30-year-old person. When children as young as three were asked which profile in a pair was the "baby," the "boy" and the "man," they chose the correct profile at greater than chance levels.

Montepare and McArthur also assessed the influence of profile shape on the behavioral affordances that children perceived in the stimulus persons. For this purpose, a storybook was constructed in which four behavioral affordances were described in a concrete manner. The story involved a child's encounters with various people who might be instrumental in helping to retrieve a kite that had been caught in a tree. It described four different behaviors and the child's task was to decide which of two pictured individuals had manifested each behavior. The behaviors were: (a) knowing the answers to a lot of questions and being smart enough to figure out a way to retrieve the kit; (b) being a boss who makes the rules and tells people what to do, and who advised the child not to fly the kite close to the trees; (c) being unabled to run very fast or jump very high and being too weak to climb the tree and get the kite; and (d) being mean and saying "go away and don't bother me." For each behavior, children were shown pairs of profiles that varied in cardioidal strain and were asked to point to the person whom they thought would exhibit that behavior. Children chose the older of the profiles as the "mean" one at a greater than chance level, but profile shape had no consistent effect on any of the other dependent measures.

The fact that children could correctly identify the baby, the boy, and the man on the basis of the information provided by the cardioidal strain indicates that even young children are sensitive to subtle and abstract age cues. However, children showed minimal ability to perceive age-related behavioral affordances. The role of perceiver attunement in detecting behavioral affordances may help to account for these findings, as individuals will differ in their sensitivity to available information as a function of its usefulness for action. It may be that information about 'meanness' is most readily extracted by children because this knowledge plays a more useful role in their daily lives than the detection of such attributes as tree-climbing ability or problem-solving ability. This interpretation is supported by a study of Fisher et al. (1984), who found that meanness is a primary dimension along which children initially base their impressions of others.

VERTICAL PLACEMENT: FOREHEAD SIZE AND CHIN SIZE

A small deficient chin stands for weakness of will and physical endurance . . . the strong, large but well-proportioned chin stands for mental backbone . . . and also tremendous physical energy and endurance. (LeBarr, 1922, pp. 73-74)

The growth process simulated by the cardioidal strain also has an impact on facial appearance as viewed from a frontal position (Mark & Todd, 1983), and these changes have an impact on perceptions of both age and craniofacial maturity. More specifically advancing age is accompanied by a raising of facial features on the vertical plane of the face, which yields a decrease in relative forehead size as well as an increase in relative chin size. Evidence that these facial changes do communicate a person's age to perceivers has been provided by McArthur and Apatow (1983-1984) who found that as the vertical placement of the features on schematic faces was lowered, the estimated age of the person decreased.

Variations in feature vertical placement and the associated changes in forehead and chin size have been found to have an impact on people's perceived affordances, as well as their perceived age. Alley (1983c, Exper. 2) applied the strain transformation to a frontal drawing of an infant face to produce a series of five schematic faces. One consequence of this transformation was a variation in the vertical placement of the facial features, with the most babyish version exhibiting the largest forehead, the smallest chin, and the lowest feature placement. Subjects were shown the five drawings and asked to rank order them in terms of which they would feel the most compelled to defend from a beating. As predicted, the lower the vertical placement of the features, the higher the ranked defense-provokingness of the face.

McArthur and Apatow (1983-1984) have provided additional evidence that the vertical placement of facial features communicates age-related affordances. Subjects in this study rated the social dominance, physical strength, intellectual naivete and physical appeal of male and female adult schematic faces.

The dependent measures included both traditional bipolar trait scales (e.g., strong/weak) and behavioral affordance questions (e.g., "Does this look like someone who would be able to move several boxes of your heaviest books?"). Persons with a lower ('younger') placement of features, and with a corresponding large forehead and small chin, were perceived as physically weaker, more socially submissive, and more naive than those with a higher ('older') placement of features. In addition, female faces with low placement were rated as cuter and warmer than those with high placement. It should be noted that partial correlation analyses indicated these relationships cannot be attributed to differences in the perceived age or physical attractiveness of faces with a low versus high vertical placement of features. Thus, it cannot be argued that the impact of vertical placement on impressions resulted from stereotypic personality prototypes elicited through changes in the age label applied to the faces or through halo effects produced by variations in their attractiveness.

size on perceived social affordances using a sample of photographed adult males as stimuli. A narrower ('younger') chin created impressions of warmth, honesty, kindness, and naivete. However, these ratings were not predicted by measures of forehead height, width, area, or measures of vertical placement. Although limited variability in the sizes of the foreheads in this sample of faces seems sufficient to account for the failure of these characteristics to influence impressions, the results do indicate that chin size, in of itself, provides sufficient information for the detection of age-related affordances. Moreover, these results suggest that variations in chin size alone may have been responsible for the effects of the vertical placement manipulations used by McArthur and Apatow (1983-1984) and Alley (1983c, Exper. 2). The impact of chin size on such judgments is also consistent with Keating, Mazur, and Segall's (1981) finding that persons with large jaws are perceived as more dominant than those with small jaws.

Using a methodology similar to that employed in their study of children's impressions of faces varying in cardioidal strain, Montepare and McArthur (1982, 1986) have investigated the impact of feature placement on children's age perceptions. Two different male faces were created by selecting two different sets of hairstyles, eyebrows, eyes, mouths, ears, and chins from a police Identi-Kit. For each face, the vertical placement of internal features was varied while keeping their relationship to one another constant to produce faces of babyish, boyish, and adult faces (see Fig. 4.2). When children as young as three were shown pairs of these faces and asked which was the baby, boy, and/or man, their choice of the correct face was significantly greater than chance. Thus, very young children are sensitive to the age information provided by feature placement.

In addition to assessing children's ability to use vertical placement information to identify a person's age, Montepare and McArthur assessed the impact

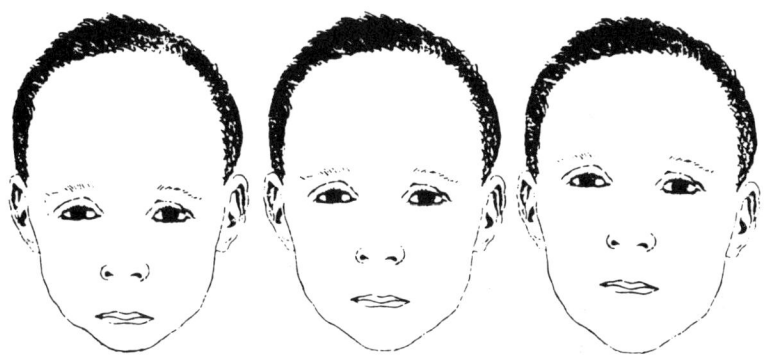

FIG. 4.2. A sample stimulus face in which vertical feature placement has been varied from low (left) to high (right). Note: from "The Impact of Age-Related Variations in Facial Characteristics on Children's Age Perceptions" by J.M. Montepare and L.Z. McArthur, 1986, *Journal of Experimental Child Psychology*. Reprinted by permission.

of such facial information on the perceived affordances of the stimulus person. For this purpose, they used a story book identical to that previously described (Montepare & McArthur 1986, Study 2) except for the addition of two behaviors: (a) sitting with the child for a while and telling him a nice story that made him feel better about the kite that was caught in the tree, and (b) telling the child that he would buy him a brand new kite. As in the study of the affordances perceived in craniofacial profiles, the children were shown pairs of faces and asked to point to the person whom they thought would exhibit the behavior.

Like craniofacial profile shape, feature placement had little impact on the perception of age-related affordances. Meanly saying "go away and don't bother me" was once again the only behavior to show systematic effects. More specifically, this behavior was attributed more often than chance to the faces that had the lower vertical placement of features. As just argued, the failure of vertical placement to communicate any of the other behavior affordances may be due to the lesser significance of the other affordances in children's everyday life. More difficult to explain is the fact that it was the "older" of the two craniofacial profiles that was perceived as affording the mean behavior, while it was the "younger" of the two feature placements that was perceived as affording the same behavior. The latter finding, which was contrary to predictions, may have been due to the tendency for the facial expression to appear more negative as the vertical placement of the features was lowered (see Fig. 4.2). If so, then children's impressions of the behavioral affordances of faces varying in feature placement may have nothing to do with the apparent age of these faces. Evidence consistent with this argument is provided by the finding that children judged the face with the lower placement of features as the meaner of the two whether or not they could accurately identify it as the younger of the two. In the case of the craniofacial profiles, on the other hand, children judged the face with the more mature profile as the meaner of the two only when they could also accurately identify the ages of the two profiles.

Although the foregoing studies have examined the impact of forehead and chin size on social perceptions, a provocative study by McCabe (1984; this volume) found evidence that children who have been physically abused display 'older' craniofacial proportions (i.e., a higher vertical placement of features) than nonabused children matched on such variables as age, gender, and race. Various explanations can be offered for the results. For example, as noted earlier, Lorenz (1943) proposed that physical characteristics typical of the young serve the function of inhibiting aggression and eliciting caregiving from adults. Perhaps infants or children who exhibit unusually mature feature characteristics do not adequately inhibit aggression or elicit caregiving and are thus at a higher risk for abuse or neglect than those who have a more 'babyish' appearance. Another possible explanation of these findings is that an age-inappropriate craniofacial appearance may elicit perceptions of the child that are discrepant with his or her true needs and abilities. This might produce parental expectations of behaviors that are beyond the child's capabilities. As a consequence, the child may be punished for failing to live up to expectations. Obviously, child abuse is a complex and multifaceted problem that involves a variety of factors. Nonetheless, the McCabe studies provide evidence that age-variant physical traits may exert an influence not only on social perceptions, but also on social behaviors.

FACIAL SHAPE

> The man of action type [whose] face . . . resembles a square . . . resorts primarily to his physical strength. The . . . 'let George do it' type is recognized by the round face . . . he is always good tempered, jolly, pleasant. (LeBarr, 1922, pp. 24–27)

In addition to the impact of chin size on the perception of age and age-related affordances, some research has suggested that the *shape* of the chin and face may exert an influence on such judgments. Berry and McArthur (1985) found that male faces rated high in angularity were perceived as less warm, less honest, and more mature than those rated as softer in shape. McArthur, Lipnick, and Rudin (1984) further investigated the impact of facial shape cues on impressions. Subjects made trait ratings for a series of schematic faces constructed from a police Identi-Kit. These included four male faces with identical features but differing jaws. The manipulation of jaw shape created two angular jaws (a rectangular and a square version) and two curved jaws (an oval and a round version). The results revealed that faces with angular jaws were perceived as older than identical faces with curved jaws. Angularity also influenced the perceived affordances of the faces. More specifically, those with angular jaws were perceived as more dominant than those with curved jaws. An additional finding in this study was that the impact of angularity on perceptions of the age and dominance of a human face was paralleled by its impact on perceptions of geometric shapes. A separate group of subjects rated a series of geometric shapes that corresponded to the shapes of the experimental faces—a rectangle, a square, oval, and a circle. Like angular faces, angular objects were perceived as older and more dominant than curved ones. Interestingly, the impact of shape on these ratings was stronger for objects than for faces.

The finding that faces with angular jaws are perceived as older than those with curved jaws is consistent with Berry and McArthur's (1985) report that angular faces are perceived to have a more mature appearance than soft faces. The finding that this 'mature' characteristic increases ratings of dominance is consistent with research indicating that faces featuring a mature-appearing chin are often judged to be dominant (Keating, Mazur, & Segall, 1981). The observation that the shape of an inanimate object has the same impact on perceived affordances as the shape of a person's face could reflect a tendency to overgeneralize impressions of persons to objects that resemble them in some manner. This finding further suggests that both age and affordances may be specified by abstract geometric information regardless of the entity it characterizes, a result consistent with research that has applied the cardioidal strain transformation to inanimate objects (Pittenger et al., 1979; chap. 1, this volume).

EYE CHARACTERISTICS

Brilliant, wide-open eyes denote sincerity, honesty, trustworthiness, and frankness. If carried to the extreme, they denote credulous and trustworthy individuals, those who take everything for granted and are easily led and often cheated by the unscrupulous . . . (LeBarr, 1922, pp. 63-63)

A higher arch of the brow [gives] a fixed air of attentiveness and receptivity. In a sense, this creates a stimulus of mild subordination. (Guthrie, 1976, p. 53)

Both eye and eyebrow characteristics have been proposed to influence age perceptions. In particular, investigators such as Hess (1970) and Lorenz (1943) have noted that round eyes and pupils that are large relative to the size of the face are typical of infants. In addition, Guthrie (1976) noted that the eyebrows of the young are lighter, finer, and characteristically higher than those of adults. Some empirical evidence that age information is available in the eyes is provided by the finding that eye size is positively associated with ratings of the 'cuteness', 'attractiveness', and 'babyishness' of an infant's face (e.g., Hildebrandt & Fitzgerald, 1979b; Maier et al., 1984; Sternglanz, Gray, & Murakami, 1977). More direct evidence for the role of eye size in age perception has been provided by the finding that as the size of the eyes in real and schematic adult faces increased, the estimated age of the persons decreased (Berry & McArthur, 1985; McArthur & Apatow, 1983–1984). In addition, both eye size and eyebrow height are negatively associated with the rated facial maturity of adult males (Berry & McArthur, 1985). Finally, Jones and Smith (1984) have reported that children make significantly more errors in rank ordering the ages of photographed persons when the eye area is masked than when other areas of the stimulus faces are occluded.

Eye size, eye roundness, and eyebrow height have been found to influence the perception of age-related affordances as well as perceived age. McArthur and Apatow (1983–1984) demonstrated that increasing the size of the eyes in adult male and female schematic faces increased perceptions of the stimulus persons' physical weakness, intellectual naivete, social submissiveness, warmth, and honesty. Furthermore, partial correlation analyses revealed that these effects were independent of any differences in the perceived age and physical attractiveness of faces with large versus small eyes. Consistent with these results are the studies of Keating (1985), who found that eyes that made male and female adult schematic faces appear mature also increased their perceived dominance, and Berry and McArthur (1985) who found that perceptions of warmth, kindness, honesty, and naivete were positively correlated with eye size in a sample of adult male faces. Berry and McArthur also found that higher eyebrows were associated with impressions of an adult male's greater warmth, kindness, and naivete. Similarly, Keating, Mazur and Segall (1977) reported that schematic cartoon faces with low eyebrows were identified as dominant more often than similar faces with high eyebrows. Additionally, Keating, Mazur, Segall, Cysneiros et al. (1981) reported that photographed adults are perceived as more dominant when their eyebrows are lowered. (See chap. 8.)

SKIN QUALITIES

It is known to the scientific world that wrinkles indicate the trend of character . . . (LeBarr, 1922, p. 59)

A variety of skin qualities have been observed to covary with age. For example, Guthrie (1976) noted that children's skin is softer and smoother than adults'. In addition, children's faces tend to be paler and to have pinker cheeks than do older faces. Although no research has considered the impact of facial coloring on perceived age and affordances, some recent work suggests that facial wrinkling is a powerful conveyor of age information. Mark et al. (1980) asked subjects to estimate the ages of a series of profile drawings of adult male faces in which wrinkling and cranial shape were independently manipulated in an age variant manner. It was found that increased wrinkling yielded linear increases in perceived age. In addition, when the age levels specified by profile shape and wrinkling were inconsistent, wrinkle information tended to have a somewhat stronger impact on age estimates than did cranial shape.

Research conducted by Montepare and McArthur 1982 investigated the impact of facial wrinkling on children's age identification and social perceptions. In the first study, 15-, 55-, 75-year-old versions of two faces were created by varying the degree of wrinkling in each. In the second, wrinkling was varied to create faces judged by adults to be 19 and 53 years old. When children were shown these faces in pairs that varied only in the extent of wrinkling, they were able to correctly identify the older faces at a rate significantly greater than chance. In addition, the storybook described earlier was again used in this research to assess the impact of the wrinkles on the perceived affordances of the faces. As was true for craniofacial profile shape and feature placement, facial wrinkling had a systematic impact on one perceived affordance: meanly saying "go away and don't bother me" was attributed more often than chance to the face in the pair that had more wrinkles.

FEATURE LENGTH

> ... the long line from the root of the nose to the tip stands, as a rule, for great energy, both mental and physical. (LeBarr, 1922, p. 67)

Another consequence of facial growth is that features become longer with increasing age. Feature length may convey age information to the perceiver. Infant faces characterized by short ears and a short nose also tend to be perceived as 'cuter' than those exhibiting longer features (Hildebrandt & Fitzgerald, 1979b). More direct evidence that feature length can convey age information is the finding that as the ear and/or nose length of schematic adult faces decreased, the estimated age of the persons also decreased (McArthur & Apatow, 1983–1984). Again, partial correlation analyses revealed that these relationships were not attributable to variations in either the physical attractiveness or the perceived age of faces with short versus long features.

OVERALL FACIAL CONFIGURATION

Facial Babyishness

Most of the work discussed to this point has concentrated on the impact of isolated feature variations on the perception of age and age-related affordances. A more complex issue involves the impact of these physical characteristics when they appear in combination, as is typically the case. As McArthur and Baron (1983) pointed out, it is likely that we extract social knowledge from complex higher order configurations of stimulus information. Therefore, overall variations in facial configuration are likely to have the greatest impact on social perception.

McArthur and Apatow (1983–1984) simultaneously manipulated feature length, vertical placement, and eye size in schematic adult faces to produce 'babyish' (low-placed, short features, and large eyes), control (medium-placed, medium length features, and medium size eyes), and 'mature' (high-placed, long features, and small eyes) versions of the faces (see Fig. 4.3). It was

FIG. 4.3. Sample schematic faces. (The top row, left to right depicts female face A with babyish features, medium features [control version], and mature features. The bottom row depicts the medium feature [control] versions of male face B, male face A, and female face B. Note: From 'Impressions of Babyfaced Adults' by L.Z. McArthur and K. Apatow, 1983/1984, *Social Cognition, 2*, p. 321. Reprinted by permission.

found that the impact of this overall manipulation on perceived age and affordances was stronger than the impact of individual variations in any of the three facial characteristics. More specifically, the simultaneous manipulation of these characteristics accounted for 74% of the variance in perceptions of physical strength, 50% of the variance in impressions of social submissiveness, and 40% of the variance in ratings of intellectual naivete. In every case, (see Table 4.2), individual feature variations accounted for less variance in these perceptions than did the overall manipulations.

Berry and McArthur (1985) investigated the simultaneous impact of a variety of facial characteristics on perceptions of age, facial maturity, and age-related affordances in a sample of real adult male faces. Subjects were asked to judge 20 faces on their physical attractiveness, and rate them on several trait dimensions. In addition, subjects estimated the chronological age of the faces, and rated them on craniofacial maturity (as measured by a 7-point scale with endpoints 'matureface' and 'babyface'). Actual measurements of the faces on a variety of physical dimensions were also obtained. Correlational analyses revealed that the indices of eye shape, eye size, eyebrow height, and chin width were significantly correlated with rated facial 'babyishness.' Furthermore, stepwise regression analyses indicated that the measures of chin width and eye size accounted for 57% of the variance in these ratings, and that the addition of other measures to these did not significantly contribute to the explained variance in this equation. A weighted linear physiognomic composite was derived from these two measures that predicted facial babyishness. This composite was simultaneously entered with ratings of the faces' perceived age and physical attractiveness into regression equations in order to predict ratings of the faces on trait dimensions (see Table 4.3). Results of these analyses revealed that the physiognomic composite exerted a strong positive

TABLE 4.2
Percent Variance in Perceived Affordance Measures
Accounted for by Facial Feature Manipulations

Affordance	Feature Manipulation			
	All Features	Vertical Placement	Eye Size	Feature Length
Physical weakness	74%	46%	26%	4%
Social submissiveness	50%	20%	36%	.04%
Intellectual naivete	40%	23%	28%	13%

Note. R^2's are averaged across two measures for each affordance and across two male and two female stimulus faces. From "Perceiving character in faces: The impact of age-related craniofacial changes on social perception" by D. S. Berry and L. Z. McArthur, 1986, *Psychological Bulletin, 100*, p. 12. Copyright 1986 by the American Psychological Association. Reprinted by permission.

TABLE 4.3
Results of Multiple Regression Analyses Predicting Trait Ratings
from the Physiognomic Composite, Perceived Age,
and Physical Attractiveness

Dependent Variable	Predictor Variable	Partial Correlation	Standardized Beta	T	R
Warmth	Composite	+.63	.58	3.26	.004
	Attractiveness	+.70	.58	3.97	.001
	Age	+.04	.03	0.14	.888
	$F(3,16) = 11.87, p < .0002, R^2 = .69$				
Honesty	Composite	+.71	.70	4.06	.001
	Attractiveness	+.73	.60	4.30	.001
	Age	+.24	.18	1.01	.328
	$F(3,16) = 13.41, p = .0001, R^2 = .72$				
Naivete	Composite	+.66	.67	3.48	.003
	Attractiveness	+.12	.08	0.49	.630
	Age	−.20	−.16	−0.81	.431
	$F(3,16) = 9.36, p = .0008, R^2 = .64$				
Kindness	Composite	+.72	.66	4.20	.001
	Attractiveness	+.72	.55	4.26	.001
	Age	+.03	.02	0.14	.893
	$F(3,16) = 16.85, p = .0001, R^2 = .76$				
Responsibility	Composite	+.33	.34	1.38	.185
	Attractiveness	+.61	.64	3.12	.001
	Age	+.29	.32	1.38	.236
	$F(3,16) = 3.57, p = .037, R^2 = .40$				

Note. From "Some components and consequences of a babyface" by D. S. Berry and L. Z. McArthur, 1985, Journal of Personality and Social Psychology, 48, p. 319. Copyright 1985 by the American Psychological Association, Inc. Reprinted by permission

impact on perceptions of warmth, honesty, kindness, and naivete, which was independent of either perceived age or attractiveness. More recent research (Berry & Brownlow, 1988) has found that facial babyishness exerts a similar impact on perceptions of adult female faces.

Berry and McArthur (in press) further examined whether facial babyishness would continue to exert an impact on social impressions when additional behavioral information is provided to subjects. More specifically, this study investigated the impact of a defendant's craniofacial maturity on judgments of his guilt or innocence in a simulated trial. Subjects read copies of fictitious pretrial reports in which a young male was charged with some offense. The reports described the incident in question as either resulting from negligence (e.g., forgetting to warn a customer about the potential hazards of a product he was selling) or intentional deception (e.g., misleading a customer about such dangers in order to make a sale). The facial maturity of the defendant was manipulated by attaching a photograph to the report. The photographed faces employed in this study were adult males who had previously been judged to be either 'babyish' or 'mature' in their facial appearance, and who differed in terms of the physiognomic features found to predict these ratings: chin size, eye size, eye shape, and eyebrow height. These faces did not differ in perceived age or physical attractiveness. Based on the finding that adults with babyish facial features are perceived to be more naive and honest than persons with more mature features (Berry & McArthur, 1985; McArthur & Apatow, 1983-1984), it was predicted that information indicating negligent criminal behavior would be more believable when the defendant was baby-faced, whereas information indicating intentional criminal behavior would be more believable when the defendant was maturefaced. Consistent with these expectations, subjects more often recommended the conviction of babyfaced men for crimes of negligence, whereas maturefaced men were more often perceived as guilty of intentional crimes (see Fig. 4.4).

Facial Attractiveness

Infantilism [of appearance] in women is attractive to men. (Guthrie, 1976, p. 77)

Although craniofacial maturity exerts an impact on social perception that is independent of attractiveness, variations in facial maturity do influence ratings of physical appeal (see chap. 3 for an extended discussion). More specifically, the available evidence indicates that facial babyishness has a divergent impact on the perceived attractiveness of men and women. Although McArthur and Apatow (1983-1984) found that male and female schematic faces that were intermediate in maturity were judged to be the most attractive, they also found that highly mature male faces were judged to be more attractive than babyish ones, whereas, the reverse was true for female faces. This pattern of results held true when facial maturity was manipulated by feature length, vertical placement, or both together with eye size. Also, although large (babyish) eyes increased the judged attractiveness of both male and female schematic faces, there was a trend for large eyes to enhance the attractiveness of females more than males. Similar results for schematic faces have also been reported by Keating (1985). Moreover, studies using photographed faces have corroborated the differential impact of facial maturity on the attractiveness of males and females. Berry and McArthur (1985) examined correlations between various measurements of a sample of male faces. The facial measures that predicted facial babyishness in this sample (large, round eyes, high eyebrows, and a small chin) were not related to ratings of the mens' attractiveness. Similarly, Berry and Brownlow (1988) found no relationship between the

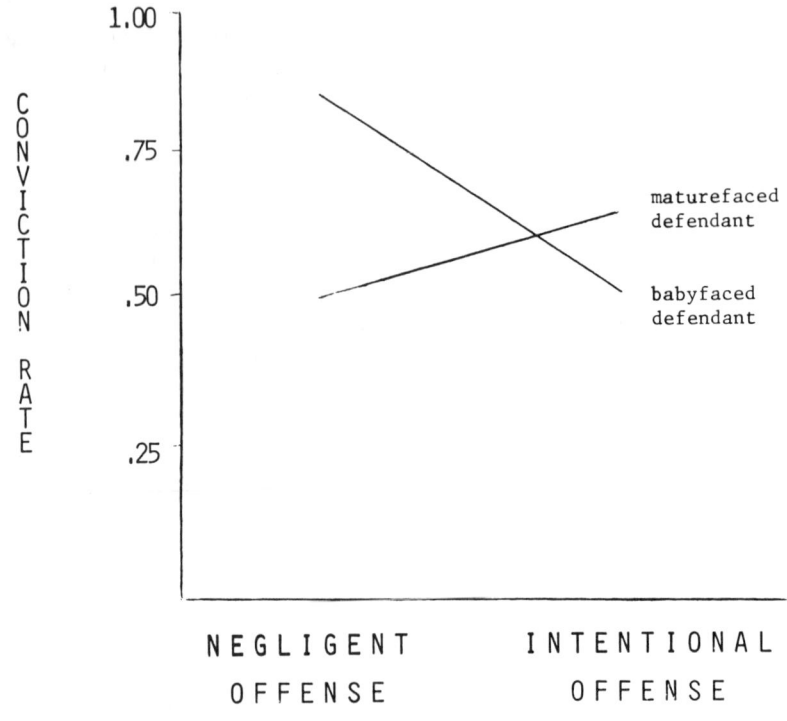

FIG. 4.4. Proportion of subjects recommending conviction as a function of criminal intent and defendant's craniofacial maturity. Note: From "What's in a face? The impact of facial maturity and defendant intent on the attribution of legal responsibility' by D.S. Berry and L. Zebrowitz-McArthur, in press, *Personality and Social Psychology Bulletin.* Reprinted by permission.

babyishness and attractiveness of male faces. On the other hand, Cunningham (1986) found that the immature features of high wide eyes, high eyebrows, and a small chin (as measured by length rather than width) did correlate significantly with the judged attractiveness of a sample of 50 female faces.

The divergent impact of babyish facial characteristics on the perceived attractiveness of male and female targets is consistent with the findings of McArthur and Apatow (1983–1984) and Keating (1985), as well as the observation that a youthful appearance is a more important determinant of female than male sexual attractiveness (e.g., Deutsch et al., 1983; Sontag, 1979). It is interesting to note that the actual morphological differences between male and female faces reflect a greater retention of infantile characteristics in the adult female than in the adult male (Gray, 1973; Liggett, 1974). Thus, the finding that a 'baby face' is more appealing on a female than on a male may reflect an aesthetic preference for faces that are prototypical for their gender.

SUMMARY AND CONCLUSIONS

The research reviewed in this chapter indicates that there is a strong consensus regarding what character traits are associated with certain facial qualities. Interestingly, this consensus bears a striking resemblance to the pronouncements of early physiognomists who have been quoted throughout this chapter. In keeping with the predictions derived from McArthur and Baron's (1983) ecological theory of social perception, people with childlike facial qualities are perceived to afford different social interactions than those with a more mature appearance. More specifically, people with an infantile craniofacial profile, low vertical placement of features, a small, and rounded chin, large round eyes, high eyebrows, smooth skin, or a short nose are perceived as affording more warmth, more submission, less physical strength, more naivete, and/or less threat (more honesty) than those with more mature versions of these facial characteristics. While these findings begin to address the question of how age-related craniofacial changes affect social perception, there are some important tenents of the ecological approach that have not yet been adequately addressed.

One unexplored issue involves potential differences among perceivers in their responses to age-variant physical characteristics. As J.J. Gibson (1979) and McArthur and Baron (1983) stress, the pick-up of useful information in the environment is in part guided by a perceiver's own needs, goals, and abilities. For example, although a babyish or immature appearance may communicate information about a particular individual's physical strength, the meaning of this information will vary as a function of a perceiver's own physical capabilities. Thus, the implications of the information provided in age-variant physical characteristics will differ for perceivers of different ages. Although a 35-year-old may readily perceive the affordance of sexual receptivity in another adult, a child would not be expected to readily extract this knowledge. The importance of perceiver characteristics in the process of detecting such adaptive information emphasizes the need for additional research focusing on developmental differences in the perception of age-related affordances.

In addition to focusing attention on individual and developmental differences in responses to age-related facial characteristics, the ecological emphasis on species-wide attunements has implications for cross-cultural research. In particular, if the responses to babyish facial characteristics that have been documented in this chapter derive from their significance for species survival, then there should be pancultural generality in responses to 'babyfaced' adults.

Recent research has revealed near-perfect agreement between U.S. and Korean subjects regarding the relative babyfacedness of schematic and real Caucasian faces, and the same facial characteristics that were correlated with U.S. subjects' ratings were also correlated with Koreans' ratings (McArthur & Berry, 1987). These results point to a shared sensitivity to age-related facial changes that are independent of racial variations in facial structure. In addition, like U.S. subjects, Koreans perceived babyfaced stimulus persons to possess more childlike psychological attributes than their maturefaced counterparts. Moreover, there was very strong agreement between Korean and U.S. perceivers' trait ratings, which indicates that a shared tendency exists for the facial configuration of babyfaced adults to elicit reactions analogous to those elicited by babies. Although these studies compared only two cultures, the fact that they differ markedly in both cultural traditions and facial structure strongly suggests that the effects will replicate in other cultures.

Another hallmark of the ecological approach is the recognition that a great deal of knowledge about the world can be revealed only in dynamic events that occur over time (cf. J.J. Gibson, 1979; chap. 2, this volume). This would seem to be especially true of social perception. Rarely do we perceive persons or faces as static stimulus displays, for they are dynamic and constantly changing by nature. The influence of such dynamic information has not been adequately treated in the research reviewed in this chapter. Rather, most of the reported findings are derived from experiments in which static facial appearance provided the only information on which to judge a person's affordances. It was necessary to limit the information made available to perceivers in order to isolate the impact of variations of particular features on social perception. However, in our everyday experiences, the information conveyed by such facial features appears in a moving face on an animate person. Research is needed to investigate the impact of age-related craniofacial characteristics on social perception when they appear in an animate person.

Another question that needs to be addressed is whether parameters of facial movement can, by themselves, convey information about age and age-related affordances. Research has indicated that characteristics of body movement can communicate important social information. For example, Cutting and his associates have demonstrated that point-light displays of a walking person, which retain only the dynamic information available in biological motion, provide sufficient information for the identification of gender and personal identity (see Cutting & Proffitt, 1981, for a review of this work). In addition, Runeson and Frykholm (1981, 1983) have demonstrated that information regarding deceptive intent can be extracted from these displays. Montepare, McArthur, and Amgott-Kwan (1984) have demonstrated that point-light gait displays also provide sufficient information for the identification of a stimulus person's relative age and have an impact on the perception of age-related social affordances. Do parameters of facial movement influence social knowledge in a similar manner? Bassili (1978, 1979) adapted the point-light technique for use with facial motion and demonstrated that perceivers can indeed identify emotion on the basis of movement cues alone. Recent research utilizing this methodology (Berry, 1987) has also provided evidence that dynamic facial qualities alone provide sufficient information for the identification of a person's age and gender. In addition, this study revealed that perceptions of a target person's physical and social power are influenced by age-related variations in facial movement, and that these perceptions are independent of the target person's perceived age.

In addition to the need to test the generalizability of existing findings to impressions of moving, talking stimulus persons, there is also the need to test their generalizability to situations other than the "first impression" paradigm that was employed in most of the research reviewed in this chapter. Some evidence that age-related facial characteristics will in fact have an impact on social perceptions in other contexts is provided by Berry and McArthur's (in press) finding that a defendant's facial maturity has an impact on judgments about his guilt or innocence in a simulated trial. More recently, McArthur and Tenenbaum (1987) found that facial maturity also has an impact on judgments about a job applicant's suitability for various types of positions. Babyfaced applicants of both sexes were rated higher than maturefaced applicants for a nurturant, teaching position at a daycare center. A babyface offered no advantage in recommendations for the position of director; these were determined by the applicant's academic performance. An even more naturalistic demonstration of the effects of facial maturity is provided by McCabe's (1984) report that abused children had more mature craniofacial proportions than nonabused children of the same age (see chap. 5).

A recent study by McArthur and Fafel (1987) suggests that unrealistically high expectations regarding the abilities of maturefaced children could contribute to their higher risk for abuse. In this study, married couples, who were parents of 11-year-old children, were asked to divide up a number of chores among 4 children, whom they were told were 11 years old. The target children were in fact equivalent in age, but varied in babyfacedness. The chores varied in difficulty from some that had been independently judged to be appropriate for 7-year-olds to others that had been judged appropriate for 15-year-olds. The results revealed that the mean age appropriateness for cognitive tasks assigned to maturefaced children was significantly higher than the age appropriateness of cognitive tasks assigned to babyfaced children, while the mean age level of physical tasks assigned to the two groups of children did not differ significantly. Although these data do suggest that facial appearance has a predictable impact on perceivers' reactions in informationally complex social situations, there is clearly a need for additional research to investigate the generalizability of appearance effects to a variety of social situations.

The finding that immature facial characteristics have a strong impact on social perception even when the perceived age of the face is held constant (e.g., Berry & McArthur, 1985; McArthur & Apatow, 1983–1984) supports the ecological view that these perceptions reflect a direct response to facial appearance rather than a response that is mediated through a process of age-labeling. Although the differential perceptions of adults who vary in facial babyishness was thus anticipated by this perspective, these data must be reconciled with another assumption of ecological theory: namely, that perception is adaptive in nature. If perception provides adaptive information to the perceiver, it would seem that perception should be accurate. Perceiving different affordances in individuals who differ in age is clearly accurate. Infants do require more nurturance and protection than adults do to insure their survival. Children are not appropriate recipients of sexual advances. Adults are more physically and intellectually capable than children. On the other hand, there is no reason to assume that *adults* who differ in craniofacial maturity actually provide different affordances. Yet, the research reviewed in this chapter clearly reveals that they are perceived to do so. The ecological theory of social perception deals with this fact in several ways.

First, because we cannot possibly process all available information, the assumption of adaptive perception suggests that people will detect the information that is the most ecologically significant. Because detecting the affordances that are communicated by an immature facial appearance is so important, these perceptions may be overgeneralized to adults who in some way physically resemble the young. Moreover, although a predisposition to pick up a particular appearance-affordance relationship may sometimes result in inaccurate perception, it may be argued that it is more adaptive to over-detect than to under-detect such a covariance. (See McArthur, 1980, for a discussion of the adaptive value of illusory correlation effects.) In short, even if impressions of babyfaced adults are erroneous, these errors reflect the functioning of a perceptual system that is basically adaptive.

A second way in which the ecological theory of social perception can account for the apparently erroneous affordances perceived in babyfaced adults is to attribute them in part to the meager stimulus information that has been provided to perceivers in most of the existing research. As noted previously, the ecological approach holds that dynamic, multimodel stimulus displays yield information beyond that which is available in static stimuli. It is further assumed that social affordances will be most accurately detected when such stimulus information is provided. Thus, one would expect that the tendency to perceive childlike affordances in adults with a babyish facial appearance would be attenuated when dynamic multimodal stimulus information is provided to perceivers. This does not obviate the importance of the existing data inasmuch as initial impressions, based on inadequate stimulus information, can affect the course of social interactions in a manner that serves to confirm those impressions (Snyder, Tanke, & Berscheid, 1977).

There is a third consideration that can reconcile the apparently erroneous affordances perceived in babyfaced adults with the accuracy assumption of the ecological theory. This involves variations which may occur in the appearance of a given person.

> . . . as we go about our daily rounds we symbolically move up and down the age scale, depending on the situation. A young woman teacher in her late 20's speaks in medium to high tones with her husband, growls in low gutteral tones at the kids . . . At school she speaks (to her class) in a medium-deep well-metered and enunciated tone with her head, back, and shoulders erect . . . at lunch with the girls, her voice rises and her shoulders and hands are mobile . . . with the superintendent her voice is high and soft, brows up and shoulders slumped slightly forward. (Guthrie, 1976, p. 143)

Although Guthrie's examples emphasize variations in vocal and gestural maturity as a person moves from one social interaction to another, there is reason to expect analogous variations in facial appearance. People may widen their eyes when they are feeling sincere or credulous. They may narrow their eyes or lower their eyebrows when they feel dominant. Through such individual variations in social maturity, people may consciously or unconsciously modulate the social affordances they present to others. As such, perceivers may be accurate when they detect honesty and naivete in wide-eyed adults, when they detect submission in adults with high eyebrows, and when they detect dominance in adults with protruding chins.

The research presented here illustrates an application of the ecological approach to the analysis of a particular area of social knowledge, the impact of age-related variations in craniofacial appearance on social perception. In addition to providing empirically testable predictions as to what stimulus information available in a person's facial appearance is likely to produce what impressions, this theoretical perspective provides us with an explanation of the origins of the readiness to detect this information. Inasmuch as persons who vary in age behave differently, and persons of similar ages may vary in the affordances they present to others with whom they interact, facial appearance may indeed provide some rudimentary guidelines for predicting how those whom we encounter are likely to behave toward us.

ACKNOWLEDGMENTS

We would like to thank Jim Todd and Tom Alley for their very helpful comments on an earlier version of this chapter. Portions of this chapter are based on "Perceiving character in faces: The impact of age-related craniofacial changes on social perception" by D.S. Berry and L.Z. McArthur, 1986, *Psychological Bulletin, 100,* 3-18. Copyright 1986 by the American Psychological Association. Adapted by permission of the publisher.

5 Facial Proportions, Perceived Age, and Caregiving

Viki McCabe
University of California—Los Angeles

I. Introduction
II. Empirical Studies
   A. Rationale
   B. Study I
   C. Study II
   D. Study III
III. Summary and Implications

INTRODUCTION

As human beings grow from small infants to larger adults, their faces undergo systematic morphological changes. Such changes are shaped by physical and biological processes, yet they provide socially pertinent information. Specifically, as people grow older their facial proportions continuously transform and produce dynamic geometric patterns that reflect their changing age-levels (cf. Enlow, 1982; Mark, Shaw, & Pittenger, this volume). Proportional facial transformations are socially relevant because the extensive period of human development mandates that decisions pertinent to the care of dependent young and other socially important interactions are age-level ordered. Thus, craniofacial proportions that correlate with particular age-levels can provide informational support for decisions pertinent to age-ordered social behaviors (McCabe, 1982c).

In addition to providing information about age, facial morphology serves as a species indicator that distinguishes humans from their nearest primate relatives (Gould, 1977). In contrast to the prognathic jaw developed in other primates, humans display dampened mandibular development and preserve over their entire life span the juvenile facial proportions characteristic only of the young in other primates.

Thus, both a person's relative age and identity as a human within the primate family are literally written on their face by the same morphological patterns created by the constraints of gravity and evolution. In sum, many biological and physical processes create morphological facial structures that specify socially relevant information; and such information may be perceived with minimum consciousness.

One particularly important social interaction that depends on the age-level information available in facial proportions is the relationship between caregivers and dependent young. This chapter reports a series of studies showing that parents and other caregivers use the informational support available from children's craniofacial proportions to make both positive and negative caregiving decisions with respect to those children, and further they may not be aware of the information they are using.

EMPIRICAL STUDIES

Rationale

In part, the following studies were designed to test an extension of a hypothesis suggested by Konrad Lorenz. Lorenz (1943) proposed that children with certain infantile morphological properties (an "infant schema") would elicit a flood of tenderness and subsequent positive caregiving responses from adult caretakers. One infant schema property that Lorenz suggested as essential is the craniofacial proportion: the large cranium to diminutive lower face characteristic of infants and young children. Although Lorenz never formally tested his theory, it makes sense because such properties, being age-specific, would indicate that a child with such proportions was developmentally immature and, therefore, dependent on adult assistance for survival. Some support for Lorenz's original hypothesis comes from studies that show that such properties elicit highly positive responses from people (chap. 4 and 6, this volume). McCabe (1984) asked whether such infant schema properties also would protect children from negative caregiving.

One might infer that, such properties might also provide information that helps inhibit adult aggression toward youngsters; aggression that might otherwise occur when small children do irritating things such as cry, wet, and vomit. An example of such aggression inhibition has been reported in chimpanzees (van Lawick-Goodall, 1968). As long as young chimps retain their dependent age-level indicators (white tail tufts), adult chimps seldom aggress against them. As soon as the tail tufts turn black, signalling the end of dependent status, adult aggression against young chimps begins. Such aggression inhibition by age-related physical characteristics of infants apparently occurs in other primate species (Alley, 1980).

Craniofacial proportions may serve the same purpose for humans as the white tail tufts do for chimps. They provide species-specific age-level information which indicates that the youngster requires protection and care (Alley, 1983c, 1986.) If craniofacial proportions specify age-level and elicit caregiving responses to children whose proportions indicate dependent status, what happens to children with atypical physical development: children whose craniofacial proportions are more characteristic of older children? Do such children elicit the same positive responses and aggression inhibition as more typical children, or can their atypical appearance elicit negative behavior?

When children are perceived as older than their chronological age, several consequences can occur. First, such children might be perceived as more capable than they actually are and be left to take care of themselves; a case of benign neglect. Personal communications from several nursery school teachers indicate that when a child looks older, they are often inadvertently left on their own much more than other children their age, and are also expected to perform in conformance with their appearance rather than their actual age.

Second, if children are perceived as older than their chronological age (or, more importantly, biological age) and therefore more capable than they actually are, they may also be subject to unrealistic age-related expectations: expectations based on their facial appearance rather than on their actual maturity and capability. Because these children probably could not meet such age-related expectations, they might elicit disciplinary or even abuse responses from their misguided caretakers. Evidence does show that abusing parents often have unrealistic expectations of their offspring and expect them to perform on levels beyond their capacities (Justice & Justice, 1976; Morris & Gould, 1963; Weston, 1974). Such misguided parental behavior may stem in part from the perception of an age-level indicator such as craniofacial proportions. As previously noted, although craniofacial proportions provide information for age-related decisions, the information may be acquired with little awareness. Such lack of awareness paired with atypical proportions that make a child appear older than their chronological age could help encourage unintentional and inappropriate responses.

Study I

In order to examine the effect of perceiving atypical proportions on caregiving responses, Study I (McCabe, 1984) looked at the relationship between such proportions and child maltreatment in two matched (for age, sex, and ethnic background) samples of nursery age children. One sample from southern California includes an experimental group of 22 youngsters between the ages of 3 and 6 that were in residence by court order at a facility for abused children, and a matched control group selected from a nursery school population. The second sample includes two matched groups, one abused and one not abused, of twenty 3- to 6-year-old Massachusetts State Social Service recipients located in Boston. Research assistants that were naive to the hypothesis of the study measured the craniofacial proportions of all the children.

The results show that the abused children in both samples have smaller cranium-to-lower-face proportions than their nonabused peers. Thus, children whose atypical craniofacial development makes them appear older than their chronological age are more likely to be maltreated. Nonetheless, the question arises as to whether the information for caretaking decision processes is in the proportional ratios of the face rather than in the facial features or facial mass as a whole and, therefore, available from photographs as well as from actual children. Study II addresses this question.

Study II

Some of the information that specifies developmental level, and thus degree of dependency, is available from topological geometric patterns (cf. chap. 2). Since this information is geometric in nature and not dependent on specific facial features, the question of whether it is invariant across modes of presentation arises. In a study conducted to test this (McCabe, 1984, Study 2), the craniofacial proportions in facial photographs of two samples of abused and nonabused youngsters were measured. The first sample consists of photographs of two groups of 2- to 7-year-old children. The 81 photographs of abused children were systematically selected from the files of a large metropolitan police department. The 121 photographs of (nonabused) children in the control group were similarly selected from the files of a large nursery school photographer with client schools in the same precincts covered in the police files and who served children with backgrounds similar to the abused group. The second sample, containing 38 abused and 50 nonabused children, was obtained in the same fashion, but included youngsters from 12 to 15 years old and used junior high school yearbook photographs for the control group. The second sample was included to see if the same results would be obtained in an older age range.

As in Study I, naive research assistants did the measurements for all photographs of 12 to 15 year old children. The smaller the cranium-to-lower-face ratio (within age-level), the more likely that child was abused. If the same information is available across age-levels and across actual and photographed children, then the question can be asked whether this invariance extends to simple line drawings of children. This question was addressed in a third study.

Study III

Study III (McCabe, 1982a) asked two questions. First, it tested Lorenz's original hypothesis by asking, What is the relationship between a craniofacial proportion and caregiving decisions? Second, it asks if the age-level information for these decisions can be perceived from two-dimensional drawings. Earlier in this chapter it was claimed that a person's developmental history and, thus, their age-level are literally written in the changing proportions of their head and face. Such changing proportions are specified by abstract patterns that provide a visual record of craniofacial change over the growth span. Study III asks whether such geometric patterns will specify the same information and support the same kind of caregiving decisions if depicted in a two-dimensional line drawing.

Study III includes three experiments that all used the same stimuli: drawings that systematically varied a 2-year-old's craniofacial proportions. The basic hypothesis tested was that if all other stimulus variables were held constant except forehead-to-face proportion, more positive and less negative caregiving responses will be given to children with relatively larger cranium-to-face proportions (i.e., proportions that look younger) whereas the reverse will hold for children with smaller cranium-to-face proportions (i.e., proportions that look older).

The first experiment paired the line drawings with descriptions of situations designed to elicit nurturant responses (e.g., the child's puppy had just run away) and asked subjects how much nurturance on a 10-point scale the subject thought appropriate for a 2-year-old in that situation. Nurturance decisions were dispensed as a function of craniofacial proportion. Significant results show that the larger the proportion of cranium to face, the more nurturance was deemed appropriate, and vice versa. The fact that subjects were influenced by the cephalic proportion despite being told that the children were 2 years old, supports the importance of cephalic information.

The second experiment paired the same drawings with descriptions of situations designed to elicit discipline responses (e.g., the child had just drawn all over freshly painted living room walls) and asked how much discipline should be administered in that situation. Discipline was dispensed as a function of craniofacial proportions: Significantly more discipline was deemed appropriate for children with smaller cranium-to-face proportions (i.e., older looking).

In the third experiment, the same drawings were paired with descriptions of situations that could elicit either a nurturance or a discipline response (e.g., the child had lost his or her teddy bear but had kept his or her parents up all night by crying). One group of subjects was asked how much nurturance they would dispense in that situation. A significant interaction between type of response and craniofacial proportion was found. Both nurturance and discipline were dispensed as a function of craniofacial proportion, but in opposite directions. As in the other experiments, significantly more discipline was deemed appropriate for children with smaller cranium-to-face proportions, whereas the larger the proportion to cranium to face, the more nurturance was deemed appropriate.

Age-level judgments were also collected in all three experiments. Although the descriptions included the fact that the child was age 2, subjects judged age-level to differ significantly as a function of craniofacial proportion: The smaller the proportion of cranium to face, the older the child was judged to be.

SUMMARY AND IMPLICATIONS

Clearly, craniofacial proportions provide compelling informational support for both positive and negative caregiving decisions. My results suggest that children with larger cranium-to-face proportions—thus, children who look younger—receive more nurturance and less discipline than their age mates who look older due to smaller cranium-to-face proportions. Unfortunately, this also makes children with atypically older craniofacial configurations more likely to receive maltreatment.

These studies also show that the craniofacial specification of information for caregiving allocation holds across modes of presentation. Such invariance supports the inference that the informational value of these specifications is in the proportion itself rather than in facial features or larger facial mass in which it is embedded. The informative nature of proportional specifications is well documented in the ethological literature (McCabe, 1982b). Consider, for example, the hawk-goose phenomena. Gallinaceous birds such as ducks and geese will flee when a head-neck proportion characteristic of predator hawks is flown above them. They will flee whether the source of proportional information is a real three-dimensional hawk or a two-dimensional cardboard cutout that simulates a hawk (Tinbergen, 1951). Similar proportional information serves as informational supports for eliciting feeding in gull chicks (Tinbergen & Perdeck, 1950) and for fighting off possible attackers of European Bitterns (Portjiele, 1921). Such evidence indicates that informative specifications can be perceived as proportions regardless of the exact form of the context in which the proportions are presented. Because of the invariance across modes of presentation, it can be inferred that the craniofacial proportions examined in two-dimensions in this chapter can specify underlying four-dimensional dynamics such as growth.

Several other implications emerge from this research. The first involves the physical (e.g., gravity) and biological (e.g., speciation) nature of socially relevant information. As long as physical, biological, and social properties are examined separately, accurate knowledge of socially relevant information and events may be obscured. Indeed, as in Study I, people may unintentionally make inappropriate caregiving decisions because they are unaware of the information they are using for guidance.

A second implication involves the proportional and patterned nature of the perceptible morphology that informs us about the underlying dynamics of human growth and aging. Such geometric specification indicates that we must look beyond the separate features or simple wholes that are typically used to describe objects and events in the world (see Garner, 1978). The fact that variation in the visible craniofacial proportion of the drawings influenced subjects' responses even when information about age-level was provided (Study III) points to the power of such specifications.

A third implication involves the fact that the abstract nature of such a socially relevant physical characteristic may lead to perceptions with little awareness. Because of the serious consequences of such lack of awareness, it is necessary to educate and inform caretakers of the nature and power of this type of perception (McCabe, 1984).

A fourth implication involves the invariant nature of craniofacial proportions across modes of presentation. This invariance calls into question the concept of schematic representation. If the exact same geometric pattern specifies the same information across real people, photographs of people, and line drawings of people, then it would appear that the "schema" one might suppose represents age-level is exactly the same as the real world specification of age-level (McCabe, 1982c). If so, why invoke the concept of schema at all?

Finally, this research highlights the importance of the human face as an information source for socially relevant decisions. This importance not only hinges on things we are often aware of, such as emotional expressions (see chap. 7), but on less conscious perceptions of information revealed in the human face.

II PSYCHOSOCIAL ASPECTS OF NORMAL VARIATION IN FACIAL APPEARANCE

Physical appearance is usually among the first sources of information available to others as a guide for social evaluation and interactions. Moreover, physical appearance is a potent, and often dominant, determinant of person perception and social cognition (Hatfield & Sprecher, 1986; McArthur, 1982). Although many aspects of the human body may be important, the face is the most important area of our bodies in the realms of psychology and social relations due to its prominence and the large amount of information available from faces. Gender is usually revealed in faces, at least those of adults. Aging and some environmental conditions (e.g., exposure to the sun) leave their mark on the face. Human facial muscles permit the face to assume hundreds of different appearances, and to rapidly change facial appearance. Thus, the face has the potential to communicate a large amount of information on a variety of interpersonal and personal dimensions (e.g., emotional, attitudinal) in a short period of time. The face actually is the chief bodily area associated with the expression of emotions and other forms of nonverbal communication. It is also generally the most important factor for aesthetic judgments. In short, the perception of others' faces is a chief component of social perception and usually exerts a major influence on social interactions.

The first chapter in this section (chap. 6) is primarily concerned with the socially significant variation in the perceived cuteness and attractiveness of "normal" human faces. Both the perceptual/judgmental process itself and the social effects of facial aesthetics are examined. Facial attractiveness is an important aspect of physical appearance and produces a wide range of psychosocial influences. In numerous studies, facial attractiveness has been found to influence the attitudes, perceptions, and behavior of both children and adults. The available research, while incomplete, overwhelmingly depicts a positive impact of facial attractiveness and a negative impact of facial ugliness or anomalies on the cognitive, affective, and behavioral reactions of others.

Although Chapter 6 largely restricts its review of facial attractiveness effects to those that have a direct impact on social relations, there are other types of facial attractiveness effects. One example is the interaction between facial attractiveness and recognition of faces; we tend to remember the faces of exceptionally attractive or unattractive others better than faces of average attractiveness (Fleishman et al., 1976), especially if they are highly attractive women or unattractive men (Shepherd & Ellis, 1973; Yarmey, 1979). As discussed in Chapter 3, there also are interactions between facial attractiveness and perceived age.

While variation in aesthetic properties is one of the most important types of variation in facial appearance across persons, emotional expression creates one of the most important types of variation in facial appearance within individuals. In the study of facial expression, the influence of face perception on human action is particularly clear. In Chapter 7, Ross Buck highlights two specific ways in which perception and action are intertwined: the central role of facial expression in social regulation, and the interrelatedness of facial perception and expression. Professor Buck proposes a resolution of the currently 'hot' issue of the primacy of affect versus cognition using some results of neuropsychological research on face perception and an ecological view of perceptual learning as the education of attention. Finally, he examines empathy and the crucial role of facial expression in this process.

It is worth noting here that the study of facial expression also brings to the forefront other basic theoretical issues dear to the hearts of perceptual psychologists. For instance, the ancient perceptual problem of perceptual constancy despite a flux in sensory stimulation is well-recognized by those who study the perception of facial expression. Given differences in both the facial structures and the patterns of expression associated with a given emotional state, how can we make judgments of emotions based on facial appearance that have any validity? "If each new face has a unique pattern of expression, not one that we have encountered before, ought we not find it quite unintelligible?" (Allport, 1937, p. 484). Although Allport refers to what he calls "intuition" to account for our ability to recognize facial expressions, what he has in mind is not an obscure and mysterious process; rather, he uses "intuition" to contrast with inference, denoting an immediate and direct form of knowledge acquisition. Allport did not make use of the concepts of structural and transformational invariants, which are necessary to understand this perceptual constancy, but like contemporary ecological psychologists he apparently believed these complex judgments were based largely on "direct perception" (1937, p. 534)! The observer does not necessarily need to *create* the meaning, he may be able to simply *receive* it; cognitive processes like imagination and inference become involved when the structure of the "outer field" is insufficient (Allport, 1937). The parallels between Allport's analysis of the perception of facial expression and the ecological analysis of perceiving age in faces (see chap. 2) are remarkable.

Chapter 8 deals with physiognomy: the attribution of psychological characteristics to people based on their facial characteristics. Although scientific evidence indicates that such judgments are seldom valid, there is considerable evidence that physiognomy is a widespread practice and that there is some consistency in the meaning attributed to some faces or facial characteristics. There is even a measure of personality that requires judgments of facial photographs: the Szondi Test (see Deri, 1949). Chapter 8 concentrates on the physiognomic judgments evoked by the normal variations in facial appearance. Physiognomic judgments play a large part in determining the psychosocial responses to individuals with facial anomalies, but most of the discussion of this topic is confined to the essay by W.C. Shaw (chap. 9).

In Chapter 8 the implications of physiognomy for an ecological theory of social perception are explored. The tack taken is primarily one of viewing physiognomically evocative facial characteristics as imperfect indices of ecologically significant states or processes. More specifically, it is proposed that certain facial characteristics produce consistent effects because they are sometimes valid traces of certain events or states that actually have predictable effects on facial appearance. Within this perspective, physiognomy is integrated with other aspects of social perception, and an underlying theme of the entire volume is repeated: The immense diversity of human facial appearance reflects, in part, detectable variations of ecological significance.

6 Determinants and Consequences of Facial Aesthetics

Thomas R. Alley
Clemson University

Katherine A. Hildebrandt
West Virginia University

I. Overview
II. Facial Attractiveness
    A. Measurement of Facial Attractiveness
        1. Facial attractiveness defined by conformity
        2. "Objective" standards of facial beauty
    B. Factors Influencing Facial Attractiveness
        1. Morphological characteristics and facial attractiveness
        2. Cosmetics and other forms of facial elaboration
        3. Facial expression
        4. Familiarity
        5. Some other influences
    C. Psychosocial Effects of Physical Attractiveness
        1. Heterosexual attraction
        2. Expectations and impression formation
        3. Aid, compliance, and reward
        4. Blame and punishment
        5. Parent–offspring, teacher–student, and peer relations
    D. Sex Differences in Facial Attractiveness Effects
III. Facial Cuteness
    A. Determinants of Facial Cuteness
    B. Some Psychosocial Effects of Facial Cuteness
IV. Closing Remarks
    A. The Sociobiology of Responses to Facial Beauty and Facial Defects
    B. Other Influences on Responses to Facial Aesthetics

OVERVIEW

Physical appearance is immediately and continuously available as a source of information in face-to-face encounters. Facial attractiveness is one important dimension of human physical appearance, and it has been found to influence the attitudes, perceptions, and behavior of both child and adult observers. Moreover, judges—even those belonging to different races, professions, sexes, or age groups (e.g., Cox & van der Linden, 1971; Cross & Cross, 1971; Dion, 1973; Iliffe, 1960; Udry, 1965)—largely agree in their ratings of facial attractiveness. The sizable agreement in people's judgments of facial beauty belies the common assertion that individual differences in aesthetic preferences vary so widely that beauty lies exclusively in the eye of the beholder.

Furthermore, people generally believe that more attractive individuals are typically more competent, likeable, and, in a very broad sense, "better" than less attractive individuals: a "beauty-is-good" stereotype. The appearance of those who are physically or facially attractive apparently fosters positive expectations and impressions, and gains for them various interpersonal advantages. Likewise, facial defects consistently evoke negative responses by others. There also may be some consistency in the effect of certain factors such as familiarity on facial attractiveness.

These aspects of the social effects of facial appearance form the main subjects of our chapter. More specifically, the focus is on the social effects of two closely related aspects of facial aesthetics: attractiveness and cuteness. Since we believe that attractiveness and cuteness are somewhat different in meaning, we will review their determinants and consequences separately. Even though some of the other terms used in the appraisal of human attractiveness—including "beautiful", "good-looking", "handsome", "pretty", and "attractive"—can be differentiated by denotation, if not by connotation, such distinctions seldom are made in this chapter.

FACIAL ATTRACTIVENESS

The vast literature on psychosocial aspects of physical attractiveness can provide insights into the more specific questions pertaining to *facial* attractiveness. Indeed, most of the studies on *"physical* attractiveness" can be interpreted as studies of *facial* attractiveness, for seldom are anything more than head-and-shoulder photographs used in "physical attractiveness" studies, and when "the stimulus person is evaluated *in vivo*, the results appear to be approximately the same" (Berscheid, 1981, p. 6). Recently, G.J. Smith (1985) reported a high correlation ($r = .72$) between attractiveness ratings of full-length and facial photographs of children. Furthermore, in most cases facial appearance is probably the most important factor contributing to overall physical attractiveness. Consider the results of a carefully controlled study based on nine photographic pairings of three faces and three clothed bodies: The attractiveness of the face and head was a significant contributor to the perception of overall physical attractiveness while the attractiveness of the variously clothed bodies was not (Nielsen & Kernaleguen, 1976). Similarly, when Lerner, Karabenick, and Stuart (1973) assessed the importance of 24 physical characteristics for own and opposite sex physical attractiveness for both males and females, they found the face to be second only to general appearance in importance.

Our goal in this section is not to provide a comprehensive review of the literature on physical attractiveness; several papers (Adams, 1977, 1982; Berscheid, 1981; Berscheid & Walster, 1974; Hildebrandt, 1982a; Langlois & Stephan, 1981; Maruyama & Miller, 1981; Sorell & Nowak, 1981) and three books (Adams & Crossman, 1978; Hatfield & Sprecher, 1986; Patzer, 1985) have reviewed this voluminous literature. Instead, we focus on some of the social effects of physical attractiveness for which facial appearance seems to be sufficient or important. Our concentration on studies that have used facial stimuli is mandated by the focus of this volume, by the risk involved in equating physical and facial attractiveness, and by evidence that facial attractiveness and the attractiveness of other bodily regions may produce different psychosocial effects (e.g., Adams, 1977; Nielsen & Kernaleguen, 1976). Facial and physical attractiveness also differ from sex appeal (see Morse, Reis, Gruzen, & Wolff, 1974). Hence, it is important to examine the psychosocial effects that have been specifically linked to *facial* attractiveness. Our discussion is limited to normal variation in facial appearance, although facial anomalies certainly have a negative impact on attractiveness and concomitant social reactions (see Part III of this volume).

Measurement of Facial Attractiveness

Facial Attractiveness Defined by Conformity of Opinion

The vast majority of studies on facial or physical attractiveness have used a consensual method to determine an individual's attractiveness: An individual is defined as attractive if a significant number of "judges" designate that individual as attractive. Usually, a person's attractiveness is taken to be the mean of the ratings obtained from a group of raters using a Likert-type scale. This method is widely accepted mainly because of the typically high level of agreement among "judges" (e.g., Hansell, Sparacino, & Ronchi, 1982; Kerr & Kurtz, 1978). Good agreement is even found among distinct types of "judges," as when Dongieux and Sassouni (1980) found good concordance of facial attractiveness judgments across three groups of raters: orthodontists, high school students, and graduate students in Art Education. Paired comparisons also yield good interrater agreement in both preference and degree of preference judgments (Milord, 1978). Although the raters are usually adults, Cross and Cross (1971) found that 7-, 12-, and 17-year-olds do not differ significantly from adults in their ratings of facial attractiveness. Even preschoolers make judgments of other children's (Dion, 1973) and adults' (Trnavsky & Bakeman, 1976) facial attractiveness that are similar to those of adult raters. Ratings of facial attractiveness which are similar to those made by unfamiliar adults can be obtained from children who are familiar with their photographically depicted peers (Styczynski & Langlois, 1977) or from acquainted adults given a list of names (Hull, 1928, p. 118). Moreover, the consensual method is particularly suitable for assessing the social impact of attractiveness, for it defines attractiveness in essentially the same manner in which it actually operates in natural contexts: as a "subjective" variable. (Note that "subjective" here refers to the individualistic nature of aesthetic judgments, but does not necessarily mean that raters will not tend to respond to the same physical characteristics in the same way, perhaps arriving at nearly identical assessments.) Nonetheless, orthodontists and others occupied with altering facial attractiveness have seldom systematically consulted the aesthetic standards of the general public (Peck & Peck, 1970).

Ratings of facial attractiveness generally have high test-retest reliability (e.g., Dongieux & Sassouni, 1980; Hansell et al., 1982, Study 1; Kerr & Kurtz, 1978). Variation in the time permitted judges to assess attractiveness probably has little effect on the ratings obtained; attractiveness ratings of facial photos made by judges with unlimited time correlated significantly with ratings made by judges who viewed the faces for as little as 150 msec (a period too short to permit eye movements), even when the target image extended beyond the central area of clear vision (Goldstein & Papageorge, 1980)! When the "sampling time" is expanded by presenting videotapes rather than photographs of faces, however, perceived attractiveness may be favorably influenced (Safier, 1983). Nonetheless, ratings of facial attractiveness based on extended videotapes are very similar to those based on a single monochromatic photograph (E.H. Fischer et al., 1982).

Given the reliability of these ratings, the two chief dangers of this approach to determining facial attractiveness are: (a) unnatural or unrepresentative stimuli (discussed in chap. 1), and (b) the systematic biases found in certain classes of raters. Among the systematic rater biases are those connected with the age and attractiveness of the judges. Older persons may tend to downgrade more youthful faces (Udry, 1965), although Walsh and Locke (1980) found no such effect in physical attractiveness ratings of waist-up photographs of women. Both of these studies indicated that middle-aged and elderly raters tend to give relatively high attractiveness ratings to more mature (female) faces; a result opposite that of a study by Nowak (1977), but confirmed for elderly raters by Johnson (1985, Study I). Older (over 55 years) raters also show less conformity of aesthetic judgment than younger adults (Iliffe, 1960; Udry, 1965). On the other hand, the interrater reliability of children's ratings when judging older children's attractiveness from full-length photos increases from kindergarten through third grade (Cavior & Lombardi, 1973). Another developmental trend is that preferences for various facial proportions, like aesthetic preferences for rectangles' proportions (G.G. Thompson, 1946), show increasing similarity to adult norms with increasing age (Taylor & Thompson, 1955).

One study (Paschall, 1975; reported in Adams & Crossman, 1978) found that extremely attractive and unattractive raters tend to give lower attractiveness ratings than raters of more average attractiveness, although another study (Gallucci & Meyer, 1984) found a consistent increase in ratings of females' facial attractiveness as the (female) raters' own attractiveness decreased. A recent study (Sugarman, Warner, & Berg, 1983) indicated that there may be individual differences, perhaps related to the judges' gender, in the effect of judges' own physical attractiveness on the attractiveness ratings they assign to others. Not surprisingly, both mothers and fathers give higher physical attractiveness ratings to their own infants than unrelated judges responding to full-length, color photographs (Keller, 1980). Similarly, mothers give higher cuteness ratings to photographs of their infants than to unfamiliar infants (Hildebrandt & Fitzgerald, 1981).

Race also influences face perception, including the judgment of facial attractiveness. Speculation that aesthetic criteria may differ between races is common and has some experimental support (e.g., Maret, 1983; Thomas, 1979; Wagatsuma & Kleinke, 1979), although the most prominent result of cross-cultural and cross-racial studies is the agreement among raters (see, e.g., Martin, 1964; Thomas, 1979; Udry, 1965). Moreover, Martin (1964) found greater similarity between ratings of the facial attractiveness of 10 Black females by American Whites and Blacks than between American Whites and Nigerian Blacks. This supports Martin's contention that "racial" differences in aesthetic standards are largely cultural or societal in origin. Also supporting this view is the finding that both occupational status and educational level are positively correlated with greater interrater conformity of facial attractiveness ratings, and more agreement may be found among American than British raters (Iliffe, 1960; Udry, 1965).

The perceived degree of aesthetic variation in cross- versus within-racial judgments might vary such that we tend to be more sensitive to facial variations in members of our own race. Travelers commonly remark that the members of other races "all look alike," and adults can recognize faces of members of their own race better than faces from other races (e.g., Malpass & Kravitz, 1969). Inspired by this finding, Bernstein, Lin, and McClellan (1982) expected to find less perceived variation in cross- versus within-racial judgments of facial attractiveness. Their results did not confirm this hypothesis, but did indicate that American Blacks and native Taiwanese may have different criteria for facial attractiveness than do American Whites.

Another racial effect may reflect the dominance of Caucasian (or American majority) standards of facial aesthetics: Whites (Bernstein et al., 1982; Cross

& Cross, 1971), Blacks (Bernstein et al., 1982), Hispanics (Hernandez, 1981), and Chinese (Bernstein et al., 1982) all tend to rate the attractiveness or cuteness of facial photographs of Whites more highly than faces of other races. Similarly, American Whites and Blacks, and to a lesser extent, Nigerian Blacks, apparently favor Caucasian over Negroid facial features in judging females' attractiveness (Martin, 1964). Hill (1944) found that Black adolescents tend to favor more Caucasian facial characteristics in their preferences for prospective spouses, friends, and acquaintances. Furthermore, there may be a developmental trend in the effect of race on facial attractiveness judgments; Langlois and Stephan (1977) found that Black and Mexican-American kindergartners rated White faces as more attractive than Black and Mexican-American faces, but White and Mexican-American fourth graders rated faces from their own ethnic group highest.

Several researchers have found that raters tend to show more interrater agreement when judging opposite-sex facial photos (e.g., Korthase & Trenholme, 1982, 1983). Also, judges may exhibit finer distinctions when assessing the facial attractiveness of opposite-sex persons than when rating same-sex persons; both male and female judges assign a significantly smaller range of values (i.e., show less differentiation) when rating the attractiveness of same- versus opposite-sex faces (Kerr & Kurtz, 1978; Sugarman et al., 1983). Other sex differences probably exist and, like attractiveness ratings in general, vary with the social context in which ratings are reported (see Berman, 1980; Berman et al., 1981; and below). More importantly, however, male and female raters largely agree in their ratings of facial attractiveness of both male and female targets (e.g., Cloonan & Ottinger, 1987; Morse et al., 1974; Udry, 1965), indicating that raters of both sexes share general standards of facial attractiveness.

"Objective" Standards of Facial Beauty

Since ancient times, a variety of other methods of determining facial beauty have been proffered. Many of these are "objective" measures in that the same specific criteria are applied regardless of any idiosyncratic facial characteristics. The underlying assumption of these approaches is that beautiful faces have certain common and measurable morphological characteristics that hold despite the wide variation in facial types and patterns.

Perhaps the best known and most frequently advocated objective measures are based on various mathematical proportions (see Liggett, 1974). Since at least the time of the ancient Greeks, people have searched for the mathematical secrets of beauty, motivated by the basic assumption that beauty is a function of proportions. Medieval artists, for example, believed that the perfect face could be neatly divided into sevenths. The hair, space between the nose and mouth, and between the mouth and chin should each occupy one seventh of total facial length; the forehead and nose were to occupy two sevenths each.

Plato believed that the essence of facial beauty lay in the "golden" proportions wherein the ratio of the whole (x) to the larger part (y) equals the ratio of y to the smaller part (z): $x/y = y/z$. A well-known orthodontist has recently revived this theory, supporting it by finding golden proportions in both the horizontal and vertical layout of features in faces of professional models (Ricketts, 1982). He also discovered golden proportions in facial profiles of beautiful women and in the dentition of dentally "ideal" subjects. Hence, it appears that golden facial proportions are compatible with high facial attractiveness, yet they cannot be sufficient (e.g., when accompanied by facial anomalies) and may not even be necessary. Moreover, unattractive (but "normal") faces may also have golden proportions.

One pitfall in evaluating the pleasingness of the golden section (or other proportions) stems from a weakness in the method of averaging judgments, as shown in a study by Valentine (1913). He found that the *average* divisions of a line into its most pleasing segments produced "almost exactly" the golden section, but noted that "no one division could rightly be said to be the most pleasing, as individuals varied so enormously" (p. 55). More generally, proportions may well be a major determinant of facial beauty, but no exact ratios determine all people's judgments of facial attractiveness. This is reflected in the substantial amount of diversity in judgments of facial attractiveness. For instance, although Cross and Cross (1971) found good overall agreement between judges of different sex, age, and race classes, they also found that at least a few of the judges would select even the least popular faces as best looking. A summary of early research on aesthetics and the golden section is consistent with this perspective:

> Many have tended to believe in it as a kind of absolute standard, with a magical claim to universal validity . . . Evidence does indicate that the golden section will often represent better than any other proportion what the average choice of a large group of people is likely to be, but . . . it also shows that certain individuals may prefer something quite remote, mathematically speaking. (Gurnee, 1936, p. 406)

To make matters worse, the complexities of facial aesthetics may be too great for a purely quantitative analysis to ever be wholly successful. Still, proportional analysis will continue to be useful as a guide for facial surgeons and orthodontists..

In recent years several methods of objectively measuring facial aesthetics or aesthetic handicap have been developed by dental and medical practitioners (e.g., Howitt, Stricker, & Henderson, 1967; Legan & Burstone, 1980; Ross & Johnston, 1972). These methods frequently rely on linear and angular cephalometrics (cf. Riedel, 1957), but such measurements often fail to discriminate attractive and unattractive faces and can display considerable variation across attractive faces (e.g., Burstone, 1975; Cox & van der Linden, 1971). In summary, the objective aesthetic standards produced by the medical and dental fields are inadequate because they (a) incompletely, and often only crudely, capture overall facial appearance; (b) often are concerned with functional as well as aesthetic impairment; (c) seldom recognize sex differences in aesthetic criteria; (d) often rely too heavily on hard tissue analysis; (e) tend to focus predominantly or exclusively on a lateral perspective (i.e., on profiles); and (f) are not grounded in socially defined aesthetic standards (cf. Albino, 1984; Albino & Tedesco, this volume; Peck & Peck, 1970). Hence, it is not surprising that Peck and Peck (1970) found some rather consistent departures from objective cephalometric standards when they examined 52 faces societally recognized as attractive (e.g., professional models and beauty contest winners). Similarly, Riedel (1957, p. 104) found that orthodontists regarded the facial profiles of most "Hollywood stars" examined as too protrusive. (Despite such notable exceptions, especially in the public's more protrusive aesthetic ideals, these studies indicate that facial aesthetic standards of orthodontists and the public are in generally good agreement.)

Some less thoroughly quantified but still largely objective methods of assessing facial aesthetics have been suggested. For instance, Peck and Peck (1970) claimed that a regular and even flow of facial curves is an essential part of an aesthetically pleasing profile, but research is needed to substantiate and clarify this criterion. Peck and Peck also introduced a method of aesthetic assessment that combines the subjective assessment provided in societally recognized exemplars of high facial attractiveness with objective assessment by "profilometric analysis." Specifically, they provide cephalometric standards of facial beauty based on analysis of faces of people perceived as exceptionally attractive by segments of the general public. This is certainly a step in the right direction, but retains problems stemming from its grounding in cephalometric standards (see previous discussion).

In conclusion, at the present time it must be recommended that assessment of facial aesthetics at least include a simple assessment by a readily available, highly sophisticated measurement system: human perception. The main weakness of a simple visual assessment of facial attractiveness, its subjectivity, can be overcome by using groups of judges, as researchers in Buffalo do with their Dental-Facial Attractiveness Scale (see Albino & Tedesco, this volume).

Factors Influencing Facial Attractiveness

A number of factors can influence the perceived facial attractiveness of a given individual. Some of these (e.g., facial expression) may be regarded as *intrinsic* factors in that they are aspects of variation in the appearance of the face itself. Other factors influencing evaluations of facial appearance are *extrinsic* in that they reflect variation within or among perceivers rather than in the perceived. In this section we examine in some detail three intrinsic factors— morphological characteristics, facial elaboration, and facial expression—and one extrinsic factor, familiarity. (Another important factor, age, was discussed in chap. 3.) Several other factors, including context and gender, are briefly discussed at the end of this section.

Morphological Characteristics and Facial Attractiveness

Some experiments have been conducted from which modest insight into the relative contribution of various facial characteristics to attractiveness can be gained. Cross and Cross (1971) tabulated the frequency with which 105 subjects, 7 to 57 years old, mentioned particular aspects of facial appearance as important aspects of facial beauty. The most frequently mentioned characteristic was the eyes, selected by 34%, followed by the mouth and/or smile (31%), facial proportions or overall facial configuration (15%), hair (10%), skin color (5%), and nose shape (5%). Remarkably similar results were obtained by Maret (1983) when he asked White Americans to name the primary criteria used in rating the attractiveness of head-and-shoulder photos of Black college students: The eyes again were cited most often (42%), followed by general facial structure (33%), smile (17%), and hair (8%). Black Cruzan raters cited rather different criteria, naming general facial structure most often (69%). The overall configuration of the face was also the criteria most frequently mentioned (73%) by a largely Black (64%) and Hispanic (26%) group of American children asked to select the more attractive child in several pairs of photos of individuals of various races (Kleck, Richardson, & Ronald, 1974).

A series of studies by Roger Terry examined the correlations between attractiveness ratings of individual facial components and ratings of overall attractiveness, following the assumption that the correlation coefficients would reflect the importance of these components in facial beauty. These studies included self-ratings (Terry & Brady, 1976), ratings of isolated facial features (Terry & Davis, 1976), and ratings of intact photographs of others (Terry, 1977). In all three studies, the correlations assumed the following order (from highest to lowest): mouth, eyes, hair, and nose. However, this ordering was clearly influenced by an eyeglass effect. For instance, females' self-ratings (Terry & Brady, 1976) indicated that eyeglasses lowered self-rated attractiveness and reduced the normally high correlation between attractiveness ratings of overall facial appearance and of the eyes.

In summary, the eyes and mouth consistently have been the specific facial regions found to be most influential for facial attractiveness ratings. Notable individual differences exist in the eye movement patterns seen used during face perception (Walker-Smith, Gale, & Findlay, 1977); nonetheless eye movement studies reveal that these two regions receive the majority of focus in both free (Yarbus, 1967) and directed (to form an impression) (Janik, Wellens, Goldberg, & Dell'osso, 1978) examination of facial photographs. When infants begin to focus on internal facial features (at about 2 months), the eyes are the feature fixated most (Haith, Bergman, & Moore, 1977). Future research should examine whether the importance of the eyes and mouth for facial aesthetics is simply due to the amount of attention they receive, or if we devote a disproportionate amount of attention to them because of their importance in determining facial attractiveness. The former now seems more likely because the eyes clearly dominate other facial features in commanding infants' attention (Maurer, 1985).

Two specific links between appearance of the eyes and perceived attractiveness or affective reaction have been reported. First, large pupils are preferred to small pupils in perception of opposite sex adults, probably because pupil dilation tends to increase with arousal or interest (Hess, 1975; Jones & Moyel, 1971; Simms, 1967). For infants, conflicting results exist regarding the effect of pupil size on attractiveness (Hess, 1975; Kirkland & Smith, 1978). Like many perceptual effects, pupil size influences our responses without our being consciously aware of it. Second, larger eyes, at least in females, produce higher ratings of attractiveness (Cunningham, 1986; Keating, 1985). This relationship probably underlies the common cosmetic practice of adding pigment to the eyelid area; a procedure which enhances the contrast of eyelids and sclera and may lower perceived age (cf. Guthrie, 1976).

Both the effects of growth-produced changes (see chap. 3) and facial feature variations in schematic drawings (e.g., Brunswik & Reiter, 1937; Maier, et al., 1984) indicate that a high forehead contributes to facial beauty while a low forehead produces an unfavorable impression. (Forehead height also appears to be an important variable in physiognomic judgments. See chap. 8.) More convex faces, especially in the mid-face region, were associated with lower facial attractiveness in a study of 72 silhouette profiles (Cox & van der Linden, 1971; cf. Poulton, 1957).

Consistent with classical writings on facial appearance, different facial characteristics seem to be required to produce aesthetically pleasing male and female faces (Feinman & Gill, 1978; Foster, 1973; Liggett, 1974; Poulton, 1957; Wagatsuma & Kleinke, 1979). In general, facial features that follow or even exaggerate trends in sexual dimorphism probably make faces more attractive (cf. Nakdimen, 1984). Likewise, the aesthetics of various facial configurations certainly vary with age; a facial characteristic that is highly attractive in a young child may be unattractive in an adult (Foster, 1973). Nonetheless, further research is needed to establish which facial features are most important for each sex and each age.

A national survey showed that the majority of Americans believe dental appearance is "very important" in social interactions, particularly in dating among young people (Linn, 1966). Other research has examined the impact of variation in oral/dental appearance on perceived attractiveness. In an ingenious experiment, Dongieux and Sassouni (1980) collected ratings of 10 Caucasian female faces, each of which appeared with 8 different mandibular positions determined by biting on special mouthpieces. Three groups of raters—orthodontists, peers, and Art Education students—largely agreed on the relative attractiveness of the positions, including finding an orthodontically normal (Class I Normal) bite to be the most attractive, and an open bite to be displeasing. Also, mandibular protrusion (Class III) was found to be less aesthetic than retrusive (Class II) mandibular position. Using a markedly different method,

Lucker and Graber (1980) found that children saw both retrusive and protrusive profiles as less acceptable than straighter profiles. Research by W.C. Shaw (1981b; this volume) and his colleagues further discloses the significant impact of dentofacial appearance on facial attractiveness, and Guthrie (1976) provides an interesting but highly speculative discussion of varieties of dental elaboration.

Some research has used a staple tool of law enforcement agencies, the Identi-Kit, to study the aesthetic impact of various facial feature variations or deviations. Ratings of the "social acceptability" of facial appearance seen in photographs are highly correlated with independent ratings of Identi-Kit constructions of these same faces (Glass, Starr, Stewart, & Hodge, 1981). (The results of this study also suggest that photographs may receive more consistent and less favorable aesthetic ratings than more schematic depictions of the same faces.) Keating (1985) used Identi-Kit materials to assess the impact of age-related variations in several facial features on facial attractiveness ratings. She found that thin lips enhanced the attractiveness of both male and female faces, although large eyes had a more favorable impact on the perceived attractiveness of female faces than did lip thickness.

The lateral symmetry of the face is another significant aspect of facial aesthetics. If perfect symmetry is an aesthetic ideal then this aesthetic ideal is certainly not based on median or normative facial appearance, for few if any people have perfect facial symmetry (Shore, 1960). Careful examination of famous women noted for their beauty reveals that perfect symmetry is *not* needed for a face to be seen as exceptionally beautiful. Indeed, the notable asymmetry in the faces of many beauty pageant winners and other persons recognized for their exceptional attractiveness (Peck & Peck, 1970) suggests that slight asymmetry in facial structure may render a face at least as attractive as a perfectly symmetrical one. The impact of this slight facial asymmetry on aesthetic judgments can be modified by familiarity: People consistently prefer photographs of familiar faces showing them with familiar images rather than laterally reversed images, but prefer the more familiar mirror-reversed images of themselves (Mita, Dermer, & Knight, 1977).

Perceptual judgment of facial symmetry in normal faces is difficult (Secord & Muthard, 1955). Nonetheless, pronounced facial asymmetry is not aesthetically pleasing. Facial structure should permit a vertical line to be drawn down the face which passes midway between the eyes and down the center of the nose, lips, and chin. Raymond (1909) discussed this and other aesthetically important facial symmetries that can be assessed by dividing the face with straight lines, noting that a wide variety of facial proportions and appearance can exist within the limits posed by these measurement.

Cosmetics and Other Forms of Facial Elaboration

At least since Darwin (1871), facial elaboration often has been seen as a universal, or nearly universal, human practice.

> The desire to alter the face is universal: in every country and in every age examples of facial elaboration can be found. Often the objective is to acquire greater beauty in the eyes of one's companions—though . . . this is by no means the only motive. Yet even the pursuit of beauty leads to an incredible variety of facial embellishments. (Liggett, 1974, p.43).

These forms of facial elaboration include scarification (cicatrization), tattooing, painting, tooth filing, deformations of facial features (ears, lips, nose, etc.), and even alteration of head shape through application of pressure to the soft skulls of infants (see Liggett, 1974; Shalleck, 1973). These often painful practices dramatically illustrate the social importance of facial appearance.

> All peoples, sophisticated as well as primitive, seem prepared to go through almost unbelievable suffering in pursuit of the purely local ideals of their particular society. Beauty must be pursued at whatever price, because it confers on its possessor profound social influence, power and respect. (Liggett, 1974, p. 46)

It is important to reemphasize that facial elaboration serves many purposes. Facial elaboration is sometimes guided by superstitious or religious beliefs. Alternatively, it may serve to indicate social, parental or marital status, courage, achievement, group membership, and so on. Even in modern Western society, our common (cosmetic) forms of facial elaboration may serve, in part, to signify social position; facial makeup usage is correlated with socioeconomic status (Schaninger, 1981). Moreover, even the great variety of aesthetic preferences evident in the remarkably diverse forms of facial elaboration does not necessarily mean that there are no universal standards of facial beauty as some (e.g., Darwin, 1871) have argued. Underlying all facial elaboration is a natural facial form, and individuals of all cultures may well agree upon certain criteria for facial beauty in the unaltered face. Likely candidates would include a degree of homogeneity in skin coloration, (at least) an approximation of bilateral symmetry, and the absence of gross, congenital facial anomalies. A poor complexion and uncleanliness are considered repulsive in (at least) a large number of societies (Ford & Beach, 1951).

Contextually variable criteria for facial beauty may also apply universally. Consider the following conclusion from an analysis of peer-nominated attractive and unattractive persons: "Any feature, if it conforms to the mode, tends to elicit a favorable reaction of median strength; but if it departs from the mode, it tends to arouse an unfavorable reaction of greater relative strength" (Perrin, 1921, p. 213). Converted to a (tentative) universal aesthetic principle, this would *demand* some interpopulation variation in aesthetic judgments of specific facial configurations. As previously noted, there is some evidence for racial differences in the criteria for facial attractiveness (Bernstein et al., 1982).

Let us turn our attention to forms of facial elaboration that are common in Western culture: namely, the use of eyeglasses, facial cosmetics, and the treatment of facial and scalp hair. Considering the widespread use of facial cosmetics, tinted contact lenses and eyeglasses, and various hair treatments, surprisingly little research has been published on their aesthetic effects. Although even within specific Western cultures wide variations can be found in the nature, frequency, and extent of these forms of facial elaboration, those who engage in these treatments may be correct in assuming that at least some of the resultant changes can have a generally positive effect on facial attractiveness. Suspecting that eyeglasses influence (probably decrease) facial attractiveness, most researchers investigating physical attractiveness have eliminated eyeglass wearers from their studies. Wearing eyeglasses does tend to decrease facial attractiveness (Hamid, 1968; Singer, 1964; Terry & Kroger, 1976), including self-rated attractiveness (Terry & Brady, 1976), although eyeglasses may have a favorable impact on other social judgments (see chap. 8).

Cosmetics are widely portrayed as devices for improving facial attractiveness, yet little research has been published to show that they can be effective in this regard. A recent review of this literature (Graham & Jouhar, 1980) found only a few studies that directly concerned the effects of cosmetics on facial attractiveness. Nonetheless, several studies have assumed that cosmetics can enhance attractiveness and have used cosmetics to manipulate physical attractiveness (see Graham & Jouhar, 1980). A study by Hamid supports this common assumption. He found that wearing "becoming make-up of lipstick, powder, eyeshadow coloring, and hair coiffured" (1972, p. 281) has a favorable impact on males', but not females', ratings of physical attractiveness. Graham and Jouhar (1981) found that "fairly standard facial make-up" can improve ratings of physical attractiveness and "pleasant-looking" for adult female targets. In this same study, hair that had been "washed, conditioned, cut and styled" did not alter attractiveness ratings compared to the same women with "unwashed casually arranged" hair, although this manipulation did increase ratings of "pleasant-looking." One might guess from this study that the appearance of the face itself has a more powerful effect on physical attractiveness than does the appearance of one's hair.

Nonetheless, in both our own and other cultures, hair is rarely allowed to grow wild. The numerous forms of hair style, and even untended hair, often provide information about the wearer's sex, age-level, degree of political conservatism, and so on (cf. Guthrie, 1976). Many hair styles are also intended to enhance facial beauty. There is evidence to support the commonplace notion that blonde or light-haired females tend to be seen as more attractive than females with darker hair (Singer, 1964), indicating that hair lightening may increase the perceived attractiveness of some females. Guthrie speculated that hair lightening (and some other cosmetic treatments such as eye makeup) is popular among women in some cultures because lighter hair fosters a more child-like appearance and, hence, "the social posture of an attractive subordinate" (1976, p. 58).

The social impact of beardedness on the perception of faces or persons certainly varies across cultures. Nonetheless Freedman has suggested, with some supportive evidence, that beards "make men more appealing to women and . . . give men more status in the eyes of other men" (1969, p. 38). Kenny and Fletcher (1973) obtained college students' ratings of a male both with and without a beard: Beardedness produced more favorable ratings (e.g., sincere, generous), but did not influence ratings of handsomeness. In contrast, two studies have found that beards increase facial attractiveness. Pellegrini (1973) photographed eight men before and after shaving off their beards, and at intermediate stages when they had goatees and moustaches. He found that the men were seen as better looking with full beards or goatees than when clean-shaven. Sprecher, Smith, and Johnson (1984, reported in Hatfield & Sprecher, 1986), using Identi-Kit faces to portray several men with and without beards, found that both young and middle-aged men were seen as better looking when bearded. The responses of 482 Caucasian females to a questionnaire about physiognomic preferences indicated that these college females did not prefer beards (Feinman & Gill, 1977). This discrepancy may be due to geographical or other cultural differences. In any case, shaving may produce effects like other means of fostering a youthful appearance because a clean-shaven face mimics the surface quality of the pre-pubertal face (cf. Pellegrini, 1973).

Skin lightening and darkening agents are often used in an attempt to improve facial attractiveness. Skin lighteners are mainly used by dark-skinned persons for whom they are probably effective in enhancing facial attractiveness in many cases; despite the "black is beautiful" saying, lightness of skin color in Black males was *positively* correlated with facial attractiveness as judged by both White and Black raters in one study (Cavior & Howard, 1973; see also Hill, 1944). Hulse (1967) concluded that social selection for light skin color among the Japanese has been strong enough to have exerted some genetic effect! Hence, the Japanese would probably assign higher attractiveness ratings to lighter skinned faces. In contrast, Americans appear to have sex differences in preferences for skin darkness with females favoring darker complexions in males, and males preferring lighter complexions in females (Feinman & Gill, 1978). In light of this, it is puzzling that Americans, particularly females, try so hard to darken their skin by tanning. It would seem that there is a socially significant and visually detectable difference between tanned and naturally dark skin. Clearly, more research is required to understand the aesthetic effects of skin coloration, particularly for intraracial variation.

Many current cosmetic practices of women in Western society can be seen as attempts to make their faces more youthful and/or feminine. Specific examples include the thinning of eyebrows, reddening of cheeks, dyeing of gray hair, masking of wrinkles and "age spots", and a variety of techniques used to make the eyes appear larger. This chapter and chapter 3 review ample evidence that increasing youthfulness or femininity is likely to increase physical attractiveness in adult women.

It is unfortunate that research on the use of facial cosmetics to enhance or alter facial appearance has not been part of the mainstream of psychological research on face perception, for this research could contribute greatly to our understanding of face perception. Fortunately, this seems to be changing (see Graham & Kligman, 1985). The existing literature already sheds light on the determinants of facial attractiveness, and we know from watching films and the theater that facial cosmetics can have a tremendous impact on perceived age.

Research on the enhancement of facial attractiveness by cosmetics (and other forms of facial elaboration) certainly can contribute to our understanding of potential cosmetic benefits, since many controlled experiments have already provided conclusions about the *casual* effects of attractiveness (see the following section). A word of caution is needed here: Like the fads of fashion, preferences for various forms of facial elaboration and the traits selected for alteration may be short-lived (Graham & Kligman, 1985). Hence, some of the studies reviewed previously may be outdated.

Facial Expression

The belief that a negative facial expression (e.g., a frown) can decrease facial attractiveness whereas a smiling or happy face may enhance facial attractiveness is very common. In a study supporting this belief (Meuser, Grau, Sussman, & Rosen, 1984), university students were shown photographs of 15 target persons posed with sad, neutral, or happy facial expressions. The target persons were judged less attractive when posing sad expressions than when posing either neutral or happy expressions (which did not differ). Facial expression has comparable effects on perceived cuteness (Hildebrandt, 1983) and may even have a significant effect on the overall assessment of physical attractiveness. Walsh and Locke (1980) found that "pleasantness of facial expression" made a significant contribution to the physical attractiveness ratings of waist-up photographs of adult women. Little is known about the impact of facial expression on facial attractiveness beyond the pleasant-unpleasant dimension of facial expression examined in the preceding studies (but see Buck, this volume; Milord, 1978).

Familiarity

Several studies have shown that familiarity with a face can increase its likeableness or attractiveness; a form of exposure effect (see Harrison, 1977). Thus, more frequent (e.g., Hamm, Baum, & Nikels, 1975; Moreland & Zajonc, 1982; Wilson & Nakajo, 1965) or longer lasting (e.g., Geiselman, Haight, & Kimata, 1984) exposure to a photograph increases the ratings of the depicted person's likeableness or attractiveness. These results parallel those found with other nonsocial stimuli, as well as the results obtained with variable exposure to real people (e.g., Saegert, Swap, & Zajonc, 1973), including nurses' exposure to premature infants (Corter et al., 1978). Wilson and Nakajo (1965) also found favorable effects of higher frequency of exposure to photos of males on females' judgments of ability, character, personality, and other aspects of social appeal. Apparently, one of the faces with which most of us are exceptionally familiar, our own face, may influence our judgments of facial attractiveness in others: People view those who are physically similar to themselves as possessing greater physical attractiveness (Sappenfield & Balogh, 1970). This influence of familiarity supports the idea that a face (or other object) must be familiar or have a familiar morphology in order to be considered attractive; the novel is ugly or repulsive (cf. Valentine, 1913). This viewpoint is consistent with adaptation level theory (Helson, 1964), which holds that we make perceptual judgments relative to a comparable stimulus to which we have become accustomed (adapted).

Cavior (1970, reported in Berscheid & Walster, 1974) noted that judges familiar with the targets depicted in full-length photos gave attractiveness ratings that, overall, were more favorable and had lower interrater reliability than the ratings of "non-knowers." Nonetheless, a large positive correlation between the judgments of familiar and unfamiliar adolescents was typically found in this research; familiarity with the targets had the greatest influence on attractiveness judgments of targets of average attractiveness compared to those at either extreme (Cavior & Dokecki, 1973). An earlier study (McCabe, 1926; reported in Hull, 1928) found that the intracorrelation of rankings of each other's beauty by acquainted women was quite high ($r = .96$), as was the intracorrelation for rankings of facial photographs of these same women by complete strangers ($r = .91$).

Styczynski and Langlois (1977) collected attractiveness judgments from nursery school children who were acquainted with the age-mates depicted in facial photos: judgments which agreed with, and did not vary more than, the judgments of unacquainted children. Their study of the effects of familiarity on attractiveness-related stereotypes in young children also suggests that it may be dangerous to generalize the results obtained using judges who are unacquainted with the ratees to judgments made by familiar others. In this study, the beauty-is-good stereotype was generally supported by the reactions of unacquainted age-mates, but was largely reversed in the ratings of familiar peers, especially boys (Styczynski & Langlois, 1977). These researchers concluded that in actual social situations facial attractiveness may actually be a social disadvantage for children, especially boys, but the results of earlier investigations (e.g., Dion & Berscheid, 1974; Lerner & Lerner, 1977) do not completely corroborate their results from peer ratings.

Some Other Influences

Although it is certainly true that the perception of facial attractiveness can produce favorable reactions, the reverse also seems to hold. That is, favorable information or reactions to others seem to increase their perceived attractiveness: a "what is good is beautiful" effect (Gross & Crofton, 1977). For instance, Shepherd, Ellis, McMurran, and Davis (1978) found that male faces described as murderers were rated less good-looking than the same faces described as photographs of lifeboatmen; an effect also found for independent ratings of Photofit constructions of the faces. Owens and Ford (1978) used favorable and unfavorable brief personality descriptions to, respectively, increase or decrease the physical attractiveness ratings of females depicted in facial photos; the ratings of males were not significantly affected by the descriptions in this study. This phenomenon is analogous to the increase in perceived height associated with greater ascribed occupational prestige (P.R. Wilson, 1968), and a "taller-is-better" stereotype seems to hold for men in Euro-American society (cf. Schumacher, 1982).

The degree of facial prominence in representations of others (i.e., the relative proportion of a depiction devoted to the face versus other body regions) may influence our evaluations of physical attractiveness. Photographs with high facial prominence receive more favorable ratings of "physical appearance" (plus intelligence and ambition) than otherwise identical photographs with low facial prominence (Archer, Iritani, Kimes, & Barrios, 1983).

As previously, noted gender has several effects on the judgment and effects of facial attractiveness. In addition to the effects already noted, attractiveness ratings may be biased in favor of one sex. In most studies in which such an effect has been reported, female faces tended to be rated as more attractive than male faces (see the following discussion). Not surprisingly, there also are consistent differences in the facial characteristics preferred in each sex. For instance, the commonplace idea that opposite sex preferences in our society favor dark colored (eyes, hair complexion) men ("tall, dark, and handsome") and light colored women ("men prefer blondes") is supported by the existing evidence (Feinman & Gill, 1978; Singer, 1964). Also, when adults from six diverse groups judged a series of profile silhouettes varying only in the protrusiveness of the lips, all six groups preferred fuller lips for adult females than for adult males (Foster, 1973).

Additionally, ratings of physical or facial attractiveness are subject to context effects. Attractiveness ratings of a female face have been lowered by concurrent or prior exposure to other very attractive females (Kenrick & Gutierres, 1980): a contrast effect. Conversely, Geiselman et al. (1984) found an *assimilation* effect of one or two female faces on the perceived attractiveness of another female face (i.e., greater similarity of ratings), but only if the other face(s) were presented simultaneously. Among the methodological differences that may account for this apparent disparity, Geiselman et al. (1984) argued that with simultaneous presentation perceivers may be less able to make independent judgments than with successive presentations. This plausible and empirically supported hypothesis should be examined in this and other areas of perception. In particular, if their hypothesis turns out to be correct, it would be interesting to know why *both* successive and simultaneous contexts in basic perceptual processes (like the perception of color and lightness) result in contrast effects (Brown & Deffenbacher, 1979). In any case, with faces there is more involved than the timing of exposures. Melamed and Moss (1975) found a contrast effect in facial attractiveness ratings of female adults when photographs of them were simply paired with either a less or more attractive female, but they found an *assimilation* effect when the context photo was described as a friend of the target.

The studies showing context effects may rightly alarm some experimenters, for these effects suggest that the physical attractiveness of the experimenter, or even the attractiveness of other raters in group testing situations, may influence ratings of attractiveness. Kenrick and Gutierres (1980) found that peers' favorable and unfavorable responses to facial appearance can increase or decrease, respectively, other raters' concurrent attractiveness ratings. This influence could artificially raise the interrater agreement on attractiveness ratings. Experimenters typically have been careful to reduce or eliminate such effects. Nonetheless, this sort of social influence may contaminate experimental settings in which evaluations are collected from groups of judges, for both nonverbal and verbal behaviors may communicate evaluations, especially of extremely attractive or unattractive faces. Of course, the evaluations of others are likely to influence aesthetic judgments in natural contexts and, therefore, merit further study.

Psychosocial Effects of Facial Attractiveness

The psychosocial effects of physical attractiveness encompass both other- and self-perception and cognition. We largely restrict our coverage of this topic to the effects of one's attractiveness on others, although these effects are not independent of the effects on oneself. More specifically, we examine two ways in which physical attractiveness influences attributions and expectations, and two areas in which physical attractiveness seems to affect social behavior. Again we rely as heavily as possible on studies that recorded judgments of *facial* attractiveness. Although factors like clothing and physique certainly can influence physical attractiveness, the available evidence indicates that such variables usually have less impact on attractiveness and its psychosocial effects than does facial appearance. For example, in the previously mentioned study of Nielsen and Kernaleguen (1976), facial attractiveness, but not body attractiveness, influenced judgments of overall physical attractiveness, social and professional happiness, and social desirability. Even more striking, G.J. Smith (1984) found correlations of facial photographs' attractiveness with several measures of treatment by peers that were consistently higher than the correlations between attractiveness ratings of full-length photographs and these behavioral variables.

To evaluate the psychosocial impact of facial attractiveness we need to know whether it is important only in the initial stages of social interaction or, alternatively, whether attractiveness remains an important influence over time despite the availability of additional information about the person. Even if attractiveness has a direct influence only during initial interactions, it can be expected to have some enduring impact because (a) many of a person's social contacts (e.g., in job interviews or jury trials) occur no more than a few times; (b) the attractiveness stereotype may give direction to the course of interaction by influencing early interactive behavior; (c) first impressions influence subsequent interactions (cf. Berscheid & Walster, 1974); (d) facial attractiveness can alter behavior via self-fulfilling prophecy (see Adams & Read, 1983; Snyder, Tanke, & Berscheid, 1977; and (e) people may distort later information to make it consistent with their early impressions (cf. Maruyama & Miller, 1981). Furthermore, unattractive persons may be viewed negatively and avoided, thus making it difficult for them to counter initially unfavorable impressions. In terms of standard psychological concepts, primacy effects, halo effects, selective attention, and implicit personality theories may each act to insure long-term effects of facial appearance (McArthur, 1982). Moreover, there is some evidence that facial attractiveness can continue to influence interactions over an extended period (e.g., Shea & Adams, 1984). One effect of facial attractiveness appears only after the passage of more than 7–35 days: After this period, recognition memory is significantly greater for female faces of high or low attractiveness than for faces of moderate attractiveness (Shepherd & Ellis, 1973).

In the remainder of this section we review studies to show that facial attractiveness has effects from birth through adulthood that appear across a variety of settings. In considering this research, keep in mind that, according to a study by Pallak (1983), physical attractiveness is likely to have a greater impact on psychosocial responses when it is highly salient (as in a high-quality colored photograph versus a low-quality xeroxgraphic copy). Of course, its influence should diminish as information from sources other than facial appearance becomes available (cf. Safier, 1983). Also, the target's sex (as discussed in the next section) or race (see Maruyama & Miller, 1981) may interact with the effects of facial attractiveness.

Heterosexual Attraction

In his 1871 book, *The Descent of Man*, Darwin discussed the influence of beauty on human sexual selection. Claiming that "in civilized life man is largely, but by no means exclusively influenced in the choice of his wife by external appearance" (p. 278); he went on to suggest that men in "semicivilized" and "savage" societies are likewise influenced. Darwin's statement refers only to men's attraction to women, but physical attractiveness certainly plays a role in the attraction of women to men. Nonetheless, there are some sex differences in the effects of facial attractiveness on interpersonal behavior (see the following section). As Darwin realized, the fact that humans universally assess physical attractiveness and universally desire attractive mates indicates that these assessments and desires have been shaped by evolutionary selection. This argument is supported by other arguments that also implicate physical attractiveness as a guide to fitness and reproductive success (see Symons, 1979 and following).

Turning to research, consider first an influential study by Walster, Aronson, Abrahams, and Rottman (1966) They randomly formed 332 heterosexual pairs of university students in a supposedly computer-matched dance. A variety of self-ratings, personality measures, and measures of scholastic aptitude were examined to assess the importance of each in contributing to a person's desirability as a date. The then surprising finding was that physical attractiveness was by far the best predictor of a partner's liking and desire to date again for both sexes. Replication and follow-up studies also have found physical attractiveness to be the only or best predictor of desire to date a partner again among numerous indices of similarity of interests, attitudes, perceived personality, and so on (see Berscheid, 1981; Berscheid & Walster, 1974). Likewise, free responses to videotaped conversing faces revealed that physical characteristics (vs. observed behaviors, etc.) were the best predictors of attraction (Lyman, Hatlelid, & Macurdy, 1981). In a study of antecedents of loving relationships among university students, males were predominantly influenced by the facial attractiveness of their partners; males' facial attractiveness also contributed to romantic love formation for females (Shea & Adams, unpublished). Several studies indicate that physically attractive men and women achieve sexual intimacy earlier in life and more frequently (see Hatfield & Sprecher, 1986).

It might be expected that beauty would have its main effect on attraction during the initial or early encounters; thereafter, as individuals get to know more about one another, the importance of physical attractiveness might decline, perhaps rather dramatically (cf. Sparacino & Hansell, 1979). Critics of the "beauty implies goodness" stereotype commonly claim that "beauty is only skin deep" and has only transitory effects. However, recent research indicates that the importance of physical attractiveness in heterosexual attraction does not decline over some fairly extended periods of time (Mathes, 1975). Shea and Adams (1984) found the influence of facial attractiveness on romantic attachment among young adults to be strongest for those who had dated the longest! A clear indication of the long-term impact of physical attractiveness is the finding that both lower and middle-class women who become upwardly mobile through marriage tend to be physically attractive (Elder, 1969; Udry, 1977). Likewise, facially attractive females tend to marry highly educated men with high income, and are less likely to remain unmarried (Udry & Eckland, 1984). This study also found that attractive males and females marry at earlier ages, probably reflecting the greater ease with which they can find satisfactory mates.

An ethological analysis of why physical attractiveness contributes to heterosexual attraction may shed light on why the effects of physical attractiveness may continue to be important in extended interpersonal relationships. For instance, one reason we desire physically attractive mates may be that attractive mates increase the chances of producing attractive offspring. Physically attractive offspring, in turn, would reap the benefits of physical attractiveness including, presumably, an increased freedom of choice of mates.

In some cases, a physical disorder underlies facial unattractiveness. For example, most individuals possessing craniofacial anomalies associated with chromosomal aberrations (such as Down's syndrome) have significant functional deficits (e.g., mental deficiency, deafness, or congenital heart anomalies). Likewise, many, if not most, other craniofacial anomalies appearing at or shortly after birth are associated with one or more functional deficiencies (Goodman & Gorlin, 1977; Gorlin, Pindborg, & Cohen, 1976). Hence, another reason that physical attractiveness may be an important determinant of heterosexual attraction is that it helps screen out individuals with genetic irregularities, disease, or other biological handicaps (see Symons, 1979; and the following discussion). Selection should favor humans who select the fittest members of the opposite sex as mates. As others have argued in explaining the colorful plumage of some birds and other physically attracting aspects of nonhuman animals (Kodric-Brown & Brown, 1985; Zuk, 1984), the real beauty of physical attractiveness may lie in its value as a guide to selecting healthy, disease-resistant mates. The selection pressure on mate selection should be greatest for females because their parental investment typically exceeds the investment by males (Symons, 1979).

Any perceptually salient craniofacial anomaly may lower the chances of sexually attracting members of the opposite sex (see Macgregor, 1974). Hence, such anomalies may tend to lower an individual's chances of mating and producing offspring. This argument for a potential reproductive impairment of the craniofacially abnormal, however, is only speculative because no data exist on the relative reproductive success of these individuals, let alone the corresponding figures for such individuals in the context of human evolutionary adaptedness which has shaped our biological constraints on the pertinent social interactions.

Expectations and Impression Formation

In a seminal study, Miller (1970) reported that both male and female judges tended to form positive impressions of highly attractive persons depicted in yearbook photographs, and negative impressions of unattractive persons. Since 1970, many additional studies have appeared that corroborate and extend Miller's results (see reviews in Adams, 1977; Berscheid & Walster, 1974; Hatfield & Sprecher, 1986), with the specific expectations even including proneness to epilepsy (Hansson & Duffield, 1976)! This "beauty-is-good" stereotype even influences adults' impressions of young infants (Stephan & Langlois, 1984) and elderly adults (Johnson, 1985) depicted in facial photographs. Most of these studies have used photographs, but a study (Mims, Hartnett, & Nay, 1975) that used a videotape presentation of two males demonstrated that facial attractiveness conveyed in more natural, dynamic displays can have similar effects on impression formation. This study also showed the potential strength of the influence of facial attractiveness on impressions, for the well-mannered but unattractive male debater received evaluative ratings no better than an attractive but "obnoxious" male debater.

Ritter and Langlois (1986) demonstrated that facial attractiveness can strongly influence global ratings of social interactions. Global ratings (e.g., relaxed, competent) of attractive adult females were higher for these targets when rated using an unaltered videotape than when rated using the same videotape in which their faces were occluded. Even more striking, these attractive adults were rated higher than unattractive adults in the unoccluded condition, but the unattractive adults were rated higher when targets' faces were occluded. In contrast, no evidence of bias due to targets' attractiveness was found for molecular (i.e., operationally defined, specific aspects of behavior like "holds close") ratings.

The evidence for a beauty-is-good stereotype has been acquired mainly in studies that used school-age or college student judges, but several studies show that this stereotype exists in older, often more sophisticated groups. For instance, the reactions of 289 Australian health professionals to facial photos have confirmed this stereotype (Nordholm, 1980). Moreover, Nordholm found that the judges' age, sex, and occupation had no effect on the positive correlation between facial attractiveness and impressions. In studies mentioned in the discussion immediately following, the beauty-is-good stereotype was exhibited by teachers and other professional groups. Other recent work has demonstrated that, in general, the beauty-is-good stereotype extends to adults' perceptions of young infants (Stephan & Langlois, 1984).

Physical attractiveness can influence a variety of evaluations and expectations of children in school settings. Among the studies that have varied *facial* attractiveness is a recent study by Elovitz and Salvia (1982). They collected evaluations from a national sampling of 324 school psychologists based on a fictitious psychological report describing a third-grade pupil whose teacher had referred him or her for poor achievement and behavioral problems. This report was accompanied by one of four facial photographs, depicting either a boy or girl of either high or low facial attractiveness. The attractive children tended to receive better prognoses than their unattractive counterparts. Comparable results have been obtained with teachers' ratings of attractive and unattractive preschool (Adams, 1978), first- (M.M. Clifford, 1975), third- (Ross & Salvia, 1975), and fifth- (M.M. Clifford & Walster, 1973) grade boys and girls depicted by facial photographs in otherwise identical psychological reports. A recent meta-analysis of the teacher-expectancy literature (Dusek & Joseph, 1983) confirmed that teachers hold both higher academic and social/personal expectations for more attractive students. A multivariate study by Rich (1975) supports these basic results, but shows that some information provided in traditional report cards can override the positive effects of facial attractiveness on teacher evaluations of children. Similarly, LaVoie and Adams (1974) showed that concrete information concerning a student's conduct can eliminate attractiveness effects. Likewise, in a study of performance evaluations of male and female undergraduates by faculty raters, the effects of facial attractiveness (as rated from yearbook photos) were overwhelmed, apparently, by information about previous performance (Morrow & McElroy, 1984).

The technique of affixing photographs varying in attractiveness to otherwise matched sets of materials has been used in several other studies. In one of these, essays supposedly written by facially attractive freshman coeds, and the alleged authors themselves, received higher evaluations by male college students than unattractive coeds (Landy & Sigall, 1974). Confirming these results, Cash and Trimer (1984) found that facial attractiveness enhanced women's evaluations of both male and female essayists and their essays. In another study, physically attractive male and female job applicants received better evaluations from both business students and professional interviewers (Dipboye, Fromkin, & Wiback, 1975). Similarly, professional personnel consultants tended to give more favorable evaluations to facially attractive job applicants than to unattractive applicants (Cash, Gillen, & Burns, 1977). Both children and adults apparently associate facial attractiveness with intelligence (W.C. Shaw, 1981b, this volume).

Several studies have provided evidence that facially attractive persons are seen as being more responsible for various kinds of successful outcome and less responsible for failures than unattractive counterparts (e.g., Seligman, Paschall, & Takata, 1974; Turkat & Dawson, 1976). That is, the failures of attractive individuals are more likely to be attributed to circumstances beyond their control than are the failures of matched unattractive persons, and relatively attractive persons are more likely to be seen as responsible for their successes. The greater competence and responsibility for success attributed to more attractive persons may account for the results of some research on counselors' physical attractiveness. Several studies (e.g., Cash & Kehr, 1978; Cash & Salzbach, 1978) indicate that the facial attractiveness of a counselor often influences the reactions of clients such that attractive counselors are more likely to obtain favorable outcomes.

Although research on the effects of physical attractiveness on impressions and expectations has been dominated by a focus on the beauty-is-good stereotype, our responses to others also are influenced by facial attractiveness in ways that do not fall on a simple good–bad continuum. For instance, greater masculinity is attributed to more attractive males, and greater femininity to more attractive females depicted by facial photographs (Gillen, 1981).

Another limitation of the beauty-is-good stereotype is that there are situations in which some negative consequences of high physical attractiveness appear. For instance, Dermer and Thiel (1975) found that socially undesirable attributions of vanity, egotism, likelihood of marital disaster, and snobbishness reliably and monotonically increased with the (independently rated) attractiveness of target persons depicted in waist-up, color photographs. Unattractive females were more likely to express such negative attributions for attractive targets and less likely to make attributions in line with the "beauty-is-good" stereotype. Gallucci and Meyer (1984), however, were mostly unable to confirm these findings of Dermer and Thiel, perhaps because their stimulus photographs only depicted heads and shoulders. Still, teachers rate less-attractive students depicted in head and neck photographs as having better work habits and personal attitudes than more attractive students (Adams & LaVoie, 1974). Nonetheless, in most of these and other studies that have found some negative effects of high physical attractiveness, positive effects have also been found. Together, these studies have verified the beauty-is-good stereotype, while highlighting some important limitations and qualifications. Other limits on the generalizability of this stereotype, such as that due to judges' familiarity with target individuals, are discussed in later sections of this chapter.

Some of the positive effects of facial attractiveness on social perceptions may in part be due to our positive valuation of beauty per se. Thus, for example, highly attractive persons may tend to be seen as generally moral or trustworthy because their beauty gives them sufficient power such that they seldom need to stoop to immoral acts to get what they want (cf. Adams & Crossman, 1978). At any rate, facial attractiveness elicits a wide variety of favorable attributions and expectations and, therefore, can be expected to promote corresponding favorable effects on social behavior.

Aid, Compliance, and Reward

One positive effect of physical attractiveness appears to be an increase in the likelihood of receiving helpful or compliant responses from others. Much of this research has involved field experiments with real people, usually females, instead of photographs, drawings, or descriptions. These studies have shown that physical attractiveness can increase one's ability to get others to follow requests or orders (e.g., Sigall, Page, & Brown, 1971; D.W. Wilson, 1978), to cooperate (e.g., Kahn, Hottes, & Davis, 1971), to provide help to an individual in need (e.g., Mims et al., 1975; West & Brown, 1975), and to persuade others to assume a certain attitude or belief when the communicator has announced her intent to influence (Mills & Aronson, 1965). These studies clearly demonstrate that physical attractiveness fosters helping behavior and compliance, and additional studies indicate that *facial* attractiveness is sufficient to produce these effects.

One such study collected female ninth-graders' responses to an editorial accompanied by a head and shoulders photograph of an attractive male, unattractive male, or no photograph (Horai, Naccari, & Fatoullah, 1974). Greater agreement with the editorial's opinions was expressed by students who read the version accompanied by an attractive photo than for the unattractive or no photograph sources (which did not differ). In a similar study, Snyder and Rothbart (1971) played a tape recorded speech which was sometimes accompanied by a facial photograph of a male alleged to be the speaker. This speech was more persuasive when heard in connection with a photograph of a facially attractive male than with unattractive or unpictured speakers. Furthermore, this effect was independent of differences in the perceived expertise or trustworthiness of the communicator. More recent experimental and theoretical work suggests that physical attractiveness influences acceptance of emotionally toned but not simply rational appeals (see Pallak, Murroni, & Koch, 1983). Further research should examine whether emotions affect the influence of physical attractiveness on other psychosocial responses, as seems likely.

High facial attractiveness can have positive effects on aid-giving. In one study (Benson, Karabenick, & Lerner, 1976), more graduate school applications left in an airport phone booth were placed in an accompanying envelope and mailed by adult callers when the application contained a facial photograph of an attractive (vs. unattractive) male or female applicant. These results, however, could be due to an increase in attention to the materials and their demand for action rather than to the attractiveness of applicants per se. In either case, the implication is that persons with attractive faces are more likely to receive aid, even if only because they are more likely to attract our attention.

The available evidence indicates that attractive persons are likely to receive greater rewards than unattractive persons under the same circumstances. For example, personnel counselors recommended that attractive males and females receive higher starting salaries than unattractive persons depicted by facial photographs in otherwise matched personnel files (Jackson, 1983).

Blame and Punishment

Actual criminal records and mock jury trials indicate that, compared to unattractive defendants, attractive individuals are less likely to be convicted of crimes that they are accused of and, if convicted, tend to receive less harsh punishment (Efran, 1974; Leventhal & Krate, 1977; Monahan, 1941, p. 103; Solomon & Schopler, 1978; Stewart, 1980). However, the effect of physical attractiveness on sentencing has been negated (E.D. Smith & Hed, 1979) and even reversed (Sigall & Ostrove, 1975) when the defendant may have used his or her attractiveness to take advantage of others (e.g., in a swindle). Further research is needed to determine whether *facial* attractiveness is sufficient to produce these effects. In the one existing study that limited physical attractiveness variation to facial appearance (Stephan & Tully, 1977), facial attractiveness did favorably influence mock jury decisions and damage awards in a personal injury suit. Also, in studying prototype formation, Goldin (1979, Exper. 4) found a strong negative correlation between rated guilt and rated attractiveness for Identi-Kit Model II faces, with "facial cues" providing the only information for the judgments of guilt.

Studies of the effects of facial attractiveness on adults' punishment of children have not yielded consistent results. In the only study of male subjects, Dion (1974) found no attractiveness effects on men's penalizations of children. The results found using female subjects are inconsistent. Berkowitz and Frodi (1979) found that women punished unattractive girls more than attractive girls, but Dion (1974) and Rich (1975) found the opposite. In addition, Dion (1974) found that women punished unattractive boys more than attractive boys. Likewise, Rich (1975) found that teachers gave harsher recommendations for punishment to unattractive boys, but Marwit, Marwit, and Walker (1978) obtained recommendations for disciplinary action which were more severe for attractive than for unattractive boys. Some apparently conflicting results can also be seen in the study by Rich (1975): A misbehavior (social aggression) was deemed more undesirable when attributed to facially attractive children, but unattractive girls were least likely (and attractive boys most likely) to be recommended for punishment.

Although these studies suggest that adult women apply differential standards in determining punishment for attractive and unattractive children, this process is influenced by the children's sex, among other factors. (Such sex differences are discussed in a separate section later in this chapter.) For example, the literature on adult interactions suggests that the nature of the transgression committed by a child will determine how attractiveness influences punishment (Sigall & Ostrove, 1975). A crucial factor that underlies some of the other discrepancies in these studies may lie in the distinction between deciding to blame or apply punishment and deciding how severe the punishment should be. A potential explanation of those cases in which unattractive children fare better with regard to receiving blame and punishment is that misbehavior by such children does not violate the beauty-is-good stereotype as much as misbehavior by attractive children. That is, misbehavior by unattractive children is more in line with our expectations than is misbehavior by attractive children. Clearly, further study is needed to determine how facial attractiveness mediates blame and punishment of children.

Parent–Offspring, Teacher–Student, and Peer Relations

As noted previously, the vital relationship between parent and offspring also may be affected by the facial attractiveness or cuteness of the offspring.

Although it seems reasonable to expect that the relationship between parent and child would be affected by the facial attractiveness of the child, almost no research on this issue has been reported.

A disproportionate amount of the existing research has focused on parents of children with facial anomalies. As most people would expect, mothers of craniofacial patients provide relatively negative ratings of their afflicted children compared to mothers of children with a less visible anomaly (cleft palate) (E. Clifford, 1979). From an evolutionary perspective, it is understandable that parents would tend to reject or at least provide poorer care for, offspring with craniofacial anomalies because such offspring are likely to be less viable and, therefore, are not (biologically speaking) as worthy of parental investment (see preceding discussion).

Like other groups, parents of facially normal children hold more positive views of attractive than unattractive unfamiliar children (Adams & LaVoie, 1975), and they expect their own preschool-age children to hold similar views (Adams & Crane, 1980). Maruyama and Miller (1981) found some relationships between parents' general evaluations and ratings of their child's motivation and parental ratings of physical attractiveness, although attractiveness interacted with ethnic group.

Remarkably, however, there is only one study of parents' reactions to their own children as a function of the children's facial attractiveness. Langlois, Sawin, and Stephan (1981) related mothers' behaviors with their newborns to ratings of facial photographs of the neonates. Mothers of more attractive newborns showed more affectionate close holding of the infants and spent more time in effective and responsive feeding during a 20-minute hospital observation. The mothers of the less attractive newborns looked at them and stimulated them more. Attitudinal measures suggested that the mothers of the unattractive neonates showed these behaviors because they were particularly concerned about and disappointed in their infants. It appears that lowered cuteness may have elicited more and perhaps better caregiving than higher cuteness, contradicting Lorenz's (1943) hypothesis, but evaluation of the effects of infants' facial attractiveness on parents should be based on observations across a larger time span than 20 minutes during the newborn period. Patterns of caregiving differing in quality probably require weeks or months to establish, and are likely to vary as a function of the stability or instability of infant facial attractiveness over time.

Studies of teachers and other caregiving adults, together with studies of adults' reactions to differentially cute infants described later in this chapter, also suggest that parent-child relations are influenced by the child's facial attractiveness. For example, Adams and Cohen (1974) reported that a seventh-grade teacher interacted more frequently with facially attractive than unattractive students during the first week of a new school year (although a similar effect was *not* found for either a kindergarten or a fourth-grade teacher observed in the same study). Evidence that facially attractive third-graders were more likely to be referred for special help by their teachers was interpreted by Barocas and Black (1974) as further evidence that more attention is paid to attractive children. Although there is some debate concerning whether or not attractive children receive higher school grades than unattractive children (see Hildebrandt, 1982a), a study by Salvia, Algozzine, and Sheare (1977) on this topic is enlightening. They selected only highly attractive and very unattractive third- to fifth-grade students and found significant difference in report card grades favoring the more attractive children. This finding could be due to differential competence of the children rather than teacher bias, but they also found that the difference was maintained even when scores on basic skills tests were held constant. These results suggest that highly attractive children were given preferential treatment by their teachers in the assignment of grades.

Considerable research has been conducted on the influence of facial attractiveness on children's peer relations. Facial attractiveness has a positive effect on peer relations from early childhood onward, while unattractive children may tend to be actively disliked by their peers. Preschool and elementary school children's perceptions of and expectations for unfamiliar peers clearly demonstrate that they hold more positive views of attractive than unattractive others (Dion, 1973; Langlois & Stephan, 1977). These positive views generally are maintained as children become acquainted. Familiar attractive peers are perceived as less frightening (Dion & Berscheid, 1974), more prosocial (Langlois & Styczynski, 1979) and, in some cases, less aggressive and antisocial (Dion & Berscheid, 1974; Langlois & Styczynski, 1979). In line with these perceptions of familiar peers is the fairly consistent observation that attractive children are more popular and socially accepted (Adams, & Roopnarine, 1987; Dion & Berscheid, 1974; Kleck, Richardson, & Ronald, 1974; Langlois & Styczynski, 1979; Lerner & Lerner, 1977; Salvia, Sheare, & Algozzine, 1975; Vaughn & Langlois, 1983), although this may not be true for Black children (Maruyama & Miller, 1981). A recent study of preschoolers suggests that this favorable effect of facial attractiveness cannot be attributed to differences in social skills; instead, the researchers conclude that the association between facial attractiveness and popularity is primarily due to differential interpersonal attraction as a function of variation in facial appearance (Adams & Roopnarine, 1987). Similarly, Zakin (1983) found physical attractiveness (judged from yearbook photographs) to be more important than sociability or athletic ability in determining selections of potential new friends by third and eighth graders. Nonetheless, the social facilitation engendered by facial attractiveness stereotypes may be fostered by a greater ability of the facially attractive to (facially) communicate affect (Buck, 1975; Larrance & Zuckerman, 1981).

Observations of peer interactions among differentially attractive children are useful in determining actual differences in both the behavior of differentially attractive children and the treatment they receive from others. A recent study by G.J. Smith (1985) revealed that attractive preschool girls were more likely to receive prosocial behaviors, and less likely to receive antisocial behaviors from peers than were unattractive girls. Another study (Langlois & Downs, 1979) found more activity and aggression in dyadic interactions when one or both of the children were unattractive. A study of older children (Dion & Stein, 1978) revealed even more clearly that attractive and unattractive children acquire different behavioral styles. These fifth- and sixth-grade children were given the task of convincing an unfamiliar peer to eat bitter-tasting crackers. Attractive children of both sexes were more successful in this task with opposite-sex partners than were unattractive children, although the attractive boys were described as assertive and coaxing, whereas the attractive girls succeeded despite a lack of persistence and forcefulness. Unattractive boys were successful with male partners, but they achieved this success through the use of commands, directives, and occasionally physical threats. This study further demonstrates that the effects of attractiveness are likely to differ for males and females. Attractive girls may learn that they can get what they want just by looking good, while unattractive boys may learn that aggression is an effective means of achieving some ends. (Such sex differences in facial attractiveness effects are examined further in the following section.)

In summary, peer relations appear to be influenced by children's facial attractiveness, although there is some variability in the effects associated with sex and age. In general it is advantageous for a child to be attractive. The fact that highly attractive children have more favorable self-concepts than unattractive children (Salvia et al., 1975) provides further evidence for this assertion.

Sex Differences in Facial Attractiveness Effects

According to the media, popular accounts, sociobiological theory, and scientific studies, the importance and impact of facial attractiveness differ for males and females. For instance, television and other media associate attractiveness and attractiveness stereotypes with females more often than with males (Adams & Crossman, 1978; Downs & Harrison, 1985). In this section, we review evidence that facial attractiveness is more important for females than males, at least in Western societies. (Also see reviews by Adams & Crossman, 1978; Freedman, 1986; Hatfield & Sprecher, 1986.)

From several sociobiological perspectives, it is expected that physical attractiveness will be more important for females than males (Buss, 1987; Buss & Barnes, 1986; Symons, 1979). For instance, since aging usually has less impact on men's reproductive capacity than on women's, heterosexual preferences for youthful appearance may carry greater selective advantage for males than females. Thus, a youthful appearance may be more important for women than for men (cf. chap. 3). After investigating sexual behavior in 190 different societies, Ford and Beach concluded that "in most societies the physical beauty of the female receives more explicit consideration . . . The attractiveness of the man usually depends predominantly upon his skills and prowess rather than upon his physical appearance" (1951, p. 86). More recent experimental studies have corroborated this (see Buss, 1987).

From at least ages 8 to 16 years, girls are less satisfied with their looks than boys and seem to be more concerned about their physical appearance (Coleman, 1961; Eme, Maisiak, & Goodale, 1979; Simmons & Rosenberg, 1975). Girls' concern with their physical appearance may be warranted because adolescent males see physical attractiveness as the primary criterion for female attractiveness (Coleman, 1961). Greater concern and dissatisfaction with physical appearance may also characterize adult females (Freedman, 1986), and older males also report that they are influenced by physical attractiveness when making dating choices, although physical attractiveness is generally not reported to be the most important determinant of adult males' heterosexual attraction (see Berscheid & Walster, 1974). Physical attractiveness seems to be slightly, but significantly, more important to males as a determinant of heterosexual attraction and liking (Miller & Rivenbark, 1970; Walster et al., 1966). In a laboratory study, facial attractiveness had a greater impact on men's preferences for women as coworkers, and potential dates or marriage partners than on the women's preferences for men (Stroebe, Insko, Thompson, & Layton, 1971). The exception that demonstrates the point is homosexual men; they are reported to be more concerned with their physical appearance because, like most women, they want to be sexually attractive to men (cf. Symons, 1979).

Buss and Barnes (1986, Study 2) found the greatest sex difference in rankings by unmarried university students of the importance of 13 potential mate characteristics for the characteristic of physical attractiveness. Married men also rate physical attractiveness and "good looking" as more important mate characteristics than their wives (Buss & Barnes, 1986, Study 1). The sex difference in the relationship between marriage and facial attractiveness is more striking. In our society there is a high negative relationship between attractiveness and percentage never married for women but not for men (Udry & Eckland, 1984). In fact, the least attractive females were almost 10 times as likely never to have married as the most attractive females in this study!

Unattractive males are viewed more favorably than unattractive females, perhaps because males are seen as more able to compensate for their looks (Miller, 1970). Indeed, a 1970 follow-up survey of over 2,000 people who were photographed as high school students in 1955 revealed that unattractive males were more educated and had higher occupational status than their more attractive peers—and male facial attractiveness was not related to parental status characteristics (Udry & Eckland, 1984). G.J. Smith's (1984) study of young children found that facially attractive girls were treated preferentially compared to less attractive girls, but in boys there was no relationship between facial attractiveness and observed treatment by peers. In addition, males tend to hold stronger physical attractiveness stereotypes than females (Downs, Reagan, Garrett, & Kolodzy, 1982). Given such sex differences in the importance placed on physical attractiveness, the greater use of cosmetics by females and the larger proportion of females seeking surgical or orthodontic treatment of facial "anomalies" (Jacobson, 1984) is to be expected.

These and many other studies (e.g., Byrne, London, & Reeves, 1968) suggest that the "beauty-is-good" stereotype may be applied more consistently to females than males in our society (cf. Bar-Tal & Saxe, 1976; Cash, 1981). Not all studies conform to this generalization, however. For instance, teachers' evaluations of children depicted in head and shoulder photos suggest that physical attractiveness makes girls *more* likely to be blamed and may tend to elicit more severe recommendations for punishment; effects opposite those found for boys (Rich, 1975). Also, some studies have found uniformly positive effects of physical attractiveness for males but mixed results for females (see review by Cash, 1981). If, on the other hand, facial attractiveness is indeed more salient for judgments of females than males, standards of facial attractiveness may be better defined and more widely shared for females; a speculation supported by a report of slightly greater test–retest reliability in ratings of females' facial attractiveness (Kerr & Kurtz, 1978).

Women apparently tend to evaluate themselves in terms of what they look like whereas men put more emphasis on what they can do (Freedman, 1986). The greater psychosocial impact of physical attractiveness for females is probably responsible for sex differences in the correlations between physical attractiveness and psychological self-reports. For instance, Mathes and Kahn (1975) found significant correlations between independently rated physical attractiveness and self-rated happiness ($r = .37$), self-esteem ($r = .24$), and psychological health (neuroticism) ($r = -.22$) for female university students, but no significant correlations for males. Likewise, the greater importance of attractiveness for females may be reflected in psychophysiological measures. Among young adults, unattractive females have significantly higher average blood pressure than attractive females, even when controlling for obesity, whereas attractiveness and blood pressure are generally unrelated in males (Hansell, Sparacino, & Ronchi, 1982).

Facial attractiveness can enhance or exaggerate perceptions of men's masculinity and women's femininity (Cash, 1981; Heilman & Saruwatari, 1979). Likewise, the favorable impact of facial attractiveness on performance evaluations of women can be modulated by task sex-typing, with attractiveness being less beneficial for "masculine" tasks (Cash & Trimer, 1984). Nonetheless, our culture and many others view physical attractiveness as a necessity for being fully feminine, but a man need not be handsome to be seen as masculine (cf. Adams & Crossman, 1978). "Good looks are prerequisite for femininity but incidental to masculinity" (Freedman, 1986, p.2). In a survey of 28,000 readers of *Psychology Today* (who are typically better educated and more liberal than the average American), almost twice as many men as women viewed physical attractiveness as a "very important" or "essential" trait of an ideal member of the opposite sex (Tavris, 1977). In our society even the pursuit of beauty is considered an aspect of femininity. The greater scarcity of males, outlawing of polygamy, and high divorce rate add competitive pressure for females to pursue physical attractiveness. Along these lines, Symons stated that compared to "preliterate peoples, modern human communities provide an enormous pool of potential sexual and marital partners, relatively few taboos, unprecedented freedom from parental influences, and thus great scope for personal attraction based on physical appearance" (1979, p. 205).

In addition to the sex difference in the social importance of beauty, there are also sex differences in the social impact of facial irregularities and aging. It is commonly believed that facial aging has a greater negative impact for females than males (cf. Adams & Crossman, 1978; Hatfield & Sprecher, 1986; Melamed, 1983), although research on this issue is somewhat inconclusive (see chap. 3). A similar sex difference may occur with facial anomalies. A broken nose or facial scar is typically no more than regrettable for a man, and may even be viewed as adding "character" to his face, whereas the same injury in a woman is likely to have a much more negative impact. A Norwegian study supports this view; some facial deformities (e.g., craniofacial asymmetry) are rated as more severe when they occur in women (Aamot, 1978).

Despite these findings, there is some evidence that in our culture facial appearance may have more influence on the evaluation of male than female physical attractiveness due to the greater importance of females' physique (Adams, 1982). Moreover, the widespread phenomenon of "face-ism"—the tendency of the face to be more prominent in representations of males than females (Archer et al., 1983)—suggests that facial *appearance*, but not necessarily facial attractiveness, may even be *more* important for men than women.

There are also sex differences in the effects of facial attractiveness on impression formation. Heilman and Saruwatari (1979) recorded personnel ratings and hiring preferences for individuals depicted by equivalent applicant folders containing yearbook photographs varying in attractiveness. They found that attractiveness was consistently advantageous for men, but was an advantage for women only when being evaluated for a nonmanagerial position; attractiveness was a disadvantage for women being evaluated for a managerial position. Morse et al. (1974) obtained ratings from both males and females which indicated that seeing a male as physically attractive is associated with seeing him as assertive, whereas physically attractive females are more likely to be viewed as friendly. In his study of adults' responses to photographs, Miller (1970) found a number of significant Sex of Stimulus × Attractiveness interactions. Although it is not clear whether these differences are qualitative or simply quantitative in nature, his results did indicate that "as one departs from high-physical attractiveness, a stimulus person's sex becomes a more influential impression determinant" (Miller, 1970, p. 242).

A final apparent sex difference is commonly seen in studies that have obtained ratings of attractiveness for faces of both sexes from raters of both sexes: Female faces are often rated more favorably than male faces (e.g., Maret, 1983; McKelvie, 1981; Nordholm, 1980). As Maret (1983) argued, this sex difference may reflect the closer association of attractiveness with femininity than masculinity: an association which makes it more acceptable to attribute physical attractiveness to females than to males. On the other hand, greater sexual selection for facial attractiveness in females (see Buss & Barnes, 1986) may have resulted in an actual, if slight, sex difference in facial attractiveness with females showing greater average facial attractiveness and, perhaps, less variability.

FACIAL CUTENESS

Perceptions of and reactions to facial cuteness have received much less attention than perceptions of and reactions to facial attractiveness. Although facial cuteness and attractiveness are undoubtedly very similar constructs, we believe that "cuteness" is more closely associated with objects of diminutive size and youthful appearance than is "attractiveness". In fact, all research on facial cuteness has used infantile stimuli. Although ratings of infant facial attractiveness and cuteness have been found to be highly correlated ($r = .88$; Hildebrandt, unpublished data; also Stephan & Langlois, 1984), comparable data are not yet available for older children and adults.

Determinants of Facial Cuteness

Some research on the perception of facial cuteness was reviewed in the preceding chapter. To summarize, this research indicates that heads or faces with relatively infantile characteristics are generally perceived as cuter than more elderly versions of these same heads. Age-related changes in the overall shape of the head, the relative size and placement of the facial features, and the proportions of various facial regions all seem to influence perceived cuteness in this manner (e.g., Alley, 1981; Hildebrandt & Fitzgerald, 1979b). Although human responses to simple line drawings have consistently pointed to a monotonic relationship between age and cuteness, a more complex relationship is suggested by a study of cuteness ratings of infants depicted in facial photographs (Hildebrandt & Fitzgerald, 1979a). Ratings of infants between 3 and 13 months were highest around 9–11 months. Although ratings declined at 13 months, the lack of data on older children precludes determining whether or not this decline continues. While facial attractiveness tends to remain fairly stable during childhood, perceived cuteness declines (Alley, chap. 3). Further, although some individuals probably remain "cute" as they grow older due to their babyish facial characteristics, most individuals will be differentiated more on the basis of attractiveness during adolescence and adulthood.

Several factors in addition to facial configurations have been found to be related to judgments of infants' facial cuteness, including familiarity. Parents (Hildebrandt, 1980; Hildebrandt & Fitzgerald, 1981) rate their own infants as more cute than other adults rate them. Furthermore, smiling infants are perceived as cuter than crying infants (Power, Hildebrandt, & Fitzgerald, 1982). Interestingly though, when the same infants are rated with both positive and negative facial expressions, the differences in ratings of individual infants are smaller than differences among infants with matched facial expressions (Hildebrandt, 1983). Thus, an infant with a positive facial expression may be perceived as less cute than an infant showing a negative facial expression if the general facial configuration of a happier infant conveys lower cuteness than the facial configuration of the more distressed infant.

Ratings of cuteness also are influenced by an infant's sex, but the relationship is not completely straightforward. Hildebrandt and Fitzgerald (1979a) obtained ratings from two groups of college students for photographs of 60 infant faces; one group was told the infants were male, the other group was told the infants were female. Higher ratings were given to infants when they were labeled male than when they were labeled female. Although female infants received slightly higher ratings than male infants when their sex was unknown, knowledge of the infant's sex had a greater influence on ratings than did actual sex. Hildebrandt and Fitzgerald (1979a) suggested that this finding indicated the operation of a physical attractiveness sex stereotype: Girls are expected to be cuter than boys, and so their cuteness is judged more stringently. Thus, a particular infant will be perceived as cuter if he or she is believed to be male since the standards for cuteness in boys are lower.

In summary, perception of an individual infant's cuteness is influenced both by their visible appearance (facial configuration and expression, and physical appearance variations associated with age and sex) and by perceivers' knowledge about the infant (in particular, the infant's sex and the adult's relationship to and familiarity with the infant). How these various factors combine to determine an adult's perception of an infant's cuteness is not known. Obviously, the perceived cuteness of an infant can change as a function of both short-term and long-term changes in the infant and the infant's relationship with the perceiver.

Some Psychosocial Effects of Facial Cuteness

There is evidence to support the claim of Lorenz (1943) and other ethologists (e.g., Hess, 1975; Wickler, 1973) that facial cuteness helps promote parental caregiving. One source of evidence comes from studies that show more positive responses to infants than to older children and adults, as well as to those who simply *appear* younger (see chaps. 3, 4, & 5). A more infantile craniofacial appearance has been shown to be associated with perceptions of cuteness (Alley, 1981), suggesting that preferential reactions to younger stimuli may be mediated by facial cuteness.

An extension of Lorenz's hypothesis suggests that individual differences in babyishness or facial cuteness will elicit preferential caregiving responses. Several studies support the proposal that cuter infants will receive more attention and more favorable caregiving than less cute infants. Adults' reactions to photographs of infants who vary in cuteness indicate that cuter infants are perceived as possessing more desirable traits (Hildebrandt & Stern, 1984; Stephan & Langlois, 1984) and receive greater amounts of adult attention. At least three studies (Hildebrandt & Fitzgerald, 1978, 1981; Power et al., 1982) have found that adults look longer at cuter infants either when photographs were presented in pairs or when the subjects had control over the length of presentation. No cuteness effects on looking were found when photographs were presented individually for set intervals (Hildebrandt & Fitzgerald, 1981). These results led Hildebrandt and Fitzgerald to propose that cuter infants will receive more attention than less cute infants, particularly in settings where there are other demands on the adult's attention.

Pursuing this hypothesis, Hildebrandt (1982b) conducted a study in which female college students were observed interacting with two 7-month-old same-sex infants. As expected, the proportion of time adults spent looking at the two infants was significantly related to differences in infant cuteness. Cuter infants were looked at more, and the difference in the time spent looking was larger when the difference in cuteness was larger. An additional finding was that cuter infants smiled more and were smiled at more. Although the causal direction was unclear, this finding suggested that the attention directed to the cuter infants was more affectively positive and that infants who vary in cuteness eventually manifest different behavioral patterns as a result of differential treatment by adults.

A follow-up study was conducted in a more natural situation: a group program for infants, where adults must continually divide their attention among several infants (Hildebrandt & Cannan, 1985). It was found that cuter infants received more attention in this setting, at least when caregivers were new to the program. The effects of cuteness on adult attention distribution dissipated over time, indicating that familiarity may moderate the influence of cuteness.

In summary, younger-appearing and cuter infants appear to have some advantages in eliciting positive responses from adults. Specifically, the available research suggests that cute infants may be given more individual attention and receive more nurturant responses from adult caregivers. Familiarity, infant age, stability of cuteness with increasing age, and behavioral responses of infants all seem to mediate the link between cuteness and quality or quantity of caregiving. Nonetheless, facial cuteness seems to be one trait that can help ensure attention and care for infants.

CLOSING REMARKS

We conclude our look at facial aesthetics with a few summarizing statements, followed by a more extended look at why facial attractiveness has such pervasive and consistent social effects. Most people probably would think it unfair that those with more attractive faces tend to be liked better, seen more favorably, and receive better treatment than those with less attractive faces; after all, facial attractiveness is largely a function of genetic endowment and environmental events not related to competence, character, or achievement. Nonetheless, our social climate places considerable weight on facial aesthetics. The evidence clearly suggests that facial aesthetics has widespread effects on social development and interpersonal relations. The studies we have reviewed show that even sophisticated members of our society—including personnel counselors, teachers, and school psychologists—are notably influenced by facial attractiveness and the "beauty-is-good" stereotype.

Two qualifications should be kept in mind when contemplating this powerful stereotype. First, exceptions exist both in the form of negative effects of high facial attractiveness, and violations of the linear relationship often assumed to hold for attractiveness effects. Second, it is likely that facial attractiveness has the greatest social impact for those who are extremely high or low on this dimension; for those of moderate facial attractiveness, other aspects of physical appearance (e.g., attire, body language, and age) are more likely to match or exceed the impact of facial attractiveness on the impressions and behaviors of others. Those at the extremes of the facial attractiveness continuum are also more likely to evoke consistent evaluations of attractiveness and other traits.

Most people believe that personality traits come in clusters. This belief, part of implicit personality theory (see Wegner & Vallacher, 1977), can account in part for the common belief that facially attractive people have many other attractive qualities (i.e., the beauty-is-good stereotype) (cf. Adams, 1982). Nonetheless, important questions about the origin and maintenance of the psychosocial effects of facial attractiveness remain. As ecological psychologists we expect the impact of facial attractiveness on our perceptions and conceptions to be pragmatic. That is, the largely favorable psychosocial impact of facial attractiveness should reflect a useful, although undoubtedly fallible, use of physical appearance as a guide to adaptive behavior. Hence, the beauty-is-good stereotype, like other forms of implicit personality theory, should help more than hinder us in guiding our social interactions. We further explore this question in the following section.

The Sociobiology of Responses to Facial Beauty and Facial Defects

Why are we attracted by facial beauty and repulsed by facial defects and ugliness? Two conjectural reasons for our response to this dimension of facial appearance have already been mentioned. First, facial attractiveness may be an important determinant of heterosexual attraction due to the desirability of producing physically attractive offspring. Second, avoidance of those with ugly or defective faces may lessen our chances of contracting certain diseases or of producing offspring with congenital defects. These two biologically based reasons suggest that the tendency to respond more favorably to facially attractive persons may, in part, reflect a hereditary reaction pattern. Moreover, there are other ways in which favorable reactions to facial attractiveness can be adaptive and, therefore, could promote evolutionary selection for this response pattern.

In addition to being associated with various biological handicaps, facial ugliness seems to be associated with character defects, mental illness and, perhaps, low intelligence. Thus, facial attractiveness may actually serve as a "symbol or harbinger of . . . less visible characteristics" like intelligence and genetic quality (Berscheid & Walster, 1974, p. 207). Although the direction of causation has not been established, the faces of both Black and White juvenile delinquents are rated as less attractive than corresponding high school students (Cavior & Howard, 1973). Recent evidence indicates that facial attractiveness is positively correlated with intelligence (Maruyama & Miller, 1981; Richardson, Koller, & Katz, 1985) and with both perceived and measured mental health.

Self, peer, and professional judgments of mental health covary with attractiveness, and this relationship apparently reflects some *actual* differences in mental health between persons varying in facial attractiveness (Cash, 1985). In one study (Farina et al., 1977), hospitalized mental patients were found to be less attractive than normal controls based on either face-to-face ratings of overall physical attractiveness or on facial attractiveness ratings of standardized colored photos. Furthermore, compared to more attractive patients, uglier patients were less socially responsive, had more severe diagnoses, were hospitalized longer, and received fewer visitors from outside. The amount of time discharged psychiatric patients stay out of the hospital is positively correlated with their attractiveness as seen in facial photographs (Farina, Burns, Austad, Bugglin, & Fischer, 1986; Farina, personal communication, 1987). It is important to note that mental or emotional disturbance often makes it difficult to look one's best, and this in turn is likely to help perpetuate the disorder (Pertschuk, 1985). Nonetheless, the pre-hospitalization, high school yearbook photos of mental patients are rated as less attractive than adjacent same-sex photos in these yearbooks (Napoleon, Chassin, & Young, 1980), strongly suggesting that being facially unattractive may predispose an individual to mental illness.

There may also be a biological (genetic) component through which we are predisposed to see certain facial types or characteristics as aesthetically pleasing. If there is a genetic component to facial aesthetics, we would expect children to make judgments of facial attractiveness which are similar to those of adults, as they do (see preceding discussion). Even 3-month-old infants show selective preference for attractive over unattractive (as rated by adults) adult faces (Langlois et al., 1986; Samuels & Ewy, 1985; Shapiro, Eppler, Haith, & Reis, 1987), making it hard to argue that facial attractiveness standards are acquired through exposure to cultural standards. Such studies and this perspective suggest that differential responses to attractive and unattractive faces may emerge early in life.

Although some people reject the notion that biological factors play a significant role in facial aesthetics simply because cross-cultural variation in facial appearance exists, there are at least two major objections to this line of argument. First, much of the remarkable cross-cultural variation in facial appearance reflects facial elaborations that are often primarily intended to denote an individual's social or marital status, accomplishments, group membership, gender, personal characteristics such as bravery, or to serve various psychological (e.g., security) or functional (e.g., camouflage) purposes (Liggett, 1974; Rubenstein, 1985). Hence, such variations should not simply be assumed to be motivated by aesthetic concerns. Besides, many treatments of facial appearance intended to increase attractiveness create the illusion of greater natural fitness (e.g., youthfulness). It remains to be seen to what degree universal standards for facial attractiveness exist. If any facial characteristics are universally indicative of health or reproductive fitness, then evolution is likely to have produced universal standards of facial attractiveness in the form of innate preferences (or predispositions for the development of such preferences) for favorable variants of these characteristics (cf. Symons, 1979). A number of facial characteristics that could serve as indicators of fitness come to mind including sound teeth, good complexion, cleanliness, and normally formed facial features and head shape. Likewise, age-related facial characteristics provide a biological basis for judging reproductive fitness and, therefore, seem likely to influence judgments of heterosexual attractiveness in a similar manner in all cultures (cf. Symons, 1979).

Second, even if little or no cross-cultural uniformity in standards of facial aesthetics could be found, biological factors may still be involved. Consider imprinting as an analogy. Imprinting is clearly controlled to a large degree by biological factors, as the characteristic "critical" or sensitive periods (among other things) show. Nonetheless, the affective responses altered by imprinting crucially depend on the perceptual experiences of the animal during early development (cf. Brown, 1975). Biological factors could conceivably play a similar role in determination of human standards of facial aesthetics and the concomitant affective responses. That is, human biology may limit the range of facial appearance that we can see as attractive, or predispose us to see certain facial characteristics as most appealing while leaving some specific aspects of our aesthetic responses to faces to be determined by experiential factors. Similarly, Symons (1979) suggested that we may have "'innate' rules" by which preferences are learned, such as a rule to prefer physical characteristics reliably associated with upper class people.

Symons' (1979) sociobiological perspective on physical attractiveness also leads him to speculate that the population means of various physical characteristics should be expected to be perceived as most attractive. There is no convincing evidence for this claim, however, beyond the good evidence that variations in physical appearance obviously beyond the normal range of variation within a population are seen as unattractive.

Other Influences on Responses to Facial Aesthetics

There are certainly other reasons why facial beauty influences our reactions to others. Focusing on heterosexual attraction, Berscheid and Walster (1974) offered four conjectures on the basis of the positive effects of physical attractiveness. First, our society, and most notably the mass media, provide norms that dictate that the physically attractive are the best targets for sexual, romantic, and marital involvement (cf. Adams & Crossman, 1978; Hatfield & Sprecher, 1986). Second, one may gain prestige and make other favorable impressions merely by associating with a physically attractive person of the opposite sex (e.g., Strane & Watts, 1977). Likewise, being seen with an ugly person may prove discrediting (Goffman, 1963). Third, due to the physical attractiveness stereotype individuals tend to assume that physically attractive people have better qualities and more promise than the unattractive. The responses of college students when asked why physical attractiveness is such a strong determinant of attraction support all three conjectures (see Adams & Crossman, 1978). Fourth, and more speculative than the first three, people may assume that those they find physically attractive will like them more and be more similar to themselves than those seen as unattractive.

Part of the explanation for the strength and pervasiveness of facial attractiveness effects may lie in the automaticity of facial attractiveness judgments. Because automatic processes are thought to be difficult to suppress and can be triggered without the necessity of conscious control or intention (see Bargh, 1984), and because people have a limited capacity to deal consciously with social information, any automatic social judgment will tend to have pervasive effects. Although the existing evidence is insufficient, it now seems plausible that facial attractiveness may be automatically, quickly, and effortlessly assessed under many circumstances. For instance, as discussed previously judgments of facial attractiveness begin to be made very early in life and can be made reliably after seeing a face for only a fraction of a second (Goldstein

& Papageorge, 1980). Furthermore, many (perhaps most) studies of facial attractiveness effects have been able to demonstrate these effects without making their subjects explicitly aware of this independent variable. Consequently, it seems likely that in some cases subjects were not consciously aware of the variation in facial attractiveness. Future research should examine whether any stimulus configuration seen as a face can automatically trigger a judgment of facial attractiveness and under what circumstances this occurs.

Facial attractiveness effects probably depend on other processes as well, such as a disproportionate amount of time spent thinking about attractive others (see Shea & Adams, 1984) or their greater ability to attract and hold our attention. We believe that there are many reasons why we tend to be attracted to people with beautiful faces and repulsed by those with ugly faces. All of the aforementioned reasons (and others) may contribute to our interpersonal attractions and produce the effects associated with the "beauty-is-good" stereotype.

Despite the quantity of existing research on attractiveness effects, further research is needed to establish the actual determinants and consequences of perceived attractiveness in real, live (and thus three-dimensional and dynamic) faces, and in settings outside the laboratory. At the moment, nonetheless, there is no doubt that facial attractiveness has important and pervasive effects on social interactions and individuals' development.

ACKNOWLEDGMENT

The authors are grateful to Gerald Adams for his comments on an earlier version of this chapter.

7 The Perception of Facial Expression: Individual Regulation and Social Coordination

Ross Buck
University of Connecticut

I. Evolution and the Perception of Bodily and Social Information
   A. The Evolution of Communication
   B. Neurological Mechanisms of Face Perception
      1. Prosopagnosia
      2. Models of facial processing
   C. Spontaneous Communication
      1. Definition
      2. Measuring spontaneous communication in humans
   D. Perception and "Subjective Experience"
II. Communication and Bioregulation
   A. Social Relationships as Biological Regulators
   B. Face Perception in Infancy
      1. The socialization of facial expression
      2. Social referencing
   C. Interpersonal Facial Feedback
      1. The other as a biofeedback device
      2. Emotional education
III. Face Perception and the Appraisal Process
   A. The "Primacy" of Affect Versus Cognition
   B. The Education of Attention
   C. Neurological Mechanisms of Perception and Attention
      1. A model of appraisal
      2. Evaluation, appraisal, and filtering
IV. Empathy: A New Perspective
   A. The Measurement of Face Perception "Accuracy"
      1. Implications
   B. A New Perspective
      1. The segmentation technique
      2. Facial expressiveness and face perception
V. Summary

Ecological psychology recognizes that organisms have evolved to be responsive to very specific aspects of the total information available in the environment: They can perceive primarily those aspects of the environment that carry biologically useful information. Perceptual mechanisms "pick up" such information directly, without the need for mediation via higher-order cognitive processes. In the words of E.J. Gibson, the perceptual process "is not one of *construction* but of *extraction* of structured information that is present in the light, in the air, on the skin, in short, in the world" (quoted in Gibbs, 1985, p. 114). The organism and its ecological niche are in effect mutually tuned to one another, and in this sense cannot be considered to be independent entities (Alley, 1985). Part of this mutual attunement is produced when organisms learn to attend to some aspects of the total information that is perceptually available, and to ignore other aspects. This "education of attention" is the basis on which skilled and unskilled perceivers differ (J.J. Gibson & E.J. Gibson, 1955).

This chapter considers the perception of facial expression from this point of view. It reviews three issues of contemporary interest: face perception and expression in infancy, the role of appraisal in face perception, and the nature of "empathy." First, however, it is necessary to deal with the more general issues of communication and "subjective experience," for it is within this context that the perception of facial expression becomes uniquely important.

EVOLUTION AND THE PERCEPTION OF BODILY AND SOCIAL INFORMATION

The perception of facial expression is different from the perception of physical objects in two critical respects. First, face perception inevitably involves communication with another, so that the perceiver comes to have knowledge of being perceived, with all that implies. Second, face perception is relevant not only to information present "in the light, in the air, on the skin . . ." but also to information present *within* the skin: to needs, to drives, to affects, in short, to motivation and emotion (Buck, 1976, 1984).

The Evolution of Communication

Communication is defined here in a very general way following Wilson (1975). A's behavior $X1$ is defined as communicative if "the conditional probability that act $X2$ will be performed by individual B given that A performed $X1$ is not equal to the probability that B will perform $X2$ in the absence of $X1$" (Wilson, 1975, p. 194). Thus, if one animal affects another animal's behavior in any way at all, communication has occurred (see Buck, 1984). This definition of communication can be applied to any species.

According to Darwin's analysis in *The Expression of the Emotions in Man and Animals* (1872), emotional expression evolved to foster social coordination necessary for survival (i.e., courting behaviors, warnings, threat and submission behaviors, etc.). There is plentiful evidence that expressive displays with important social functions are innately organized in many species (see Camras, 1982; Zivin, 1985). Andrew (1963, 1965) and Redican (1983) have discussed the evolution of facial expression in humans and other primates in this regard. However, communication demands a receiver as well as a sender: displays are useless unless receiving tendencies exist that are sensitive to those displays and that alter behavior tendencies accordingly. In the terms of Gibsonian theory, emotional displays are social affordances. They have evolved hand-in-hand with the behavior tendencies of the receiver so that the nature of the display specifies the receiver's reaction in important ways (Buck, 1983b).

There is not as much direct evidence for the presence of innately organized receiving mechanisms as there is for sending mechanisms, but such evidence is beginning to accumulate. For instance, Sackett (1966) demonstrated that infant rhesus monkeys isolated from other monkeys since birth react with appropriate fear to a photograph of a large male monkey making a threat display. Several studies have demonstrated significant discrimination of affective facial expressions by human neonates (Field, 1982, Field & Walden, 1982; LaBarbara, Izard, Vietze, & Parisi, 1976; Nelson, Morse, & Leavitt, 1979). For example, Field, Woodson, Greenberg, and Cohen (1982) demonstrated that neonates at an average age of 36 hours can discriminate happy, sad, and surprised expressions posed by a model, as evidenced by their imitations of those expressions.

Ohman and Dimberg have demonstrated that human facial expressions of anger and fear are more readily associated with aversive events in classical conditioning studies than are happy or neutral expressions (Dimberg, 1983; Ohman & Dimberg, 1978; see also Lanzetta & Orr, 1980, 1981). They interpret these findings as supporting Seligman's (1970) notion that species are biologically prepared (predisposed) to associate some events with each other (see Ohman & Dimberg, 1984). It is noteworthy that this effect occurs only when the face is oriented toward the responder (Dimberg & Ohman, 1983). Dimberg suggested that the direction of the facial display is as critical as its emotional quality because "direction indicates whether the recipient is the target of attention" (Dimberg, 1983, p. 6).

Neurological Mechanisms of Face Perception

The burgeoning literature in neuropsychology will surely have an increasing impact upon the analysis of face perception. There are specific neural systems that are particularly responsive to the face. Perrett, Rolls, and Cann (1982) found cells in an area of the temporal lobe of monkeys that respond only to faces, and they found reductions in response as the facial stimulus is rotated away from a direct orientation.

There is also evidence that for most right-handed and many, if not most, left-handed individuals, the comprehension of facial information is typically faster and more accurate in the right-hemisphere than in the left-hemisphere (see Borod & Koff, 1984; Borod, Koff, & Buck, 1986; Bryden & Ley, 1983; R. Campbell, 1978, 1982; Tucker, 1981, 1986). Studies employing normal subjects have shown that there is a left-visual-field (i.e., right hemisphere) superiority for the recognition and processing of faces, and right-hemisphere damaged patients often have difficulty with the recognition and discrimination of faces. The latter condition is known as prosopagnosia.

Prosopagnosia

Agnosias in general are modality-specific disorders of recognition that are not due to sensory dysfunction or unfamiliarity with the stimulus: The normal perceptual process is somehow "stripped of meaning" (Bauer, 1984, p. 457). In prosopagnosia the patient is often unable to recognize the faces even of familiar family members. In one recent study, Etcoff (1984) asked brain-damaged patients to discriminate photographs of faces according to the identity of the individual depicted and the nature of the emotion displayed on the face. Patients with right hemisphere damage showed impairments in discriminating both identity and expression relative to left-hemisphere-damaged and control groups. These patients however did not show comparable impairments in discriminating the color and shape of geometric figures: The deficit was specific to faces.

There is suggested evidence that the prosopagnosic patient may discriminate faces on an "unconscious" level. Bauer (1984) showed a male prosopagnosia patient pictures of family members and famous personalities and gave him five names, one of which was correct. The patient was unable to recognize any of the pictures, and performed at a chance level when given multiple choices. However, the patient did show electrodermal responses to the correct names, suggesting that the facial identity was "recognized" at some level.

Bauer's result was replicated on two female patients by Tranel and Damasio (1985), who related such "covert" recognition to a model of face recognition and learning (Damasio, Damasio, & Van Hoesen, 1982). This model suggests that conscious face recognition involves four steps: (a) perception; (b) the arousal by the perceptual event of a "template" based on the elaboration of past visual perceptions of that face; (c) the activation of multimodal memories associated with the face; and (d) a conscious "readout" including feelings of familiarity and an ability to give pertinent verbal accounts or to perform relevant nonverbal matching tasks. Tranel and Damasio (1985) suggested that prosopagnosia is associated with a defect in the template system: The template may be (a) intact but inaccessible to ongoing percepts; (b) destroyed; or (c) intact but prevented from activating multimodal memory stores. They argued that their findings suggest the latter alternative—that prosopagnosia involves "a complete or partial blocking of the activation that normally would be triggered by template matching" (p. 1454). They suggested further that the blocking is probably not caused by damage to visual or association cortices *per se*, but rather to connecting white matter. Finally, they noted that the blocking of the associated memories does not block the autonomic response, and suggested that the anatomic substrate of the latter phenomenon remains to be elucidated. We consider other examples of "unconscious perception" in the following discussion, when analysing the appraisal process.

Modes of Facial Processing

The Damasio et al. (1982) model implies that the association between face perception and right-hemisphere processing is not a simple one. There is evidence in fact that instructions and expectations can alter the pattern of hemispheric asymmetry in some subjects, perhaps by a process of "metacontrol" involving neural mechanisms that control the direction of cognitive operations *prior* to actual information processing (Levy & Trevarthen, 1976; Safer, 1984).

Ross-Kossak and Turkewitz (1984) presented data suggesting that, at least in female subjects, face recognition involves three levels of processing that come into play successively as the face becomes more familiar. The first level is a relatively "primitive" undifferentiated holistic processing, which is associated with the right-hemisphere. As the face becomes more familiar, a more analytic left-hemisphere processing occurs, which involves the recognition of distinctive features of the face. Finally there is a more advanced integrated type of right-hemisphere processing that involves the incorporation of distinctive features into an integrated whole. Ross-Kossak and Turkewitz noted differences in processing between better- and poorer-performing subjects, and they caution that the results may not apply to males, as there is evidence of both sex and age differences in the face-recognition process (Turkewitz & Ross-Kossak, 1984).[1]

---

[1] It is conceivable that the shifts in processing at the different steps of the Damasio et al. (1982) model and the different levels of the Ross-Kossak and Turkewitz (1984) model represent a basic change in the way that the facial stimulus is "known." Specifically, they may represent a shift from knowledge-by-acquaintance to knowledge-by-description (see Buck, 1984, pp. 11–15; 1985). See footnote 2.

Spontaneous Communication

Definition

The nature of the communication process involved in innately organized sending and receiving mechanisms is distinct from symbolic and linguistic communication, and it has been termed *spontaneous communication* (Buck, 1982, 1984). It is distinguished from symbolic communication by several criteria. First, the elements of symbolic communication are symbols, which have arbitrary relationships with their referents; the elements of spontaneous communication are signs, which are externally accessible aspects of the referent. An example of a sign can be seen in the statement "dark clouds are a sign of rain": The darkness of the clouds is an externally accessible aspect of the moisture within the clouds blocking the sunlight. Second, symbolic communication is learned (one must learn the meaning of the symbols), whereas spontaneous communication is biologically built-in to the organism. Humans have evolved so that certain patterns of facial movements are expressive of motivational-emotional states—they are externally accessible signs of those states. In addition, because there is no communication without a receiver, it is logically necessary to assume that humans have also evolved to be perceptually attuned to those patterns of facial movements. Third, although symbolic communication is intentional at some level, spontaneous communication is entirely automatic and spontaneous, with no intentional aspect except in interaction with symbolic communications systems. Fourth, the content of symbolic communication involves propositions—statements that are capable of logical analysis. The simplest form of logical analysis is the test for truth or falsity, so that propositions can, in principle, be false. Spontaneous communication, in contrast, cannot be false, because if the sign is an externally accessible aspect of the referent, the referent is there by definition if the sign is present. Thus, the content of spontaneous communication is nonpropositional, consisting of signs of desires and feelings (i.e., motives and emotions).

It has been suggested that the distinction between spontaneous and symbolic communication implies a simple dichotomy or continuum between the two (Zivin, 1985). That is not the case. The relationship between spontaneous and symbolic communication is biological rather than logical (Buck, 1982, 1984) in that spontaneous communication must be present in any situation in which organisms influence one another in any way, while symbolic communication is present only to the extent that there is intention and a use of learned symbols.

Measuring Spontaneous Communication in Humans

Spontaneous communication is most clearly apparent in lower animals, as in insect communication systems. The complex social structure of ants demonstrates how successfully the behavior of individuals can be coordinated by way of entirely innate and wholly nonintentional communication systems (see E.O. Wilson, 1975). In "higher" animals symbolic communication systems become progressively more important, and in humans it often seems that communication is dominated by language. However, recent evidence indicates that spontaneous nonverbal communication is extremely important and powerful, and that it may actually carry the burden of meaning transferred between individuals in many normal interpersonal communication situations (Buck, 1984). Of the channels of nonverbal behavior, the face is particularly important in primates.

Many studies of spontaneous communication via facial expression in humans have used a slide-viewing technique derived from R.E. Miller's cooperative conditioning studies in rhesus monkeys (e.g., Miller, Caul, & Mirsky, 1967). In the slide-viewing technique, a "sender" views a series of emotionally-provocative slides, and reports on the emotional experience that they evoke while being filmed by a hidden camera. The slides may include sexual scenes showing nudes, pleasant scenes showing landscapes, scenes showing persons familiar to the sender, unpleasant scenes of burns and serious injuries, and unusual scenes showing strange camera effects. "Receivers" view the filmed expressions and try to guess the nature of the slide shown on each trial and the emotional experience reported by the sender.

These studies have demonstrated a number of relevant findings, including the following: (a) females are more expressive (i.e., are better "senders") than males; (b) there is no significant gender difference in receiving ability in this task; (c) facially expressive persons are also more expressive in their verbal descriptions of their feelings; (d) facially expressive persons often have *smaller* skin conductance and heart rate responses to the slides than do nonexpressive persons; (e) the gender difference in facial expressiveness in preschool children is smaller than that in adults; (f) as boys get older (between 3.5 to 6 years) they become *less* facially expressive; (g) left hemisphere brain damage results in symbolic communication deficits, whereas right-hemisphere brain damage appears to cause deficits in spontaneous facial expressiveness (see Buck, 1979, 1982, 1983a, 1984).

These studies demonstrated strong and consistent individual differences in facial expressiveness that were related to other measures in meaningful ways. In contrast, measures of facial receiving ability have shown little consistent variation from person to person. This may well be due to the nature of face perception, as we see in the following discussion.

Perception and "Subjective Experience"

The ecological theory of direct perception provides a framework for understanding the nature of knowledge of the environment, both the environment external to the body *and that inside the body*. Thus Goldfield (1983) argued that information for perception must be defined relative to the situation and the physical dimensions, capabilities, and needs of the perceiver. The needs of the perceiver actually involve information "within the skin" that can in many ways be thought of as analogous to external information, except that the information in question is internal rather than external to the body. I have argued that relevant information about the state of bodily needs, drives, and affects is directly available to the perceiver, just as is relevant information in the external environment (Buck, 1984, 1985).[2] This is a process of subjective experience (Emotion III) which evolved in a manner analogous to the process of spontaneous communication (Emotion II). Subjective experience may be defined as the extraction of structured information present within the body. Such information includes, but is not limited to, sensations of pain and temperature (as in bodily symptoms and fever), drives of hunger, thirst, and sexual arousal, and most relevant to face perception, primary affects such as happiness, sadness, fear, anger, surprise, and disgust (Ekman & Friesen, 1975; Tomkins, 1962, 1963).

From the ecological point of view, perceiving is the act of noticing the potential uses of objects (the activities they afford) relative to the perceiver's capabilities and *needs* (Neisser, 1976; J.J. Gibson, 1966a, 1979). These *affordances* constitute situation- and perceiver-specific meanings of objects according to their value to the perceiver. This implies that organisms simultaneously and interactively gather information *external and internal to the body*. During development, the infant becomes increasingly efficient at noticing potentially available affordances (Goldfield, 1983). This is the education of attention, and as we shall see there is increasing evidence that much of this early development involves face perception and the relationship of the facial expressions of others to those of the infant. It is important to recognize that with face perception the infant is learning not only about faces as objects, or even as objects that change as a function of the infant's behavior. The infant is also learning about the relationship between these objects and the whole world of information internal to the body. This implies that face perception is intimately involved both in the coordination of social behavior—via spontaneous communication—and in the regulation of the physiology of the individual—via the connection between facial expression and information present within the body.

Next, we consider recent findings from several quite different fields of inquiry that shed light on the role that the perception of facial expression and

---

[2] I have argued elsewhere that the disagreement between Gibsonians and those (e.g., Piagetians) who argue that knowing involves the use of representations to give meaning to acts or percepts may be resolvable if it is recognized that there are two sorts of knowledge: knowledge by acquaintance and knowledge by description (see Buck, 1984, pp. 40–46; 1985). These may respectively be associated in most persons with the right and left cerebral hemispheres (see Tucker, 1981). Gibsonian theory is most applicable to knowledge by acquaintance, whereas more traditional information-processing views are more applicable to knowledge by description.

other spontaneous nonverbal displays has in the maintenance of individual physiology and of social structure. These include studies of the role of facial communication in the bioregulatory functions of social relationships in infancy, the influence of appraisal in face perception, and the fate of attempts to measure face perception "accuracy."

COMMUNICATION AND BIOREGULATION

Social Relationships as Biological Regulators

There is evidence from a wide variety of sources that the individual organism is open to social influences that are qualitatively different from those commonly recognized. Specifically, it appears that social stimuli participate directly in the physiological regulation of the individual. This fact has important implications for the understanding of both individual and social regulation. In many species, including humans, face perception is a major channel by which these influences are manifest, although it is by no means the only channel. This section briefly discusses the evidence for this emerging point of view.

Love as an Addiction. There is evidence from a variety of species that social attachment is based in part upon endorphinergic neural systems at the level of the hypothalamus (Panksepp, 1981, 1982). A number of social behaviors have been linked to opiate activity, including separation-induced crying in infant mice (Panksepp, 1981) and the schooling behavior of fish (Karaliers, 1981). If this is the case, social attachment must involve a motivational phenomenon as basic as the needs for food and water, mediated by naturally occurring morphinelike substances. This would explain the solitary nature of the opiate addict, whose needs for other persons are satisfied by the drug. This theory also suggests that in normal persons the existence of close relationships with others may be associated with increased levels of endogenous morphines so that we are, in a sense, addicted to close personal attachments with others. Love may well be, in a sense, an addiction.

Social Deprivation in Development. There is plentiful evidence that the deprivation of normal social experience in infancy has widespread negative consequences in both animals and humans. In the early 1960s, a number of investigators showed that maternal separation in infant mice led to a "maternal deprivation syndrome," which included slowed growth, impaired immune system responding, and a lack of resistance to stress (Denenberg, 1981; Levine, 1969). Subsequent studies showed that this pattern of response is similar across different species, and Harlow and his colleagues documented the disastrous effects of early social isolation in rhesus monkeys (Harlow & Mears, 1983). More recently, Hofer (1984) demonstrated that the syndrome of maternal separation is not caused by the generalized stress associated with separation, as had often been supposed; rather it is caused by the elimination of a variety of *specific* regulatory social stimuli. By systematically providing some stimuli associated with the mother's presence but withholding others, Hofer was able to demonstrate the specific function of each. For example, the lack of growth hormone and subsequent slowed growth is associated with a lack of activity normally provided by the mother, and the lack of the warmth of the mother's body appears to interfere with the normal levels of norepinephrine and dopamine in the infant's nervous system. Thus, deprivation of *specific aspects* of the mother–infant interaction appear to cause *specific biological deficits* in the infant. This suggests in turn that the infant's homeostatic system does not function independently, but rather is open to social influence. In Hofer's terms, "biologic regulation is delegated in part to the mother" (1984, p. 186).

Hofer noted that there is evidence for the social regulation of biological functions in humans as well as animals. For example, a group of people isolated together will develop its own circadian rhythm (Vernikos-Danellis & Wingert, 1979), and young women living together develop synchrony in their menstrual cycles (McClintock, 1971). He also discussed the phenomenon of separation and bereavement from this point of view, noting that supportive social relationships are a powerful buffer against stress in both humans and animals (Bovard, 1959; Cobb, 1976). Separation from those supports has widespread negative impact upon the body, leading to muscular, cardiovascular, endocrine, and immune system changes and increased susceptibility to stress and disease (Hofer, 1984). Hofer concluded that bereavement involves the withdrawal of "multiple regulators woven into the fabric of the relationship" and that "independent self-regulation may not exist, even in adulthood. Social interactions continue to play an important role in the everyday regulation of internal biologic systems throughout life" (p. 194). He also suggested that these bioregulating functions of social relationships are mediated by nonverbal signals that are outside the awareness of the participants—facial expressions, gestures, touches, smells—in short, by spontaneous communication.

Face Perception in Infancy

The Socialization of Facial Expression

The face plays a central role in this regulatory process in humans, and in addition may well be involved in the earliest symbolic communication that eventually emerges as language. There has been much interest in recent years in the process by which spontaneous expressions become socialized and used in instrumental social communication. There is considerable evidence that emotional expressions in infants are responsive to rewarding and punishing contingencies (Campos et al., 1983) and that infants' capabilities for imitating facial expressions benefit from practice (Malatesta & Izard, 1984). Also, many studies have documented the attempts by mothers to alter the emotional expessions of infants during face-to-face play (Brazelton, Koslowski, & Main, 1974; Malatesta & Haviland, 1982; Tronick, Als, & Adamson, 1979). Malatesta and Haviland, for example, found a preponderance of positive expression modeling by mothers, with less frequent responses to negative expressions. Panksepp and Hofer's analyses allow us to regard these data as demonstrating not only socialization of emotional expression, but more generally a socialization of bioregulation unique to the particular mother–infant relationship.

This process varies markedly as a function of the particular qualities of the infant and mother involved. For example, preterm infants are often fussy, easily overstimulated, and possibly less able to tolerate playful face-to-face interaction. Malatesta and Haviland (1982) noted that mothers of normal infants encourage eye contact and show expressive behavior when the infant is looking. However, Field (1982) found that preterm infants are more irritable during such play and engage in more gaze averting. Consequently, she suggested that they may be at risk for developmental deficits in the socialization of expressive behavior. This in turn may contribute to problems in attachment: Parents of preterm infants tend to engage in less face-to-face play, smile at them less, touch them less, make fewer bodily contacts, and show evidence of emotional withdrawal (Crnic, Ragozin, Greenberg, Robinson, & Basham, 1983; Field, 1982; Ungerer & Sigman 1983). Papousek and Papousek (1983) discussed how such initially minor deviances can come to have major consequences in that they may start a chain of reciprocal consequences—a vicious circle—leading to deprivation, rejection, and even abuse of the child (see Thoman, 1975, 1981).

Malatesta and her colleagues examined the facial expressions of infants and their mothers during face-to-face interaction, coding the expressions on a second-by-second basis using Izard's (1979) discrete emotion coding system (Malatesta, Grigoryev, Lamb, Albin, & Culver, 1986). The study included preterm infants and was longitudinal, with testing at the ages of 2.5, 5, and 7.5 months. Results included a linear increase with age in positive affect (i.e., interest and joy) and a decrease in negative affect (pain and knit brow). The mother's modeling of joy and interest predicted increases in infant joy and interest expressions from 5 to 7.5 months, whereas in the case of anger, the infant's expressions appeared to influence those of the mother. Persistently irritable and angry babies may produce angry mothers. In addition, the mothers showed increases in contingent responding to interest expressions and decreases in contingent responding to pain expressions over time. A cross-lagged panel analysis suggested that the rate of maternal-contingent responding to the infant's expressions was associated with age increases in positivity of infant expression (rates of joy, interest, and surprise expressions) and overall infant expressivity (rate of facial change).

Malatesta and her colleagues noted that the mothers responded to infant expressions with expressions of their own within 0.5 seconds; a lag that is known to be optimal for instrumental learning.[3] Malatesta concluded that mothers behave in ways that "could easily affect the course of infant emotional expression" (1985, p. 19), and that there is evidence of "mutual emotional influence" in the mother–infant interaction (1985, p. 20. See Fig. 7.1).

A recent analysis of data from the Malatesta et al. (1986) study investigated the relationships between maternal facial contingency and attachment (Malatesta, 1985). Twelve months after the third testing period (at 18–20 months) the security of the infant's attachment to the mother was tested by the "strange situation" (Ainsworth, Blehar, Waters, & Wall, 1978). Results indicated a curvilinear relationship between facial contingency and attachment: Moderate contingency rates predicted insecure attachment. Malatesta argued that, taken together, her results suggest that the contingency of facial response on the part of the mother is part of a pattern of "emotional engrossment" whose presence or absence could have an enormous influence on the infant's social and emotional development (Malatesta, 1985). Security of attachment at 18–20 months was also related to the rate of smiling of the infant while interacting with the mother over the three earlier testing periods. Infants who increased their rates of smiling relative to other infants in the study were termed "increasers," whereas infants who decreased in relative smiling were labeled "decreasers". Most (86%) of the increasers showed secure patterns of attachment, whereas most (60%) decreasers manifested insecure attachment (Malatesta, 1985).

In another relevant study, Slee (1984) investigated mother–infant gaze patterns as a function of emotional expression, finding that both mothers and infants modified the timing of their gaze behavior as a function of the emotional expression of the other. Between the ages of 6 to 8 months, infants' time looking decreased for mothers' "neutral" expressions but not for "warm" expressions. On the other hand, over this age span mothers' time looking decreased as a function of infants' "warm" and "neutral" expressions, but not "cold" expressions.

---

[3] The infant's smile to the mother resulting from this process may be the earliest form of symbolic–intentional communication (Buck, 1984, pp. 4–11). Fox and Davidson (1985) reported that infant smiles in response to the mother, but not strangers, are associated with left-sided EEG activity. Whether this is due to an association with positive affect, as they suggest, or with an early form of symbolic communication, is open to question.

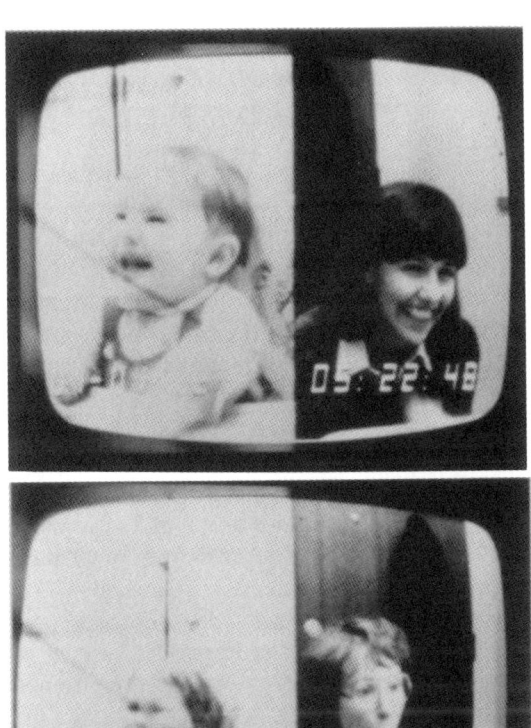

FIG. 7.1 Maternal facial and bodily responses to expressions of positive affect (upper) and negative affect (lower) on the part of their infants. Photographs courtesy Carol Malatesta.

Social Referencing

There is evidence that, as the infant grows, it begins to seek out emotional information from others in ambiguous situations. Several researchers have studied *social referencing*, in which the infant looks at the face of others, apparently to gain expressive information to aid in the appraisal of a situation (Campos, 1983; Campos & Stenberg, 1981; Camras, 1977; Klinnert, Campos, Sorce, Emde, & Svejda, 1983). A broader view of social referencing has been suggested by Feinman (1982, 1983, 1986; Feinman & Lewis, 1983). Whereas Campos and his colleagues restricted social referencing to situations where people use the affective responses of others, Feinman also included the actions and judgments of others that are employed in the construction of "social reality" (see Bandura, 1986; Bretherton, 1984). Both agree that by 10 months the infant shows behavior indicating that it is capable of using its mother's emotional expression to appraise an ambiguous event.

In one study of social referencing, Klinnert (1984) presented 12- and 18-month-old infants with an unusual toy designed to elicit uncertainty. When the infant looked at the mother she posed the discrete emotional expression of joy or fear, or held a neutral expression. At both ages the infant moved toward the mother when she posed fear but away from her when she posed joy. Another study found individual differences in the social referencing of 19.5-month-old infants that were related to the security of attachment to the mother (Dickstein, 1984).

Sorce, Emde, Campos, and Klinnert (1985) put 12-month-olds in a 4-foot visual-cliff situation in which the infant was placed on the shallow side of the cliff while the mother smiled at the infant from across the deep side. When the infant reached a point near the edge of the cliff, the mother changed her expression in a way consistent with one of the discrete emotions. When she increased her expression of joy or expressed interest, most of the infants crossed the deep side of the cliff to her side (74% and 73%, respectively). When she changed to an expression of sadness 33% crossed, with anger 11% crossed, and with fear none crossed. Significantly, data from a control condition in which no cliff existed could not be collected because the infants did no social referencing: They did not look at the mother's face unless the ambiguous situation of the cliff was present (Klinnert et al., 1983).

Campos (1985) suggested that social referencing increases as the infant achieves self-produced locomotion. The latter is an important event for a number of reasons. First, the achievement of self-produced locomotion produces a major increase in the infant's perceptual experience. Second, it is associated with a dramatic change in the mother's emotional communication with the infant, with more use of fear, particularly when the child is in danger of falling, and anger, particularly when the child "gets into things." Third, this event alters the social world of the infant, with adults now obliged to spend more time watching the infant, teaching it about the dangers of the environment, and less time holding the infant, for it is much less tolerant of restriction of activity. Thus, this may be the time when the infant begins to *use* its face-perception abilities as an aid to the exploration of the environment.

Interpersonal Facial Feedback

The Other as a Biofeedback Device

Panksepp's and Hofer's analyses suggest that social stimuli have previously unrecognized bioregulatory functions, and the studies of facial expression in mother–infant interaction suggest that facial interaction is crucial in the development of these functions. In effect, the presence of others may function in ways analogous to a biofeedback device. I have argued in other contexts that spontaneous nonverbal behavior, including facial expression, is generally more accessible to others than it is to the responder (Buck, 1984, pp. 140–146).[4] If this is the case, one of the major means by which an individual comes to know the nature of his or her own facial expressions and other displays is by interpersonal feedback: by the response to those displays on the part of others. Ekman and Friesen (1974) discussed the process by which the individual learns to control nonverbal displays, suggesting that channels that others respond to quickly and reliably (such as facial expressions) become controlled by "display rules," whereas nonverbal behaviors that are ignored by others (such as many body movements) are less controlled and may thus "leak" the individual's true feelings. This process is, in effect, an education of attention, where the individual's attention is drawn to those aspects of his or her own display that are responded to by others. A potentially less accessible response is rendered more accessible by feedback provided by others' behavior. This interpersonal feedback is directly analogous to the feedback provided by a biofeedback device, where a relatively inaccessible physiological response is rendered more accessible because of its association with the feedback signal and consequent education of attention (see Fig. 7.2).

If the face functions as an interpersonal feedback device, the expressiveness of the faces involved and the attention patterns of the persons involved must determine the efficiency of that device. As discussed previously, there is evidence that interpersonal facial feedback must often be deficient in the preterm infant, and this may have important lasting consequences. Specifically, in the case of a child (C) who has just been frustrated and feels annoyed and angry, the ability of an adult (A) to respond to those feelings appropriately is first determined by the clarity of C's spontaneous expressions and the degree of A's attention to those expressions. If C is facially expressive and A is attentive, A will come to know C's emotional state via the direct perception of facial expression. A may then express his or her reactions to C's display in a variety of ways. A may or may not spontaneously express feelings about C's display. If A is facially expressive and C is attentive, C can come to know A's affective response to C's display via direct face perception. It is clear from this that face perception is a necessary but by no means sufficient condition for feedback to occur.

---

[4] There is not universal agreement on this point. The facial feedback hypothesis, for example, emphasizes that the individual has direct access to his or her facial expression, and indeed, argues that this is the basis of emotional experience (see Buck, 1980). I feel this to be potentially misleading, for it takes facial expression out of the social context and views it as entirely within the individual. Although some feedback from facial expression may occur and have cuing effects for the responder, I believe that the "readout" function of facial expression is more important, and that the most important "facial feedback" is *interpersonal* feedback from others in reaction to the responder's expressions (see Buck, 1984, pp. 46–67).

BIOFEEDBACK:

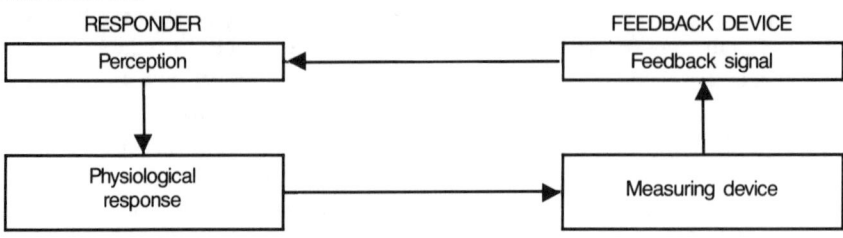

EMOTIONAL COMMUNICATION;

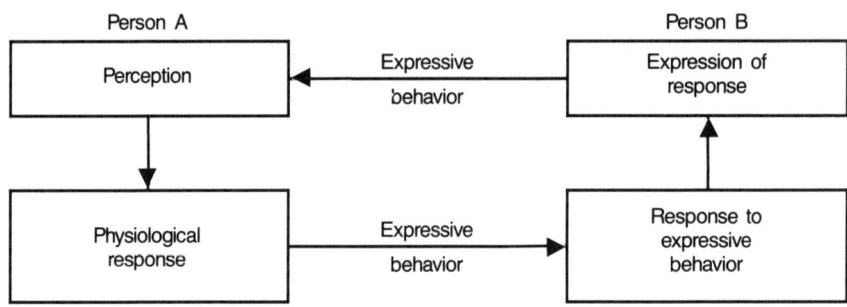

FIG. 7.2 The social biofeedback process. See text for description.

It is noteworthy in this regard that persons with expressive faces may be preferred over unexpressive persons in much the same way, and to perhaps the same degree, as physically attractive persons are preferred over less-attractive persons. There is much evidence for a generalized physical attractiveness stereotype, in which attractive persons are rated as more positive on a wide array of social characteristics (Adams, 1977; Alley & Hildebrandt, this volume). There is evidence that this may be true of expressiveness as well. For example, nonverbally expressive counselors are rated to be more interpersonally attractive, likable, warm, agreeable, genuine, and empathic (Bayes, 1972; LaCrosse, 1975; Strong, Taylor, Bratton, & Loper, 1971).

Sabatelli and Rubin (1985) studied this issue by assembling sequences of facial displays taken from a study by Sabatelli, Buck and Dreyer (1982) on which expressiveness data (i.e., sending accuracy data) were available. They then obtained ratings of physical attractiveness for 15 male and 15 female senders portrayed on the sequences by showing them to a group of raters. Other groups of raters then viewed the sequences and rated the senders in warmth and likeability: dimensions often found to distinguish attractive and less-attractive persons. They found, as usual, that attractive persons were judged higher on these dimensions, but they also found an effect for expressiveness that was as strong as the attractiveness effect. This effect remained significant after the effects of physical attractiveness were removed from the expressiveness scores by partial correlation and stepwise regression analyses (see Table 7.1). In other words, expressive persons are judged to be warm and likable, independent of their physical attractiveness. This may be associated with the ability of expressive persons to give clear and unambiguous interpersonal feedback. It should be noted that, although significant for the combined sample, the results in this study were stronger for females than males. Thus, as Table 7.1 indicates, the attractiveness–evaluation relationship and the expressiveness–evaluation relationships were stronger when the raters were judging females.

Emotional Education

The net result of experience in social relationships is that the individual comes to respond effectively in social contexts, being able to control his or her displays appropriately while the social relationships perform important bioregulatory functions in their own right. This occurs in animals as well as humans. In humans, an additional level of complexity is added by the capacity for language. Humans appear to be unique in their abilities to encode experiences into words, allowing the contemplation of experiences that one has not had and that may even be impossible. Humans use their verbal and logical abilities in their exploration of the external physical environment, a process that has been long acknowledged and is much studied. At the same time, humans must make connections between verbal labels and reasoning and the

TABLE 7.1
Partial correlations of interpersonal evaluation with nonverbal expressiveness controlling for physical attractiveness and physical attractiveness controlling for expressiveness. Pearson rs between evaluation and these variables are given in parentheses.

	Evaluation and Expressiveness		Evaluation and Attractiveness	
	Attractiveness Controlled	Pearson rs	Expressiveness Controlled	Pearson rs
Males	.21	(.33)	.37	(.45**)
Females	.51*	(.56**)	.50*	(.55**)
Total	.36*	(.44**)	.42**	(.49**)

*$p < .05$
**$p < .01$

Note: From *Nonverbal Expressiveness and Physical Attractiveness as Mediators of Interpersonal Perceptions* by R. Sabatelli and M. Rubin, 1986, *Journal of Nonverbal Behavior*, *10*(2), Summer 1986, 120–133.

internal environment of their own bodies—the information of feelings and desires. The resulting process of *emotional education* has received much less attention (Buck, 1983a), but it is clear that face perception must play a major role in this process.

In the example given previously, the adult *A* may respond to the child *C*'s annoyed expression linguistically as well as spontaneously. For example, *A* may say, "You seem to be angry." This would give *C* a lesson in accurate emotional labeling: *C* could connect the subjective experience of anger with its verbal label. Alternatively, *A* might say, "You should not feel like that. It's naughty," and *C* would receive another sort of lesson in emotional labeling. As in other kinds of education, emotional education may provide *C* with the wrong labels, or no labels at all, for certain experiences. That is not, however, incompatible with the notion that the perception of facial expression per se is always direct and vertical.

If the foregoing is correct, it would follow that persons and situations that enrich and clarify one's knowledge of internal reality would be as intrinsically interesting and rewarding as are persons and situations that enrich and clarify one's knowledge of external reality. The ability of a leader to elicit and label feelings may be the basis of charisma. The ability of a novel, play, film, or song to elicit and foster the understanding of strong emotions may determine its commercial success. This may be the case even for "negative" emotions like fear and sadness, as with horror shows and "tear-jerkers." Also, throughout the history of art, facial expressions and bodily displays have been used to evoke strong feelings. The artistic expression of a culture may uniquely reflect the emotional education experienced by its members.

FACE PERCEPTION AND THE APPRAISAL PROCESS

At some point, the perception of facial expression, and the affective responses thus engendered, may become transformed into cognitive judgments concerning those expressions. The distinctions between attention, perception, emotion, and cognition are fuzzy indeed, and important conceptual work remains to be done in this area.

The "Primacy" of Affect versus Cognition

The aforementioned evidence suggests that the capacity to receive information from the face is partially innate: It largely constitutes "knowledge by inheritance," rather than by experience (LeDoux, 1986). This makes face perception an interesting case for the analysis of the recent controversy regarding the appraisal process. There are individual differences in the perception of some stimuli, and these differences are determined by some process within the individual, but there is much disagreement concerning the nature of that process. Richard Lazarus and his colleagues have argued for the centrality of an "appraisal process" in coping with the environment, which involves the evaluation by the individual of the harmful or beneficial significance of events in the person–environment interaction (Folkman, 1984; Lazarus, 1984). Others have argued that affective processes precede appraisal: that the organism in effect responds affectively to stimuli before it can identify their nature (Zajonc, 1980, 1984). In the foregoing discussion, we saw that there is evidence of "unconscious recognition" or "unconscious perception," in that some prosopagnosic patients who cannot consciously recognize a familiar face may respond to it physiologically (Bauer, 1984; Tranel & Damasio, 1985). People also can respond physiologically to stimuli presented at exposure durations below absolute threshold (Lazarus & McCleary, 1951), show preferences for stimuli not consciously recognized (Kunst-Wilson & Zajonc, 1980), recognize unattended material that cannot be verbally identified (Allport, Antonis, & Reynolds, 1972), and become conditioned (i.e., conditioned taste aversion) while unconscious (Garcia & Rusiniak, 1980).

Lazarus' view implies that appraisal is an active process in which incoming stimuli are evaluated for their harmful or beneficial significance. However, if one assumes that the organism is in any way active in its initial processing of incoming stimuli, one quickly runs into the problem of explaining how the organism knows which incoming stimuli to process one way and which to process another. Gibsonian perceptual theorists have shown how an infinite regress of processing mechanisms is avoided only if one assumes direct registration of initial stimuli (see J.J. Gibson, 1966a, 1979; Neisser, 1976; Shaw & Bransford, 1977; Turvey, 1977).

The Education of Attention

The Gibsonian view of a direct perceptual process is able to accommodate individual differences in the information extracted from a given stimulus complex by suggesting that different persons attend to different aspects of the stimulus array. E.J. Gibson (1969) suggested that a skilled perceiver does not process information differently from an unskilled perceiver, but rather extracts more information from the stimulus complex. The skilled perceiver attends to the right things and ignores irrelevant information, and is thus able to detect features and higher order structures in the stimulus array that the naive perceiver cannot detect. For example, an older child may learn to note important information that a younger child ignores and to ignore confusing information (Neisser, 1976). J.J. Gibson (1966) referred to the perceptual selection of relevant information as the *education of attention.*

The education of attention assures that the organism will come to attend to stimuli that have in the past been associated with harm or benefit. When combined with the notion that some stimuli, including facial stimuli, intrinsically draw attention, the need for an *active* evaluation of environmental stimuli by the process of appraisal becomes unnecessary. This view avoids the logical problems noted previously.

Neurological Mechanisms of Perception and Attention

A Model of Appraisal

Recent work in the neurosciences suggests that increasing knowledge about the neural mechanisms of attention and emotion may reveal structures by which to anchor the concepts of perception, attention, and appraisal (McGuinness & Pribram, 1980; Pribram & McGuinness, 1975; Schneider & Shiffrin, 1977; Tucker & Williamson, 1984). For example, LeDoux's (1986) account of the role of the amygdala provides us with a neurological model of appraisal. LeDoux noted that bilateral amygdalectomy results in a dissociation between the sensory–perceptual and affective qualities of stimuli: "objects are still perceived and emotional reactions are still expressed, but these functions are no longer coupled in the brain" (LeDoux, 1986). An example is the Kluver–Bucy syndrome, where an amygdalectomized monkey might mouth a burning match or innately–feared snake.

LeDoux summarized a number of studies of the role of the amygdala in the evaluation of stimuli from a variety of sources: visual stimuli, auditory stimuli, visceral stimuli, and even stimuli from the neocortex. He suggested that the amygdala receives sensory input directly from the thalamus, and also from the neocortex, but that the thalamic pathway is several synapses shorter. The early input reaching the amygdala may "prime the area to receive the better analysed neocortical inputs, providing a crude picture of what is to come, narrowing the affective possibilities, and perhaps even organizing possible and actual responses" (LeDoux, 1986, pp. 345–346). If the system is disrupted, as in bilateral amygdalectomy, the sensory–perceptual qualities of stimuli are divorced from their emotional qualities. LeDoux also suggested that there are different levels of appraisal at the neurological level; that is, that the processing may take place at the amygdala without cortical involvement, or that the cortex may be involved in interaction with the amygdala mechanism. Perhaps the former is appraisal as a "primitive evaluative perception" in Lazarus' (1984, p. 124) terms, whereas the latter is appraisal as a conscious, rational, symbolic process.

Evaluation, Appraisal, and Filtering

As noted in the preceding discussion, everyone agrees that something happens early in the emotion process that determines the impact of a particular stimulus for a particular individual, but the terms used—stimulus evaluation, appraisal, filtering—have widely differing connotations. It could be argued that both "evaluation" and "appraisal" have cognitive connotations, suggesting a conscious process of deciding upon the personal relevance of an event. For this reason, the term *filter* may be more appropriate here.

In the Readout Model of emotion (Buck, 1984, 1985), the handling of initial stimuli is accomplished by the notion of a relatively passive stimulus filter. The notion of a filter might be clarified by an example. There is evidence that sensory information is processed at the cortex only if it is accompanied by nonspecific influences from subcortical systems (the reticular formation or amygdala). Thus, we are not aware of the feeling of comfortable shoes because even though the sensory information about the feeling of those shoes is available to the brain (you are probably feeling your shoes as you read this), it is usually ignored. Presumably, neither the reticular formation nor the amygdala *know* what the sensory stimuli are like, rather they use certain decision rules to pass the information on or not. Thus, if the stimulation is weak or repetitive, it is ignored; consequently, these subcortical systems are not evaluators or appraisers—they are filters. Basic decision rules are involved in attaching emotional relevance to incoming stimuli. A "hard stare" directed at the receiver will excite a very different subcortical response than if the stare is directed a few degrees away. "In this way, it can be seen that we feel *more* than we know, we feel *before* we know, and in an important sense, feeling *determines what we know*" (Buck, 1986, p. 541).

EMPATHY: A NEW PERSPECTIVE

The foregoing view of emotional perception and communication has implications for the analysis of empathy, which until recently has been conceptualized as an "ability" or "skill." In fact, most attempts to measure empathy have used techniques adapted from the measurement of cognitive abilities. Most recently, these have involved the study of what might be termed face perception *accuracy*. These attempts have not succeeded in providing a simple, widely accepted measure of empathy, and this section examines the reasons for this failure.

The Measurement of Face Perception "Accuracy"

In the aforementioned studies of spontaneous facial expression using the slide-viewing procedure, it was noted that stable and meaningful individual differences in facial expressiveness or "sending accuracy" have been found repeatedly, but that that has not been the case with receiving ability. In fact, a concerted attempt was made to develop a test of nonverbal receiving ability using the slide-viewing situation: The Communication of Affect Receiving Ability Test (CARAT) was constructed using traditional item-analytic techniques from a set of 600 videotape sequences showing a particular sender viewing a particular slide (Buck, 1976). This instrument was designed to assess a phenomenon that in the history of psychology has been intensively investigated but remains poorly understood: The phenomenon of skill in gaining information from others. It has gone under a variety of names—empathy, accuracy in person perception, social sensitivity—and has recently been reborn in a variety of measures of nonverbal skill (Buck, 1983b). Other measures of nonverbal receiving ability include the Profile of Nonverbal Sensitivity (PONS) developed by Robert Rosenthal and his colleagues, and the Brief Affect Recognition Test (BART) developed by Paul Ekman and his colleagues (Ekman & Friesen, 1974; Rosenthal, Hall, DiMatteo, Rogers, & Archer, 1979).

CARAT, PONS, and BART were created to measure the same conceptual variable: accuracy at decoding facial expression. One of the primary requirements for the validity and scientific utility of a concept is the demonstration that it can be operationally measured by a variety of methods that relate meaningful with one another. Thus, one would expect that these different instruments should correlate significantly. That is not the case. Buck and Carroll (1974) found an r of .04 between CARAT and the long form of PONS. One of the few encouraging results was reported by Klaiman (1979) who found a significant correlation between CARAT and the face score of the PONS short form for females ($r = .24, p < .01$). The results for males were not significant: $r = .09$. Fields and O'Sullivan (1976) reported a pattern of low and nonsignificant correlations between BART and PONS. Attempts to relate other measures of face perception accuracy with one another have found similar results (Buck, 1983b, 1984).

Implications

The fact that a variety of measures designed to assess the same conceptual variable do not significantly correlate with one another raises questions about the adequacy of that conceptual variable. All of these instruments conceptualized the perception of facial expression as a skill, and attempt to measure it by procedures derived from the measurement of cognitive abilities. Gibsonian perceptual theory suggests why this is unsatisfactory, by arguing that as soon as one's attention is drawn to the facial display, the "meaning" of the display is directly perceived. All of these instruments specifically direct the receiver to attend to the facial display, and in this way they may be missing the most important determinant of face perception accuracy—the education of attention. That is, it may be that in real life the most important determinant of face perception accuracy is whether or not the receiver has learned to attend to facial cues (Buck, 1983b, 1984). If this is the case, it may be argued that new approaches must be developed for the study of face perception accuracy.

A New Perspective

The Segmentation Technique

Reuben Baron and I have used Darren Newtson's (1976) segmentation procedure to assess the patterns of attention to facial displays (Buck, Baron, & Barrette, 1982; Buck, Baron, Goodman, & Shapiro, 1980). Briefly, receivers are instructed to make a response (press a button) when they see "something meaningful" as they view a film of spontaneous facial/gestural expression (CARAT). The definition of what is meaningful is left to the receiver, but it is important to note that there is a high degree of consensus among receivers when "something meaningful" occurs, despite the complexity of the facial/gestural display that they are watching. For example, the correlation of the number of segmentation points given to CARAT items in our 1980 and 1982 studies was .79, despite considerable differences in procedures between the studies.

The studies demonstrated meaningful relationships between segmentation measures and the gender of the sender and receiver, the senders' expressive behaviors, and the receivers' ability to guess the kind of slide being viewed. Also, a new kind of accuracy measure was developed, involving whether the receiver "hit" or "missed" events of the videotape that were judged by most receivers to be meaningful.

In another study employing the segmentation technique, Goodman (1980) employed a videotape of a person showing both emotional expressions (frowns, smiles, shrugging the shoulders) and instrumental behaviors (sitting down, lighting a cigarette, picking up a magazine). Subjects segmented the videotape in three conditions. In the Action Focus condition they were instructed to press a button when the person on the film made a meaningful action; in the Emotion Focus condition they were told to press when the person showed emotions; and in the No Focus condition they were simply told to press when "something meaningful" occurred. Results indicated that segmentation patterns in the Action and Emotion Focus conditions were quite different, with facial expressions occurring at all of the Emotion Focus segmentation points. Action Focus segmentation points involved more manipulation of objects and changes in bodily position in space, and fewer facial expressions, compared with Emotion Focus segmentation points. Interestingly and significantly, the pattern of segmentation points in the No Focus condition was quite similar to that of the Action Focus condition and dissimilar to the Emotion Focus condition, suggesting that in the circumstances of this study subjects mainly attended to instrumental actions and ignored the emotional expressions. I suggest that it is individual differences in this latter tendency—to spontaneously attend to instrumental actions versus emotional expressions *when given a choice*—that may be most similar to the conceptual variable of "empathy."

Facial Expressiveness and Face Perception

The discussion of expressiveness suggests another potential dimension of empathy: that a facially expressive person (P) may encourage expressiveness in those that P interacts with, thus providing P with cues about the other's feelings (Sabatelli, Dreyer, & Buck, 1979). Indeed, it may be that the most reliable way to increase one's ability at face perception is to become more facially expressive, thus encouraging increased expressiveness in others.

This suggests that the "empathic" person may be one who (a) is facially expressive, thus encouraging expression in others; and (b) is attentive to those expressions in others thus encouraged. This perspective suggests that empathy can be properly studied only in an interactive situation, in which the sender and receiver can influence each other's expressive behavior directly, and in which each is given a choice of focusing upon the expressive behavior of the other or upon other potentially relevant information in the situation. The studies of mother–infant interaction reviewed previously exemplify the kind of research design that is necessary (e.g., Malatesta, 1986). Only when this is done can we expect to have at hand empirical data truly relevant to empathy.

SUMMARY

This chapter reviews evidence from a variety of sources concerning the perception of facial expression, suggesting first that face perception inevitably involves communication—specifically spontaneous communication—and that it is intimately involved with the exploration of information present within the body—subjectively experienced motives and emotions. It argues that spontaneous facial communication is directly involved in bioregulatory processes, and that interpersonal facial feedback plays a more central regulatory role than does intrapersonal facial feedback. Recent studies of mother–infant facial communication and the phenomenon of social referencing are discussed from this point of view. The relationship of face perception and appraisal is discussed, suggesting that directly perceived information is "filtered" by neurochemical systems that use relatively specific decision rules to pass on information to higher centers. Attempts to measure empathy in terms of face perception "accuracy" are reviewed, with the suggestion that, taken together, they demonstrate that face perception is not an "ability" analogous to cognitive abilities. Instead, face perception is a direct pick-up of biologically relevant information. It is suggested that empathy instead involves whether one attends to facial cues and whether one is oneself facially expressive, thus encouraging expression in others.

ACKNOWLEDGMENTS

Portions of this chapter were presented in the paper "Nonverbal Expression and Communication: The Social Regulation of Emotion." T. Field (Chair), symposium on *Emotional Expression in Infants and Young Children*. Society for Research in Child Development convention, Toronto, Canada, April 27, 1985. Research reported in this chapter was supported by the University of Connecticut Research Foundation.

8 Physiognomy and Social Perception

Thomas R. Alley
Clemson University

I. Introduction
II. Theory and Metatheory
III. Facial Features as a Guide to Character:
   The Issue of Validity
IV. Reliability: Physiognomic Judgments
   as Facial Stereotypes
   A. Physiognomy and Facial Anomalies
   B. Stereotypes and Normal Variations in Facial Appearance
      1. Judgments based on overall facial appearance
      2. Stereotypes associated with specific facial features or regions
   C. Stereotypes Concerning Forms of Facial Elaboration
V. Concluding Remarks

INTRODUCTION

By the face one knows not only the beauty or ugliness of the entire body but also the customs and affections of the soul, good or bad, ugly or beautiful; in as much as, in the face, all the affections of the soul or of the spirit imprint some sign and significance of their issue
—Jean Liebault, 1582, quoted in Shalleck, 1973, p. 27

This chapter examines *physiognomy*: the practice of trying to judge character and other psychological qualities by observation of facial features.[1] Physiog-

---

[1] Judgments based on the physical appearance of other bodily regions or on a wholistic assessment of physique form an additional, but secondary aspect of physiognomy (see Allport, 1937) and are not discussed in this chapter. My use of the term *physiognomy* also differs from its occasional (mis)use (e.g., Cohen, 1973; Secord & Muthard, 1955) to refer to facial characteristics themselves.

nomy is an ancient and widespread practice, the history of which has been reviewed by Burr (1935), Evans (1969), Liggett (1974), and Brandt (1980). The earliest known systematic written treatment of physiognomy is a book entitled *Physiognomonica*, which is commonly attributed to Aristotle. Even earlier works may have existed, for it is likely that as soon as our ancestors had evolved far enough mentally to have human relations with each other, they began to try to read character in each others' faces (cf. Allport, 1937; Burr, 1935).

Most of the literature on physiognomy is not based on scientific study. As Gordon Allport noted 50 years ago, and is still true today, "the quantity of literature on the subject is far more striking than its quality, for the practical nature of its appeal brought it early under the patronage of quacks and charlatans, where unfortunately it has largely remained" (1937, p. 66). The existing research on physiognomy has addressed two separate issues: (a) the veridicality of physiognomic judgments and (b) the existence of consistent, stable or widespread impressions of psychological characteristics based on facial appearance (i.e., facial stereotypes).

In brief overview, the literature on physiognomy reveals that, with few exceptions, scientific research has failed to find relationships between (normal) variations in facial features and psychological characteristics. Nonetheless, there is good evidence that the general public continues to believe in and, at least in some circumstances, practice physiognomy (cf. Brandt, 1980; Mainwaring, 1980). Hence, the psychosocial effects of facial appearance (especially for those with abnormal facial characteristics) cannot be fully understood without consideration of physiognomy. Moreover, consideration of this practice can provide insight into the processes of face perception and stereotyping.

In this chapter, the theories and underlying assumptions of various perspectives on physiognomy are briefly discussed, with most approaches being dismissed as implausible. Following this discussion, a second section briefly examines the validity of physiognomy. In the third and most extensive section, the practice of physiognomy is viewed as a form of stereotyping that is surely a significant influence on social interactions.

THEORY AND METATHEORY

> Whatever amount of truth the so-called science of physiognomy may contain, appears to depend . . . on different persons bringing into frequent use different facial muscles, according to their dispositions; the development of these muscles being perhaps thus increased, and the lines or furrows on the face, due to their habitual contraction, being thus rendered deeper and more conspicuous.
>
> —Darwin, 1872, pp. 364–365

This view of Darwin is but one of several general perspectives on physiognomy. A variety of beliefs about the significance of resemblances of faces have been used as the basis for the practice of physiognomy. The common approaches to physiognomy are (a) seeking resemblances in appearance between humans and animals, assuming similarities in appearance indicate shared psychological qualities (e.g., a person whose face is reminiscent of a fox is believed to be sly and cunning); (b) an inductive process whereby others sharing distinctive facial characteristics with a known person (or group) are believed to share some of the familiar person's (group's) psychological characteristics; (c) an approach based on functional analogies whereby inferences are made according to the size, shape, or presence of facial features and their common function(s); and (d) an approach based on the facial expressions engendered by various emotional and cognitive states that looks for *traces* of these expressive facial postures as clues to the common emotional and cognitive states of an individual (e.g., Bellak & Baker, 1981).

This fourth approach differs from the first three in that it is based primarily on muscular patterns rather than bony or cartilaginous structures. Since these structures are largely determined by heredity (genotypic) whereas our facial expressions are chiefly evoked by our experiences, it is reasonable to suppose that they may support two distinct types of physiognomic diagnosis: the relatively fixed structural aspects correlated with native (innate) psychological factors (e.g., temperament and intelligence), whereas the aspects of facial appearance modified by expression may serve as an index of acquired aspects of personality (Allport, 1937). As Allport noted, in everyday physiognomic judgments we do not take note of the differing diagnostic significance of hard and soft tissue structures, and dividing facial characteristics along these lines has not proven useful in understanding their relevance to physiognomic judgments (Secord, Dukes, & Bevan, 1954). This distinction may nonetheless be useful in evaluating physiognomic theories, but a recent supplement to the standard facial expression account of physiognomy makes it a rather fuzzy distinction. This supplemental argument is that the mechanical pressures of facial muscles may alter the skeletal structure of the face in ways reflecting personality (Squier & Mew, 1981).

Physiognomy based on perceived traces of the cumulative effects of common facial expressions has the soundest theoretical and empirical basis of the four aforementioned approaches. The other three all assume that there are genetic relationships between facial characteristics and personality. Even if such relationships existed, training, self-discipline, or experience could modify or reverse these genetic tendencies. Moreover, it is dubious that genetic relationships between personality and facial characteristics exist except in some varieties of facial anomaly (e.g., Down's syndrome). Further, each of these approaches is plagued by additional theoretical difficulties.

There is simply no good reason to suppose that external resemblances between humans and animals reflect psychological similarities, especially since the comparisons are made between intraspecific variants of human faces and interspecific forms of animal faces. The second (inductive) method, besides being based on the dubious and implicit assumption that normal variation in human facial appearance has consistent personality or dispositional correlates, is subject to the weaknesses of hypotheses or beliefs based on inductive generalization (see Kahane, 1969). (Nonetheless, inductive generalization may provide a seemingly plausible ground to support facial stereotypes acquired and transmitted by power of "authority.") There is even less reason to believe that functional analogies have any validity. For example, contrary to a common attribution (see Secord & Muthard, 1955), lip thickness is highly unlikely to be a useful guide to persons' talkativeness.

Even though all three of these approaches stem from theoretically and empirically dubious premises, each may play a significant, even fairly consistent role in physiognomic judgments (cf. McArthur, 1982). The approaches taken to justify physiognomic theories and the origins of physiognomic judgments are two separate issues. Physiognomic judgments may be made frequently, and even reliably, without valid grounds. The origins of facial stereotypes are discussed elsewhere (see Berry & McArthur, this volume; McArthur, 1982; Secord, 1958), as well as in this chapter.

Returning to the physiognomic method based on facial musculature, note that its theoretical grounding is supported by two assumptions. The first is that universal patterns of facial expression exist; an assumption supported by cross-cultural studies showing significant invariance in the expression and perception of emotions in faces (e.g., Darwin, 1872; Ekman & Oster, 1979). The second assumption is that common facial expressions produce a cumulative record in the form of detectable patterns (traces) left in the soft tissues of the face. If this is true then, for example, people who are often worried should acquire, say, relatively wrinkled foreheads. Perception of such facial wrinkles (i.e., relatively permanent wrinkling of the forehead) could then rightfully indicate, at least some of the time, that the perceived face is that of an anxious person. Relationships between facial muscle activity and facial morphology have been reported (e.g., Moller, 1966), and the apparent bilateral asymmetry of perceived emotional content in "neutral" faces suggests that such asymmetry is a result of facial expression (McGee & Skinner, 1987). To date, however, facial expression has not been directly linked to permanent alterations of facial appearance. Furthermore, there are several factors that impair the theoretical underpinnings of this approach to physiognomy.

First, because of the natural constraints of various facial structures on the dynamics of facial expression, individual differences exist in the facial patterns produced by specific emotional and cognitive states. In addition, facial structure may also affect the cumulative impact of facial expression, further masking the accumulated effects of expression on facial appearance.[2] Addi-

---

[2] Of course, structural characteristics that distort or exaggerate one's emotional expression are likely to be highly significant influences on *perceived* character or emotional state; that is, they may be a major determinant of (largely invalid) physiognomic judgments.

tional masking could result from variation (regional or racial) in the conventional standards of expression which individuals adopt as a consequence of socialization. Affected (feigned) facial expression, such as the smile forcefully maintained by a morose receptionist, could conceivably leave traces that provide *misleading* indications about psychological characteristics. Finally, due to the time-dependent nature of the process presumed, from this perspective, to underlie physiognomy, physiognomic judgments about infants and children should be difficult or impossible to make. Perhaps this is part of the reason why advocates of physiognomy have focused on adults in their examples and clientele. On the other hand, if facial muscle activity is to influence hard tissue structures, then it should exert the greatest effect during infancy and childhood when these structures are relatively pliable and dynamic. This, in turn, enhances the possibility that any indications of personality created by facial muscle activity could reflect outdated traces from an earlier developmental stage.

Although all four of the aforementioned perspectives on physiognomy have serious flaws or weaknesses, there is a fifth perspective that is more reasonable and plausible. This perspective focuses on the variations in facial appearance commonly produced by biological anomalies (e.g., genetic defects), developmental processes, and environmental interactions (e.g., tanning). Stated simply, this perspective holds that physical traces of these events or states, or facial features that merely resemble such traces, will engender a reaction appropriate for typical individuals with the corresponding history or biology. Thus, the squinted eyes, sun-bleached (i.e., light) hair, and weathered skin typical of people who work outdoors may foster the impression of ruggedness and vitality that usually characterize outdoor workers; and these physical characteristics may foster the same impression even when they result from genetics rather than from exposure to the elements. Likewise, as argued several places in this book (e.g., Berry & McArthur, chap. 4; McCabe, chap. 5), the presence of immature facial features in a mature person, or vice versa, can alter our age-related responses.

This perspective integrates physiognomy with the more general process of "person perception" and is compatible with the "kernel of truth hypothesis" used to explain other stereotypes (see McArthur, 1982; Vinacke, 1956). Physiognomy is no longer based on special analogical, inferential, or perceptual processes. Instead, like other aspects of "person perception", physiognomic judgments are "simply" classifications based on perceptual or descriptive information of varying degrees of reliability. As seen in the next section, physiognomy usually seems to rely on quite unreliable information.

FACIAL FEATURES AS A GUIDE TO CHARACTER: THE ISSUE OF VALIDITY

Is facial structure related to personality? Folklore, literary characterizations, and requests for photographs from job applicants, not to mention the practice and promulgation of physiognomy for centuries, indicate that such relationships exist. Scientific research, however, has generally found little or no validity in physiognomy. For instance, in a relatively recent and thorough study, Cohen (1973) "found it impossible to discover any meaningful relations—even through use of multiple correlations—between physiognomic and psychological characteristics, which could maintain their statistical significance in cross-validation on other data" (p. 107).

Two related issues govern this question of validity: (a) Are there relationships between facial morphology and personality or dispositional traits? And assuming such relationships exist, (b) can people detect these facial characteristics and correctly interpret them? So, for example, although Squier and Mew (1981) found a few statistically significant relationships between lateral facial height and self-reported personality traits, whether such relationships influence physiognomic judgments has yet to be determined. On the other hand, physiognomic judgments may tend to become valid through a self-fulfilling prophecy effect, especially if there is consistency in these judgments. That is, people who are reliably stereotyped may tend to fulfill the expectations of others.

Most of the research on the validity of physiognomy was conducted before the second half of this century. The search for reliable relationships between specific facial characteristics and psychological characteristics proved to be so fruitless (see, e.g., Cleeton & Knight, 1924) that little research on this topic has been performed since the 1940s. Rather than simply review these studies, I take the most positive approach and discuss the few apparently credible studies that seem to show that somewhat valid physiognomic judgments can be made, albeit under restricted sets of circumstances.

Some of the most promising results have been obtained in studies on the facial appearance of abnormal (e.g., mentally deficient) individuals. A once popular question of this sort is whether criminals have a distinctive facial appearance. In what may be the only carefully controlled study of this issue, Thornton (1939) showed that most college students could judge the crimes committed by male criminals depicted in facial photographs with an accuracy exceeding statistical significance, but still so slight as to have negligible practical importance. A study done in Germany (Kozeny, 1962) used photographs of over 700 convicted criminals to produce composite portraits according to the type of crime committed. The facial characteristics of these composites were related to the crime category, thus showing some relationship between facial appearance and criminality. Exposure of individuals with certain facial appearance to a less-favorable social environment (e.g., via self-fulfilling prophecy) may account for the apparent link between the face and records of criminal activity (cf. Bull & Green, 1980), just as self-fulfilling prophecy probably contributes to the formation and retention of other facial stereotypes (cf. Snyder et al., 1977). That is, facial appearance and personal traits may be related because the traits are partly determined by social stereotyping which, in turn, is influenced by facial morphology. During the course of development, behavior is modified so as to conform to these stereotypes.

Several researchers have found that groups of adults can make gross judgments of intelligence based on facial appearance at statistically significant levels (see Anderson, 1921; Hull, 1928). The correlations between intelligence test scores and intelligence estimates of these persons' as seen in facial photographs are so low, however, that it is unlikely that intelligence can be usefully assessed by examination of facial appearance (cf. Hull, 1928). Nonetheless, Hull and others have found small, positive correlations between a variety of craniofacial measurements and academic success (see Hull, 1928). Such morphological characteristics may provide the informational support for the typically better than chance physiognomic estimates of intelligence.

Empirical results for other physiognomic judgments are generally worse than those for intelligence, although small positive correlations between impressions based on facial appearance and more objective measurements of those traits have frequently been found (see Cohen, 1973; Hull, 1928). Terry and Snider (1972) found that males were able to correctly identify female college students who were active in extracurricular activities, noted for their physical attractiveness, inactive in extracurricular activities, and honor students (listed in descending order) only using monochromatic yearbook photos; females in this study identified male athletes and males active in extracurricular activities, but were unable to identify inactive or honor student males at better than chance levels. This study was replicated and extended by Terry (1975), this time eliminating targets wearing eyeglasses and adding same-sex judgments. Both male and female viewers identified females noted for their physical attractiveness, male athletes, and female honor students, and both active and inactive males, but females were identified by extracurricular activity levels only by males, and then barely above chance. For the most part, these results are not surprising and do not suggest that most other physiognomic judgments would have validity, for much of the success of the viewers in these two studies probably stems from the fact that membership in the selected social categories (e.g., athlete) is largely a function of physical attributes. Of course it is interesting that we are able to consistently get the information needed to make these judgments from facial photographs.

RELIABILITY: PHYSIOGNOMIC JUDGMENTS AS FACIAL STEREOTYPES

Although scientific efforts to uncover relationships between specific categories of facial appearance and psychological characteristics have waned, researchers have continued to explore the relationship between *attributed* psychological characteristics and facial appearance. In fact there seems to be a current surge of interest in physiognomic judgments as perceptual stereotypes. Underlying these studies, and supported by them, is the view that people, even highly literate ones, adhere to various facial stereotypes (cf. Roll & Verinis, 1971). When you consider that many variations in, and modifications of, facial appearance produce resemblances to certain facial expressions, and that we instantly and automatically evaluate others' facial expressions, some facial stereotyping seems inevitable. In short, the use of facial characteristics for stereotyping and other inferential–judgmental processes is probably common and, therefore, may have a significant impact on social interactions.

Categorizing others on the basis of facial appearance can **potentially** help us predict social interactions. As Brandt (1980) pointed out, in principle (but seldom in practice) physiognomy meets our needs and desires to see into the minds and personalities of others; to see beyond what is given in their potentially misleading facial expressions, utterances, and other behaviors. Moreover, in many situations, particularly first encounters, little behavioral information will be available with which to judge others.

An early review of this topic concluded that "social standards" for physiognomic judgments seem to exist "which, if crude, are yet rather widely accepted and practiced" (Gurnee, 1936, p. 187). More recently, a survey of university students revealed that a majority believe that the face (especially the mouth) provides a helpful guide to personality and social class; only 10% believed that there are "no important facial guides to character" (Liggett, 1974)! Common parlance ("an honest face") and the widespread use of facial photographs in personnel departments also testify to the prevalence of belief in the usefulness of facial appearance to predict behavior.

Furthermore, facial stereotypes may be relatively powerful. Secord, Bevan and Dukes (1953) provided evidence that facial appearance is more influential than occupational stereotypes when forming impressions from photographs accompanied by occupational labels. One early study (Wallace, 1941) suggests that, as many suspect, the face may dominate other aspects of appearance in guiding judgments based on physical appearance. Mazur, Mazur, and Keating (1984) found a significant correlation between perceived dominance of cadets depicted in facial photographs and their military rank while at West Point Military Academy. Earlier research on judgments of silhouette profiles indicates that facial appearance may be particularly powerful in forming impressions within the sphere of "the will" (e.g., judgments of self-confident or energetic) and the "intellectual sphere" (Wolff, 1943).

Finally, as we see shortly, judges very often agree in the impressions attributed to certain faces or facial features. Consistent physiognomic impressions have even been found in cross-cultural studies. Secord and Bevan (1956) found general agreement between Norwegians and Americans on personality judgments of facial photographs. More recently, Keating, Mazur and Segall (1981) reported that Americans reliably sort facial photographs along a dominance–submissiveness dimension, and that these portraits are given similar ratings in a wide variety of cultures across the globe. McArthur and Berry (1986) found strong agreement between American and Korean adults regarding the traits attributed to both schematic drawings and photographs of faces varying in babyishness. Such findings imply that the study of attributions based on specific facial characteristics is worth pursuing, even if the search for actual relations between facial features and character or personality is not. Before proceeding, however, some forewarning is needed.

Past research on physiognomic effects has been dominated by interest in personality impressions, with little attention devoted to the role of physiognomy in actual social situations. For ecologically minded psychologists, the significance of attributing traits to faces is limited to the extent to which these attributions reflect perceivers' behavioral intentions or the perception of social affordances. Although it may seem obvious, we should not simply assume that the traits attributed to faces necessarily have implications for other responses. Like most other areas of research on psychosocial effects of perceiving faces, research on the implications of physiognomic attributions lags behind research on the attributions themselves. Hochberg and Galper (1974) directly confronted this issue, finding that photographs of faces have differing but reliable effects on perceivers' expectations of behavioral intentions. Furthermore, these "attributions of intention", in terms of sexuality or social desirability in their studies, conformed to the personality traits attributed to the same faces. So physiognomic judgments of personality traits do seem to have the expected implications for other responses to faces, but considerably more research is needed to assess the actual consequences of physiognomy for social interaction.

A sociobiological perspective on human physical appearance has enabled theorists (e.g., Guthrie, 1970, 1976) to ascribe a purpose (i.e., some contribution to fitness) to numerous facial characteristics and forms of facial elaboration (see the following discussion), but the as yet largely speculative work of sociobiology is often prone to what may be called the "adaptationist fallacy" (Gould & Lewontin, 1979): the faulty speculative interpretation of unitary traits of an organism as adaptations to selection pressures. Thus, most sociobiological interpretations of facial appearance need to be supported at least by evidence that facial characteristics actually produce the social effects attributed to them.

Also be forewarned that nearly all of the studies on physiognomy have used photographs or drawings. As noted in chapter 1, there are many dangers inherent to the strategy of using research based on photographs or other static depictions to develop theories or hypotheses about perceptual or cognitive processes operating in everyday interactions with actual people, for their faces are naturally and multidimensionally dynamic. In addition to the aforementioned dangers, judgments of photographs may be influenced by the "social function of photographs in our culture" (Cohen, 1973, p. 55). For instance, people usually are supposed to appear "at their best" (e.g., smiling) in photographs. Despite the often recognized problem of generalization to real faces, researchers have used, and will continue to use, two-dimensional depictions of faces due to the convenience and, more importantly, control such depictions afford (cf. Secord, 1958).

Physiognomy and Facial Anomalies

The impact of facial features on the judgments of others is surely greatest among those with facial anomalies. These unfortunate individuals are often the victims of faulty attributions (Macgregor, 1974). Marked facial deformities frequently lead others to suspect these aesthetically handicapped individuals of criminality or mental deficiency. More specific links have been reported between attributions of alcoholism and a reddened nose, and at least one individual was commonly seen as being a "tough" character due to his partial facial paralysis (Macgregor, Abel, Bryt, Lauer, & Weissman, 1953). Sex differences in the impact of facial anomalies probably exist: Bull (1979) found that one or two facial scars made a man's face appear less honest, less "warm and affectionate", and less sincere, whereas a female was rated as less honest and having no sense of humor when she was depicted with a scarred face.

Research is needed on physiognomic judgments related to other specific facial anomalies. Individuals with repaired cleft lips, though dramatically improved, do tend to have a thin repaired (generally upper) lip whereas the lower lip is usually moderately thick and protrusive (Ross & Johnston, 1972). Do these results produce consistent social reactions? Cleft lip is not uncommon and is usually treated in developed countries, yet we still cannot answer this basic question. (Additional discussion of physiognomy and facial anomalies appears in the following chapter by W.C. Shaw.)

Stereotypes and Normal Variations in Facial Appearance

In experiments using both photographs (see Hull, 1928; Secord, 1958) and schematic drawings (e.g., Brunswik & Reiter, 1937), researchers repeatedly have found evidence that adults make, and largely agree upon, physiognomic judgments. In the following review of some of these studies, the findings are divided according to whether the judgments reflect a response to the overall appearance of the face or to some specific facial feature(s). Keep in mind that physiognomic judgments influence, and are influenced by, other aspects of face perception, most notably by the perception of facial expression. Indeed, people tend to agree about the emotions represented in facial photographs *even when their judgments are incorrect* (Tomkins & McCarter, 1964), so accuracy does not distinguish physiognomic judgments from perception of emotions.

Some physiognomic judgments cannot be traced to specific facial features, but instead seem to arise from perception of the whole craniofacial complex (see Secord et al., 1954). People often make judgments of others based on physical appearance without being able to ascribe their impressions to specific physical characteristics. Indeed, many researchers (e.g., Hull, 1928; Samuels, 1939; Secord et al., 1954) have noted that perceivers often find it difficult or impossible to state just what facial characteristics produce their impressions, even when they are highly confident of their judgments. Moreover, lay adults seem to be able to render physiognomic judgments easier and faster than they can rate the morphological characteristics of faces, although they end up with roughly equivalent levels of agreement, overall, in these two types of ratings (Secord et al., 1954).

Likewise, for objects as variable and complex as human faces it is difficult for perceptual psychologists to know which characteristics or combination of characteristics are most important to perceivers required to make a given judgment. Even when specific facial features are linked to physiognomic judgments, the overall appearance of the face still will play an influential role; in part because we normally attend to at least several facial regions when viewing faces (Yarbus, 1967), and in part because it forms the context within which each individual facial feature is perceived. Wolff (1943) demonstrated that left and right, and upper and lower halves of the same face could produce impressions that distinctly differed from each other and from the impression produced by a full-face photograph. Using pairs of front and side view photographs of heads and shoulders, Warr and Knapper (1968, Exper. 34-35) found that photographic angle significantly influenced some physiognomic judgments for most targets, although they were unable to identify any systematic effect. Altering a single facial feature will often influence the perception of other facial features in photographs (Stritch & Secord, 1956). Compounding this complexity are the facial expressions and other behaviors of the perceived faces, various context effects, and the motivational and emotional states of perceivers (cf. Warr & Knapper, 1968). Other available information (e.g., rankings of intelligence) can also influence physiognomic judgments (Asch, Block, & Hertzman, 1938).

Judgments Based on Overall Facial Appearance

Many of the studies performed to examine the influence of facial attractiveness on impressions or expectations (see Alley & Hildebrandt, this volume) can be seen as research on a type of physiognomic phenomenon: namely, the differential ascription of personality or behavioral traits to others varying in an overall assessment of facial attractiveness. With this in mind, consider one such study (Unger, Hilderbrand, & Madar, 1982). They had college students make judgments of other students' sexual preferences, job aspirations, and political radicalism based solely on facial photographs. Although in this and other similar studies it is not clear how readily raters will make such physiognomic assessments without pressure (e.g., experimenter requests) to do so, these studies do show that adults readily comply with requests to make these sorts of judgments. Unger et al. noted that "few subjects refused to participate because they could not make judgments about group membership on the basis of physical appearance" (1982, p. 298). Moreover, the raters in these studies display some agreement about facial appearance in that less favorable traits (e.g., epilepsy, social deviance) usually are ascribed to less attractive faces. Still, there is little evidence for the validity of these physiognomic judgments, particularly for judgments of political orientation or sex roles (cf. Unger et al., 1982).

Age-related variations in facial appearance are often associated with variations in physiognomy, including some readily explained changes in perceived dominance (Keating, 1985) and responsibility (McArthur & Apatow, 1983–1984). For instance, the age-related trait of a receding hairline, which may have evolved to signal seniority status (Guthrie, 1976), tends to produce attributions of dominance (Keating & Bai, 1986; Keating, Mazur, & Segall, 1981). In a seminal study of physiognomy based on photographs of males' faces (Secord et al., 1954), perceived age was among the 4 most influential aspects of facial appearance among the 23 characteristics assessed for their influence on personality judgments. The effects of age-related facial changes on many other judgments are discussed earlier in this volume (Alley, chap. 3; Berry & McArthur, chap. 4).

Several studies, including the previously discussed study of Thornton (1939), suggest that facial stereotypes exist for various types of criminals. Shoemaker, South, and Lowe (1973) had subjects select from 12 facial photographs of middle-aged White males 2 men that were most likely and 2 that were least likely to have committed one of four types of crime. Agreement in the selections of photographs indicate that specific stereotypes exist for those most and least likely to have committed each of the four crimes. These researchers also asked other subjects to evaluate the guilt or innocence of men based on an ambiguous written vignette, presented either with or without a facial photograph allegedly depicting the accused man. Stereotype-congruent photographs received as many as 30% more guilty verdicts. A more recent and thorough study (Bull & Green, 1980) examined the frequency with which 10 male faces (noncriminal) were chosen to match each of 11 types of crime. For 7 of these crimes (including illegal possession of drugs, mugging, and indecency), but not all (e.g., arson, theft, rape), one face was selected much more frequently than the others, and different faces were selected for different crimes. A small sample of policemen selected the same faces to match these 7 crimes.

Defining a facial stereotype in terms of the agreement across judges in the selection of same or similar features in Identi-kit (Model II) constructions of the face of a given criminal type, Goldin (1979) found that different crimes are associated with distinctly different facial characteristics. The appearance of the eyes, hair, chinline (or face shape), and age accounted for most of the variability. Moreover, her results indicated that each criminal stereotype was "dominated by a few critical features that are strongly associated with the crime and viewed as diagnostic of the criminal type", and that "other features may be "filled in" using normative features" when people are asked to construct a facial image (1979, p. 38).

Goldstein, Chance, and Gilbert (1984) found that certain faces in 20-face arrays were selected at well above chance levels for each of three types of criminal, as well as three types of high-status occupation. Goldstein et al. (1984) also reported that the faces commonly selected as criminals were also seen as more dirty, insane, brash, cruel, vulgar, bad, and unfriendly by an independent group of judges. Together these studies clearly indicate that crime-specific facial stereotypes may introduce bias into both criminal identification and trial situations.

Some other work on overall facial appearance and physiognomy exists. For instance, the left side of the human face is more likely to evoke attributions of emotion (McGee & Skinner, 1987). Secord et al. (1954) found males' facial tension to be correlated with impressions of aggressiveness, quick-temper, determination and several other traits. Adults with broad faces tend to be perceived as dominant, perhaps due to a correction between facial width and body build (Keating & Bai, 1986; Keating, Mazur & Segall, 1981). Although physiognomic judgments in everyday life no doubt often rely on such variations in overall facial appearance, a majority of the research on physiognomy has been concerned with the impact of variation in specific facial regions or features.

Stereotypes Associated
with Specific Facial Features or Regions

Psychologists, for the most part, have avoided research on the validity of physiognomic judgments, especially judgments of "normal" people, but there is a long line of research investigating which factors in faces influence these judgments. In this section, results of that research are reviewed, with the findings categorized by facial area. As you will see, this is in keeping with the predominant research method used in this field: a method which relies on variation in, or analysis of, specific local facial features as independent variables. Keep in mind, however, that such a spatial classification may not provide the best taxonomy for physiognomic judgments. Development of an adequate taxonomic system for physiognomy, if possible, awaits further research and greater understanding of these judgments.

Scalp and Facial Hair. Cross-cultural and cross-generation differences in the significance of various hairstyles may be far more important than the specific stereotypes uncovered by modern psychologists; thus, a very limited discussion of these follows. A European study (Seiller-Tarbuk, 1951; reported in Cohen, 1973) found that people who were bald or had parts in the middle were seen as less energetic than those with unparted hair or hair parted on the side. Using 11 semantic differential scales, Roll and Verinis (1971) found significant consistency in the judgments of male faces varying in the quantity and quality of hair on all five of the dimensions they examined: hair color, length, distribution (regular, balding, bald), quality (straight, wavy, curly), and facial hair (clean-shaven, mustachioed, bearded). In our fast-changing society it seems likely that the effects of these variables change from time to time along with the popularity of various hairstyles and of the prominent men and women associated with each. Furthermore, Lawson (1971) found variation in the hair color stereotypes held by raters varying in hair color and sex, although statistically significant general stereotypes (e.g., dark-haired males were seen as superior to redhead or blonde males) also emerged.

Research on hair care has revealed what is probably a more stable and generalizable finding: hair care (versus untreated hair) can produce more favorable ratings of personality (Graham & Jouhar, 1981). Also, Hallpike (1969) has gathered cross-cultural evidence that long hair signifies being partially or wholly outside society while the cutting of hair symbolizes re-entering society or adherence to a disciplinary regime within society. If so, long hair may tend to produce an impression that the individual is unsociable, unconforming or the like, whereas short hair may foster physiognomic judgments of conformity or discipline.

Human ethology provides some hypotheses about the social significance of facial hair. Facial hair provides a sign of males' age-related status, since facial hair does not become apparent until puberty and changes in density and coloration during adulthood. Thus, facial hair is likely to foster impressions of dominance, wisdom and other traits associated with adult male status. Guthrie (1970, 1976) has suggested that male facial hair also serves to increase the apparent mass of the lower face, thus helping them (or at least our bearded ancestors) to intimidate other males and (thereby) increase their reproductive (i.e., mating) success. In other words, Guthrie argued that beards are agonistic display organs. Thus, Guthrie's theory suggests that beards increase adult males' ability to intimidate other males, and beards do increase ratings of courageousness and dominance (Pellegrini, 1973), as well as masculinity and strength (Kenny & Fletcher, 1973; Pellegrini, 1973). We still need to determine whether beards increase the perceived mass of men's chins or the perceived utility (e.g., bite strength) of their mouths.

Facial hair influences other impressions; bearded men are again generally seen more favorably than men with less facial hair. Beards have increased perceptions of intelligence, likableness, health, popularity, sensitivity to others, and sexual appeal (Sprecher et al., 1984, reported in Hatfield & Sprecher, 1986), as well as enthusiasm, sincerity, generosity, inquisitiveness and dirtiness (Kenny & Fletcher, 1973). Compared to their clean-shaven appearance, bearded men also are seen as more mature, self-confident, liberal, nonconformist, and industrious (Pellegrini, 1973). Additional results of these studies indicate that men with moustaches or goatees tend to evoke impressions intermediate between those of fully bearded and clean-shaven men. For no clear reason, Bull (1979) failed to find any significant differences in ratings on 10 scales of a man seen in three states: fully bearded, moustached, and clean shaven.

Forehead Size and Contour. One study (Cohen, 1973) found that foreheads narrowing upwards and hairline height were both negatively correlated with ratings of dominance. Most studies of the forehead area, however, have concerned mental ability. Studies done in both Europe and America have found that the contour and width of the forehead is commonly taken to be indicative of mental ability, with higher or larger foreheads associated with greater intelligence (Brunswik & Reiter, 1937; Gurnee, 1936; Kiener & Hofer, 1971). The forehead may well be the major feature underlying the "considerable agreement" among judges as to which people depicted in facial photographs are the brightest and dullest (Anderson, 1921; Gurnee, 1936), but other factors (probably including facial expression) are certain to be involved as well. Related to the association of forehead size with mental ability is the claim of many physiognomists that an elongated or triangular (with base at top) face is characteristic of an intellectual personality (see Allport, 1937). In any case, as noted earlier, "the pattern of the face, in so far as it is revealed in a photograph, bears practically no relation to intelligence . . . as measured by standardized tests" (Gurnee, 1936, p. 185).

The Eyes. Although the forehead is the primary facial region used as an index of mental ability, the eyes are commonly taken to represent the motive or emotive (e.g., Raymond, 1909). Despite the central role played by the eyes in face perception, little research has been conducted on the physiognomy of eyes (excepting study of the effects of eyeglasses). Secord et al. (1954) did find a correlation between protruding eyes in males and an impression of excitability, but no significant correlations for narrowed eyes or wrinkles at eye corners. Cohen (1973), however, found a correlation between narrow eyes and raters' attributions of arrogance, whereas Kuhnel (1954, reported in Cohen, 1973) found that narrow eyes in schematic faces were commonly associated with the judgment "not likable". Jones and Moyel (1971) also found that male college students are more likely to see photographs of adult males as friendly if they have light-colored irises. Large eyes increase the perceived warmth and kindness of photographed and schematic adult faces (Berry & McArthur, 1985; McArthur & Berry, 1986), whereas both male and female students rate faces with small eyes as more dominant (Keating, 1985), thus supporting Guthrie's (1970) hypothesis that large eyes connote submissiveness.

Nakdimen (1984) argued that the typically higher and more arched eyebrows (among other sexual dimorphic facial traits) of women foster stereotyped impressions of submissiveness, credulity, and so on; and women often use cosmetics to enchance these traits. Although Keating (1985) reported that eyebrow thickness had no significant impact on their ratings, low eyebrows do increase perceived dominance for children and adults in Western cultures, probably due to the use of lowered eyebrows to express dominance or aggressiveness (Keating & Bai, 1986; Keating, Mazur, Segall et al., 1981). Similarly, the perceived warmth and submissiveness of faces increases with naturally high eyebrows (Berry & McArthur, 1985; McArthur & Berry, 1986).

Nasal Size and Shape. The availability of rhinoplasty and the publicity surrounding it demonstrate public belief in psychosocial effects of nasal appearance, yet little research has been conducted on the social impact of variations in nasal morphology. Samuels (1939), using schematic drawings, found a long nose to be associated with impressions of sadness, bad character, intelligence, age, and energy and determination. Her own research (1939), however, suggests that these results may not apply to real or even photographed faces. The existing research does support the view that current plastic surgical procedures (mainly rhinoplasty) can alter nasal shape so as to improve social perceptions of others, such as their judgments of the patients' likability and life success (Cash & Horton, 1983).

Mouth, Lips, and Teeth. The oral region is apparently at least one of the most important areas for physiognomy. Adults commonly believe it to be particularly revealing (Liggett, 1974) and seem to rely on it when forming physiognomic impressions of both men and women (Secord & Muthard, 1955; Wolff, 1943). Brunswik and Reiter (1937) found the height of the mouth to be the most important single characteristic in influencing judgments of seven qualities. In brief, a high mouth tended, depending on the pattern of other associated features, to produce the impression of a gay, young, unintelligent, unenergetic person; an impression opposite that produced by a low mouth, but like that produced by a short nose and eyes far apart. Samuels (1939) was able to replicate these results, but found only moderate carryover to judgments of photographs of faces with the characteristics varied in the schematic drawings. Further, her subjects seldom referred to these controlled variables in their reports of the bases for their judgments. Thus, for at least some physiognomic judgments, the features used by Brunswik and Reiter are inadequate (cf. Cohen, 1973).

More specific oral characteristics have been studied. For instance, using facial photographs, Secord found that bowed lips produced an impression of a conceited, demanding, immoral, and heterosexually receptive women (Secord & Muthard, 1955), and thin lipped males were seen as conscientious (Secord et al., 1954). Thin lips also make targets more likely to be seen as dominant (Cohen, 1973; Keating, 1985), as well as sociable and energetic (Cohen, 1973).

Other research shows that the presence of a smile is an important aspect of oral-facial appearance. A smile consistently has a favorable effect on assessment of such factors as intelligence (Allport, 1937), happiness (e.g., Keating, Mazur & Segall, 1981), humor and kindliness (Thornton, 1943) and, usually, honesty (Thornton, 1943). Smiling also reduces perceived dominance (Keating & Bai, 1986; Keating, Mazur, Segall et al., 1981; Mazur et al., 1984). Although such facial expression effects are beyond the scope of this chapter, they are worth citing in this context because a related but more purely structural variable, mouth curvature, seems to produce similar effects. Upward mouth curvature in photographed males produced impressions of friendly, cheerful, easygoing, kind, likable, unaggressive, unhostile, and slow to anger personality traits (Secord et al., 1954). Likewise, other oral-facial variables influencing apparent emotional expression can be expected to produce consistent physiognomic judgments. For instance, a protrusive lip might foster the impression of a defiant or hostile personality since the lower lip is protruded in times of anger (cf. Guthrie, 1976).

Protrusive and Retrusive Chins. A common facial stereotype is that a protrusive chin (prognathic profile) indicates strength of will, ambition, or determination, whereas a retrusive chin (retrognathic profile) indicates weakness of will or lack of determination (Bellak & Baker, 1981; Cohen, 1973; Gurnee, 1936). This probably is related to ethologists' observation that humans jut out their chins as a signal of belligerence, whereas those shrinking from aggressive encounters retract their jaws back toward their necks: the "grimace of acquiescence" (Guthrie, 1970, p. 263). Also, the chin becomes larger and more prognathic with growth. Children select faces with large jaws as appearing dominant disproportionately often (Keating & Bai, 1986). As noted previously, a beard or protrusive lower lip may enhance the social impact of a protruding chin.

Stereotypes Concerning Forms of Facial Elaboration

There are numerous forms of facial elaboration that may influence physiognomic judgments. Many of these alterations do influence perceived facial attractiveness (see Alley & Hildebrandt, this volume). The existing research has been concerned mainly with the impact of facial cosmetics and eyeglasses.

Cosmetics, even in normal everyday use, are thought by some to be capable of altering physiognomic judgments. In support of this notion, Graham and Jouhar (1981) found that the use of facial make-up by adult females led to improved ratings on 8 of the 14 personality dimensions tested. As is generally true for the study of psychosocial effects of various forms of facial elaboration, it remains unclear whether facial make-up has a direct effect on personality judgments (a "what has been cared for is good" stereotype) or operates indirectly by altering facial attractiveness (cf. Graham & Jouhar, 1981).

The effects of most specific types of cosmetic treatment are also unclear. For instance, even though females commonly "make-up" artificially raised eyebrows, perhaps increasing their perceived attentiveness and submissiveness (Guthrie, 1970), insufficient psychological research exists to evaluate the social effect of this common facial alteration. McKeachie (1952) reported significant effects of lipstick on college males' first impressions of females for 5 (out of 22) personality dimensions. Asking different questions, Secord and Muthard (1955) found a positive relationship between rated sexuality and the amount of lipstick worn.

Hamid (1972) found that the traits ascribed to females by New Zealand males were influenced by the use of facial make-up and wearing eyeglasses. Female viewers displayed weaker, as well as qualitatively different, stereotypes associated with eyeglasses and make-up. In a pilot study by Hamid (1968), ratings of eight female faces displayed no consistent stereotypes other than an effect of eyeglasses: Faces with eyeglasses were rated less attractive and sophisticated, and more conventional, shy, and religious. Elman (1977) found that both males and females rated a photographed male as more of a follower, softer, more sensitive, and gentler when he wore glasses. Wearing eyeglasses affected other trait ratings in this study only when the male was described as short, demonstrating again the importance of context for physiognomic judgments.

It is commonly thought that wearing eyeglasses often produces the impression of greater intelligence, but research on the impact of glasses on judgments of intelligence has produced conflicting results. Thornton found that a person shown in a photograph (1943, 1944) or seen briefly in person (1944) while wearing glasses was judged more intelligent (and industrious) than when not wearing them. Likewise, students with eyeglasses were more likely to be identified as honor students in a physiognomic study (Terry & Snider, 1972). Conversely, Argyle and McHenry (1971), using short videotapes of people engaged in conversation, found that wearers of eyeglasses were seen as *less* intelligent. Geographical or methodological differences may have contributed to this discrepancy.

In at least several of the aforementioned studies (Graham & Jouhar, 1981; Hamid, 1968, 1972; McKeachie, 1952), the judges had little or no recognition that cosmetics or eyeglasses were influencing their ratings. As ecological psychologists frequently point out, perception is *not* dependent on conscious awareness either in the form of specific environmental properties identified as crucial components or simply consciously experienced sensations (see J.J. Gibson, 1966a). Furthermore, perceivers are relatively unlikely to recognize the specific underpinnings for perceptual judgments of highly complex perceptual arrays like faces.

CONCLUDING REMARKS

Physiognomy is an important aspect of person perception. Yet perhaps as much as any branch of social or perceptual psychology, scientific knowledge of physiognomic diagnosis lags behind naive belief and credulous practice. For instance, we know nothing about the role of physiognomy in established interpersonal relationships. In everyday interpersonal relations, judgments of other persons can be continually corrected and adjusted in light of their behavior. Hence, facial stereotypes are likely to have their greatest impact in our dealings with strangers and in the formation of first impressions, particularly when little information about them is available (e.g., when simply shown in a photograph). Likewise, physiognomy seems unlikely to dominate our judgments of those with whom we are well acquainted. Nevertheless, no research exists to support or negate these notions, and the surprisingly long-term effects of facial attractiveness (see Alley & Hildebrandt, this volume) suggest that physiognomy too may have a significant impact even after long periods of interpersonal relations.

Reiterating the main points of this chapter, physiognomy is, with few and nearly negligible exceptions, an invalid practice, yet consistent facial stereotypes exist such that certain faces or facial characteristics produce remarkably uniform impressions in perceivers. Perceivers typically recognize the structural bases of their physiognomic impressions only vaguely, if at all. Psychologists, too, remain largely in the dark about the determinants of facial stereotypes or more idiosyncratic physiognomic judgments. A review of studies on physiognomy reveals a bewildering hodgepodge of more specific findings on facial stereotyping.

A major pitfall of most studies has been that they have inquired into relationships between facial appearance and perceptual impressions without asking what relationships ought to be found although several recent studies on physiognomy do address this question and, therefore, proceed from a theoretical basis (see Berry & McArthur, 1985, this volume; Cunningham, 1986; Keating, 1985). In the absence of guidelines provided by theory, it is especially important that faces and attributes be representatively sampled. A method for systematically selecting relevant traits that may be attributed to faces has been explored by Hurwitz, Wiggins, and Jones (1975). Existing cephalometric norms may be used to insure representative sampling of faces, while systematic and controlled variation of one or more facial features (e.g., Alley, 1983c; Brunswik, 1956) must be used to assess the impact of variability in specific facial characteristics on social reactions and impressions. Nonetheless, systematic sampling of faces and relevant attributes has seldom been attempted. As a result, most studies lack generalizability and comparability.

Despite these shortcomings, some general conclusions and expectations can be gleaned from the literature in addition to those discussed so far. First, individuals with more abnormal or eccentric facial characteristics produce physiognomic impressions that are more extreme or eccentric, whereas those with average face characteristics tend to receive physiognomic judgments of average personality characteristics (e.g., Secord et al., 1954; Secord & Muthard, 1955). Second, the traits judges agree upon best differ for male and female targets (Secord & Muthard, 1955). Third, for reasons as yet unknown, some faces produce much more reliable (i.e., consistent) physiognomic reactions than others (e.g., Goldstein et al., 1984; Hochberg & Galper, 1974). Fourth, greater concensus for physiognomic judgments is produced for general categories such as "good guys" and "bad guys" than for more specific categories like engineer or rapist (Goldstein et al., 1984).

The existing findings leave many questions unanswered. The most interesting or important of these include: (a) an explanation of the veridicality, albeit slight, of some physiognomic judgments; (b) explanation of actual physiognomic effects, including an account of their reliability; (c) the relationship between trait attributions and patterns of social interaction; (d) the general theoretical orientation(s) that can account for the role of physiognomy in social perception; (e) the extent and direction of modification of physiognomic effects by facial expressions, observations of behavior, and other sources of information; and (f) other aspects of the generalizability of conclusions about physiognomy based on two-dimensional, static depictions of faces to physiognomy based on dynamic presentations (e.g., videotapes) or in real face-to-face interactions. In sum, much work remains to be done before we can begin to answer more questions than are raised by research on physiognomy.

ACKNOWLEDGMENT

Thanks are due to Diane Berry for her helpful comments on an earlier version of this chapter.

III PERCEIVING ABNORMAL FACES

INTRODUCTORY REMARKS

Every knowledgeable person would agree that facial anomalies often have severe psychosocial consequences, yet there is remarkably little research on this topic. Moreover, the majority of the existing literature has focused on the limited domains of self- and parent-perception rather than on the interpersonal arena (cf. Macgregor, 1974). Individuals with mental retardation (Richardson, Koller, & Katz, 1985) and certain other psychological impairments (cf. chap. 6) are more likely to have facial anomalies. Nonetheless, as Macgregor (1974) stressed, most facial anomalies by themselves present little or no problems for the victim: It is the reactions of others that create the major problems and provide minor irritants such as nicknames and teasing (cf. W.C. Shaw, Meek, & Jones, 1980).

Research on children's social preferences highlights the serious social handicap that facial disfigurement can create: Children consistently prefer other children with one of several types of handicap—including crutches and a brace, wheelchair, or missing hand—to a facially disfigured child (Giancoli & Neimeyer, 1983; Richardson, Goodman, Hastorf, & Dornbusch, 1961). Similar research has found rather consistent ordered preferences for faces with various anomalies, all of which are less preferred than a normal face (e.g., Lansdown & Polak, 1975).

Clinical interviews also often reveal that facial defects can have severe and pervasive effects, rendering some individuals incapable of engaging in normal interactions with any but a few individuals. Many victims of facial anomalies cannot find employment or achieve or maintain close friendships. Macgregor noted that there are exceptional individuals who are remarkably well-adjusted and who function in a fairly normal manner. Even these people, however, must resort to special tactics (like joking about their faces to break the tension of a first social encounter) to become socially acceptable. Furthermore, like all of the patients with facial paralysis in one study (Hirschenfang, Goldberg, & Benton, 1969), people with obvious facial anomalies are all likely to show some degree of depression and/or withdrawal. All adults with facial anomalies, but perhaps especially females (see chap. 6, this volume), will have fewer potential people from whom to select friends and mates.

Modern developments in surgical and orthopedic techniques bring to the study of facial attractiveness a new realm of importance, for it is now possible to make alterations in facial appearance that dramatically increase physical attractiveness. At least since the 14th century surgeons have been able to improve the appearance of some grossly damaged or malformed facial features, but now plastic surgeons and orthodontists are able to improve the appearance of most individuals with significant facial defects and can even alter unaesthetic but medically normal facial characteristics so as to make them more pleasing to the eye. With these advances, our society's current concern for physical attractiveness and the general acceptance of numerous techniques of improving one's appearance, many individuals, unhappy with their facial appearance, are now able and willing to seek and find ways of improving matters (see Graham & Kligman, 1985). The fact that about 75% of cosmetic surgery patients are women over 40 (Melamed, 1983) probably reflects our society's double standards of beauty and aging (see chaps. 3 and 6).

Clinicians generally agree (and there is some good evidence) that poor aesthetics rather than poor function typically serves as the main motivation for patients seeking orthodontic or other dentofacial treatments or plastic surgery (Jacobson, 1984). This perspective on patient motivation has had an unfortunate side-effect: Clinicians and psychiatrists have too frequently jumped to the conclusion that patients seeking surgery for aesthetic reasons are displaying a symptom of psychopathology. We now know that these patients have good reason to believe in the social significance of facial appearance (see chaps. 6, 8, 9, and 10). Although the reception for these patients in surgeons' offices may have improved, we are left with a body of research on psychological aspects of facial anomalies and facial surgery which has emphasized uncovering patients' motives and personalities in order to weed out those with psychopathology; research on other issues is still quite sparse (cf. Berscheid & Gangestad, 1982). Moreover, earlier clinical accounts of persons suffering from various facial anomalies may have been too quick to report paranoia (e.g., Hirschenfang et al., 1969) or other forms of psychopathology because the authors had underestimated the degree of handicap posed by facial anomalies (cf. Bull & Stevens, 1981). Both the severity of facial anomalies and the effectiveness of treatments of them can only be properly evaluated when the social impact of facial appearance is considered (cf. Stricker et al., 1979), and we still have much to learn in these areas (cf. W.C. Shaw, Addy, & Ray, 1980).

The social effects of facial anomalies are examined in a chapter by William Shaw, an orthodontist who has initiated a series of important studies on this topic. The research reviewed in his chapter demonstrates convincingly that the social difficulties surrounding those with facial anomalies do not just stem from a simple negative reaction to facial defects; rather, individuals with facial defects are stigmatized and viewed as flawed in character and worth as well as in physical appearance. In other words, physiognomic judgments play a large part in determining the psychosocial responses to individuals with facial anomalies. Hence, improved facial appearance should improve patients' social environments, and most facial surgery patients believe their surgery produced positive effects on their social lives (Jacobson, 1984; Lefebvre & Munro, 1986).

Two specific aspects of Shaw's own research, reviewed in this chapter, merit mention. First, the photographs he has used to portray various oral-facial anomalies are extraordinarily good; only the facial defects themselves vary from photograph to photograph (see Figs. 9.2 and 9.3). Second, his discussion of the influence of facial appearance on teacher expectancy (Investigation 5) highlights the question of ecological validity that should be raised in connection with many other studies of facial appearance effects.

The chapter by Judith Albino and Lisa Tedesco examines the role of perception in the evaluation and treatment of facial disorders. Their analysis shows that perception actually plays a number of distinct roles in these processes. The questions of whether and when to treat facial disorders often depend on perception. Patients' desire for treatment is largely determined by their **perception** of the nature and degree of anomaly, which may differ drastically from judgments of others (Lefebvre & Barclay, 1982), together with the reactions of others to their facial appearance. The reactions of others, in turn, mainly depend on their **perception** of the potential patient's face. Perception is also a fundamental part of the evaluation of the need for treatment by professionals. Following treatment, the perception of facial appearance by the patient, significant others, and the general public helps determine the "success" of treatment. These issues, together with an examination of some specific methods for evaluating the severity of facial anomalies and some influences on these evaluations, constitute the principle foci of Albino and Tedesco's chapter, and further highlight the pervasive importance of face perception in human society.

9 Social Aspects of Dentofacial Anomalies

William C. Shaw
University of Manchester

I. Introduction
II. Part One: The Origins of Facial Prejudice
   A. Instinctive Rejection
   B. Social Conditioning and Reinforcement
   C. Primitive Beliefs
      1. Cleft lip
      2. Birthmarks
   D. Attribution of Personality
   E. Conclusion
III. Part Two: Current Research
   A. Investigation 1: A Survey of Present-Day Beliefs
   B. Investigation 2: A Survey of Nicknames, Teasing, and Harassment among School Children
   C. Investigation 3: The Influence of Children's Dentofacial Appearance on Their Social Attractiveness
   D. Investigation 4: The Influence of Dentofacial Appearance on the Social Attractiveness of Young Adults
   E. Investigation 5: The Influence of Children's Dentofacial Appearance on Teacher Expectations
   F. Investigation 6: The Effect of Facial Deformity on Petitioning
   G. Investigation 7: A Longitudinal Study of Children with Special Reference to Dentofacial Features
      1. Assessment procedures
      2. The physical attractiveness stereotype (at age 12 years)
      3. The impact of dentofacial anomalies
IV. Concluding Remarks

INTRODUCTION

In the pioneer study by Macgregor et al. (1953), extended interviews with facially deformed patients revealed the serious psychosocial difficulties that could be encountered in everyday life. This view was elaborated by Goffman (1963) who held that facial deformity was one of several conditions that could stigmatize individuals, making them less acceptable to the rest of society. The desire to overcome social prejudice is certainly an important motive for patients who seek corrective craniofacial surgery (Jensen, 1978) or orthodontic treatment (W.C. Shaw, Gabe, & Jones, 1979).

Hostility toward the facially deformed is no longer as extreme as in 1708 when Frederick V of Denmark ruled that no individual with a facial deformity might show himself to a pregnant woman (Weiser-Aall, 1963). Yet in some parts of the world, open prejudices still persist. Among some African tribes a deformed man is prohibited from elevation to chieftaincy (Babalola, 1978). Among rural communities in the Indian subcontinent, the family that begets a deformed child is held in low esteem until certain purifying rituals have been performed (R. Dehragoda, personal communication).

Even in modern society, feelings of aversion are still aroused by deformities of the face, particularly severe deformities, though the modifying effect of other emotions such as sympathy and curiosity are poorly understood (W.C. Shaw, Humphreys, McLoughlin, & Shimmin, 1980). In the less inhibited society of childhood, disapproval of deviant physical features is openly voiced (W.C. Shaw et al., 1980), and in interviews held at out-patient clinics for children with deformities such as cleft lip and facial burns, most of the children were reported to be victims of frequent teasing and harassment (Jones, Gabe, & Shaw, 1979).

The first part of this chapter deals with the possible origins of facial prejudice; the second part reviews recent investigations of social response to facial and dental anomalies.

PART ONE:
THE ORIGINS OF FACIAL PREJUDICE

Facial deformity is particularly stigmatizing because of the unique importance of the various functions of the face. It is not only the primary means of personal identification, but facial expression (at rest and in action) is an enormously rich source of nonverbal information (Buck, this volume; Ekman, 1978). According to Morris (1967) the face provides a highly important focus of erotic interest in sexual encounters and there is a primitive and profound association in the mind between the whole integrated pattern of the face and the pattern of the torso.

Deformities of the face may interfere with the normal transmission of social information in several ways. Certain defects such as ptosis or Bell's palsy clearly interfere with the transmission of a vast range of nonverbal messages. For the individual with a tightly repaired cleft lip, a broad engaging smile may be unattainable. In addition, transient expressions characteristic of mood may be permanently imitated by morphological features. For example, the intention bite (Grant, 1969) may be noted in an individual with mandibular prognathism and lower incisor display and give him an "aggressive look".

Disentangling the instinctive and learned origins of facial prejudice is not straightforward, but a number of headings may be suggested as a framework for consideration.

Instinctive Rejection

Modern man undoubtedly retains a legacy of instinctive behavior handed down from a time when natural selection shaped behavioral as well as physical attributes (E.O. Wilson, 1975), and instincts that limited procreation by deficient partners would have been desirable in evolutionary terms (Dawkins, 1976). As facial deformities may be a visible indication of more profound mental or physical disorder (Gorlin et al., 1976), some degree of instinctive sexual aversion could be expected. It is less clear however, why aversion operates within the sexes as well as between them, and against acquired facial deformities which cannot be genetically transmitted.

Wright (1960) suggested that a normal person's unconscious body image could be threatened by the appearance of an individual with a deformity, inasmuch as the perceiver identifies to some extent with that person. The truly instinctive nature of fear arousal is suggested by the observation of Hebb (1946) that spontaneous fear of mutilated bodies experienced by man and chimpanzee alike is due to neurophysiological conflict, and there is some evidence that initial reactions to deformed faces are autonomic in character (Aamot, 1978).

Social Conditioning and Reinforcement

As Darwin (1871) pointed out, one cultural group's concept of a pleasing appearance may vary from another's, but within the group there is pressure to conform to a socially defined norm, even if this involves expense, discomfort, or physical trauma (Jenny, 1975). Distortions and elaborations, which include neck elongation, head molding, scarring, and the wearing of lipdiscs have been reported among primitive peoples, but modern civilization is also replete with examples of cosmetic ritual. How else should we regard the use of cosmetics, the control and cultivation of facial hair, and the grooming of scalp hair? Sadly, the commercial exploitation by the advertising media of the desire to be beautiful merely serves to perpetuate myths about the qualities of the individual behind the face.

It requires little imagination to see how much the various prejudices and instincts already considered are compounded by popular imagery. Distortions of the human form associated with evil and terror were part of oral and written tradition long before the arrival of horror films, whereas the comic face has long attracted amusement in circus, theatre, caricature, and cartoon.

Primitive Beliefs

Throughout the history of man, the birth of a child with a congenital deformity must have stimulated speculation as to the cause. The beliefs held since primitive times have been many and varied, and attitudes to the deformed child, governing at times his very survival, have depended upon them. These are more fully dealt with elsewhere (W.C. Shaw, 1981a), but two distinctive facial deformities will be considered here.

Cleft Lip

In the case of this deformity, often called "harelip," a belief that recurs commonly in the folk history of many European countries is that the defect arises when the mother sees a hare during pregnancy. A variation of this tale is that the mother need only step over a hare's lair to induce the deformity, but that she can break the spell by tearing her petticoat or dress in a prescribed manner.

One vivid account recorded in the North of Scotland in 1893 was as follows: "An unmarried woman in Kingussie became pregnant. She was shearing in the harvest field, and came upon a hare's lair. Her companions suspected her condition, and said she ought to take a snip from the border of her petticoat. To conceal her shame, she, so far from taking the advice of her companions, put her foot in the lair, stepped over it, and then back. The child had a double hairlip" (A. Bruford, 1978).

Such beliefs were shared elsewhere in the British Isles (Briody, 1978; Evans, 1972; Hole, 1961; S.E. Sanderson, 1978) and in Denmark (Fogh-Andersen, 1942), Sweden (A. Nyman, 1978; E. Schon, 1978) and Norway (I. Christensen, 1978), where an old Norwegian law for the protection of pregnant women forbade butchers from displaying hares in public (Reed, 1956). This curious association between cleft lip and the hare is represented by the terminology of the condition in many languages (Table 9.1) and the true antiquity of the association is revealed in the writings of Galen in the second century by usage of the term *lagocheilos* (Weiser-Aall, 1963).

The natural form of the hare's upper lip lends itself appropriately to description of untreated cleft lip in man, but the same is true for the snout of many other mammals (Bateman, 1977) and there appear to be additional reasons for the hare–cleft lip association. Together with the cat, the hare in folklore is regarded as a common witches' familiar, or form assumed by a witch, in order to avoid detection during the execution of some malevolent act. Tales of such witch–hares are abundant in various parts of the British Isles (R. Gwyndaf, 1977; McPherson, 1929; L. Smith, 1978).

TABLE 9.1
Implied Association Between Cleft Lip and the Hare in Several Languages

Language	"Harelip"	Translation
Dutch	*Hazenlip*	Harelip
German	*Hasenlippe*	harelip
	Hasenscharte	*Scharte:* crack, fissure, gap, notch
Danish	*Hareskarr*	Hare cut
French	*Bec de lievre*	Hare's mouth
Swedish	*Harmynthet*	Harelipped
Spanish	*Labio leporino*	Harelip
Italian	*Labbro leporino*	Harelip
Irish	*Bearna*	Slash (in dress), gap, chasm
Old English	*Haersceard*	Hare cleft
Old Frisian	*Hasskerde*	Hare lipped

Looking further into the past, most folklore surrounding the hare supports its connection with an ancient religion (the worship of Diana, goddess of childhood and the moon) and a universal complex of moon–hare myths can be traced (Evans, 1972). The hare was associated with the moon in ancient Egypt and among the North American Indians, and Asian and Chinese children are still told bedtime stories about the hare and the moon, rather than the man and the moon. In African mythology, it is believed that the moon in anger actually split the hare's lip and similar tales are recounted in Tibet (Layard, 1944). These interwoven beliefs are also revealed in the pre-Columbian culture of Mexico, where to the present day, lunar eclipse, rather than the hare is considered responsible for cleft lip (Ortiz-Monasterio & Serrano, 1971).

Thus the folklore surrounding the aetiology of cleft lip appears to represent a fusion of several of the primitive beliefs reviewed by Ballantyne (1904); supernatural influences, lunar influence, hybridity, and maternal impressions.

Birthmarks

In several modern languages the equivalent word for birthmark again implies a supposed causal inference between experiences of the mother and the anomaly (Table 9.2). Various maternal impressions have been implicated, such as the witnessing of a conflagration or the slaughter of animals, especially when the woman is unwise enough to simultaneously touch her own face.

Even more common is the belief that birthmarks are produced when a mother craves for or eats vividly colored food, such as strawberries. Indeed dietary cravings or indiscretions of this kind are represented in the pregnancy taboos of every corner of the world (Ferrera, 1969). Not surprisingly, many such tales have been transported by North American immigrants where "marking theories" have been comprehensively recorded (Fife, 1976; W.D. Hand, 1979). Here, an additional recurring belief was that deformity of the child was induced by the mother previously mocking someone similarly afflicted, therefore implying a form of punishment.

Historically, the significance of these superstitions and beliefs has been their impact on the perception of affected individuals, for the supposition that evil influences had teratrogenic powers was widespread (W.C. Shaw, 1981a); deformity of any kind might be regarded as retribution for sins of the parents, evidence of witchcraft, or collusion with the devil. In the Middle Ages, fetal abnormalities which had some perceived animal resemblance, could be considered to be the issue of human and animal union, with the practice of executing the affected individual being recorded as late as the 17th century.

Attribution of Personality

Although there is no sound evidence that personality can be accurately read from individual physiognomic cues (Ekman, 1978), first impressions of a face can produce an extraordinary consensus of opinion concerning the subject's personal characteristics (Alley, chap. 8; Secord, 1958).

Perhaps the most important facial cue in influencing first impressions is the aggregate quality of attractiveness. Almost 200 investigations conducted over the last decade have demonstrated the ubiquitous effect of facial attractiveness

TABLE 9.2
Implied Causal Inference from the Etymology
of "Birthmark" in Several Languages

Language	"Birthmark"	Translation
Dutch	*Moedervlek*	*Moeder:* mother
		Vlek: spot, stain, mark, mole
German	*Geburtmal*	*Mutter:* mother
	Muttermal	*Mal:* mole, mark, spot
Danish	*Modermaerke*	*Moder:* mother
		Maerke: mark, sign
French	*Envie*	Desire, longing
Spanish	*Estigma*	Birthmark, mother's mark stigma, slur
Italian	*Voglia*	Wish, desire, craving,
	e.g., *voglia*	Longing, strawberry
	de fragola	Birthmark
Norwegian	*Branflekk*	*Brann:* fire
		Flekk: mark
Czech	*Materskeznameni*	*Matersky:* mother's
		Znameni: mark

in many social settings. These include friendship, dating and marriage choice, scholastic assessments, helping behavior, criminal identification, and simulated court settings (Adams, 1977; Alley & Hildebrandt, this volume; Berscheid & Walster, 1974).

The possibility that particular features of the human face might serve in some way to reveal facets of character and personality has been considered seriously from ancient times to the present day (Fischer, 1976). The so-called art of physiognomy was espoused by such philosophers as Pythagoras and Aristotle and subsequently developed in ad hoc fashion, appealing to any principles that appeared superficially relevant. Although eventually outlawed in England by the Parliament of George II, physiognomy flourished in Europe, and in 1783 Lavater published an influential work containing guidelines for prognostication. The validity of reading character from features of the human face has never been established, however. Despite this, popular interest in the idea can still be found (Lefas, 1975; Mar, 1974).

In one of the earliest scientific attempts to determine which components of facial appearance influence first impressions, judgments of a series of simplified facial diagrams were obtained (Brunswik & Reiter, 1937). Although high interjudge consensus was found for estimates of personality evoked by variations in the diagrammatic faces, subsequent investigation revealed that the findings could not be translated back to real faces (Samuels, 1939).

Secord et al., (1954) used photographs of real faces and again accumulated evidence that people share a variety of beliefs about the personality characteristics associated with facial appearance. These authors were less successful in determining which facial features had been associated with personality judgments and failed to distinguish between static facial morphology and transient facial expressions. More positive findings were obtained by examining the effect on attribution of altering a single physiognomic cue: pupil size (Hess, 1975). Male subjects judged a standardized photograph of a young woman's face to be more attractive when pupil size had been artificially enlarged. This was explained on the basis of autonomic sexual responses. (Further discussion of physiognomy can be found in chap. 8).

In considering the influence of dentofacial features on judgments of personality and social acceptability, it may be speculated that such features will have impact via two perceptual processes. First, the attractiveness of the dentofacial area must contribute to the total attractiveness of the face, indirectly influencing the type of response engendered by the physical attractiveness stereotype previously referred to. There is, indeed, some evidence that the oral region is of considerable importance in determining overall facial attractiveness (Alley & Hildebrandt, this volume). Second, certain variations of dentofacial morphology may operate as specific cues along selected personality dimensions, such as the perceived "intention bite" of mandibular protrusion, which may prompt the attribution of aggressiveness (W.C. Shaw, 1981a).

Previous investigations of lay perceptions of dentofacial features have been limited mainly to establishing a hierarchy of preference or treatment need, no attempt being made to disguise this primary interest from the participants. Various media used to represent dentofacial features have been chosen to elicit responses, including study casts, drawings, dental photographs, facial photographs and motion picture film. Profile preferences per se have also been sought by having participants rate drawings, silhouettes, cardboard shapes, and photographs. A striking observation from these studies is the high level of consensus reached by a wide variety of judges on the most preferred dentofacial characteristics, with the most popular arrangement of incisors being that regarded as ideal by orthodontists (see Alley & Hildebrandt, this volume; W.C. Shaw 1981b).

Of perhaps greater relevance, it has been demonstrated that minor variations in tooth position can be a significant determinant of the overall aesthetic impression of a face (Sergl & Stodt, 1970). In this experiment, photographs of a young woman were retouched to depict her with a variety of arrangements representing closure of a lateral or central incisor space. Subsequent ranking of her attractiveness within a group of 23 other photographs was highest for the normal condition. This finding is particularly significant since the manipulation of dental features had not been disclosed to the judges.

Collectively, the preceding investigations suggest that a widely held "form concept" (Peck & Peck, 1970) prevails, so that orthodontic concepts of ideal occlusion are also shared by the public. It is necessary, of course, to distinguish these public perceptions of ideal occlusion from the range of occlusion regarded as acceptable by the public, if not the orthodontist (Prahl-Anderson, Boersma, van der Linden, & Moore, 1979; W.C. Shaw, Lewis, & Robertson, 1975). Similarly, there is a general preference for the straighter profile, but this need not conform to traditional cephalometric norms (Cox & van der Linden, 1971; Peck & Peck, 1970). Similarities and discrepancies among evaluations of facial attractiveness by dental professionals, peers, and self-perception are discussed more fully by Albino and Tedesco (chap. 10, this volume).

The influence of dental features on judgments of personality has received little attention. In one exploratory investigation, 14 adults were asked to name, from their own acquaintances, persons falling at each of five points along a continuum of the following dimensions: protrusion of upper teeth, protrusion–recession of the chin, and straightness–crookedness of teeth (Secord & Backman, 1959). For only 8 of 45 possible combinations, however, did reasonably clear linear associations between reported dentofacial characteristics and perceived personality emerge, and even here the actual presence of the reported dental and personality traits could not be checked.

Conclusion

On the basis of the foregoing evidence it would seem reasonable to suppose that significant variations from normal facial and dental appearance often will present a considerable social disadvantage for the individual concerned. Not only would the subject's social acceptance be reduced with diminished opportunities for successful interaction, but personal development might be marred by unfavorable self-fulfilling prophecy. In other words, consistent experience of negative stereotyped response might lead to impaired self-perception of personal worth and ability and, in turn, to lower aspiration and attainment.

This being so, correction of physiognomic imperfections via surgery and/or orthodontics is of great social relevance, and using the investigation techniques of social psychology, it should be possible to determine guidelines for advising individuals about the merits of treatment in individual cases. Furthermore, in the common circumstances of limited resources or cost–benefit analysis, it should be possible to develop criteria for assessing urgency or priority of treatment need. In this context a series of applied studies was undertaken. These are outlined in Part Two.

PART TWO: CURRENT RESEARCH

Investigation 1: A Survey of Present-Day Beliefs

In order to examine current beliefs and knowledge relating to facial deformities, 200 women in the age range 20–69 years were privately interviewed, either at their place of work (schools and factories) or in their own homes (W.C. Shaw 1981a). They were shown color photographs of six individuals who demonstrated a distinct type of facial deformity (Fig. 9.1). These deformities were a repaired bilateral cleft lip, portwine stain, mandibular protrusion, mandibular retrusion, mandibular asymmetry, and acromegaly. The women were asked to give a description of each deformity, their beliefs as to its cause and any other causes that they may have heard of. In addition, they were asked to comment on the kind of personality that they thought the photographed individual might have and whether they knew anyone with such a condition.

Precise or reasonably accurate descriptions were given for all demonstrated conditions with the exception of acromegaly. Of the respondents 7.5% simply regarded acromegaly as a manifestation of subnormality while 15.5% used such bizarre descriptions as "boxer," "rugby player," "mongol," "spastic," "prehistoric man."

Although many respondents were unable to suggest a cause for the various conditions, a reasonable proportion offered various medical or quasimedical explanations. Included under the heading "genetic" were various replies such as "hereditary," "just born like that," or "fault at conception." Intrauterine pressure was considered a potential cause for all the conditions; more specifically thumb sucking (in the case of cleft lip) and, according to one respondent, tight corsets during pregnancy (for mandibular retrusion).

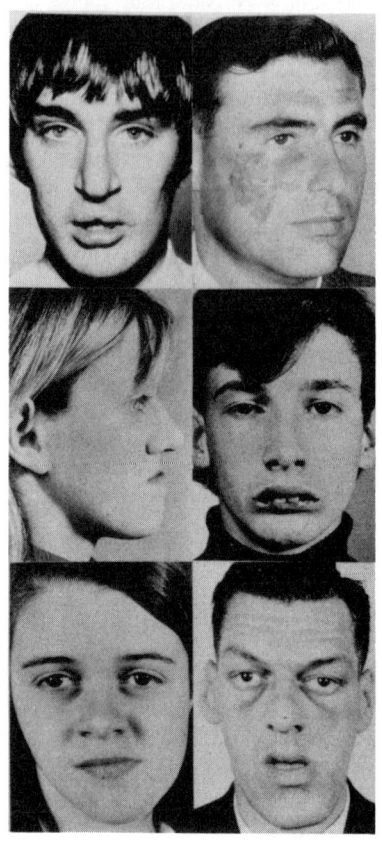

FIG. 9.1 Facial photographs of six individuals, originally in color, to demonstrate facial deformities. Bilateral cleft lip; portwine stain; mandibular protrusion; mandibular retrusion; mandibular asymmetry; acromegaly. *Note:* From "Folklore Surrounding Facial Deformity and the Origins of Facial Prejudice" by W. C. Shaw. *British Journal of Plastic Surgery,* 1981, *34,* 237-246. Copyright 1981 by the trustees of British Association of Plastic Surgeons. Reproduced by permission.

Six respondents mentioned attempted abortion as a cause of cleft lip, mandibular asymmetry, and acromegaly. A few respondents also mentioned excessive smoking and consumption of alcohol in pregnancy as causes of acromegaly. Relatively few respondents considered maternal impressions to be an important cause of the deformity, except in the case of portwine stain. Twenty percent of the respondents thought this condition was due to the mother's consumption of strawberries or red cabbage, or to an unsatisfied craving for such foods. Less often it was considered to be due to the mother being frightened by an animal, her contact with blood during pregnancy, or some extra-abdominal injury. Only two respondents admitted personal conviction that maternal impressions caused cleft lip, though many more were familiar with the old tales. Only a few women believed that the mother had been frightened by a hare or rabbit, and only one respondent blamed the mother's failure to observe the spell-breaking ritual of tearing her dress.

Popular faith in the efficacy of surgical treatment was revealed for all conditions, and in orthodontic or dental treatment in the case of mandibular retrusion. Medical solutions included the use of pills or, for acromegaly, hormone treatment. Suggestions to provide psychiatric therapy or emotional support underline expectations of mental subnormality (see the following discussion). Not surprisingly, cosmetic disguise of portwine stain was suggested. A minority of respondents recommended physiotherapy or rather unorthodox approaches, such as prayer or a change of environment. It was interesting to note that about 25% of respondents considered the repaired cleft lip as an untreated condition, though the result was typical for anomalies of this kind (Fig. 9.1).

This approach, which adopted interviews based on photographs, clearly failed to incorporate a wide range of methodological controls. Nevertheless, the replies seem to reveal common preconceptions of the personality of individuals with deformed faces. Of course, some respondents (10%-15%) felt it impossible to predict personality from a photograph, and others (20%-50%) reported that the individual would be unaffected, yet it was widely anticipated that the deformed individuals would be self-conscious or shy. Personality assessments of a more discrediting kind however, were reported by the remainder of the sample; the individuals displaying acromegaly and mandibular retrusion were regarded as being subnormal by 22% and 8% of respondents, respectively. The acromegalic and, to a lesser degree, the other deformed individuals were considered by some to be aggressive. A substantial minority anticipated that the photographed individuals would have personalities that were in some other way odd or disturbed.

The results suggest that many misconceptions about facial deformity persist, even when there is prior knowledge of the deformity. Almost all the various ancient and medieval explanations reviewed by Ballantyne (1904) were mentioned by one or more respondents. The role of maternal impressions in producing facial birthmarks was more commonly believed by the older women. Folklore beliefs appear to be dying out and are being replaced instead by sometimes accurate, sometimes inaccurate, quasimedical explanations. On the other hand, unfavorable preconceptions about the personality of individuals with facial deformities are still prevalent.

Attitudes to facially deformed individuals appear to arise from a complex of deep-seated preconceptions and cultural pressures. In addition, a legacy of confused folk belief persists so that to the present day understanding of the nature and causes of facial deformity remains imprecise.

Investigation 2: A Survey of Nicknames, and Harassment Among School Children

Confidential interviews with 531 school children between 9 and 13 years were conducted in six different schools (W.C. Shaw et al., 1980). The nature of the interview was explained to each child, but the affiliation of the interviewers and the underlying interest in dental features was not disclosed. The individual children were asked whether they had a nickname, its origin, and their feelings about the nickname. They were asked whether and how often they were teased about a variety of characteristics, who did the teasing and how they felt about this. If the child was teased about a certain characteristic, the interviewer made a subjective judgment of the "justification" for the taunt. For example, was the child conspicuously tall or short in the case of teasing about height? Finally, respondents were asked whether they were "picked on" by other children and the nature of the persecution.

Using a 7-point scale, the teacher of each child was asked to rate the subject on the following dimensions: extrovert/introvert; happy/unhappy; assertive/unassertive. The relationship of these scores to the frequency of nicknaming, teasing, and harassment was examined by the chi-square test.

Sixty-seven percent of the children reported having a nickname, 19% of which were derived from physical characteristics. Most (63.3%) of the nicknames were derived from the childrens' names. Only in three children were dental characteristics the clear origin of the nickname. Nicknames were used mainly by peers and, in general, seemed to cause little upset, with only 7% of subjects with nicknames expressing strong dislike (13% in the case of subjects whose nickname was derived from a physical feature). No relationship emerged between nicknaming experience and other characteristics examined (age, sex, extroversion, happiness, and assertiveness).

Sixty-six percent of the sample were teased about one or more characteristics. Height and weight were the most common targets for teasing; dental features were fourth (Table 9.3). Thirty-seven children (7%) reported being teased about their teeth once per week or more, and of these, 19 suffered comments about incisors' prominence (Goofy, Bugs Bunny, Stickyout teeth), and 3 about crowding (Crooked, Cronky, Fang). The remaining 15 children were teased about dental characteristics unrelated to alignment (e.g., dirty teeth, broken tooth, big teeth). In the opinion of the interviewers, 30 of these 37 children did possess a conspicuous dental deviation. Comments about the teeth appear to be more hurtful than those about other features, with 60% of the group teased about teeth admitting that they disliked or were upset by it (Table 9.4). Though most of the teasing was done by male peers (responsible for 46% of all teasing), an equal number of boys and girls were victims. Slightly more 9- and 10-year-old children suffered teasing compared with 12- and 13-year-olds (73% versus 65%, $p < 0.05$), but there was no relationship between the incidence of teasing and the teachers' judgments of extroversion, assertiveness, or happiness.

Twenty-nine percent of the sample reported that they suffered persecution either in the form of verbal intimidation (26.5%), physical intimidation (59%), or in being victimized by their peers in other ways (14.5%). Considerably more 9- and 10-year-olds report harassment than did 12- and 13-year-

TABLE 9.3
Frequency of Teasing Directed at Different Features
(once per week or more)

Feature	Frequency (Percentage)
Height	11.9
Weight	11.3
Hair	8.9
Teeth	7.0
Strength	6.6
Nose	5.5
Freckles	3.8
Ears	3.8
Others	3.6
Glasses	2.7
Eyes	2.5
Brace	2.3
Clothes	1.7
Lips	1.5

olds (49% versus 8% $p < 0.001$), and equal numbers of boys and girls were victims. Twice as many introverted children as extroverted ones reported harassment (39% versus 19%, $p < 0.025$), but no relationship between harassment and teachers' judgments of the child's assertiveness or happiness could be demonstrated.

For any child the playground environment may at times be hostile. The principle aim of the present study was to explore the extent to which deviant

TABLE 9.4
Distress Reported by Children Teased about Different Features

Feature	Children Who Disliked or Were Upset by Teasing (Percentage)
Teeth	60.7
Clothes	53.8
Ears	51.7
Strength	42.9
Weight	41.5
Freckles	37.0
Brace	33.3
Glasses	33.3
Hair	31.0
Nose	29.3
Eyes	27.7
Other [a]	26.7
Height	25.3

[a] Various other features occasionally mentioned.

dental features may expose children to ridicule and embarrassment. So commonplace were nicknames that their use could be regarded as part of the normal relationships of childhood. Only rarely did they appear to be hurtful (85% reported no negative reactions) and such was their diversity that it is hardly surprising that they were seldom inspired by dental features.

On the other hand, dental deviations did appear to attract a reasonable amount of teasing. The fact that dental features came fourth in the hierarchy of "target" features for teasing is particularly significant because none of the children interviewed were aware of the true nature of the investigation. Similarly, the finding that children teased about their teeth were particularly upset by it and were also twice as likely to suffer general harassment is of interest, though unintentional recording bias may be partly responsible because the background of the investigation was known to the interviewers. However, it has been observed previously that unattractive children are more likely to be the victims of bullying (Lowenstein, 1978).

The issue is further complicated by the fact that other features and qualities of the child are likely to ameliorate or compound the perceived stigma. For example, the general attractiveness of the face may influence the perception of dental features (see the following discussion). It is notable that children judged by their teachers to be introverted were more likely to complain about harassment by peers. The actual dynamics of the situation could not be extrapolated further, but it seems likely that certain children are regarded as more "suitable" targets for abuse. It is also probable of course, that some children will be better equipped, physically or psychologically, to cope with various forms of insult and shrug them off or otherwise deal with them without undue concern.

The long-term effects of teasing on the development of personality are undetermined, but one may readily imagine that for some children sustained ridicule and insult may promote lower self-confidence and alienation. The available empirical data support this (Berscheid, Walster, & Bohrnstedt, 1973). In this respect, the contribution of orthodontic treatment should not be underestimated where a conspicuous dentofacial deviation has attracted the hurtful mockery of peers.

Investigation 3:
The Influence of Children's Dentofacial Appearance on Their Social Attractiveness

An experimental design that would maximize the effect of dentofacial cues in impression formation was adopted in order to explore possible stereotyping mechanisms regarding social acceptance (W.C. Shaw, 1981b). Portrait photographs of two boys and two girls, preselected by a panel of 60 adult judges as representing high or low attractiveness for each sex, were modified so that, for each face, five different photographic versions were available. In each version, the child's face was standardized except that a different dentofacial arrangement was demonstrated (Fig. 9.2).

Eight hundred and forty children and 840 adults were shown 1 of the 20 photographs and asked to rate the represented child's suitability as a friend, likely aggressiveness, and attractiveness using visual analogue scales. The adults were also asked to rate intelligence.

The results are presented in Tables 9.5 and 9.6 and a full discussion is presented elsewhere (W.C. Shaw, 1981b). Essentially, the hypothesis that photographs of children with a normal dental appearance would be judged by peers and lay adults to be better looking, more desirable as friends, and less likely to behave aggressively than children with a dentofacial anomaly was upheld. Background attractiveness of the face, however, emerged as a factor

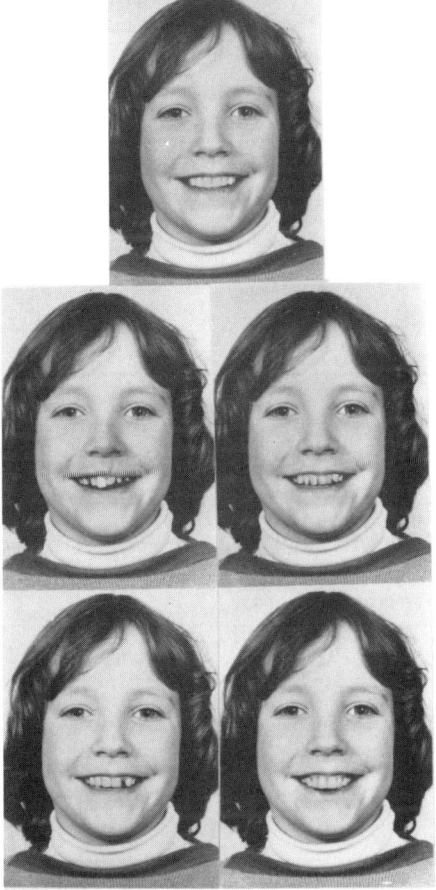

FIG. 9.2 Stimulus photographs of an attractive girl, showing normal incisors, harelip, crowded incisors, missing lateral incisor, and prominent incisors. *Note:* "The Influence of Children's Dentofacial Appearance on Their Social Attractiveness as Judged by Peers and Lay Adults" by W. C. Shaw. *American Journal of Orthodontics, 1981, 79,* 399-415. Copyright 1981 by C. V. Mosby Co. Reproduced by permission.

TABLE 9.5
Mean Peer Judgments

Significant Effects of Attractiveness

Characteristic	Attractive Face	Unattractive Face	p
Attractiveness	40.0	26.9	< 0.001
Desirability as a friend	49.0	43.8	< 0.01
Perceived aggressive tendency[a]	73	62.0	< 0.001

Significant Effects of Dentofacial Features

Characteristic	Normal Incisors	Harelip	Crowded Incisors	Missing Incisor	Prominent Incisors	p
Attractiveness	43.1	24.9	33.7	31.1	35.0	< 0.001
Desirability as a friend	52.1	44.4	41.7	46.3	47.7	< 0.01
Perceived aggressive tendency[a]	73.5	64.8	67.4	61.1	72.3	< 0.001

[a] Higher ratings signify more favorable attribution (i.e., less aggressive).

TABLE 9.6
Mean Lay Adult Judgments

Significant Effects of Attractiveness

Characteristic	Attractive Face	Unattractive Face	p
Attractiveness	69.1	52.8	< 0.001
Desirability as a friend	76.0	65.4	< 0.001
Perceived aggressive tendency[a]	77.2	66.9	< 0.001
Perceived intelligence	67.6	61.2	< 0.001

Significant Effects of Dentofacial Features

Characteristic	Normal Incisors	Harelip	Crowded Incisors	Missing Incisor	Prominent Incisors	p
Attractiveness	69.4	62.4	61.0	57.0	54.0	< 0.001
Desirability as a friend	76.9	72.8	71.0	67.9	65.4	< 0.001

[a] Higher ratings signify more favorable attribution (i.e., less aggressive).

of greater potential influence than dental appearance. On the "good looks" ratings, for example, there were many instances in which the attractive children with dentofacial anomalies still gained more generous ratings than unattractive children with normal dental appearance. On perceived intelligence, dentofacial variations had no statistically significant effect on biasing judgments, but background facial attractiveness did, low attractiveness being associated with low intelligence ($p < 0.001$).

Investigation 4: The Influence of Dentofacial Appearance on the Social Attractiveness of Young Adults

In a replication of the foregoing study, photographs of four young adults were modified (Fig. 9.3) and presented for rating to students from a wide range of social backgrounds (W.C. Shaw, Rees, Dawe, & Charles, 1985). Each of the 20 photographs was independently rated by 40 students ($N = 800$), and again the design allowed an assessment of four independent variables and their interactions: sex of photographed individual ($X2$), dental variations

FIG. 9.3 Stimulus photographs of an attractive male, showing normal incisors, prominent incisors, missing lateral incisor, crowded incisors, and harelip. *Note:* "The Influence of Dentofacial Appearance on the Social Attractiveness of Young Adults" by W. C. Shaw et al. *American Journal of Orthodontics, 1985, 87,* 21-26. Copyright 1985 by C. V. Mosby Co. Reproduced by permission.

represented ($X5$), and sex of judge ($X2$). The significant main effects for dentofacial and background facial appearance are listed in Table 9.7.

Faces displaying a normal incisor relationship gained the most favorable ratings for 8 of the 10 social characteristics examined, and in 4 of these (perceived friendliness, social class, popularity, and intelligence) differences across the range of dental conditions were statistically significant. Once again, background facial attractiveness was often more powerful than the individual's dental condition.

In studies such as this and its forerunner, conducted so as to exclude the myriad of variables attending genuine human interaction, only guarded extrapolation is appropriate. In the two following investigations, which incorporate a greater "real-life" component, stereotyping phenomena are not so readily demonstrable.

Investigation 5:
The Influence of Children's Dentofacial Appearance on Teacher Expectations

A recurring doctrine in educational psychology is that a teacher's attitudes toward an individual, and more specifically, preconceived expectations of

TABLE 9.7
Mean Peer Judgments

	Significant Effects of Attractiveness		
Characteristic	Attractive Face	Unattractive Face	p
Extrovert/Introvert	53.7	50.8	0.05
Social Class[a]	44.8	52.2	< 0.001
Popular/Unpopular	40.0	47.9	< 0.001
Interesting/Boring[a]	43.8	51.0	< 0.001
Intelligent/Unintelligent	54.8	50.5	< 0.01
Sexually Attractive/ Unattractive[a]	51.8	67.7	< 0.001

	Significant Effects of Dentofacial Features					
Characteristic	Normal Incisors	Harelip	Crowded Incisors	Missing Incisor	Prominent Incisors	p
Friendly/Unfriendly[a]	31.8	40.6	40.3	39.2	37.1	< 0.0001
Social Class[a]	44.3	53.2	48.2	50.9	46.0	< 0.01
Compliant/Aggressive	59.4	52.7	55.5	57.4	62.3	< 0.01
Popular/Unpopular[a]	39.1	47.2	46.1	43.9	45.9	< 0.01
Intelligent/Unintelligent	56.9	49.0	50.2	53.0	54.0	< 0.05

[a] Lower ratings signify more favorable attribution.

their scholastic potential and behavior, may significantly influence actual performance; that is, a self-fulfilling prophecy is established (Brophy & Good, 1974). *Pygmalion in the Classroom*, the much quoted work of Rosenthal and Jacobson (1968), provides an important reference point for this argument. These authors misled teachers in an American school into believing that certain (randomly selected) children showed, on recent screening, exceptional scholastic potential. Remarkably, subsequent objective I.Q. testing revealed that the appointed children had in fact "bloomed." These observations initiated an abundance of investigations and, though much controversy still surrounds the issue, the contention that teachers' expectations can influence the child's eventual attainment has found some support in British junior schools (Crano & Mellon, 1978).

Researchers investigating the physical attractiveness stereotype were among those to undertake experimentation into teacher expectations, the prototype study being that of Clifford and Walster (1973). Teachers in 404 Missouri schools were issued report cards of a fictitious child and asked to make estimates of future scholastic and social performance. The only manipulated variable was the child's facial attractiveness, depicted in a small (routinely) attached photograph. It was found that the child's attractiveness was significantly and positively associated with the teacher's expectations about how intelligent the child was, how interested in education his parents were, how far he was likely to progress in school, and how popular he would be with his peers. A confirmatory study of Salvia et al. (1977) is especially relevant, since genuine teachers' reports completed at the end of a full academic year still revealed favorable bias related to the child's attractiveness. This study, however, failed to find any difference in the child's actual performance as assessed by objective evaluation, bearing out the findings of a second study by Clifford (1975) which concluded that, although attractiveness probably does have an extended influence on teachers' opinions, it is not a predictor of long-term academic success.

Investigation 5 (W.C. Shaw & Humphreys, 1982) was a replicate of the study of Clifford and Walster (1973). A four-factor experimental design was used to determine the effect of sex of child, sex of teacher, attractiveness of child, and child's dentofacial condition on teacher expectations. Copies of the 20 stimulus photographs used in Investigation 3 (discussed previously) were attached to school record cards containing a fictitious report. The report represented the academic progress of an average child (boy or girl) and was held constant for all record cards. In addition, a 16-item questionnaire, dealing with anticipated academic ability, social and family relationships, and personality was prepared. One record card and questionnaire were issued to each of 320 teachers uninformed as to the true nature of the study.

Analysis of variance *failed* to demonstrate any significant main effects; that is, in contrast to the foregoing studies, neither facial attractiveness nor dental condition had bearing on teachers' responses. Only for sex of child, sex of the teacher, and age of teacher were minor effects apparent. A full discussion of the nonoperation of the attractiveness stereotype is presented elsewhere (W.C. Shaw & Humphreys, 1982). The essential point for the present review is that material that successfully evoked stereotyped responses in a highly controlled experimental setting failed to do so in an experimental context of greater real-life validity.

Investigation 6:
The Effect of Facial Deformity on Petitioning

The aim of this project was to examine the effect of three different types of facial deformity in a situation incorporating an element of interaction. Petitioning was chosen to test the effect of facial deformity upon compliance because of the obvious face-to-face interaction involved, the ease of classifying responses to such direct confrontation, the commonplace nature of the situation, and the brevity of each encounter, enabling a large number of responses to be tested.

Since normal individuals seem to avoid those with physical handicaps (Kleck et al., 1968; McGarry & West, 1975, Novak & Lerner, 1968), it was hypothesized that a deformed petitioner would be avoided more than a normal one. A second hypothesis concerned the number of signatures secured by the petitioner. We viewed the experimenter, the subject, and the petition as elements of a triadic system, such as those studied within the framework of balance theory (Heider, 1958; Rosenberg, Hovland, McGuire, Abelson, & Brehm, 1960). Suedfeld, Bochnepl, and Matas (1971), for example, found that dress congruence between petitioner and subject can have the effect of overriding belief congruence, though Bryant (1975) later suggested that this was true only when the beliefs involved are of little importance to the subject. Thus, it was hypothesized that the deformed petitioner would secure fewer endorsements than the normal one when the petition was presented, particularly where the petition statement would evoke low subject involvement.

Responses made by passersby to a request for a signature endorsing a petition were recorded as they related to a number of variables: sex of subject ($X2$), sex of petitioner ($X2$), strength of petition ($X2$), and appearance of petitioner ($X4$). For each condition, the number of signatures, evasions, and refusals were noted.

Two pairs of actors, one male and one female in each pair, were recruited from a local drama college. In order for the actors to provide their own control, for half of the experimental period each was made-up to exhibit a superficial facial deformity. The deformities exhibited were markedly protruding front teeth, a red birthmark on the left cheek, or a burn scar on the left cheek. For the remainder of the experiment the actors appeared in their normal states. The protruding front teeth were carried on an overdenture which seated firmly over the actors' own teeth and left the roof of the mouth uncovered in order that there would be no interference with speech. A television make-up artist created the burn scars with theatrical wax and the birthmarks (portwine stain haemangioma) with textured wax and coloring sticks.

The subjects were 7,200 unaccompanied adult members of the general public. The two petitions used were either (a) judged to be fairly neutral, thus maximizing the deformity cue, or (b) judged to evoke greater strength of feeling, in order to investigate the possibility of reduced effectiveness of such cues in a "high-involvement situation". The former petition was accordingly worded: "We the undersigned believe that there should be a total ban on cigarette advertising", whereas the second petition stated: "We the undersigned believe that possession of a small amount of cannabis (30g) should be legalized." (In the U.K., the ban on cigarette advertising is almost total whereas legalization of cannabis remains an extremely controversial issue. Our choice of the latter as a topic of "high-involvement" was born out by the frequent discussions that ensued between the actors and passersby).

Each signature sheet initially contained five signatures, which functioned as a perceived reference group norm and also maintained the appearance of authenticity. The actors also carried genuine propaganda leaflets on their clipboards appropriate to the respective statement. Full details of the experimental procedure and results are presented elsewhere (W.C. Shaw et al., 1980).

The principle finding was the surprising noneffect of facial deformity with regard to the number of evasions, signings, and refusals obtained. Yet the petition model did prove to be sensitive to variables of interpersonal perception, for one of the female actors did secure consistently more endorsements than the other three actors and both females obtained more endorsements than the males.

A number of explanations were considered for the noneffect of deformity. When the actor first obtained the attention of a passerby, it was hypothesized that aversion to facial disfigurement would cause a greater desire to avoid contact with the deformed actor. This did not prove to be so. Similarly, in keeping with Heider's balance theory (Heider, 1958), it was hypothesized that the deformed actor would secure fewer endorsements when soliciting signatures. There was only limited support for this hypothesis (when the results were collapsed across sex of subject and actor) and this was overridden when the more controversial proposal was presented. Perhaps the type of encounter staged was too sudden and brief to allow underlying stereotyped reactions to affect behavioral responses, or the facial deformities tested were not viewed as sufficiently stigmatizing. Other possibilities are that conflicting responses such as curiosity and sympathy operated to counterbalance aversion.

Experimental evidence indicates that in situations where the norms against staring are suspended, subjects will freely indulge their curiosity (Langer, Fiske, Taylor, & Chanowitz, 1976). Indeed, Langer and coworkers proposed that prior opportunity to stare at physically disabled individuals reduces tension in subsequent interaction. Therefore, the subjects of the present study might have resisted their desire to avoid contact with the deformed petitioner in order to take a better look at the disfigurement.

We may also consider sympathetic response. Under the pretext of a door-to-door survey, and using the presence or absence of an eye patch as a stigmatizing cue, Doob and Ecker (1970) found that the normal subjects were equally willing to submit to an interview regardless of the experimenter's condition. Compliance was actually higher when the experimenter in the eye-patch condition asked subjects to complete the questionnaire in their own time. Similarly, Levitt and Kornhaber (1977) found that a female wearing an orthopedic brace or leg cast secured greater compliance with a request for money than when normal. On the other hand, Soble and Strickland (1974) observed less compliance with a subsequent interview request by a hunch-backed experimenter. It has also been shown that an actor, apparently collapsing in a subway train, elicited less help from fellow passengers when he exhibited a facial birthmark (Piliavin, Piliavin, & Rodin, 1975).

The reaction of normal individuals to those with facial deformities is undoubtedly complex. Whatever aversion is present, this apparently may be modified by other responses such as curiosity and sympathy, and actual behavior may be influenced by factors such as the severity and permanency of the stigma, the cost of helping, the extent of anticipated further contact, and age of subject. Clearly, further research is indicated to examine the influence of facial deformity in extended interactions and, in particular, those involving physical contact and those leading to friendship formation and romantic bonding. Certainly no firm conclusions can be reached yet about the extent to which the prejudice reported by stigmatized individuals is the result of their own unease in interaction (Comer & Piliavin, 1972; Farina, Allen, & Saul, 1968) or negative social stereotyping.

A salutary point arising from this investigation relates to the value and validity of structured, contrived, social–psychological studies of stereotyped response. Although it may be possible in studies allowing little or no interaction to demonstrate possible mechanisms of attribution, the richness and complexity of genuine social intercourse and personality development will overwhelmingly determine the personal and social impact of variations from "normal" or "ideal" facial appearance. This is especially relevant in the clinical context when attempting to determine guidelines for estimation of treatment need; a matter of no little importance given the considerable disadvantages of surgical and orthodontic intervention: expense, pain, time, and inconvenience, and the official stamp of abnormality.

Well-structured, longitudinal, naturalistic studies must be performed to determine meaningful estimates of cosmetic treatment need. The final investigation being reported represents an initial foray in this direction.

Investigation 7:
A Longitudinal Study of Children
with Special Reference to Dentofacial Features

This investigation began in 1981 when a cohort of 12-year-old children was selected by disproportionate stratified sampling in order that dental features of low prevalence, but high orthodontic interest would be well represented. Using preselected criteria, 3420 children were screened, 663 with dental features of high interest were selected and an additional 355 children free of specific anomalies randomly allocated on a pro-rata basis. This gave a final study population of 1018.

Baseline dental data and study casts were collected. Standardized photographs of the face and dentition were also collected and examined by a panel of six lay judges to provide a rating of dental and facial attractiveness (Howells & Shaw, 1985). In addition to demographic and social class data, standardized social–psychological profiles were obtained. Full details of design and procedure are presented elsewhere (W.C. Shaw, Addy, Dummer, Ray, & Frude, 1986).

Assessment Procedures

Child Appraisal. Initially in each school all the children who had been selected to take part in the survey were grouped together and given a classroom administered "package." This consisted of three self-report questionnaires together with a test of cognitive development. The first questionnaire, "The Way I Feel About Myself", is a well-established instrument used to examine children's self-concepts (Piers & Harris, 1969). This questionnaire yields scores on six factors: popularity, happiness and satisfaction, behavior (good or bad), intellectual status, physical appearance, and anxiety. The children were instructed to respond to the statements according to how they felt most of the time, in order to reveal a reliable profile of their self-concept. This was followed by the Goodenough–Harris "Draw-a-person" test (Goodenough & Harris, 1963). The complex scoring procedure of the drawings produces an indication of cognitive development. A second questionnaire was an adaptation of the Olweus (1978) instrument for examining children's attitudes toward, and experience of, aggression. This consists of 57 statements, each followed by a 7-point rating scale for the children to indicate how well each statement applied to them personally. A third questionnaire dealt with smoking behavior and health related issues.

Subsequently each child was interviewed individually for about 20 minutes, and part of the interview was tape-recorded for further analysis. During the interview, after a suitable "warm-up" session, the children were required to describe their own faces, with the aid of a mirror. The children chose from a list their best and worst facial features and were asked to give an indication of their satisfaction with their body size (both height and weight). They were also asked to rate their self-attractiveness on a 5-point scale (from "one of the worst looking" to "one of the best looking"). Another "game" was devised for the interview to reveal each child's person perception constructs (i.e., the way in which they "view the social world"), using the triad method initiated by Kelly (1955). The constructs obtained were later classified into such categories as physical appearance, sporting ability, possessions, and so on. The children were also asked if they had been teased about anything and whether they had ever been given a nickname. The interviewer rated each child on both facial and general attractiveness scales as well as rating each child's social ease during the interview.

A sociometric test was used to reveal each child's popularity amongst the rest of the class. Each child was provided with a numbered list of all the children in the class. They then selected up to six children whom they felt were their friends, and placed these in order of preference.

Teacher Questionnaire. The teachers completed a standard Rutter questionnaire for each child in their class who had been selected for the study (Rutter, Tizard, & Whitmore, 1970). The aim was to assess whether the child exhibited any emotional or behavioral disturbances while at school. Secondly, the teachers were asked to rate each child on a 7-point rating scale for leadership, confidence, popularity, intellect, physical attractiveness and sociability.

Parental Questionnaire. Parents of the children also were asked to complete a questionnaire concerning any behavioral problems displayed by their child. This Rutter parental questionnaire is more comprehensive than the one for teachers, following the assumption that parents have different and more detailed information about their own children. Some items are the same in both the teachers' and parents' questionnaires, enabling direct comparison of results. Both questionnaires include items that yield subscores on such disorders as neuroticism, antisocial behavior, and other behavioral problems.

The cohort has now been reassessed at age 15-16 years by the same team, and detailed synchronic and diachronic analysis are being prepared at the time of writing. Some preliminary observations can be made however.

The Physical Attractiveness Stereotype (at Age 12 Years)

In order to improve the chances of determining clear effects for high-versus-low facial attractiveness, the dichotomy of the 50 most- and 50 least-attractive children was examined. The social-psychological parameters for which a statistically significant difference emerged are listed in Table 9.8.

Unattractive children demonstrated a recognition of this aspect of their own appearance, and in line with the physical attractiveness stereotype, teachers rated their general social characteristics less favorably. Notably however,

TABLE 9.8
High-versus-Low Facial Attractiveness

Significant differences between the 50 most and 50 least
attractive children in the cohort

		Children		
		Boys & Girls (N = 50)	Boys (N = 50)	Girls (N = 50)
Teacher Ratings:	Leadership	$p < 0.001$	$p < 0.05$	$p < 0.05$
	Confidence	$p < 0.051$	$p < 0.05$	$p < 0.01$
	Popularity	$p < 0.001$	$p < 0.01$	$p < 0.001$
	Academic Brightness	NS	NS	NS
	Physical Attractiveness	$p < 0.001$	$p < 0.001$	$p < 0.001$
	Sociability	$p < 0.001$	$p < 0.001$	$p < 0.01$
Self-concept:	Physical Appearance	$p < 0.05$	NS	$p < 0.01$
Interview:	Self Attractiveness	$p < 0.01$	$p < 0.001$	$p < 0.05$

judgments of academic brightness were not biased. This is particularly interesting because these were the registration teachers of the subjects (responsible for checking attendance, etc., but only limited teaching) and would have a general knowledge of subjects' performance over the range of school work from various sources.

No effects were demonstrable for the teacher and parent Rutter scores for school and home behavior, nor for scores of cognitive development. Subjects' self-concepts in respect to popularity, happiness and satisfaction, general social behavior, intellectual status, and anxiety did not differ significantly and the objective popularity of the unattractive children, as measured in the sociometric tests, was not adversely affected.

A small number of isolated differences from individual items of the Olweus questionnaire also emerged, but these did not conform to any recognizable pattern. In sum, perhaps the most striking finding is the noneffect of attractiveness over a broad group of features for the cohort at 12 years.

The Impact of Dentofacial Anomalies

The impact of the most severe variations of dentofacial appearance was also appraised by comparing groups of subjects with conspicuous anomalies against a group of subjects with normal dental appearance. For example, in one group of 65 subjects with severe overjet (incisor prominence) in excess of 9mm, the data indicate that this dental anomaly reduced the childrens' general attractiveness and that this was recognized by the subjects and their parents. However, no important differences distinguished the group in terms of self-esteem, teacher and parent perceptions of behavior and adjustment, objective popularity, and the other social–psychological parameters recorded.

The analysis of this material continues and the effects during the teenage years of treated versus not-treated dentofacial anomalies and high-versus-low attractiveness will receive particular attention.

CONCLUDING REMARKS

Studies that have pointed to the operation of a physical attractiveness stereotype have on the whole been noninteractive and have maximized the effect of attractiveness by presenting extremes of the attractiveness continuum. But attractiveness effects have to be studied very critically. In Investigation 4, the "beautiful-is-good" stereotype did not operate uniformly in favor of the attractive woman; that is, she was judged to be less friendly, less kind, and less honest than her unattractive counterpart (W.C. Shaw et al., 1985). A similar reversal of the physical attractiveness hypothesis was found in a study of American students, in which attractive women were expected to be more conceited, egotistical, likely to engage in adultery, and unsympathetic (Dermer & Thiel, 1975).

For studies conducted so as to exclude the myriad of variables attending genuine human interaction, only guarded extrapolation is appropriate. The degree to which first impressions continue to operate in subsequent interaction when the perceiver has the opportunity to process further information about the subject is uncertain. Certainly some investigations have suggested that initial impressions may have an extended influence, at least over the short term. For example, in the supposed setting of a computer dating program among college students, the physical attractiveness of a partner was a stronger predictor of the continuing desire to sustain a relationship than any of a large number of other attributes or interests (Walster et al., 1966). A similar conclusion was reached in a study of friendship in a summer camp setting (Kleck et al., 1974). This effect however, did not emerge from the study described previously (Investigation 7), where sociometric choice was based on attitudes formed over an extended period of everyday school life.

A particular issue requiring detailed attention is the place of facial deformity, generalized or local, with regard to the physical attractiveness stereotype. Perhaps the general assumption that deformity is simply at the lower end of the continuum is too simplistic, and instead deformity-versus-normality should be regarded within another framework. Certainly, many fundamental issues remain to be settled in this field, and the existing body of knowledge is an unsatisfactory basis for public health planning. We have hardly begun to understand the enormous variation in personal response and adjustment to imperfections of appearance, or the impact of other qualities of the individual in ameliorating the effect of a facial flaw.

Duly sensitive naturalistic studies involve considerable methodological difficulties and complex evaluation. In the view of this author, however, they are essential if we are to arrive at meaningful estimates of treatment priority that are appropriate to the needs of individual patients.

10 The Role of Perception in Treatment of Impaired Facial Appearance

Judith E. Albino
Lisa A. Tedesco
State University of New York at Buffalo

I. Social Meanings of Facial Attractiveness and Disfigurement
II. Evaluating the Aesthetic Impairment of Malocclusion
III. Professional, Peer, and Self-Perceptions of Malocclusion
   A. Professional Perceptions of Malocclusion
   B. Peer Perceptions of Malocclusion
   C. Self-Perceptions of Malocclusion
IV. Perceptions and Treatment Outcomes
V. Developmental Influences
VI. Familial Influences
VII. A Final Comment

Congenital craniofacial anomalies and other medical and dental conditions that result in disfigurement or impaired appearance of the head and facial structures present some particularly challenging problems for health-care professionals, as well as for those affected by these conditions. Not the least of these problems is that of determining the full psychological and social, as well as physical and functional, impact of such conditions. This is true whether the impairment is the result of one of the relatively mild and commonly occurring forms of malocclusion or of a more severe congenital abnormality, acute disease, or traumatic injury. Furthermore, treatment of virtually all of these conditions requires complex procedures that are long term, often repetitive, and invariably expensive. Commitment to treatment on the part of the patient is usually essential to a successful outcome. For these reasons, treatment decisions must include a consideration of the subjective perception and meaning of disfigurement to the patient, as well as consideration of the reactions of others.

Health-care professionals working with craniofacially impaired patients have long accepted the fact that degree of disfigurement and, consequently, the potential psychological and social effects of disfigurement, must be evaluated in terms of individual response, as well as clinical assessment of the severity of impaired appearance. One individual with a relatively mild form of facial disfigurement may be affected far more profoundly than another with a seemingly more significant defect. Although theory suggests that individual expectations, social experiences, social support, personality, and cognitive variables, as well as development, may play a role in determining response to impaired facial appearance, the available data do not as yet provide for prediction of individual responses. The specific ways in which personal and social variables interact to mediate individual response remain largely undefined. We can state with assurance only that it is the *perceived* degree of disfigurement that is critical, rather than the extent of impairment in any absolute sense.

This chapter focuses on those variables that are hypothesized to be associated with social and psychological responses to impaired facial appearance, particularly in terms of desire for treatment and satisfaction with its results. Some data and findings are presented from a selected group of studies, and these are discussed against the background of a social–psychological explanation of the role of appearance in interpersonal interactions.

SOCIAL MEANINGS OF FACIAL ATTRACTIVENESS AND DISFIGUREMENT

It has been suggested that concepts of physical attractiveness are biogenetic in origin. This has never been adequately demonstrated, however, and it is clear only that aesthetic preferences with respect to facial characteristics are expressed very early in life. Kagan, Henker, Hen-Tov, Levine, and Lewis (1966) demonstrated that infants as young as 4 months can discriminate, and respond differentially to pleasant and unpleasant representations of faces. Studies by Dion (1973) and Dion and Berscheid (1974) of preschool children showed that attractiveness influences how much even every young children are liked by their peers. Other research has demonstrated the positive relationship of physical attractiveness to interpersonal popularity in adults (e.g., Kleck & Rubenstein, 1975); and to others' favorable evaluations of personality (e.g., Walster, Aronson, Abrahams, & Rottmann, 1966); social behavior; and academic ability (e.g., Clifford & Walster, 1973). Results and implications of these investigations have been discussed at length elsewhere (Adams, 1977, 1981, 1982; Alley & Hildebrandt, this volume; Berscheid & Walster, 1974). It suffices to say, therefore, that there is ample evidence that facial attractiveness is a construct that can be reliably measured and is relatively stable across social settings and tasks. There is also considerable research evidence to suggest that people actually behave differently toward attractive and unattractive individuals (Alley & Hildebrandt, this volume). For example, Kleck and Rubenstein (1975) found that attractive individuals elicit more smiles and longer periods of visual attending from those interacting with them than do less attractive ones. Brundage, Derlega, and Cash (1977) found that participants in their studies shared more information about themselves with attractive than with unattractive individuals.

Such findings from the empirical basis for a social psychology of attractiveness that helps us to understand the ways in which appearance affects social behavior. Adams (1977) provided a summary of this process in the form of four assumptions about outer appearance and inner-personal experiences. These are: (a) attractiveness and unattractiveness elicit different social expectations from others; (b) more attractive individuals are the recipients of more favorable social interactions; (c) as a result of these more frequent favorable social experiences, attractive individuals are more likely to develop positive expectations and social images, as well as personality styles and behaviors that reflect this; and (d) as a result of their positive social experiences and greater self-confidence, attractive persons are more likely to initiate and maintain satisfying interpersonal behaviors and relationships with others.

Research on social and psychological responses to disfiguring handicaps has often resulted in findings consistent with those of the studies on attractiveness. Moreover, studies on perceptions of handicaps conducted by Richardson (1970, 1971; Richardson, Goodman, Hastorf, & Dornbusch, 1961) have revealed that children with far more severe and physically disabling handicaps are rated more favorably by others than are children with handicaps such as facial scars and obesity that are primarily impairments of appearance. Based on his studies of individuals stigmatized by visible physical handicaps, Kleck (1966, 1969) concluded that handicapped individuals view themselves as ineffective in social situations. Studies of children with cleft lip and/or palate, the most frequently occurring congenital craniofacial defect, have revealed these children to be more socially restrained and lacking in social skills (McWilliams, 1982; Peter, Chinsky, & Fisher, 1975; Richman, 1976, 1978; Richman & Harper, 1978, 1979; Simonds & Heimburger, 1978; Spriesterbach, 1973). Furthermore, when compared with normal control subjects, children with facial clefts have reported feeling less accepted by their parents (Brantley & Clifford, 1979a, 1979b), more dissatisfied with their appearance (Kapp, 1979), and more inhibited (Starr, 1978). In addition, when Heller, Tidmarsh, and Pless (1981) interviewed 96 Canadian young adults born with cleft lip and/or cleft palate, more than half reported that their conditions had negatively affected their social lives. Approximately 10% were judged to have inadequate psychosocial adjustment, and another 23% were judged to be functioning only marginally in this respect. Although psychosocial functioning was not related to objective assessment of the severity of impairment, it was strongly related to dissatisfaction with appearance. These findings suggest again that it is the aspects of impairment that are *perceived* as most likely to interfere with social interaction that will cause distress. Although the literature fails to support the notion that either general intellectual or personality deficits are associated with cleft palate (Clifford, 1983; Tobiasen, 1984), findings such as those described here do point to frequent and significant psychosocial problems that generally fit within the same explanatory models used in understanding the effects of normal variation in attractiveness on behavior.

The broad range of more commonly occurring malocclusions have been less frequently studied than facial clefts. Yet there is reason to believe that problems of social adjustment also occur in those whose appearance is impaired by malocclusion, that broad range of conditions in which the teeth are poorly aligned and do not close together properly. Macgregor (1970) has suggested that children with these milder forms of facial disfigurement may actually be at greater risk for developing psychological problems. She reasoned that for these individuals the responses of others are less predictable, thereby creating a higher degree of uncertainly and anxiety in the anticipation of social reactions. This suggests less consistency in the feedback received from social interactions and the possibility that those affected will develop neither the self-confidence and high self-esteem accruing to the physically attractive, nor the coping skills forged by the severely impaired who must adjust to the inevitability of others' responses.

EVALUATING THE AESTHETIC IMPAIRMENT OF MALOCCLUSION

Although data directly addressing the issue of psychosocial response to malocclusion are sparse, there are some studies that demonstrate the effects of malocclusion on appearance. Research involving various procedures for evaluating dental–facial attractiveness has shown that when other facial features are held constant, normal occlusion is perceived as more attractive than various forms of malocclusion. In most such studies the effects of malocclusion have been represented in photographs or drawings (Albino, 1981; Cohen & Horowitz, 1970; Jenny, Cons, Kohout, & Frazier, 1980; Lucker, Graber & Pietromonaco, 1981; Prahl-Andersen, 1978; Shaw, 1981b; Tedesco, Albino, Cunat, Green, Lewis, & Slakter, 1983; Tedesco, Albino, Cunat, Slakter, & Waltz, 1983). In a study of 774 school children that was focused on assessing the relative salience of health and appearance motives, Gochman (1972, 1975) found that some children preferred straight, evenly spaced teeth with noticeable carious lesions to healthy, but crowded and poorly aligned dentition. Children over 12 and suburban residents generally made this choice, although inner-city children under the age of 12 preferred the healthier teeth. Only 20% of all subjects clearly preferred the healthier, but more crowded teeth.

Shaw (1981b) altered photographs of children to show either normal occlusion or occlusal malrelations within the same face. He found that both children and adults identified the faces with normal occlusion as more attractive, more intelligent, less inclined to aggression, and more desirable as friends than were the faces with any of four types of occlusal impairment. When other facial features were varied to influence attractiveness, however, subjects always preferred the more attractive face, regardless of occlusal features. These results suggest that although attractiveness of other features of the face may be more salient than dental appearance, visible aspects of occlusion do influence perceptions of general attractiveness. This conclusion is consistent with Lucker, Graber, and Pietromonaco's (1981) description of occlusal malrelations as detectable "signals" that influence facial aesthetics.

Based on confidential interviews with 531 children 9 to 13 years old, Shaw, Meek, and Jones (1980; reviewed in chap. 9) found that teeth represented the fourth most common target of teasing, after height, weight, and hair. They reported that young children with malocclusion are sometimes the targets of teasing, harassment, and unflattering nicknames related to problems of occlusion and dental–facial appearance. Interestingly, teasing about the teeth resulted in strong feelings of upset and the sense of being harassed significantly more often than did other types of teasing. Although few children reported such teasing, the data certainly suggest that unattractive occlusal appearance can result in negative social interactions.

Dating was the situation for which dental–facial appearance was perceived as most important by young people, according to a study reported by Linn (1966). Only 15% of respondents indicated that dental–facial appearance was not important in the social situations described to them. Samuels and Proshek (1973) found that dental–facial appearance was considered especially important in occupations that their subjects had ranked as high in prestige or visibility.

In other studies, investigators have attempted to demonstrate the effects of malocclusion on psychosocial functioning by examining changes in self-image and other personality measures that follow orthodontic treatment. Rutzen (1973) studied 252 persons 5 years after they completed orthodontic treatment and compared them with 67 individuals who had not received treatment for diagnosed malocclusions. Those treated reported significantly more positive assessments of their appearance, and far less frequently mentioned oral features as their worst facial characteristics. Rutzen also found that treated subjects had achieved a slightly, but significantly, higher level of occupational status than had nontreated subjects, even though they did not differ on social class or educational level. Treated subjects had lower levels of anxiety but did not obtain higher scores on Rosenberg's Self-Esteem Scale or on measures of extraversion or neuroticism.

Dennington and Korabik (1977) found positive changes on Tennessee Self-Concept Scale scores for a group of 77 patients measured before treatment and 7 months after being fitted with orthodontic bands. On the other hand,

Klima, Wittemann, and McIver (1979) found no significant differences on measures of body image or self-concept between groups of orthodontic patients whose fixed appliances recently had been removed, prospective patients, and individuals not receiving treatment.

In summary then, it is clear that normal occlusion generally is perceived as more attractive than dental-facial malrelations, both by those affected and by others. In addition, it appears that there is probably some negative social feedback associated with highly visible and less-attractive forms of dental-facial malrelations. For some individuals these negative experiences may result in defensive responses such as withdrawal, isolation, and even depression. Because malocclusions are often very highly visible and yet may not represent an overriding determinant of facial attractiveness, these conditions offer some interesting challenges. Responses to malocclusion, either by the individual affected, or by those with whom he or she associates, will probably not be directly related to the objective severity of impairment. Rather, response will be mediated by a variety of psychological and social variables that may affect treatment decisions, as well as perceptions of and satisfaction with appearance.

PROFESSIONAL, PEER, AND SELF-PERCEPTIONS OF MALOCCLUSION

Although congenital defects and traumatic injuries are generally considered to cause greater disfigurement than do most forms of malocclusion, these latter types of facial impairment affect enormous numbers of people. Estimates based on epidemiological research indicate, conservatively, that 70% to 75% of the population are affected by some form of occlusal malrelations that could be treated beneficially by orthodontic techniques (Jago, 1974; Kelly & Harvey, 1977).

Among those who actually seek treatment, an estimated 80% do so for cosmetic reasons (Rosenberg, 1974). Practicing orthodontics also generally acknowledge that the need for orthodontic treatment is based most often on aesthetic factors, rather than on concerns for health or function (Foster & Menezes, 1976). As a result, guidelines for determining the need for orthodontic treatment often have been expanded to include those who appear to suffer impaired self-esteem or other personal or social difficulties as the result of perceived malocclusion. Indeed, it now appears that while malocclusion refers by definition to physical deviations from ideal occlusion, the effects of these conditions for those who experience them are almost entirely psychological or social in impact (Macgregor, 1951, 1970; Secord & Backman, 1959; Stricker, 1970; Stricker et al., 1979).

At the State University of New York at Buffalo School of Dental Medicine, a series of studies have been focused on identifying and assessing the social and psychological correlates of malocclusion, including the assessment of perceived effects on appearance. The first studies at Buffalo, completed during 1977 to 1981, involved the development of methods to measure psychological and social variables that appeared to be related to decisions to seek treatment for adolescents. Data were collected from 50 eighth- and ninth-grade children who planned to begin orthodontic treatment within 6 months and from a comparison group of 113 children who were randomly selected from school rosters and did not seek such treatment. A second study involved 52 children planning treatment and a comparison group of 102. Data also were collected from the mothers and fathers of these children, as well as from their nearest in age siblings, in order to study the social context and familial influences related to children's perceptions of malocclusion and the need for treatment.

The initial selection of variables to be studied was based on extensive review of relevant research and theories of human behavior, as well as on informal, open-ended interviews with children seeking orthodontic treatment (Albino, 1977). The measures and variables studied fell into two very general categories. The first comprised dental-specific measures, including perceptions of malocclusion and attitudes toward malocclusion and its treatment, as well as objective measures of dental–facial appearance and occlusion, and cooperation in orthodontic treatment. The second group of variables included measures of psychosocial content, including personality and general attitude measures not directly related to malocclusion and orthodontic treatment. Using treatment-seeking versus nonseeking as a criterion measure, discriminant analyses were conducted on the two sets of variables (Albino et al., 1981).

Eight measures from the dental-specific group and four measures from the psychosocial group of variables were found to significantly discriminate between the adolescents seeking treatment and those not seeking treatment. Additional discriminant analyses were then conducted using only those variables that had provided significant discrimination in the earlier analyses. In these final analyses, the psychosocial measures added little to the strong discrimination provided by the measures that were focused directly on malocclusion. Fully 82% of the cases could be identified correctly as seeking or not seeking treatment on the basis of these four measures. The measures providing the greatest discrimination, in order of contribution to the discriminant function, were:

1. *Treatment Priority Index* (TPI) (Grainger, 1967). This objective measure of severity of malocclusion produces a score based on a weighted sum of actual measurements made in the mouth. Higher scores reflect more severe occlusal malrelations.

2. *Concern About Occlusion* (Albino, 1981). This is a subscale of a longer questionnaire covering many aspects of malocclusion and orthodontic treatment. It provides direct self-reports in response to questions regarding attitudes toward malocclusion and its treatment. Higher scores reflect greater levels of concern about occlusal appearance and functioning.

3. *Dental–Facial Attractiveness* (DFA) (Tedesco, Albino, Cunat, Green, Lewis, & Slakter, 1983; Tedesco et al., 1983). This measure is based on assessments of the attractiveness of subjects' dental–facial features, as seen in photographs. Ratings are made by age peers who rate each photograph on a scale of 1 to 5, using standard reference photographs that represent 5 levels of attractiveness. Higher scores indicate more negative assessment.

4. *Child's Perception of Occlusion* (CPO) (Albino et al., 1981). This measure produces a self-perception score that is based on children's rankings for attractiveness of eight drawings of discrete occlusal types and selection of a "self-image" from among these types. Higher scores indicate more negative perceptions of appearance.

These results from discriminant analyses led the investigators to conclude that an understanding of treatment decisions as a response to malocclusion would be most productively studied by focusing on how adolescents, their peers, and significant others, as well as professionals, view dental–facial attractiveness. To that end, an investigation of relationships among the various assessments of malocclusion and dental–facial appearance was undertaken, as well as a thorough study of each approach to assessment.

These studies involved three basic approaches to evaluating orthodontic treatment, as already described: professional assessment of severity (TPI), peer evaluations of appearance (DFA), and self-perception of occlusal appearance (CPO). Each of these measures represents a very different perspective, and correlations among the three reflect this. Table 10.1 shows the correlations between these measures for subjects in each of the two studies described.

The objective measurements of severity of malocclusion (TPI) are related at moderate levels to peer evaluations of the attractiveness of photographs (DFA), but at lower levels to children's perceptions of their own dental–facial attractiveness (CPO). The somewhat higher correlations between children's self-ratings and peer ratings may reflect a shared understanding of cultural norms for occlusal appearance and the strong influence of adolescent peer

TABLE 10.1
Correlations Between Professional, Peer,
and Self-Evaluations of Malocclusion in Two Studies

	DFA (Peer)	CPO (Self)
TPI (Professional)	.42, .47	.26, .31
DFA (Peer)		.34, .38

Note: All correlations are significant ($p < .05$).

groups in the internalization of such standards. These data, however, are based on the two studies that included both children seeking orthodontic treatment and larger groups who were not seeking treatment. When correlations between these scores for the two groups were calculated separately, however, the relationships were especially weak for children seeking treatment.

The same pattern was found in a more recent study involving 93 children, all of whom were seeking treatment (Albino, Davis, Tedesco, Cunat, Lewis, & Slakter, 1985). Those correlations are presented in Table 10.2. Here the correlation between CPO and TPI is not significant, and the relationship between DFA and CPO is stronger than that between TPI and DFA. The lower correlations overall produced by this sample are assumed to be a function of smaller sample size and the restriction of range resulting from sample characteristics. Because all subjects were seeking treatment, it can be assumed that all measures reflect greater degrees of malocclusion or perceived malocclusion.

TABLE 10.2
Correlations Between Professional, Peer, and Self-Evaluations of Malocclusion for 93 Children Seeking Treatment

	DFA (Peer)	CPO (Self)
TPI (Professional)	.17*	.11
DFA (Peer)		.33*

*$p < .05$

Again, these results are not surprising. The TPI scores involve measurements of less visible, posterior relations of the teeth, as well as the highly visible, anterior ones. Although scoring of the TPI provides added weight to visible deviations, it is not intended to evaluate attractiveness of occlusion per se, but rather, severity of malocclusion.

Professional Perceptions of Malocclusion

There has been considerable discussion about how malocclusion should be evaluated for the purpose of identifying treatment need, and a number of indices have been developed in attempts to standardize these evaluations. Carlos (1970), Katz (1978), and Helm (1977) have reviewed available measures and examined their reliability and validity. Efforts to consider the aesthetic effects of occlusal malrelations have been included in a number of such standardized indices. These have included the Draker Labiolingual Deviations Index (Draker, 1960), the Grainger Treatment Priority Index (Grainger, 1967), the Salzmann AAO Handicapping Malocclusion Assessment Record

(Salzmann, 1971), the Occlusal Index (Summers, 1971), and the Eastman Esthetic Index (Howitt, Stricker, & Henderson, 1967). Despite such efforts, however, standardized measures tend to be perceived as inadequate, in part because of their lack of grounding in socially defined aesthetic standards. Furthermore, clinicians prefer to rely on their own judgments of the aesthetic, as well as functional, impairment suffered by their patients (Albino, 1984). Because treatment is individually prescribed, these professional evaluations of facial aesthetics will directly affect both treatment decisions and outcome; thus, the orthodontist plays a pivotal role in the relationship between appearance and treatment.

The components of clinical evaluations made by orthodontists were the subject of a study by Lewis, Albino, Cunat, and Tedesco (1982), who also compared these clinical evaluations with a standardized measure of malocclusion (TPI). They asked five dentists enrolled in a graduate specialty program on orthodontics to rate plaster study casts of occlusal characteristics for 21 children seeking orthodontic treatment and 29 not seeking treatment. Six sets of ratings were made blind by each dentist to provide a score of one to five on each of the following criteria: need for treatment, degree of malocclusion, potential for tissue loss, occlusal stability, dental–facial attractiveness, and interference with masticatory function. Ratings on the first two criteria were repeated after 9 weeks, and dentists also examined the casts to obtain standardized Treatment Priority Index scores 6 weeks after the initial set of ratings were made. Results indicated interrater reliabilities on these measures ranging from .42 to .81, with most above .75. Retest reliabilities were in the .80's. All of the ratings based on clinical judgments were significantly correlated at moderately high levels with TPI scores, with dental–facial attractiveness assessments attaining the highest correlation ($r = .70$). Need for treatment and degree of malocclusion ratings produced correlations with TPI scores of .65 and .64, respectively. Dental–facial attractiveness ratings were also highly correlated with both need for treatment ($r = .80$) and degree of malocclusion ($r = .80$).

In addition to providing general support for the reliability of clinical judgments of malocclusion, this work confirms a central role for aesthetic factors in the determination of these judgments. In fact, the data seem to indicate that neither functional nor aesthetic manifestations of malocclusion can be clearly separated from judgments about general severity of a condition.

These findings suggest that professional evaluations of the severity of malocclusion place strong emphasis on appearance, as well as on function, and this may account for some of the correlation between professional and lay assessments. Nevertheless, the intercorrelations of standardized clinical measures of malocclusion (TPI), peer ratings of dental–facial attractiveness (DFA), and self-perceptions of occlusion (CPO), also indicate important discrepancies among these three different sources of evaluation.

Peer Perceptions of Malocclusion

Measures of peer perceptions of dental–facial attractiveness reflecting normative standards of an appropriate reference group would seem to provide an important element for understanding responses to malocclusion. Jenny and Cons and their colleagues (Cons, Jenny, Freer, Eismann, & Kohout, 1982; Jenny et al., 1980) have recently reported on the development of measures of dental–facial appearance based on normative ratings of the attractiveness of photographs of plaster study casts. In the Albino studies at Buffalo (Albino, 1981; Tedesco, Albino, Cunat, Green et al., 1983; Tedesco, Albino, Cunat, Slakter, & Waltz, 1983), the dental–facial attractiveness (DFA) measures reflect social standards based on ratings of photographs of subjects' mouths. This group has demonstrated the association between their measure of dental–facial attractiveness (DFA) and indices of severity of occlusal malrelations, as already described.

In developing the DFA measures, eighth- and ninth-grade children seeking orthodontic treatment and those not seeking treatment were rated for dental–facial attractiveness by adolescent peer judges and by dentists (Tedesco et al., 1983). As described previously, standard reference photographs comprising a 5-point scale were used to assign attractiveness scores to photographs of study participants. Scale-point photographs and study participants' photographs were three-quarter views of the mouths and jaws, and reference photographs were selected separately for males and females, and for Blacks and Whites. One set of such reference photographs is shown in Fig. 10.1. The photographed children also had been assessed for severity of occlusal malrelations using the Treatment Priority Index (Grainger, 1967). Not only did children seeking treatment have significantly higher malocclusion severity (TPI) scores than those not seeking treatment; they also were perceived as significantly less attractive by their peers. Significant correlations between severity of malocclusion and dental–facial attractiveness ranged from the teens to the high 40s, depending on the study sample. These data suggest that judgments of facial aesthetics are not completely captured by clinical indices of malocclusion.

The study by Lewis and his colleagues (Lewis et al., 1982) described earlier also included an examination of relationships between component scores on the TPI and clinical judgments of dental–facial attractiveness. TPI components that were most strongly related to peer perceptions of facial aesthetics, as measured by the DFA, were those that measure the most obvious occlusal malrelations, such as crowding and spacing problems that occur in the anterior section of the mouth. When orthodontists' ratings for dental–facial attractiveness were compared with adolescent peer ratings, correlations between the two sets were high ($r = .72$ to $.83$). However, orthodontists consistently judged the occlusal conditions of children with malocclusion as more attractive than did the adolescent peer raters. This suggests either that adolescents are harsher judges of malocclusion or, alternatively, that adoles-

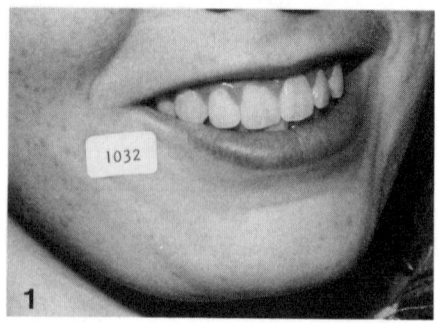

Most Attractive

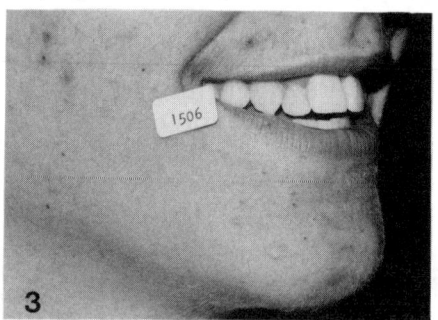

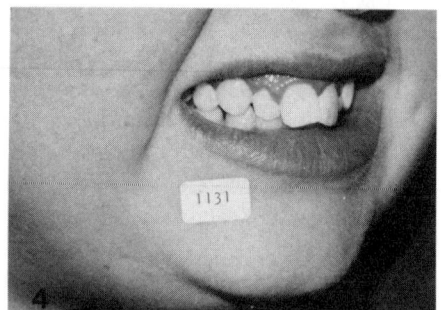

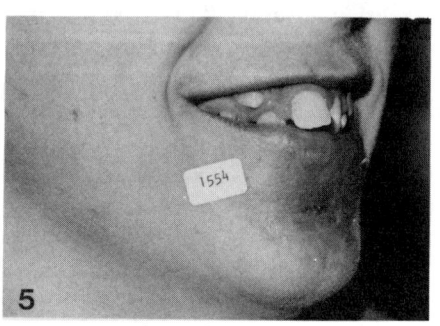

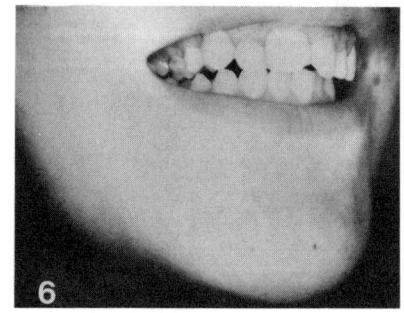

Least Attractive

This child received a score of 4.00 for dental–facial attractiveness

FIG. 10.1 Standard photographs for dental–facial attractiveness scale

cent standards for attractiveness are more sensitive to highly visible, but not necessarily severe, indications of malocclusion (Tedesco, Albino, Cunat, Green et al., 1983; Tedesco, Albino, Cunat, Slakter, & Waltz, 1983).

These studies of the DFA measure have also indicated that the judgments involved in these scores are generally understood and that photographs are consistently evaluated. Intraclass reliability coefficients of .61 to .90, depending on the sex and race of faces in the photographs, have been obtained.

Although peer evaluations may be highly suggestive of social judgments of attractiveness, such peer judgments are not necessarily tied to a standard of ideal occlusion. Consequently, an individual's desire for treatment cannot be equated with his or her clinical need for treatment. With this in mind, professional perceptions and peer perceptions of appearance can be thought of as parts of a social-clinical dynamic that the individual uses to develop and maintain his or her self-perception.

Research on the relationship of peer evaluations and self-evaluations of occlusal appearance has not demonstrated a causal connection. Yet, empirical data and theoretical work suggest that assessment of self-evaluations of dental-facial attractiveness should be made with reference to internalized standards that are forged from standards of the relevant peer group. This seems particularly true in dealing with adolescents and young adults who tend to be extremely peer-oriented in their expressions of values and attitudes.

Self-Perceptions of Malocclusion

The technique for assessing perceived occlusal appearance that was developed at Buffalo (Albino, 1981) is embedded in a task that allows comparison with normative standards. Adolescents' rankings of pictures demonstrating eight general types of occlusal features (see Fig. 10.2) revealed a consistent hierarchy of preferences, both for those seeking and those not seeking treatment. With very few, and only minor, changes in the rank orders, this hierarchy was also found in the ratings of attractiveness made by siblings of the adolescents in the study and by their mothers and fathers. Comparisons of rankings by male and female, and Black and White subjects, revealed similar consistency in rankings among these groups. These data strongly support the concept of general social standards for occlusal attractiveness. Moreover, these rankings were almost identical to those obtained 10 years earlier by Cohen and Horowitz (1970) in their study using different illustrations of the same occlusal types. Regardless of which instrument was used and regardless of rater characteristics, problems of crowding, spacing, and protrusion of the maxilla or both mandible and maxilla were seen as more objectionable than mandibular protrusions, open bite, midline deviations or, of course, normal occlusion.

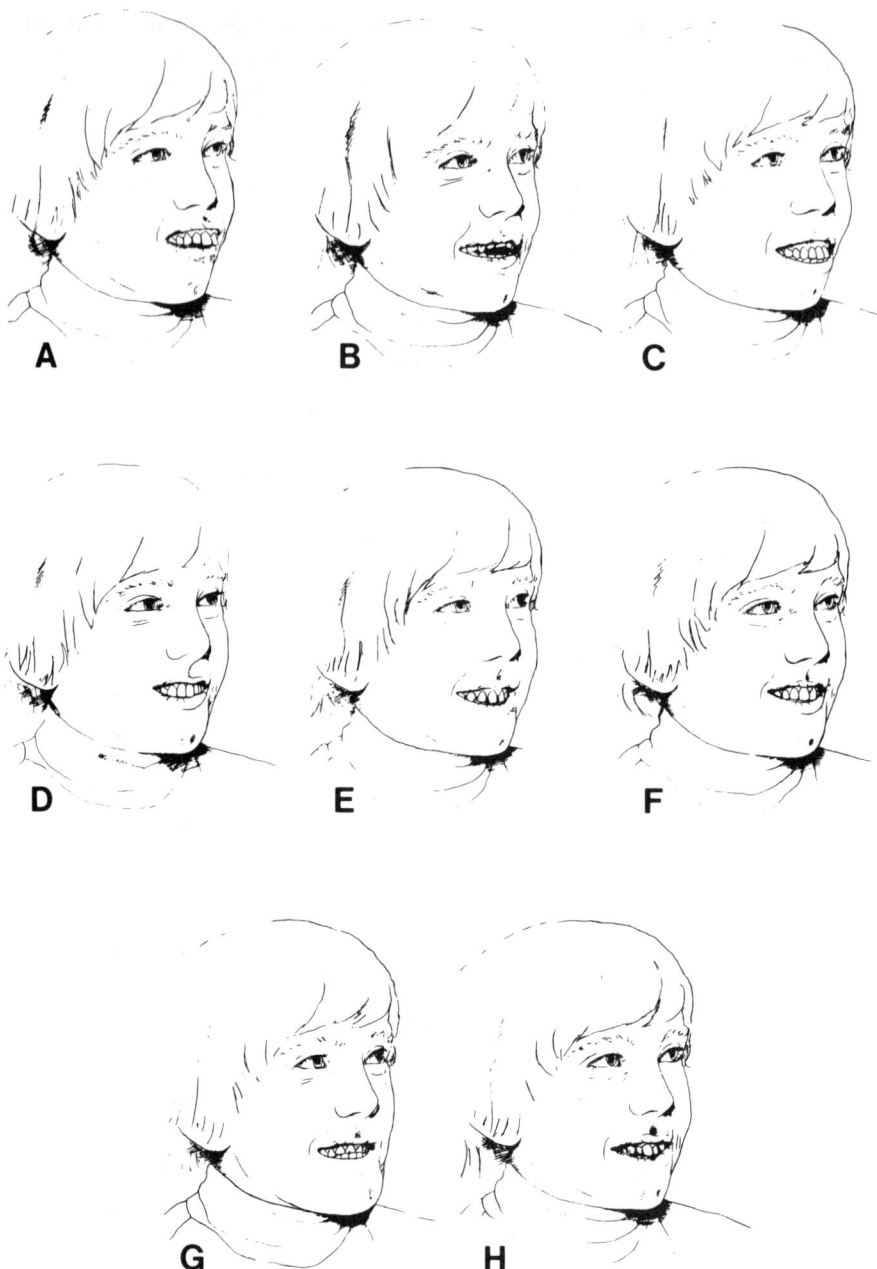

FIG. 10.2 Drawings used to assess perception of child's occlusion (White males). These drawings represent: (A) maxillary protrusion, (B) open bite, (C) bimaxillary protrusion, (D) midline deviation, (E) excess spacing, (F) ideal occlusion, (G) mandibular protrusion, and (H) crowding.

In additional studies of the self-perception method for evaluating malocclusion, Albino, Lewis, Wu, Slakter, and Fox (1979) reported that when only those children seeking treatment were considered, there were no significant correlations between professional (TPI), peer (DFA), and self-assessments (CPO). This suggests that some psychological distortion is present in the responses made by children seeking treatment, and perhaps in the values underlying their responses. For children not seeking treatment, however, dental–facial attractiveness was related both to TPI scores ($r = .34$) and to self-perception scores ($r = .23$). When TPI scores were used as a covariable, thereby statistically adjusting for subject differences on objective severity of malocclusion, Albino and Tedesco (1981) found that children not seeking treatment had significantly more positive perceptions of the acceptability of their occlusal characteristics than did children seeking treatment. Their DFA scores, reflecting peer evaluations of dental–facial attractiveness, were also more positive. On close examination of the Buffalo self-perception data (Lewis, Fox, Albino, Slakter, and Wu, 1979), it appeared that when a rank order approach was used, children seeking treatment evaluated the attractiveness of their particular type of malocclusion very much as others did. Children not seeking treatment, however, tended systematically to overestimate the relative attractiveness of the occlusal characteristics that they perceived to be most like their own. So although children seeking treatment seem to evaluate their appearance in terms of the same hierarchy of attractiveness of occlusal types, the data suggest that they may be harsh in their judgments of where their own appearance fits into that hierarchy.

The results of studies in which children have been asked to evaluate their own dental–facial attractiveness have suggested that they have difficulty performing such tasks with accuracy. Shaw (1981b) found that the majority of 200 children tested could neither identify photographs of their own teeth and jaws, nor accurately describe their anterior occlusal features. In contrast, fairly accurate evaluations were reported by Graber and Lucker (1980), who asked 481 children who were 10 to 13 years old to assess the "straightness" of their teeth. When asked to assess their level of satisfaction with the appearance of their teeth, however, these same children demonstrated a distinctly positive bias, thereby suggesting the possibility of a general response set. Pitt and Korabik (1977) found that children with high self-esteem judged their profiles to be closer to an ideal than they actually were, whereas those with low self-esteem judged their profiles to be further from the ideal than they actually were.

Several conclusions can be drawn from this consideration of various sources of aesthetic evaluations of dental–facial appearance. First, professional evaluations are reasonably stable and seem to be rather closely tied to severity of condition. Second, peer ratings of attractiveness based on photographs are also reasonably stable, but are related at somewhat lower levels to assessments of condition severity. Self-perceptions of occlusion, however—at least in adolescence—appear to lack consistency in their relationship to either of the other types of evaluation. Although social and cultural standards are important, they do not adequately account for children's perceptions of their appearance. It is self-perceptions that are most important in determining demand for treatment, however, and because correction of aesthetic impairment is generally considered elective, in determining need for treatment as well.

PERCEPTIONS AND TREATMENT OUTCOMES

Having examined the relationship between perception of appearance and decisions to seek and provide treatment for the correction of aesthetic defects related to malocclusion, it remains to explore the role of perceptions in determining treatment results. Although few studies have directly addressed this issue, there are some indications that perceptions could affect treatment.

Maxillofacial and plastic reconstructive surgeons have long expressed concern that psychological problems may follow treatment of patients with distorted perceptions of the severity of aesthetic impairments (Peterson & Topazian, 1974, 1976). Research focused on responses to the correction of oral–facial defects, however, has shown that patients are generally satisfied with the results achieved. Hutton (1967) found that all of his patients expressed satisfaction with the results of their surgery for mandibular protrusion, that 90% believed there were major improvements in aesthetics, and that 50% thought their personalities had improved. Crowell, Sazima, and Elder (1970) reported that 94% of their 33 subjects were satisfied when questioned from 3 to 42 months after surgery. Olson and Laskin (1980) also found high levels of satisfaction among a group of patients receiving orthognathic surgery.

Kiyak, West, Hohl, and McNeill (1982) found that although satisfaction was high immediately following surgery for 55 adult orthognathic patients, satisfaction declined significantly from a 4-month posttreatment assessment to the 9-month assessment. This pattern was found for measures of self-esteem using the Tennessee Self-Concept Scale and facial body image using a modification of Secord and Jourard's body cathexis scale which included assessment of satisfaction with specific facial features. In these cases 9-month posttreatment assessments yielded self-esteem and facial–body image scores even lower than at the pretreatment assessment. It was interesting to note, however, that the results for facial body image reflected an improvement in chin image simultaneously with the decline in facial–body image. The investigators suggested that this pattern may indicate a refocusing of concerns. As patients adjust to improvements in the appearance of corrected dental–facial features, the salience of these features for body image may recede. As a result, the individual may become more aware of, and less satisfied with, other features. Kiyak and her coauthors pointed out that these changes did not appear to be related to the severity of impairment, or to postsurgical pain and functional problems. In discussing the decline in satisfaction between posttreatment intervals, the investigators also reported interview content that suggested that many patients did not feel fully prepared for surgery. Although they reported having received adequate information about the surgical process and its side effects, many felt they had not absorbed it, or they had not fully understood the potential impact. The delayed response on satisfaction measures may simply be a function of the time required for structural changes to stabilize and for patients to confront the actual end result of surgery.

Although Ouellette (1978) found that most of his patients were satisfied with their surgical results, he also emphasized the importance of expectations in ultimate satisfaction with the outcome of treatment and has elaborated on the clinician's role in defining realistic expectations. The work of Hirsch, Levin, and Tiber (1972, 1973) with denture patients demonstrated that when these patients were involved in treatment planning they were more likely to be satisfied with the aesthetic properties of their final dentures. Patients who were asked their preferences for four denture-teeth arrangements, or set-ups, prior to treatment were randomly assigned to receive dentures that resembled either their first, second, third, or last preferences. Although these groups did not differ on their adaptation to dentures, results indicated that the lower a patient had initially rated the denture set-up that was ultimately received, the greater was the change in their preference rating at the posttreatment assessment. The authors offered an explanation for these results based on cognitive dissonance theory. They suggested that in order to satisfy the need for consistency among values, beliefs, and behaviors, patients had changed their evaluations to conform to the reality confronting them. In their later study, Hirsch, Levin, and Tiber (1973) found that the positive changes in acceptance they had identified were enhanced when dentists were lower in authoritarian personality traits. The authors suggested that more authoritarian dentists may appear to have already made up their minds and to be uninterested in the patients' perceptions. This explanation suggests that one must go beyond inner cognitive processes to understand patient responses to treatment. Clearly, the social dynamics of the treatment setting must be considered.

Albino, Tedesco, and Conny (1984) reviewed the shared concerns related to aesthetics in the clinical specialities of orthodontics and prosthodontics. The expectations in prosthodontics, which involves the fabrication and placement of fixed and/or removable replacements for teeth, tend to be especially complex because there may be expectations related to the size, color, and shape, as well as the alignment, of teeth. Conny et al. (1985) reported a strong focus by prosthodontic patients on aesthetic issues as contrasted with issues of function, and Brisman (1980) found significant differences on preference ratings by dentists, dental students, and men and women patients, when they viewed photographs of teeth showing variations in proportion and symmetry.

Although some have suggested that clinicians' views of aesthetics tend to reflect the perspective of art reproducing nature, this view is no doubt tempered by an understanding of the limitations of materials, techniques and, one would assume, the patients' perceptions and preferences. For their part, patients seem to be influenced, on the one hand, by attentiveness to very narrow aspects of appearance and, on the other hand, to some global sense of acceptability or nonacceptability. The clinical–social dynamic, therefore, is most productive when it functions to minimize the incongruencies among these perspectives within the context of some normative values related to appearance.

DEVELOPMENTAL INFLUENCES

Although the foregoing discussion has emphasized perceived degree of facial impairment as most important in determining demand and need for treatment, as well as expectations and satisfaction with treatment, it is important to recognize that these perceptions may be influenced by life-stage variables. The relative importance of professional, peer, and self-perceptions of facial appearance may change as a function of age, cognitive development, and the social developmental tasks of various ages. As the roles of the individual change across the life span, so may the meaning of facial appearance and response to facial impairment as well. This is true both in terms of the responses of others, and the responses one has about his or her own facial appearance.

For example, adolescents express concern about their physical appearance in general, and facial appearance in particular. Because of a life-stage experience of intense biological growth that involves physical, emotional, and cognitive development, responses to appearance can be easily distorted (Adams, 1977; Hamburg, 1980). As a function of the emphasis and importance placed on attractiveness by the peer culture, negative self-perceptions of facial appearance may be greatly exaggerated (Rosenberg, 1974). During adolescence, the individual is shaping an adult self-image that depends on identification with peer standards (Hamburg, 1980). Again, the interplay of self and peer perceptions is evident, and the stability of these perceptions must be considered when investigating psychosocial responses to facial impairment during adolescence (Albino, Tedesco, & Phipps, 1982). Thus, we must know how perceptions and other psychosocial responses change in the "normal" appearing adolescent as well as in the facially impaired.

Adults also may hold self-perceptions that are strongly influenced by peer perceptions, but their concerns about appearance generally are more stable. Clinicians are aware of these differences and, consequently, may be less hesitant to treat the mild facial impairment of an adult patient who has lived with and experienced concern about his or her condition for years than to provide treatment for the same problem in an adolescent who may "outgrow" the concern. It is not clear, however, whether the intensity of concern remains constant across the life span. Changes in physical appearance become important markers for aging adults, and concerns about age-related changes in appearance may be manifested by intense, and even frantic, searches for cosmetic treatment during certain periods of adult midlife development. In later life stages, however, dental–facial concerns might be expected to shift again toward those of comfort and function, rather than appearance (Davis, Portenoy, & Ortman, 1985).

FAMILIAL INFLUENCES

Experiences within the social unit of the family have important and profound influences on the perception of facial appearance. The attitudes, beliefs, and perceptions of parents and siblings provide a background against which the individual designs his or her self-perception of facial appearance. Although parents have been found to vary in their reasons, they nevertheless consider the occlusal attractiveness of their children very important (Linn, 1966). Maternal characteristics such as achievement need, social aspirations, self-image, and identification with their children's occlusion have been shown to be associated with the decision to seek orthodontic treatment (Baldwin & Barnes, 1965, 1966).

Lewit and Virolainen (1968) investigated a rather complex model of social factors in connection with perception of occlusal malrelations and need for treatment. Incorporating both personality characteristics and social pressures from parents, peers, and self, they hypothesized these variables would predict the treatment-seeking behavior of 129 eighth-grade subjects. Although this investigation assessed only self-reports of intention to seek treatment, rather than actual treatment seeking, several interesting findings emerged. For middle-class adolescents with high dependency needs, desire for orthodontic treatment was related to parental pressures and need for parental approval. When parental dependency needs were low, however, high need for peer approval was related to desire for treatment. Objective orthodontic standards most influenced adolescents with low need for peer approval.

The Albino (1981) investigations also strongly suggest that parents' attitudes and values influence both the child's self-perception of dental–facial attractiveness and the decision to seek orthodontic treatment. Mothers' attitudes toward orthodontic treatment and their perception of their children's occlusion were associated with the decision to seek treatment at higher levels than either the children's self-perceptions of facial appearance or peer assessments of dental–facial attractiveness, although these two variables were also strongly related to mothers' perceptions.

Albino and her colleagues also found assessments of perceptions in high agreement among family members (Albino, Gale, Lewis, & Slakter, 1980). Positive and significant correlations were found for children's self-perceptions of facial appearance with those of their mothers' and siblings' perceptions, but not with their fathers'. However, fathers' and mothers' perceptions were significantly associated. Whether children were in the treatment or nontreatment-seeking group these correlations were similar. This finding suggests that agreement among family members for perception of the child's occlusal status is not solely a function of the process of treatment seeking, or of the orthodontist's recommendations. In addition, when the effects of the objective clinical assessment of malocclusion (TPI scores) were removed, the correlations between family members' perceptions of the child's occlusion did not change. Hence, severity of malocclusion does not account for perceptual agreement among family members. Other researchers (Baldwin & Barnes, 1965, 1966) have described the importance of maternal influences on children's attitudes toward dental treatment. The relationships described previously for perception of facial appearance confirm the importance of family influences with regard to dental–facial aesthetics as well.

A FINAL COMMENT

In this chapter we have attempted to describe and document some determinants of face perception and to examine how those perceptions are related to decisions regarding the treatment of dental–facial impairment. Although we began with the premise that self-perceptions of facial appearance are socially learned and are dependent on normative values for facial aesthetics, the possibility of corrective treatment introduces still another dimension to face perception. Clinical assessments of the severity of aesthetic impairment both influence, and are influenced by, patients' views of the acceptability or nonacceptability of their appearance. Yet these different evaluations of perceptions cannot be viewed as emanating from the same set of values. Instead, they represent the convergence of two cultures, the clinical and the social. Self-perceptions are founded in the individual's experiences with face-to-face interactions that are mediated by personal interpretations of peer and family values. Clinicians' perceptions, on the other hand, are shaped by a different set of experiences that are based on familiarity with a much broader range of defects and greater variability with respect to aesthetic impact. Their perceptions are mediated by an awareness of treatment possibilities and an understanding of the limitations of techniques and results. Yet, in the clinical setting and during the decision making that occurs there, these different perspectives and the concerns that underlie them will influence one another, both directly and indirectly. We have considerable anecdotal evidence that surgeons and other practitioners listen carefully to their patients' concerns about appearance and, on the other hand, that patients' perceptions and expectations are shaped by their providers' views.

Data from research completed over the past 10 years have substantially enhanced our understanding and skill in measuring facial appearance from a variety of perspectives. We also now have considerable information about the relationships among these various perceptions. New research in this area can now be expected to turn toward predicting outcomes, in terms of need and demand for treatment and predicting satisfaction with the results of treatment. Previous work suggests that this should be a richly productive field for inquiry, with implications for enhancing our more general understanding of such diverse areas as the implications of facial attractiveness for social behavior and the development of coping responses by individuals with disabilities.

References

Aamot, S. (1978). Reactions to facial deformities: Autonomic and social psychological. *European Journal of Social Psychology, 8,* 315-333.

Adams, G. R. (1977). Physical attractiveness research: Toward a developmental social psychology of beauty. *Human Development, 20,* 217-239.

Adams, G. R. (1978). Racial membership and physical attractiveness effects on preschool teachers' expectations. *Child Study Journal, 8,* 29-41.

Adams, G. R. (1981). The effects of physical attractiveness on the socialization process. In G. W. Lucker, K. A. Ribbens, & J. A. McNamara (Eds.), *Psychological aspects of facial form* (pp. 25-47). Ann Arbor, MI: Center for Human Growth.

Adams, G. R. (1982). Physical attractiveness. In A. G. Miller (Ed.), *In the eye of the beholder: Contemporary issues in stereotyping* (pp. 253-304). New York: Praeger.

Adams, G. R., & Cohen, A. S. (1974). Children's physical and interpersonal characteristics that effect student-teacher interactions. *Journal of Experimental Education, 43,* 1-5.

Adams, G. R., & Crane, P. (1980). An assessment of parents' and teachers' expectations of preschool children's social preference for attractive or unattractive children and adults. *Child Development, 51,* 224-231.

Adams, G. R., & Crossman, S. M. (1978). *Physical attractiveness: A cultural imperative.* Roslyn Heights, NY: Libra.

Adams, G. R., & LaVoie, J. C. (1974). The effect of students' sex, conduct and facial attractiveness on teacher expectancy. *Education, 95,* 76-83.

Adams, G. R., & LaVoie, J. C. (1975). Parental expectations of educational and personal-social performance and childrearing patterns as a function of attractiveness, sex, and conduct of the child. *Child Study Journal, 5,* 125-142.

Adams, G. R., & Read, D. (1983). Personality and social influence styles of attractive and unattractive college women. *Journal of Psychology, 114,* 151-157.

Adams, G. R., & Roopnarine, J. L. (1987, April). *Physical attractiveness, social skills, and peer popularity.* Paper presented at the meeting of the Society for Research in Child Development, Baltimore.

Ainsworth, M. D. S., Blehar, M. C., Waters, E., & Wall, S. (1978). *Patterns of attachment.* Hillsdale, NJ: Lawrence Erlbaum Associates.

Albino, J. E. (1977). *Report of procedures for selection and testing of variables and items: Development of methodologies for behavioral measurements related to malocclusion.* Unpub-

lished manuscript, (Department of Behavioral Science, State University of New York at Buffalo, NY.)
Albino, J. E. (1981). *Development of methodologies for behavioral measurements related to malocclusion* (Final Report: Contract No. N01-DE-27499). Bethesda, MD: National Institute of Dental Research.
Albino, J. E. (1984). Psychosocial aspects of malocclusion. In J. D. Matarazzo, N. E. Miller, S. M. Weiss, J. A. Herd, & S. M. Weiss (Eds.), *Behavioral health: A handbook of health enhancement and disease prevention* (pp. 918-929). New York: Wiley.
Albino, J. E., Cunat, J. J., Fox, R. N., Lewis, E. A., Slakter, M. J., & Tedesco, L. A. (1981). Variables discriminating individuals who seek orthodontic treatment. *Journal of Dental Research, 60*, 1661-1667.
Albino, J. E., Davis, E. L., Tedesco, L. A., Cunat, J. J., Lewis, E. A., & Slakter, M. J. (1985). Occlusal impairment and self-image in adolescents. *Journal of Dental Research, 64* (Abstract No. 1057), p. 292.
Albino, J. E., Gale, N. E., Lewis, E. A., & Slakter, M. J. (1980). Self and family perceptions of children's malocclusion. *Journal of Dental Research, 59*(B) (Abstract No. 169), p. 216.
Albino, J. E., Lewis, E. A., Wu, T. H., Slakter, M. J., & Fox, R. N. (1979). Comparisons of professional and public assessments of malocclusion. *Journal of Dental Research, 58* (Abstract No. 1136), p. 375.
Albino, J. E., & Tedesco, L. A. (1981, August). *Adolescents' self-perceptions of dental-facial appearance and orthodontic treatment.* Paper presented at the annual meeting of the American Psychological Association, Los Angeles.
Albino, J. E., Tedesco, L. A., & Conny, D. J. (1984). Patient perceptions of dental-facial esthetics: Shared concerns in orthodontics and prosthodontics. *Journal of Prosthetic Dentistry, 52*, 9-13.
Albino, J. E., Tedesco, L. A., & Phipps, G. T. (1982). Social and psychological problems of adolescence and their relevance to dental care. *International Dental Journal, 32*, 184-193.
Alley, T. R. (1980). Infantile colouration as an elicitor of caretaking behaviour in Old World primates. *Primates, 21*, 416-429.
Alley, T. R. (1981). Head shape and the perception of cuteness. *Developmental Psychology, 17*, 650-654.
Alley, T. R. (1983a). Age-related changes in body proportions, body size and perceived cuteness. *Perceptual and Motor Skills, 56*, 615-622.
Alley, T. R. (1983b). Growth-produced changes in body shape and size as determinants of perceived age and adult caregiving. *Child Development, 54*, 241-248.
Alley, T. R. (1983c). Infantile head shape as an elicitor of adult protection. *Merrill-Palmer Quarterly, 29*, 411-427.
Alley, T. R. (1984, September). *Facial attractiveness from early childhood to young adulthood: A longitudinal study.* Paper presented at the XXIII International Congress of Psychology, Acapulco, Mexico.
Alley, T. R. (1985). Organism-environment mutuality, epistemics, and the concept of an ecological niche. *Synthese, 65*, 411-444.
Alley, T. R. (1986). An ecological analysis of the protection of primate infants. In V. McCabe & G. J. Balzano (Eds.), *Event perception: An ecological perspective* (pp. 239-258). Hillsdale, NJ: Lawrence Erlbaum Associates.
Alley, T. R., & Baron, R. M. (1986). Young adults' caregiving and the age level of a potential recipient. *Journal of Psychology, 120*, 567-580.
Allport, D. A., Antonis, B., & Reynolds, P. (1972). On the division of attention: A disproof of the single-channel hypothesis. *Quarterly Journal of Experimental Psychology, 24*, 225-235.
Allport, G. W. (1937). *Personality: A psychological interpretation.* New York: Holt.
Anderson, L. D. (1921). Estimating intelligence by means of printed photographs. *Journal of Applied Psychology, 5*, 152-155.

REFERENCES 241

Andrew, R. J. (1963). The origin and evolution of the calls and facial expressions of the primates. *Behaviour, 20,* 1-109.

Andrew, R. J. (1965). The origins of facial expression. *Scientific American, 213,* 88-94.

Archer, D., Iritani, B., Kimes, D. D., & Barrios, M. (1983). Face-ism: Five studies of sex differences in facial prominence. Journal of Personality and Social Psychology, 45, 725-735.

Argyle, M., & McHenry, R. (1971). Do spectacles really affect judgements of intelligence? *British Journal of Social and Clinical Psychology, 10,* 27-29.

Asch, S. E. (1956). Studies of independence and conformity: A minority of one against a unanimous majority. *Psychological Monographs, 70* (9, Whole No. 416).

Asch, S. E., Block, H., & Hertzman, M. (1938). Studies in the principles of judgments and attitudes: I. Two basic principles of judgment. Journal of Psychology, 5, 219-251.

Asendorpf, J. (1982). Contributions of the German "Expression Psychology" to nonverbal communication research. Part II: The face. *Journal of Nonverbal Behavior, 6,* 199-219.

Babalola, A. (1978). Personal communication from the Department of African Languages and literatures, University of Lagos, Nigeria.

Baldwin, D. C., & Barnes, M. L. (1965). Psychosocial factors motivating orthodontic treatment. *IADR Abstracts* (Abstract No. 461), p. 153.

Baldwin, D. C., & Barnes, M. L. (1966). Patterns of motivation in families seeking orthodontic treatment. *IADR Abstracts* (Abstract No. 412), p. 142.

Ballantyne, J. W. (1904). *Manual of antenatal pathology and hygiene: The embryo.* Edinburgh: William Green & Sons.

Bandura, A. (1986). Social cognitive theory and social referencing. In S. Feinman (Ed.), *Social referencing and social construction of reality.* New York: Plenum.

Barclay, C. D., Cutting, J. E., & Kozlowski, L. T. (1978). Temporal and spatial factors that influence gender recognition. *Perception and Psychophysics, 23,* 145-152.

Bargh, J. A. (1984). Automatic and conscious processing of social information. In R. S. Wyer & T. S. Srull (Eds.), *Handbook of social cognition* (Vol. 3, pp. 1-43). Hillsdale, NJ: Lawrence Erlbaum Associates.

Barocas, R., & Black, H. K. (1974). Referral rate and physical attractiveness in third-grade children. *Perceptual and Motor Skills, 39,* 731-734.

Bar-Tal, D., & Saxe, L. (1976). Physical attractiveness and its relationship to sex-role stereotyping. *Sex Roles, 2,* 123-133.

Bartlett, J. C., & Leslie, J. E. (1986). Aging and memory for faces versus single views of faces. *Memory and Cognition, 14,* 371-381.

Bassili, J. W. (1978). Facial motion in the perception of faces and of emotional expression. *Journal of Experimental Psychology: Human Perception and Performance, 4,* 373-379.

Bassili, J. W. (1979). Emotion recognition: The role of facial movement and the relative importance of the upper and lower areas of the face. *Journal of Personality and Social Psychology, 37,* 2049-2058.

Bateman, G. (1977). Personal communication from the Zoology Department, National Museum of Wales.

Bauer, R. M. (1984). Autonomic recognition of names and faces in prosopagnosia: A neuropsychological application of the guilty knowledge test. *Neuropsychologia, 22,* 457-469.

Bayes, M. A. (1972). Behavioral cues of interpersonal warmth. *Journal of Consulting and Clinical Psychology, 30,* 333-339.

Beier, E. G., Izard, C. E., Smock, C. D., & Tougas, R. R. (1957). "Response to the human face as a standard stimulus": A re-examination. *Journal of Counseling Psychology, 2,* 165-170.

Bellak, L., & Baker, S. S. (1981). *Reading faces.* New York: Holt, Rinehart & Winston.

Benson, P. L., Karabenick, S. A., & Lerner, R. M. (1976). Pretty pleases: The effects of physical attractiveness, race, and sex on receiving help. *Journal of Experimental Social Psychology, 12,* 409-415.

Berkowitz, L., & Frodi, A. (1979). Reactions to a child's mistakes as affected by her/his looks

and speech. *Social Psychology Quarterly, 42,* 420-425.
Berman, P. W. (1980). Are women more responsive than men to the young? A review of developmental and situational variables. *Psychological Bulletin, 88,* 668-695.
Berman, P. W., Goodman, V., Sloan, V. L., & Fernander, L. (1978). Preferences for infants among black and white children: Sex and age differences. *Child Development, 49,* 917-919.
Berman, P. W., O'Nan, B. A., & Floyd, W. (1981). The double standard of aging and the social situation: Judgments of attractiveness of the middle-aged woman. *Sex Roles, 7,* 87-96.
Bernick, N. (1966). *The development of children's preferences for social objects as evidenced by their pupil responses.* Unpublished dissertation, University of Chicago.
Bernstein, I. H., Lin, T-D., & McClellan, P. (1982). Cross- vs. within-racial judgments of attractiveness. *Perception & Psychophysics, 32,* 495-503.
Berry, D. S. (1987). *Perceiving faces: Contributions of dynamic information.* Unpublished dissertation, Brandeis University.
Berry, D. S., & Brownlow, S. (1988). *Were the physiognomists right? Personality correlates of facial babyishness.* Manuscript submitted for publication.
Berry, D. S., & McArthur, L. Z. (1985). Some components and consequences of a babyface. *Journal of Personality and Social Psychology, 48,* 312-323.
Berry, D. S., & McArthur, L. Z. (1986). Perceiving character in faces: The impact of age-related craniofacial changes on social perception. *Psychological Review, 100,* 3-18.
Berry, D. S., & McArthur, L. Z. (in press). What's in a face? The impact of facial maturity and defendent intent on the attribution of legal responsibility. *Personality and Social Psychology Bulletin.*
Berscheid, E. (1981). A review of the psychological effects of physical attractiveness. In G. W. Lucker, K. A. Ribbens, & J. A. McNamara (Eds.), *Psychological aspects of facial form* (pp. 1-23). Ann Arbor, MI: Center for Human Growth.
Berscheid, E., & Gangestad, S. (1982). The social psychological implication of facial physical attractiveness. *Clinics in Plastic Surgery, 9,* 289-296.
Berscheid, E., & Walster, E. (1974). Physical attractiveness. *Advances in Experimental Social Psychology, 7,* 157-215.
Berscheid, E., Walster, E., & Bohrnstedt, G. (1973). The happy American body: A survey report. *Psychology Today, 7,* 119-131.
Borod, J. C., & Koff, E. (1984). Asymmetries in affective facial expression. In N. Fox & R. Davidson (Eds.), *The psychobiology of affective development* (pp. 293-323). Hillsdale, NJ: Lawrence Erlbaum Associates.
Borod, J. C., Koff, E., & Buck, R. (1986). The neuropsychology of facial expression: Data from normal and brain-damaged adults. In P. Blanck, R. Buck, & R. Rosenthal (Eds.), *Nonverbal communication in the clinical context* (pp. 198-222). University Park, PA: Pennsylvania State University.
Bovard, E. (1959). The effects of social stimuli on the response to stress. *Psychological Review, 66,* 267-277.
Bowman, P. C. (1979). Physical constancy and trait attribution: Attenuation of the primacy effect. *Personality and Social Psychology Bulletin, 48,* 61-64.
Brandt, A. (1980). Face reading: The persistence of physiognomy. *Psychology Today, 14*(7), 90-96.
Brantley, H. J., & Clifford, E. (1979a). Cognitive, self-concept, and the body image measures of normal cleft palate and obese adolescents. *Cleft Palate Journal, 16,* 177-182.
Brantley, H. J., & Clifford, E. (1979b). Maternal and child locus of control and field-dependence in cleft palate children. *Cleft Palate Journal, 16,* 183-187.
Brazelton, T. B., Koslowski, B., & Main, M. (1974). The origins of reciprocity: The early mother-infant interaction. In M. Lewis & L. A. Rosenblum (Eds.), *The effect of the infant on its caregiver* (pp. 49-77). New York: Wiley.

Bretherton, I. (1984). Social referencing and the interfacing of minds: A commentary on the views of Feinman and Campos. *Merrill-Palmer Quarterly, 30,* 419–427.
Briody, M. (1978). Personal communication on the archives of the Department of Irish Folklore, University of Dublin.
Brisman, A. (1980). Esthetics: A comparison of dentists' and patients' concepts. *Journal of the American Dental Association, 100,* 345.
Brooks, V., & Hochberg, J. (1960). A psychophysical study of cuteness. *Perceptual and Motor Skills, 11,* 205.
Brophy, J. E., & Good, T. L. (1974). *Teacher–student relationships: Causes and consequences.* New York: Holt, Rinehart & Winston.
Brown, E. L., & Deffenbacher, K. (1979). *Perception and the senses.* New York: Oxford University Press.
Brown, J. L. (1975). *The evolution of behavior.* New York: W.W. Norton.
Bruce, V. (1982). Changing faces: Visual and non-visual coding processes in face recognition. *British Journal of Psychology, 73,* 105–116.
Bruford, A. (1978). Personal communication on the archives of the School for Social Studies, Edinburgh.
Brundage, L. E., Derlega, V. J., & Cash, T. F. (1977). The effects of physical attractiveness and need for approval on self-disclosure. *Personality and Social Psychology Bulletin, 3,* 63–66.
Brunswik, E. (1956). *Perception and the representative design of psychological experiments.* Berkeley: University of California.
Brunswik, E., & Reiter, L. (1937). Eindruckscharaktere schematisierter Gesichter. *Zeitschrift für Psychologie, 142,* 67–134.
Bryant, N. J. (1975). Petitioning: Dress congruence versus belief congruence. *Journal of Applied Social Psychology, 5,* 144–149.
Bryden, M. P., & Ley, R. G. (1983). Right-hemispheric involvement in the perception and expression of emotions in normal humans. In K. M. Heilman & P. Satz (Eds.), *Neuropsychology of human emotion* (pp. 6–44). New York: Guilford.
Buchman, H. (1971). *Stage makeup.* New York: Watson–Guptill.
Buck, R. (1975). Nonverbal communication of affect in children. *Journal of Personality and Social Psychology, 31,* 644–653.
Buck, R. (1976). *Human motivation and emotion.* New York: Wiley.
Buck, R. (1979). Individual differences in nonverbal sending accuracy and electrodermal responding: The externalizing-internalizing dimension. In R. Rosenthal (Ed.), *Skill in nonverbal communication: Individual differences.* Cambridge, MA: Oelgeschlager, Gunn & Hain.
Buck, R. (1980). Nonverbal behavior and the theory of emotion: The facial feedback hypothesis. *Journal of Personality and Social Psychology, 38,* 811–824.
Buck, R. (1982). Spontaneous and symbolic nonverbal behavior and the ontogeny of communication. In R. S. Feldman (Ed.), *Development of nonverbal behavior in children* (pp. 29–62). New York: Springer-Verlag.
Buck, R. (1983a). Emotional development and emotional education. In R. Plutchik & H. Kellerman (Eds.), *Emotion in early development* (pp. 259–292). New York: Academic Press.
Buck, R. (1983b). Nonverbal receiving ability. In J. M. Wiemann & R. P. Harrison (Eds.), *Nonverbal interaction* (pp. 209–242). Beverly Hills, CA: Sage.
Buck, R. (1984). *The communication of emotion.* New York: Guilford.
Buck, R. (1985). Prime theory: An integrated view of motivation and emotion. *Psychological Review, 92,* 389–413.
Buck, R. (1986). Discussion of J. LeDoux, "Neurobiology and emotion". In J. E. LeDoux & W. Hirst (Eds.), *Mind and brain: Dialogues in cognitive neuroscience.* New York: Cambridge University.
Buck, R., Baron, R., & Barrette, D. (1982). The temporal organization of spontaneous emotional

expression: A segmentation analysis. *Journal of Personality and Social Psychology, 42,* 506–517.
Buck, R., Baron, R., Goodman, N., & Shapiro, B. (1980). The unitization of spontaneous nonverbal behavior in the study of emotion communication. *Journal of Personality and Social Psychology, 39,* 522–529.
Buck, R., & Carroll, J. (1974). *CARAT and PONS: Correlates of two tests of nonverbal sensitivity.* Unpublished paper, Carnegie-Mellon University, Pittsburgh.
Bull, R. (1979). The psychological significance of facial deformity. In M. Cook & G. Wilson (Eds.), *Love and attraction* (pp. 21–25). London: Pergamon.
Bull, R. H. C., & Green, J. (1980). The relationship between physical appearance and criminality. *Medical Science Law, 20,* 79–83.
Bull, R., & Stevens, J. (1981). The effects of facial disfigurement on helping behavior. *Italian Journal of Psychology, 8,* 25–33.
Burr, C. W. (1935). Personality and physiognomy. *Dental Cosmos, 77,* 556–560.
Burstone, C. J. (1975). Soft tissue factors in treatment planning. In J. T. Cook (Ed.), *Transactions of the Third International Orthodontic Congress* (pp. 26–34). St. Louis, MO: C. V. Mosby.
Buss, D. M. (1987). Sex differences in human mate selection criteria: An evolutionary perspective. In C. Crawford, M. Smith, & D. Krebs (Eds.), *Sociobiology and psychology: Ideas, issues and applications* (pp. 335–351). Hillsdale, NJ: Lawrence Erlbaum Associates.
Buss, D. M., & Barnes, M. (1986). Preferences in human mate selection. *Journal of Personality and Social Psychology, 50,* 559–570.
Byrne, D., London, O., & Reeves, K. (1968). The effects of physical attractiveness, sex, and attitude similarity on interpersonal attraction. *Journal of Personality, 36,* 259–271.
Campbell, A., Converse, P. E., & Rodgers, W. L. (1976). *The quality of American life.* New York: Russell Sage Foundation.
Campbell, R. (1978). Asymmetries in interpreting and expressing a posed facial expression. *Cortex, 14,* 327–342.
Campbell, R. (1982). The lateralization of emotion: A critical review. *International Journal of Psychology, 17,* 211–229.
Campos, J. J. (1983). The importance of affective communication in social referencing: A commentary on Feinman. *Merrill-Palmer Quarterly, 29,* 83–87.
Campos, J. J. (1985, June). *Self-produced locomotion in development.* Colloquium presented to the Department of Psychology, University of Connecticut, Storrs, CT.
Campos, J. J., Barrett, K. C., Lamb, M. E., Goldsmith, H. H., & Stenberg, C. (1983). Socioemotional development. In P. H. Mussen (Ed.), *Handbook of child psychology* (Vol. 2, pp. 783–916). New York: Wiley.
Campos, J. J., & Stenberg, C. (1981). Perception, appraisal, and emotion: The onset of social referencing. In M. Lamb & L. Sherrod (Eds.), *Infant social cognition.* Hillsdale, NJ: Lawrence Erlbaum Associates.
Camras, L. (1977). Facial expressions used by children in a conflict situation. *Child Development, 48,* 1431–1435.
Camras, L. (1982). Ethological approaches to nonverbal communication. In R. S. Feldman (Ed.), *Development of nonverbal behavior in children* (pp. 3–28). New York: Springer-Verlag.
Carlos, J. P. (1970). Evaluation of indices of malocclusion. *International Dental Journal, 20,* 606–617.
Cash, T. F. (1981, August). *The interface of sexism and beautyism.* Paper presented at the Annual Meeting of the American Psychological Association, Los Angeles.
Cash, T. F. (1985). Physical appearance and mental health. In J. A. Graham & A. M. Kligman (Eds.), *The psychology of cosmetic treatments.* New York: Praeger.
Cash, T. F., Gillen, B., & Burns, D. S. (1977). Sexism and "beautyism" in personnel consultant decision making. *Journal of Applied Psychology, 62,* 301–310.

Cash, T. F., & Horton, C. E. (1983). Aesthetic surgery: Effects of rhinoplasty on the social perception of patients by others. *Plastic and Reconstructive Surgery, 72,* 543-548.
Cash, T. F., & Kehr, J. (1978). Influence of nonprofessional counselors' physical attractiveness and sex on perceptions of counselor behavior. *Journal of Counseling Psychology, 25,* 336-342.
Cash, T. F., & Salzbach, R. F. (1978). The beauty of counseling: Effects of counselor physical attractiveness and self-disclosures on perceptions of counselor behavior. *Journal of Counseling Psychology, 25* 283-291.
Cash, T. F., & Trimer, C. A. (1984). Sexism and beautyism in women's evaluations of peer performance. *Sex Roles, 10,* 87-98.
Cavior, N., & Dokecki, P. R. (1973). Physical attractiveness, perceived attitude similarity, and academic achievement as contributors to interpersonal attraction among adolescents. *Developmental Psychology, 9,* 44-54.
Cavior, N., & Howard, L. R. (1973). Facial attractiveness and juvenile delinquency among black and white offenders. *Journal of Abnormal Child Psychology, 1,* 202-213.
Cavior, N., & Lombardi, D. A. (1973). Developmental aspects of judgment of physical attractiveness in children. *Developmental Psychology, 8,* 67-71.
Christensen, I. (1978). Personal communication from the Institute of Folklore, Oslo.
Cleeton, G. U., & Knight, F. B. (1924). Validity of character judgments based on external criteria. *Journal of Applied Psychology, 8,* 215-231.
Clifford, E. (1979). Psychologic aspects of the craniofacial surgical experience. In J. M. Converse, J. G. McCarthy, & D. Wood-Smith (Eds.), *Symposium on diagnosis and treatment of craniofacial anomalies* (pp. 117-122). St. Louis, MO: C. V. Mosby.
Clifford, E. (1983). Why are they so normal? *Cleft Palate Journal, 20,* 83-84.
Clifford, M. M. (1975). Physical attractiveness and academic performance. *Child Study Journal, 5,* 201-209.
Clifford, M. M., & Walster, E. (1973). The effect of physical attractiveness on teacher expectation. *Sociology of Education, 46,* 248-258.
Cloonan, H. A., & Ottinger, D. R. (1987, April). *Physical attractiveness and the effects of labeling on adult perceptions of preterm infants.* Paper presented at the meeting of the Society for Research in Child Development, Baltimore.
Cobb, S. (1976). Social support as a moderator of life stress. *Psychosomatic Medicine, 38,* 300-314.
Cohen, L. K., & Horowitz, H S. (1970). Occlusal relations in children born and reared in an optimally fluoridated community. II. Social-psychological findings. *Angle Orthodontist, 40,* 159-169.
Cohen, R. (1973). *Patterns of personality judgment.* New York: Academic Press.
Coleman, J. S. (1961). *The adolescent society.* New York: Free Press.
Comer, R. J., & Piliavin, J. A. (1972). The effects of physical deviance upon face-to-face interaction: The other side. *Journal of Personality and Social Psychology, 23,* 33-39.
Conny, D. J., Tedesco, L. A., Brewer, J. D., & Albino, J. E. (1985). Changes of attitude in fixed prosthodontic patients. *Journal of Prosthetic Dentistry, 53,* 451-454.
Cons, N. C., Jenny, J., Freer, T. J., Eismann, D., & Kohout, F. (1984). Perceptions of occlusal conditions in Australia, the German Democratic Republic, and the United States of America. *International Dental Journal, 33,* 200-206.
Cook, T. A. (1911). *The curves of life.* New York: Dover.
Corter, C., Trehub, S., Boukydis, C., Ford, L., Celhoffer, L., & Minde, K. (1978). Nurses' judgments of the attractiveness of premature infants. *Infant Behavior and Development, 1,* 373-380.
Cox, N. H., & van der Linden, P. G. M. (1971). Facial harmony. *American Journal of Orthodontics, 60,* 175-183.
Crano, W. D., & Mellon, P. M. (1978). Causal influence of teachers' expectations on children's

academic performance: A cross-lagged panel analysis. *Journal of Educational Psychology, 5,* 39-49.

Crnic, K. A., Ragozin, A. S., Greenberg, M. T., Robinson, N. M., & Basham, R. B. (1983). Social interaction and developmental competence of preterm and full-term infants during the first year of life. *Child Development, 54,* 1199-1210.

Cross, J. F., & Cross, J. (1971). Age, sex, race and the perception of facial beauty. *Developmental Psychology, 5,* 433-439.

Crowell, N. T., Sazima, M. J., & Elder, S. T. (1970). Survey of patients' attitudes after surgical correction of prognathism: Study of 33 patients. *Journal of Oral Surgery, 28,* 818-822.

Cunningham, M. R. (1986). Measuring the physical in physical attractiveness: Quasi-experiments on the sociobiology of female facial beauty. *Journal of Personality and Social Psychology, 50,* 925-935.

Cutting, J. E., & Kozlowski, L. T. (1977). Recognizing friends by the way they walk: Gait perception without familiarity cues. *Bulletin of the Psychonomic Society, 9,* 333-356.

Cutting, J. E., & Proffitt, D. R. (1981). Gait perception as an example of how we may perceive events. In R. D. Walk & H. L. Pick (Eds.), *Intersensory perception and sensory integration* (pp. 249-273). New York: Plenum.

Damasio, A. R., Damasio, H., & Van Hoesen, G. W. (1982). Prosopagnosia: Anatomic basis and behavioral mechanisms. *Neurology, 32,* 331-341.

Darwin, C. R. (1871). *The descent of man and selection in relation to sex.* London: John Murray.

Darwin, C. R. (1872). *The expression of the emotions in man and animals.* London: D. Appleton.

Davies, G., Ellis, H., & Shepherd, J. (1981). *Perceiving and remembering faces.* New York: Academic Press.

Davis, E. L., Portenoy, B. S., & Ortman, L. F. (1985). Expectations and satisfaction of denture patients in a university clinic. *Journal of Dental Research, 64* (Abstract No. 1063), p. 293.

Dawkins, R. (1976). *The selfish gene.* Oxford: Oxford University.

Denenberg, V. H. (1981). Hemispheric laterality in animals and the effects of early experience. *Behavioral and Brain Sciences, 4,* 1-49.

Dennington, R. J., & Korabik, K. (1977). Self-concept changes in orthodontic patients during initial treatment. *American Journal of Orthodontics, 72,* 461.

Deri, S. (1949). *Introduction to the Szondi Test.* New York: Grune & Stratton.

Dermer, M., & Thiel, D. L. (1975). When beauty may fail. *Journal of Personality and Social Psychology, 31,* 1168-1176.

Deutsch, F. M., Clark, M. E., & Zalenski, C. M. (1983, April). *Is there a double standard of aging?* Paper presented at the 54th Annual Meeting of the Eastern Psychological Association, Philadelphia.

Dickstein, S. (1984). Social referencing and the security of attachment. *Infant Behavior and Development, 7,* 507-516.

Dimberg, V. (1983). Emotional conditioning to facial stimuli: A psychobiological analysis. *Acta Universitet Uppsala: Abstracts of Uppsala Dissertations from the Faculty of Social Sciences, 29.* Uppsala: University of Uppsala.

Dimberg, V. & Ohman, A. (1983). The effects of directional facial cues on electrodermal conditioning to facial stimuli. *Psychophysiology, 20,* 160-167.

Dion, K. K. (1973). Young children's stereotyping of facial attractiveness. *Developmental Psychology, 9,* 183-188.

Dion, K. K. (1974). Children's physical attractiveness and sex as determinants of adult punitiveness. *Developmental Psychology, 10,* 772-778.

Dion, K. K., & Berscheid, E. (1974). Physical attractiveness and peer perception among children. *Sociometry, 37,* 1-12.

Dion, K. K., & Stein, S. (1978). Physical attractiveness and interpersonal influence. *Journal of Experimental Social Psychology, 14,* 97-108.

Dipboye, R. L., Fromkin, H. L., & Wiback, K. (1975). Relative importance of applicant sex, attractiveness, and scholastic standing in evaluation of job applicant resumes. *Journal of Applied Psychology, 60,* 39-43.

Dongieux, J., & Sassouni, V. (1980). The contribution of mandibular positioned variation to facial esthetics. *Angel Orthodontist, 50,* 334-339.

Doob, A. N., & Ecker, B. P. (1970). Stigma and compliance. *Journal of Personality and Social Psychology, 14,* 302-304.

Downs, A. C., & Harrison, S. K. (1985). Embarrassing age spots or just plain ugly? Physical attractiveness stereotyping as an instrument of sexism on American television commercials. *Sex Roles, 13,* 9-19.

Downs, A. C., Reagan, M. A., Garrett, C., & Kolodzy, P. (1982). The Attitudes Towards Physical Attractiveness Scale (ATPAS): An index of stereotypes based on physical appearance. *Psychological Documents, 12,* 4. (Ms. No. 2502)

Downs, A. C., & Walz, P. J. (1981). Sex differences in preschoolers' perceptions of young, middle-aged, and elderly adults. *Journal of Psychology, 109,* 119-122.

Draker, H. L. (1960). Handicapping labiolingual deviations: A proposed index for public health purposes. *American Journal of Orthodontics, 46,* 295-305.

Dusek, J. B., & Joseph, G. (1983). The bases of teacher expectancies: A meta-analysis. *Journal of Educational Psychology, 75,* 327-346.

Efran, M. G. (1974). The effect of physical appearance on the judgment of guilt, interpersonal attraction, and severity of recommended punishment in a simulated jury task. *Journal of Research in Personality, 8,* 45-54.

Ekman, P. (1978). Facial signs: Facts, fantasies and possibilities. In T. A. Sebeok (Ed.), *Sight, sound, and sense.* Bloomington: Indiana University.

Ekman, P., & Friesen, W. V. (1974). Detecting deception from the body or face. *Journal of Personality and Social Psychology, 29,* 288-298.

Ekman, P., & Friesen, W. V. (1975). *Unmasking the face.* Englewood Cliffs, NJ: Prentice-Hall.

Ekman, P., & Oster, H. (1979). Facial expressions of emotion. *Annual Review of Psychology, 30,* 527-554.

Elder, G. H., Jr. (1969). Appearance and education in marriage mobility. *American Sociological Review, 34,* 519-533.

Ellis, H. D., Jeeves, M. A., Newcombe, F., & Young, A. (Eds.). (1986). *Aspects of face processing* Dordrecht: Martinus Nijhoff.

Elman, D. (1977). Physical characteristics and the perception of masculine traits. *Journal of Social Psychology, 103,* 157-158.

Elovitz, G. P., & Salvia, J. (1982). Attractiveness as a biasing factor in the judgments of school psychologists. *Journal of School Psychology, 20,* 339-345.

Eme, R., Maisiak, R., & Goodale, W. (1979). Seriousness of adolescent problems. *Adolescence, 14,* 93-99.

Enlow, D. H. (1968). Wolff's law and the factor of architectonic circumstance. *American Journal of Orthodontics, 54,* 803-822.

Enlow, D. H. (1982). *Handbook of facial growth* (2nd ed.). Philadelphia: W. B. Saunders.

Etcoff, N. I. (1984). Selective attention to facial identity and facial emotion. *Neuropsychologia, 22,* 281-295.

Evans, E. C. (1969). Physiognomics in the ancient world. *Transactions of the American Philosophical Society, 59,* Pt. 5.

Evans, G. E. (1972). *The leaping hare.* London: Faber.

Farina, A., Allen, J. G., & Saul, B. B. B. (1968). The role of the stigmatized person in affecting social relationships. *Journal of Personality, 36,* 169-182.

Farina, A., Burns, G. L., Austad, C., Bugglin, C., & Fischer, E. H. (1986). The role of physical attractiveness in the readjustment of discharged psychiatric patients. *Journal of Abnormal*

Psychology, 95, 139-143.
Farina, A., Fischer, E. H., Sherman, S., Smith, W. T., Groh, T., & Merman, P. (1977). Physical attractiveness and mental illness. *Journal of Abnormal Psychology, 86,* 510-517.
Feinman, S. (1982). Social referencing in infancy. *Merrill-Palmer Quarterly, 28,* 445-470.
Feinman, S. (1983). How does baby socially refer? Two views of social referencing: A reply to Campos. *Merrill-Palmer Quarterly, 29,* 467-471.
Feinman, S. (Ed.). (1986). *Social referencing and social construction of reality.* New York: Plenum.
Feinman, S., & Gill, G. W. (1977). Females' response to males' beardedness. *Perceptual and Motor Skills, 44,* 533-534.
Feinman, S., & Gill, G. W. (1978). Sex differences in physical attractiveness preferences. *Journal of Social Psychology, 105,* 43-52.
Feinman, S., & Lewis, M. (1983). Social referencing at 10 months: A second-order effect on infants' responses to strangers. *Child Development, 54,* 878-887.
Ferrera, A. (1969). *Prenatal environment.* Springfield, IL: Thomas.
Field, T. (1982). Individual differences in the expressivity of neonates and young infants. In R. W. Feldman (Ed.), *Development of nonverbal behavior in children.* New York: Springer-Verlag.
Field, T. M., & Walden, T. A. (1982). Perception and production of facial expressions in infancy and young childhood. In H. Reese & L. Lipsett (Eds.), *Advances in child development and behavior* (Vol. 16). New York: Academic Press.
Field, T. M., Woodson, R., Greenberg, R., & Cohen, D. (1982). Discrimination and imitation of facial expressions by neonates. *Science, 218,* 179-181.
Fields, B., & O'Sullivan, M. (1976, April). *Convergent validation of five person perception measures.* Paper presented at a meeting of the Western Psychological Association, Los Angeles.
Fife, A. E. (1976). The marking of children and psychic imprinting. In W. O. Hand (Ed.), *American folk medicine: A symposium.* Los Angeles: University of California.
Fischer, E. H., Farina, A., Council, J. R., Pitts, H., Eastman, A., & Millard, R. (1982). Influence of adjustment and physical attractiveness on the employability of schizophrenic women. *Journal of Consulting and Clinical Psychology, 50,* 530-534.
Fischer, G. H. (1976). *Early studies of person perception.* Unpublished paper, Department of Psychology, University of Newcastle-upon-Tyne, England.
Fisher, K. W., Hand, H. H., Watson, M. W., Van Parys, M. M., & Tucker, J. L. (1984). Putting the child into socialization: The development of social categories in preschool children. In L. G. Katz (Ed.), *Current topics in early childhood education* (Vol. 5, pp. 27-71). Norwood, NJ: Ablex.
Fiske, S. T., & Cox, M. G. (1979). Person concepts: The effect of target familiarity and descriptive purpose on the process of describing others. *Journal of Personality, 47,* 136-161.
Fleishman, J. J., Buckley, M. L., Klosinsky, M. J., Smith, N., & Tuck, B. (1976). Judged attractiveness in recognition memory of women's faces. *Perceptual and Motor Skills, 43,* 709-710.
Fogh-Andersen, P. (1942). *Inheritance of harelip and cleft palate.* Copenhagen: Nyt Nordisk Forlag.
Folkman, S. (1984). Personal control and stress and coping processes: A theoretical analysis. *Journal of Personality and Social Psychology, 46,* 839-852.
Ford, C. S., & Beach, F. A. (1951). *Patterns of sexual behavior.* New York: Harper & Row.
Foster, E. J. (1973). Profile preferences among diversified groups. *Angle Orthodontist, 43,* 34-40.
Foster, T. D., & Menezes, D. M. (1976). The assessment of occlusal features for public health planning purposes. *American Journal of Orthodontics, 69,* 83-90.
Fox, N. A., & Davidson, R. (1985, April). EEG correlates of early facial expressions. In T. Field (Chair), *Emotional Expressions of Infants and Young Children.* Symposium conducted at the meeting of the Society for Research in Child Development, Toronto.

Freedman, D. G. (1969). The survival value of the beard. *Psychology Today, 3*(5), 36–39.
Freedman, R. (1986). *Beauty bound.* Lexington, MA: D. C. Heath.
Friedrich, W. N., & Boriskin, J. A. (1976). The role of the child in abuse: A review of the literature. *American Journal of Orthopsychiatry, 46,* 580–590.
Fullard, W., & Reiling, A. M. (1976). An investigation of Lorenz's "Babyness." *Child Development, 47,* 1191–1193.
Gallucci, N. T., & Meyer, R. G. (1984). People can be too perfect: Effects of subjects' and targets' attractiveness on interpersonal attraction. *Psychological Reports, 55,* 351–360.
Garcia, J., & Rusiniak, K. W. (1980). What the nose learns from the mouth. In D. Muller-Schwarze & R. M. Silverstein (Eds.), *Chemical signals.* New York: Plenum.
Garner, W. R. (1978). Aspects of a stimulus: Features, dimensions, and configurations. In E. Rosch & B. B. Lloyd (Eds.), *Cognition and categorization.* Hillsdale, NJ: Lawrence Erlbaum Associates.
Geiselman, R. E., Haight, N. A., & Kimata, L. G. (1984). Context effects on the perceived attractiveness of faces. *Journal of Experimental Social Psychology, 20,* 409–424.
Giancoli, D. L., & Neimeyer, G. J. (1983). Liking preferences toward handicapped persons. *Perceptual and Motor Skills, 57,* 1005–1006.
Gibbs, J. E. (1985). The problem of knowledge, still: A review of Libeu's *Piaget and the foundations of knowledge. Merrill-Palmer Quarterly, 31,* 111–115.
Gibson, E. J. (1969). *Principles of perceptual learning and development.* New York: Appleton-Century-Crofts.
Gibson, J. J. (1947). *Motor picture testing and research.* (AAF Aviation Psychology Research Rep. No. 7). Washington, DC: Government Printing Office.
Gibson, J. J. (1950). *The perception of the visual world.* Boston: Houghton–Mifflin.
Gibson, J. J. (1961). Ecological optics. *Vision Research, 1,* 253–262.
Gibson, J. J. (1966a). *The senses considered as perceptual systems.* Boston: Houghton–Mifflin.
Gibson, J. J. (1966b). The problem of temporal order in stimulation and perception. *Journal of Psychology, 62,* 141–149.
Gibson, J. J. (1979). *The ecological approach to visual perception.* Boston: Houghton-Mifflin.
Gibson, J. J., & Gibson, E. J. (1955). Perceptual learning: Differentiation or enrichment? *Psychological Review, 62,* 32–41.
Gibson, J. J., Kaplan, G. A., Reynolds, H. N., & Wheeler, K. (1969). The change from visible to invisible: A study of optical transitions. *Perception and Psychophysics, 5,* 113–116.
Gillen, B. (1981). Physical attractiveness: A determinant of two types of goodness. *Personality and Social Psychology Bulletin, 7,* 277–281.
Glass, L., Starr, C. D., Stewart, R. E., Hodge, S. E. (1981). Identikit Model II—A potential tool for judging cosmetic appearance. *Cleft Palate Journal, 18,* 147–151.
Gochman, D. S. (1972). The organizing role of motivation in health beliefs and intentions. *Journal of Health and Social Behavior, 13,* 285–293.
Gochman, D. S. (1975). The measurements and development of dentally relevant motives. *Journal of Public Health Dentistry, 35,* 160–164.
Goffman, E. (1963). *Stigma.* Englewood Cliffs, NJ: Prentice-Hall.
Goldberg, S., Blumberg, S. L., & Kriger, A. (1982). Menarche and interest in infants: Biological and social influences. *Child Development, 53,* 1544–1550.
Goldfield, E. (1983). The ecological approach to perceiving as a foundation for understanding the development of knowing in infancy. *Developmental Review, 3,* 371–404.
Goldin, S. E. (1979). *Facial stereotypes as cognitive categories.* Unpublished doctoral dissertation, Carnegie-Mellon University, Pittsburgh.
Goldstein, A. G. (1983). Behavioral scientists' fascination with faces. *Journal of Nonverbal Behavior, 7,* 223–255.
Goldstein, A. G., Chance, J. E., & Gilbert, B. (1984). Facial stereotypes of good guys and bad guys: A replication and extention. *Bulletin of the Psychonomic Society, 22,* 549–552.

Goldstein, A. G., & Papageorge, J. (1980). Judgments of facial attractiveness in the absence of eye movements. *Bulletin of the Psychonomic Society, 15,* 269–270.

Gonzalez-Ulloa, M., & Flores, E. S. (1965). Senility of the face—Basic study to understand its causes and effects. *Plastic and Reconstructive Surgery, 36,* 239–246.

Goodenough, F. L., & Harris, D. B. (1963). *Goodenough–Harris drawing test.* New York: Harcourt, Brace & World.

Goodman, N. R. (1980). *Determinants of the perceptual organization of ongoing action and emotion.* Unpublished doctoral dissertation, University of Connecticut, Storrs, CT.

Goodman, R. M., & Gorlin, R. J. (1977). *Atlas of the face in genetic disorders* (2nd ed.). St. Louis, MO: C. V. Mosby.

Gorlin, R. J., Pindborg, J. J., & Cohen, M. M. (1976). *Syndromes of the head and neck* (2nd ed.). New York: McGraw-Hill.

Gould, S. J. (1971). D'Arcy Thompson and the science of form. *New Literary History, 2,* 229–258.

Gould, S. J. (1977). *Ontogeny and phylogeny.* Cambridge, MA: Harvard University.

Gould, S. J., & Lewontin, R. C. (1979). The spandrels of San Marco and the Panglossian paradigm: A critique of the adaptationist programme. *Proceedings of the Royal Society of London, 205*B, 581–598.

Graber, L. W., & Lucker, G. W. (1980). Dental esthetic self-evaluation and satisfaction. *American Journal of Orthodontics, 77,* 163–173.

Graham, J. A., & Jouhar, A. J. (1980). Cosmetics considered in the context of physical attractiveness: A review. *International Journal of Cosmetic Science, 2,* 77–101.

Graham, J. A., & Jouhar, A. J. (1981). The effects of cosmetics on person perception. *International Journal of Cosmetic Science, 3,* 199–210.

Graham, J. A., & Kligman, A. M. (Eds.). (1985). *The psychology of cosmetic treatments.* New York: Praeger.

Grainger, R. M. (1967). *Orthodontic Treatment Priority Index* (PHS Publication No. 1000, Series 2, No. 25). Washington, DC: U.S. Government Printing Office.

Grant, E. C. (1969). Human facial expression. *Man, 4,* 525–536.

Gray, H. (1973). *Anatomy of the human body* (20th American ed.). Philadelphia: Lea & Febiger.

Gross, A. E., & Crofton, C. (1977). What is good is beautiful. *Sociometry, 40,* 85–90.

Gurnee, H. (1936). *Elements of social psychology.* New York: Farrar & Reinhart.

Guthrie, R. D. (1970). Evolution of human threat display organs. In T. Dobzhansky, M. K. Hecht, & W. C. Steere (Eds.), *Evolutionary biology* (Vol. 4, pp. 257–302). New York: Appleton-Century-Crofts.

Guthrie, R. D. (1976). *Body hot spots.* New York: Van Nostrand Reinhold.

Gwyndaf, R. (1977). Personal communication on the archives of the Welsh Folk Museum, Cardiff.

Hagg, U., & Taranger, J. (1985). Dental development, dental age, and tooth counts. *Angle Orthodontist, 55,* 93–107.

Haith, M., Bergman, T., & Moore, M. (1977). Eye contact and face scanning in early infancy. *Science, 198,* 853–855.

Hallpike, C. R. (1969). Social hair. *Man, 4,* 256–264.

Hamburg, B. A. (1980). Early adolescence as a life stress. In S. Levin & U. Holger (Eds.), *Coping and health: Vol. 12. Nato conference series: Human factors.* New York: Plenum Press.

Hamid, P. N. (1968). Style of dress as a perceptual cue in impression formation. *Perceptual and Motor Skills, 26,* 904–906.

Hamid, P. N. (1972). Some effects of dress cues on observational accuracy, a perceptual estimate, and impression formation. *Journal of Social Psychology, 86,* 279–289.

Hamm, N. H., Baum, M. R., & Nikels, K. W. (1975). Effects of race and exposure on judgments of interpersonal favorability. *Journal of Experimental Social Psychology, 11,* 14–24.

Hand, W. D. (1979). Personal communication on the unpublished files of the *Dictionary of American Popular Beliefs and Superstitions.*

Hansell, S., Sparacino, J., & Ronchi, D. (1982). Physical attractiveness and blood pressure: Sex and age differences. *Personality and Social Psychology Bulletin, 8,* 113-121.

Hansson, R. O., & Duffield, B. J. (1976). Physical attractiveness and the attribution of epilepsy. *Journal of Social Psychology, 99,* 233-240.

Harlow, H. R., & Mears C. E. (1983). Emotional sequences and consequences. In R. Plutchik & H. Kellerman (Eds.), *Emotion: Theory, research and experience* (Vol. 2). New York: Academic Press.

Harrison, A. A. (1977). Mere exposure. *Advances in Experimental Social Psychology, 10,* 39-83.

Hatfield, E., & Sprecher, S. (1986). *Mirror, mirror: The importance of looks in everyday life.* Albany, NY: State University of New York.

Hebb, D. O. (1946). On the nature of fear. *Psychological Review, 53,* 259-276.

Heider, F. (1958). *The psychology of interpersonal relations.* New York: Wiley.

Heider, F., & Simmel, M. (1944). An experimental study of apparent behavior. *American Journal of Psychology, 57,* 243-259.

Heilman, M. E., & Saruwatari, L. R. (1979). When beauty is beastly: The effects of appearance and sex on evaluations of job applicants for managerial and nonmanagerial jobs. *Organizational Behavior and Human Performance, 23,* 360-372.

Heller, A., Tidmarsh, W., & Pless, I. B. (1981). The psychosocial functioning of young adults born with cleft lip or palate. *Clinical Pediatrics, 20,* 459-465.

Helm, S. (1977). Epidemiology and public health aspects of malocclusion. *Journal of Dental Research* (Special Issue C), *56,* C27-C30.

Helson, H. (1964). *Adaptation-level theory.* New York: Harper & Row.

Hernandez, O. A. (1981). *A cross-cultural comparison of adults' perceptions of infant sex and physical attractiveness.* Unpublished doctoral dissertation, Michigan State University, East Lansing.

Hess, E. H. (1970). Ethology and developmental psychology. In P. Mussen (Ed.), *Carmichael's manual of child psychology* (Vol. 1). New York: Wiley.

Hess, E. H. (1975). *The tell-tale eye.* New York: Van Nostrand Reinhold.

Hildebrandt, K. A. (1980, April). *Parents' perceptions of their infants' physical attractiveness.* Paper presented at the International Conference on Infant Studies, New Haven, CT.

Hildebrandt, K. A. (1982a). The role of physical appearance in infant and child development. In H. E. Fitzgerald, B. M. Lester, & M. W. Yogman (Eds.), *Theory and research in behavioral pediatrics* (Vol. 1). New York: Plenum.

Hildebrandt, K. A. (1982b, April). *Who gets more attention when an adult plays with two 7-month-old infants?* Paper presented at the Annual Meeting of the Eastern Psychological Association, Baltimore.

Hildebrandt, K. A. (1983). Effect of facial expression variations on ratings of infants' physical attractiveness. *Developmental Psychology, 19,* 414-417.

Hildebrandt, K. A., & Cannan, T. (1985). The distribution of caregiver attention in a group program for young children. *Child Study Journal, 15,* 43-55.

Hildebrandt, K. A., & Fitzgerald, H. E. (1978). Adults' responses to infants varying in perceived cuteness. *Behavioural Processes, 3,* 159-172.

Hildebrandt, K. A., & Fitzgerald, H. E. (1979a). Adult perceptions of infant sex and cuteness. *Sex Roles, 5,* 471-481.

Hildebrandt, K. A., & Fitzgerald, H. E. (1979b). Facial feature determinants of perceived infant attractiveness. *Infant Behavior and Development, 2,* 329-339.

Hildebrandt, K. A., & Fitzgerald, H. E. (1981). Mothers' responses to infant physical appearance. *Infant Mental Health Journal, 2,* 56-61.

Hildebrandt, K. A., & Stern, M. (1984). *Infants' physical appearance and labeled sex: Effects on adults' perceptions.* Paper presented at the Annual Meeting of the American Psychological Association, Toronto.

Hill, M. C. (1944). Social status and physical appearance among Negro adolescents. *Social Forces, 22,* 443-448.

REFERENCES

Hirsch, B., Levin, B., & Tiber, N. (1972). Effects of patient involvement and esthetic preference on denture acceptance. *Journal of Prosthetic Dentistry, 28,* 127.

Hirsch, B., Levin, B., & Tiber, N. (1973). Effects of dentist authoritarianism on patient evaluation of dentures. *Journal of Prosthetic Dentistry, 30,* 745.

Hirschenfang, S., Goldberg, M. J., & Benton, J. G. (1969). Psychological aspects of patients with facial paralysis. *Memory and Cognition, 2,* 39-42.

Hochberg, J., & Galper, R. E. (1974). Attribution of intention as a function of physiognomy. *Memory and Cognition, 2,* 39-42.

Hofer, M. A. (1984). Relationships as regulators: A psychobiologic perspective on bereavement. *Psychosomatic Medicine, 46,* 183-198.

Hogarth, B. (1965). *Drawing the human head.* New York: Watson-Guptill.

Hole, C. (1961). *Encyclopaedia of superstitions.* London: Book Club Associates.

Horai, J., Naccari, N., & Fatoullah, E. (1974). The effects of expertise and physical attractiveness upon opinion agreement and liking. *Sociometry 37,* 601-606.

Howells, D. T., & Shaw, W. C. (1985). The validity and reliability of ratings of dental and facial attractiveness for epidemiological use. *American Journal of Orthodontics, 88,* 402-409.

Howitt, J. W., Stricker, G., & Henderson, R. (1967). Eastman Esthetic Index. *New York State Dental Journal, 33,* 215-220.

Huckstedt, B. (1965). Experimentelle untersuchungen zum "Kindchenschema". *Zeitschrift fur Experimentelle und Angewandte Psychologie, 12,* 421-450.

Hull, C. L. (1928). *Aptitude testing.* Yonkers-on-Hudson, NY: World Book.

Hulse, F. S. (1967). Selection for skin color among the Japanese. *American Journal of Physical Anthropology, 27,* 143-156.

Hurwitz, D., Wiggins, N. H., & Jones, L. E. (1975). A semantic differential for facial attribution: The face differential. *Bulletin of the Psychonomic Society, 6,* 370-372.

Hutton, C. E. (1967). Patients' evaluation of surgical correction of prognathism: Survey of 32 patients. *Journal of Oral Surgery, 25,* 225-228.

Iliffe, A. H. (1960). A study of preferences in feminine beauty. *British Journal of Psychology, 51,* 267-273.

Izard, C. E. (1979). *The maximally discriminative facial movement coding system (MAX).* Newark, DE: University of Delaware, Instructional Resources Center.

Jackson, L. A. (1983). The influence of sex, physical attractiveness, sex role, and occupational sex-linkage on perceptions of occupational suitability. *Journal of Applied Social Psychology, 13,* 31-44.

Jacobson, A. (1984). Psychological aspects of dentofacial esthetics and orthognathic surgery. *Angle Orthodontist, 54,* 18-35.

Jago, J. D. (1974). Epidemiology of dental occlusion: A critical approach. *Journal of Public Health Dentistry, 34,* 80-93.

Janik, S. W., Wellens, R., Goldberg, M. L., & Dell'osso, L. F. (1978). Eyes as the center of focus in the visual examination of human faces. *Perceptual and Motor Skills, 47,* 857-858.

Jenny, J. (1975). A social perspective on need and demand for orthodontic treatment. *International Dental Journal, 25,* 248-256.

Jenny, J., Cons, N. C., Kohout, F., & Frazier, P. J. (1980). Test of a method to determine socially acceptable occlusal conditions. *Journal of Dental Research, 59* (Abstract No. 11), p. 270.

Jensen, S. H. (1978). The psychological dimensions of oral and maxillofacial surgery: A critical review of the literature. *Journal of Oral Surgery, 36,* 447-453.

Johansson, G. (1973). Visual perception of biological motion and a model for its analysis. *Perception and Psychophysics, 14,* 201-211.

Johansson, G. (1975). Visual motion perception. *Scientific American, 232,* 76-88.

Johnson, D. F. (1985). Appearance and the elderly. In J. A. Graham & A. M. Kligman (Eds.), *The psychology of cosmetic treatments* (pp. 152-160). New York: Praeger.

Jones, B. M., Gabe, M. J., & Shaw, W. C. (1979). *Experience of teasing and harassment in children attending plastic surgery clinics.* Unpublished project report, Dental School, Welsh National School of Medicine, Cardiff.

Jones, G., & Smith, P. K. (1984). The eyes have it: Young children's discrimination of age in masked and unmasked facial photographs. *Journal of Experimental Child Psychology, 38,* 328–337.

Jones, Q. R., & Moyel, I. S. (1971). The influence of iris color and pupil size on expressed affect. *Psychonomic Science, 22,* 126–127.

Justice, B., & Justice, R. (1976). *The abusing family.* New York: Human Sciences Press.

Kagan, J., Henker, B. A., Hen-Tov, A., Levine, J., & Lewis, M. (1966). Infants' differential reactions to familiar and distorted faces. *Child Development, 37,* 519–532.

Kahane, H. (1969). *Logic and philosophy.* Belmont, CA: Wadsworth.

Kahn, A., Hottes, J., & Davis, W. L. (1971). Cooperation and optimal responding in the prisoner's dilemma game: Effects of sex and physical attractiveness. *Journal of Personality and Social Psychology, 17,* 267–279.

Kaplan, G. (1969). Kinetic disruption of optical texture: The perception of depth at an edge. *Perception and Psychophysics, 6,* 193–198.

Kapp, K. (1979). Self-concept of the cleft lip and/or palate child. *Cleft Palate Journal, 16,* 171–176.

Karaliers, M. (1981). Schooling behavior in fish: An opiate-dependent activity. *Behavioral and Neural Biology, 33,* 379–401.

Kassin, S. M. (1977). Physical continuity and trait inference: A test of Mischel's hypothesis. *Personality and Social Psychology Bulletin, 3,* 637–640.

Kassin, S. M., & Baron, R. M. (1986). On the basicity of social perception cues: Developmental evidence for adult processes? *Social Cognition, 4,* 180–200.

Katz, R. V. (1978). Relationships between eight orthodontic indices and oral self image satisfaction scale. *American Journal of Orthodontics, 73,* 328–334.

Keating, C. F. (1985). Gender and the physiognomy of dominance and attractiveness. *Social Psychology Quarterly, 48,* 61–70.

Keating, C. F., & Bai, D. L. (1986). Children's attributions of social dominance from facial cues. *Child Development, 57,* 1269–1276.

Keating, C. F., Mazur, A., & Segall, M. H. (1977). Facial features which influence the perception of status. *Sociometry, 40,* 374–378.

Keating, C. F., Mazur, A., & Segall, M. H. (1981). A cross-cultural exploration of physiognomic traits of dominance and happiness. *Ethology and Sociobiology, 2,* 41–48.

Keating, C. F., Mazur, A., Segall, M. H., Cysneiros, P. G., Divale, W. T., Kilbride, J. E., Komin, S., Leahy, P., Thurman, B., & Wirsing, R. (1981). Culture and the perception of social dominance from facial expression. *Journal of Personality and Social Psychology, 40,* 615–626.

Keller, L. E. (1980). *Effects of physical attractiveness of infants on parental behavior.* Unpublished doctoral dissertation, California School of Professional Psychology, Berkeley.

Kelly, G. (1955). *The psychology of personal constructs.* New York: Norton.

Kelly, J. E., & Harvey, C. R. (1977). *An assessment of the occlusion of the teeth of youths 12–17 years, United States* (DHEW Publication No. HRA 77-1644). Washington, DC: U.S. Government Printing Office.

Kenny, C. T., & Fletcher, D. (1973). Effects of beardedness on person perception. *Perceptual and Motor Skills, 37,* 413–414.

Kenrick, D., & Gutierres, S. E. (1980). Contrast effects and judgments of physical attractiveness: When beauty becomes a social problem. *Journal of Personality and Social Psychology, 38,* 131–140.

Kepler, J. (1611). *Dioptric seu demonstratio eorum quae visui & visibilibus propter conspicilla non its pridem inventat accidunt.* Ausburg.

Kerr, N. L., & Kurtz, S. T. (1978). Reliability of "the eye of the beholder": Effects of sex of beholder and sex of beheld. *Bulletin of the Psychonomic Society, 12,* 179–181.

Kiener, F., & Hofer, B. (1971). Modifikation der Personwahrnehumung durch nicht bewusste Lernvorgange. *Psychologische Rundschau, 23,* 30–40.

Kirkland, J., & Smith, J. (1978). Preferences for infant pictures with modified eye-pupils. *Journal of Biological Psychology, 20,* 33–34.

Kiyak, H. A., West, R. A., Hohl, T., & McNeill, R. W. (1982). The psychological impact of orthognathic surgery: A 9-month follow-up. *American Journal of Orthodontics, 81,* 404–412.

Klaiman, S. (1979). *Selected perceptual, cognitive, personality, and socialization variables as predictors of nonverbal sensitivity.* Unpublished doctoral dissertation, University of Ottawa.

Klatzky, R. L., & Forrest, F. H. (1984). Recognizing familiar and unfamiliar faces. *Memory & Cognition, 12,* 60–70.

Klaus, M. H., & Kennell, J. H. (1976). *Mother–infant bonding.* St. Louis, MO: C. V. Mosby.

Kleck, R. E. (1966). Emotional arousal in interactions with stigmatized persons. *Psychological Reports, 19,* 1226.

Kleck, R. E. (1969). Physical stigma and task oriented interactions. *Human Relations, 22,* 53–60.

Kleck, R. E., Buck, P. L., Goller, W. L., London, R. S., Pfeiffer, J. R., & Vukcevic, D. P. (1968). Effect of stigmatizing condition on the use of personal space. *Psychological Reports, 23,* 111–118.

Kleck, R. E., Richardson, S. A., & Ronald, L. (1974). Physical appearance cues and interpersonal attraction in children. *Child Development, 45,* 305–310.

Kleck, R. E., & Rubenstein, C. (1975). Physical attractiveness, perceived attitude similarity, and interpersonal attraction in an opposite-sex encounter. *Journal of Personality and Social Psychology, 31,* 107–114.

Klima, R. J., Wittemann, J. K., & McIver, J. E. (1979). Body image, self-concept, and the orthodontic patient. *American Journal of Orthodontics, 75,* 507–516.

Klinnert, M. D. (1984). The regulation of infant behavior by maternal facial expression. *Infant Behavior and Development, 7,* 447–465.

Klinnert, M. D., Campos, J. J., Sorce, J. F., Emde, R. N., & Svejda, M. (1983). Emotions as behavior regulators: Social referencing in infancy. In R. Plutchik & H. Kellerman (Eds.), *Emotion: Theory, research and experience* (Vol. 2, pp. 57–86). New York: Academic Press.

Kodric-Brown, A., & Brown, J. H. (1985). Why the fittest are prettiest. *Sciences, 25*(5), 26–33.

Koffka, K. (1935). *Principles of gestalt psychology.* New York: Harcourt Brace.

Korthase, K. M., & Trenholme, I. (1982). Perceived age and perceived physical attractiveness. *Perceptual and Motor Skills, 54,* 1251–1258.

Korthase, K. M., & Trenholme, I. (1983). Children's perceptions of age and physical attractiveness. *Perceptual and Motor Skills, 56,* 895–900.

Kozeny, E. D. (1962). Experimentelle untersuchungen zur ausdruckskunde mittels photographisch-statistischer methode. *Archiv fur die gesamte Psychologie, 114,* 55–71.

Kunst-Wilson, W. R., & Zajonc, R. B. (1980). Affective discrimination of stimuli that cannot be recognized. *Science, 207,* 557–558.

LaBarbera, J. D., Izard, C. E., Vietz, P., & Parisi, S. A. (1976). Four- and six-month-old infants' visual responses to joy, anger, and neutral expressions. *Child Development, 47,* 535–538.

LaCrosse, M. B. (1975). Nonverbal behavior and perceived counselor attractiveness and persuasiveness. *Journal of Counseling Psychology, 22,* 563–566.

Landy, D., & Sigall, H. (1974). Beauty is talent: Task evaluation as a function of the performer's physical attractiveness. *Journal of Personality and Social Psychology, 29,* 229–304.

Langer, E. J., Fiske, S., Taylor, S. E., & Chanowitz, B. (1976). Stigma, staring, and discomfort: A novel stimulus hypothesis. *Journal of Experimental Social Psychology, 12,* 451–463.

Langlois, J. H. (1986). From the eye of the beholder to behavioral reality: Development of social behaviors and social relations as a function of physical attractiveness. In C. P. Herman, M. P. Zanna, & E. T. Higgins (Eds.), *Physical appearance, stigma, and social behavior: Vol. 3.*

Ontario Symposium on Personality and Social Cognition (pp. 23-51). Hillsdale, NJ: Lawrence Erlbaum Associates.

Langlois, J. H., & Downs, A. C. (1979). Peer relations as a function of physical attractiveness: The eye of the beholder or behavioral reality? *Child Development, 50,* 409-418.

Langlois, J. H., Roggman, L., Casey, R. J., Ritter, J. M., Rieser-Danner, L. A., & Jenkins, V. (1986, April). *Infant preferences for attractive faces: Rudiments of a stereotype?* Paper presented at the International Conference on Infant Studies, Los Angeles.

Langlois, J. H., Sawin, D. B., & Stephan, C. W. (1981). *Infant physical attractiveness as an elicitor of differential parenting behavior.* Paper presented at the biennial meeting of the Society for Research in Child Development, Boston.

Langlois, J. H., & Stephan, C. W. (1977). The effects of physical attractiveness and ethnicity on children's behavioral attributions and peer preferences. *Child Development, 48,* 1694-1698.

Langlois, J. H., & Stephan, C. W. (1981). Beauty and the beast: The role of physical attractiveness in the development of peer relations and social behavior. In S. S. Brehm, S. M. Kassin, & F. X. Gibbons (Eds.), *Developmental social psychology* (pp. 152-168). New York: Oxford University.

Langlois, J. H., & Styczynski, L. (1979). The effects of physical attractiveness on the behavioral attributions and peer preferences in acquainted children. *International Journal of Behavioral Development, 2,* 325-341.

Lansdown, R., & Polak, L. (1975). A study of the psychological effects of facial deformity in children. *Child: Care, Health and Development, 1,* 85-91.

Lanzetta, J. T., & Orr, S. P. (1980). Influence of facial expressions on the classical conditioning of fear. *Journal of Personality and Social Psychology, 39,* 1081-1087.

Lanzetta, J. T., & Orr, S. P. (1981). Stimulus properties of facial expressions and their influence on the classical conditioning of fear. *Motivation & Emotion, 5,* 225-234.

Larrance, D. T., & Zuckerman, M. (1981). Facial attractiveness and vocal likeability as determinants of nonverbal sending skills. *Journal of Personality, 49,* 349-362.

Lavater, J. C. (1783). *Essays on physiognomy.* London: Ward, Lock & Co.

LaVoie, J. C., & Adams, G. R. (1974). Teacher expectancy and its relation to physical and interpersonal characteristics of the child. *Alberta Journal of Educational Research, 22,* 122-132.

Lawson, E. D. (1971). Hair color, personality, and the observer. *Psychological Reports, 28,* 311-322.

Layard, J. (1944). *The lady of the hare.* London: Faber & Faber.

Lazarus, R. S. (1984). On the primacy of cognition. *American Psychologist, 39,* 124-129.

Lazarus, R. S., & McCleary, R. A. (1951). Autonomic discrimination without awareness: A study of subception. *Psychological Review, 58,* 113-122.

LeBarr, G. H. (1922). *Why you are what you are.* Boston: Author.

LeDoux, J. E. (1986). Neurobiology and emotion. In J. E. LeDoux & W. Hirst (Eds.), *Mind and brain: Dialogues in cognitive neuroscience.* New York: Cambridge University.

Lefas, J. (1975). *Physiognomy: The art of reading faces.* Barcelona: Ariane.

Lefebvre, A., & Barclay, S. (1982). Psychosocial impact of craniofacial deformities before and after reconstructive surgery. *Canadian Journal of Psychiatry, 27,* 579-584.

Lefebvre, A., & Munro, I. R. (1986). Psychosocial adjustment of patients with craniofacial deformities before and after surgery. In C. P. Herman, M. P. Zanna, & E. T. Higgins (Eds.), *Physical appearance, stigma, and social behavior: Vol. 3. Ontario Symposium on Personality and Social Cognition* (pp. 53-62). Hillsdale, NJ: Lawrence Erlbaum Associates.

Legan, H. L., & Burstone, C. J. (1980). Soft tissue cephalometric analysis for orthognathic surgery. *Journal of Oral Surgery, 38,* 744-751.

Lerner, R. M., Karabenick, S. A., & Stuart, J. L. (1973). Relations among physical attractiveness, body attitudes, and self-concept in male and female college students. *Journal of Psychology, 85,* 119-129.

Lerner, R. M., & Lerner, J. V. (1977). Effects of age, sex, and physical attractiveness on child-peer relations, academic performance, and elementary school adjustment. *Developmental Psychology, 13,* 585-590.

Leventhal, G., & Krate, R. (1977). Physical attractiveness and severity of sentencing. *Psychological Reports, 40,* 315-318.

Levine, S. (1969). An endocrine theory of infantile stimulation. In A. Ambrose (Ed.), *Stimulation in early infancy.* London: Academic Press.

Levitt, L., & Kornhaber, R. C. (1977). Stigma and compliance: A re-examination. *Journal of Social Psychology, 103,* 13-18.

Levy, J., & Trevarthen, C. (1976). Metacontrol of hemispheric function in human split-brain patients. *Journal of Experimental Psychology: Human Perception and Performance, 2,* 299-312.

Lewis, E. A., Albino, J. E., Cunat, J. J., & Tedesco, L. A. (1982). Reliability and validity of clinical assessments of malocclusion. *American Journal of Orthodontics, 81,* 473-477.

Lewis, E. A., Fox, R. N., Albino, J. E., Slakter, M. J., & Wu, T. H. (1979). Accuracy of self-perception of occlusal state. *Journal of Dental Research, 58* (Abstract No. 1180).

Lewis, M., & Brooks, J. (1974). Self, other, and fear: Infants' reactions to people. In M. Lewis & L. A. Rosenblum (Eds.), *Origins of fear* (pp. 195-227). New York: Wiley.

Lewit, D. W., & Virolainen, K. (1968). Conformity and independence in adolescents' motivation for orthodontic treatment. *Child Development, 39,* 1189-1200.

Liggett, J. (1974). *The human face.* London: Constable.

Linn, E. L. (1966). Social meanings of dental appearance. *Journal of Health and Human Behavior, 7,* 289-295.

Livesley, W. J., & Bromsley, D. B. (1973). *Person perception in childhood and adolescence.* London: Wiley.

Livson, N. (1979). The physically attractive women at age 40: Precursor in adolescent personality and adult correlates from a longitudinal study. In M. Cook & G. Wilson (Eds.), *Love and attraction* (pp. 55-59). New York: Pergamon.

Lorenz, K. (1943). Die angeborenen formen möglicher arfahrung. (Innate forms of possible experience.) *Zietschrift fur Tierpsychologie, 5,* 233-409.

Lowenstein, L. R. (1978). The bullied and non-bullied child. *Bulletin of the British Psychological Society, 31,* 316-318.

Lucker, G. W., & Graber, L. W. (1980). Physiognomic features and facial appearance judgments in children. *Journal of Psychology, 104,* 261-268.

Lucker, G. W., Graber, L. W., & Pietromonaco, P. (1981). The importance of dentofacial appearance in facial esthetics: A signal detection approach. *Basic and Applied Social Psychology, 2,* 261-274.

Lucker, G. W., Ribbens, K. A., & McNamara, J. A. (Eds.). (1981). *Psychological aspects of facial form.* Ann Arbor, MI: Center for Human Growth.

Lyman, B., Hatlelid, D., & Macurdy, C. (1981). Stimulus-person cues in first-impression attraction. *Perceptual and Motor Skills, 52,* 59-66.

Mace, W. M. (1977). J. J. Gibson's strategy for perceiving: Ask not what's inside your head, but what your head's inside of. In R. Shaw & J. Bransford (Eds.), *Perceiving, acting, and knowing: Toward an ecological psychology* (pp. 43-65). Hillsdale, NJ: Lawrence Erlbaum Associates.

Macgregor, F. C. (1951). Some psycho-social problems associated with facial deformities. *American Sociological Review, 16,* 629-638.

Macgregor, F. C. (1970). Social and psychological implications of dentofacial disfigurement. *Angle Orthodontist, 40,* 231-233.

Macgregor, F. C. (1974). *Transformation and identity.* New York: Quadrangle.

Macgregor, F. C., Abel, T. M., Bryt, A., Lauer, E., & Weissmann, S. (1953). *Facial deformities and plastic surgery: A psychosocial study.* Springfield, IL: C. C. Thomas.

Maier, R. A., Holmes, D. L., Slaymaker, F. L., & Reich, J. N. (1984). The perceived attractiveness of preterm infants. *Infant Behavior and Development, 7*, 403-414.

Mainwaring, M. (1980). "Phys/phren'—why not to take each other at face value. *Smithsonian, 11*(8), 193-212.

Malatesta, C. (1985). The concept of adaptation in developmental research: Contemporary paradigms and historical perspective. *Early parent-child interaction and later competence*. Symposium conducted at the 8th Biennial Meeting of the International Society for the Study of Behavioral Development, Tours, France.

Malatesta, C. Z., Grigoryev, P., Lamb, C., Albin, M., & Culver, C. (1986). Emotion socialization and expressive development in preterm and full term infants. *Child Development, 57*, 316-330.

Malatesta, C. Z., & Haviland, J. M. (1982). Learning display rules: The socialization of emotion expression in infancy. *Child Development, 53*, 991-1003.

Malatesta, C. Z., & Izard, C. E. (1984). the ontogenesis of human social signals: From biological imperative to symbol utilization. In N. Fox & R. Davidson (Eds.), *The psychobiology of affective development* (pp. 161-206). Hillsdale, NJ: Lawrence Erlbaum Associates.

Malpass, R. S., & Kravitz, J. (1969). Recognition of faces of own and other races. *Journal of Personality and Social Psychology, 13*, 330-334.

Mar, T. T. (1974). *Face reading: The Chinese art of physiognomy*. New York: Dodd, Mead.

Maret, S. M. (1983). Attractiveness ratings of photographs of blacks by Cruzans and Americans. *Journal of Psychology, 115*, 113-116.

Mark, L. S., Pittenger, J. B., Hines, H., Carello, C., Shaw, R. E., & Todd, J. T. (1980). Wrinkling and head shape as coordinated sources of age-level information. *Perception and Psychophysics, 27*, 117-124.

Mark, L. S., Shapiro, B. A., & Shaw, R. E. (1986). Structural support for the perception of growth. *Journal of Experimental Psychology: Human Perception and Performance, 12*, 149-159.

Mark, L. S., & Todd, J. T. (1983). The perception of growth in three dimensions. *Perception and Psychophysics, 33*, 193-196.

Mark, L. S., & Todd, J. T. (1985). Describing geometric information about human growth in terms of geometric invariants. *Perception and Psychophysics, 37*, 249-256.

Mark, L. S., Todd, J. T., & Shaw, R. E. (1981). Perception of growth: A geometric analysis of how different styles of change are distinguished. *Journal of Experimental Psychology: Human Perception and Performance, 7*, 855-868.

Martin, J. G. (1964). Racial ethnocentrism and judgment of beauty. *Journal of Social Psychology, 63*, 59-63.

Maruyama, G., & Miller, N. (1981). Physical attractiveness and personality. In B. A. Maher & W. B. Maher (Eds.), *Progress in experimental personality research* (Vol. 10, pp. 203-280). New York: Academic Press.

Marwit, K. L., Marwit, S. J., & Walker, E. (1978). Effects of student race and physical attractiveness on teachers' judgements of transgressions. *Journal of Educational Psychology, 70*, 911-915.

Mathes, E. W. (1975). The effects of physical attractiveness and anxiety on heterosexual attraction over a series of five encounters. *Journal of Marriage and the Family, 37*, 769-773.

Mathes, E. W., & Kahn, A. (1975). Physical attractiveness, happiness, neuroticism, and self-esteem. *Journal of Psychology, 90*, 27-30.

Maurer, D. (1985). Infants' perception of facedness. In T. M. Field & N. A. Fox (Eds.), *Social perception in infants* (pp. 73-100). Norwood, NJ: Ablex.

Mazur, A., Mazur, J., & Keating, C. (1984). Military rank attainment of a West Point class: Effects of cadets' physical features. *American Journal of Sociology, 90*, 125-150.

McArthur, L. Z. (1980). Illusory causation and illusory correlation: Two epistemological accounts. *Personality and Social Psychology Bulletin, 6*, 507-519.

McArthur, L. Z. (1982). Judging a book by its cover: A cognitive analysis of the relationship between physical appearance and stereotyping. In A. H. Hastorf & A. M. Isen (Eds.), *Cognitive social psychology* (pp. 149-211). New York: Elsevier.

McArthur, L. Z. (unpublished). [*Impressions of human profiles varying in craniofacial maturity*]. Unpublished data, Brandeis University.

McArthur, L. Z., & Apatow, K. (1983-84). Impressions of baby-faced adults. *Social Cognition, 2,* 315-342.

McArthur, L. Z., & Baron, R. M. (1983). Toward an ecological theory of social perception. *Psychological Review, 90,* 215-238.

McArthur, L. Z., & Berry, D. S. (1987). Cross-cultural agreement in perceptions of babyfaced adults. *Journal of Cross-cultural Psychology, 18,* 165-192.

McArthur, L. Z., & Fafel, J. B. (1987). *The impact of children's babyfacedness on the tasks that parents assign to them.* Unpublished data, Brandeis University.

McArthur, L. Z., Lipnick, J., & Ridin, D. (1984). *The impact of curvature and angularity on the perception of faces and objects.* Unpublished data, Brandeis University.

McArthur, L. Z., & Tenenbaum, D. R. (1987). *The impact of facial maturity and academic achievement on evaluations of job applicants.* Unpublished data, Brandeis University.

McCabe, V. (1982a, April). *Abstract perceptual information for the social act of caregiving.* Paper presented at the Annual Meeting of the Eastern Psychological Association, Baltimore, MD.

McCabe, V. (1982b). Invariants and affordances: An analysis of species typical information. *Ethology and Sociobiology, 3,* 79-92.

McCabe, V. (1982c). The direct perception of universals: A theory of knowledge acquisition. *Synthese, 52,* 495-513.

McCabe, V. (1984). Abstract perceptual information for age level: A risk factor for maltreatment? *Child Development, 55,* 267-276.

McCall, R. B., & Kennedy, C. B. (1980). Attention of 4-month old infants to discrepancy and babyishness. *Journal of Experimental Child Psychology, 29,* 189-201.

McClintock, M. K. (1971). Menstrual synchrony and suppression. *Nature, 229,* 244-245.

McGarry, M. S., & West, S. C. (1975). Stigma among the stigmatized: Resident mobility, communicative ability, and physical appearance as predictors of staff-resident interaction. *Journal of Abnormal Psychology, 84,* 399-405.

McGee, A-M., & Skinner, M. (1987). Facial asymmetry and the attribution of personality traits. *British Journal of Social Psychology, 26,* 181-184.

McGuinness, D., & Pribram, K. (1980). The neuropsychology of attention: Emotional and motivational controls. In M. C. Witbrock (Ed.), *The brain and psychology.* New York: Academic Press.

McKeachie, W. J. (1952). Lipstick as a determiner of first impressions of personalities: An experiment for the General Psychology course. *Journal of Social Psychology, 36,* 241-244.

McKelvie, S. J. (1981). Sex differences in memory for faces. *Journal of Psychology, 107,* 109-125.

McPherson, J. M. (1929). *Primitive beliefs in the north east of Scotland.* London: Longmans Green & Co.

McWilliams, B. J. (1982). Social and psychological problems associated with cleft palate. *Clinics in Plastic Surgery, 9,* 317-326.

Melamed, E. (1983). *Mirror mirror: The terror of not being young.* New York: Simon & Schuster.

Melamed, L., & Moss, M. K. (1975). The effect of context on ratings of attractiveness of photographs. *Journal of Psychology, 90,* 129-136.

Miller, A. G. (1970). Role of physical attractiveness in impression formation. *Psychonomic Science, 19,* 241-243.

Miller, H. L., & Rivenbark, W. H. (1970). Sexual differences in physical attractiveness as a determinant of heterosexual liking. *Psychological Reports, 27,* 701-702.

Miller, R. E., Caul, W. F., & Mirsky, I. A. (1967). Communication of affects between feral and socially isolated monkeys. *Journal of Personality and Social Psychology, 7,* 231–239.

Mills, J., & Aronson, E. (1965). Opinion change as a function of the communicator's attractiveness and desire to influence. *Journal of Personality and Social Psychology, 1,* 173–177.

Milord, J. T. (1978). Aesthetic aspects of faces: A (somewhat) phenomenological analysis using multidimensional scaling methods. *Journal of Personality and Social Psychology, 36,* 205–216.

Mims, P. R., Hartnett, J. J., & Nay, W. R. (1975). Interpersonal attraction and help volunteering as a function of physical attractiveness. *Journal of Psychology, 89,* 125–131.

Mita, T. H., Dermer, M., & Knight, J. (1977). Reversed facial images and the mere exposure hypothesis. *Journal of Personality and Social Psychology, 35,* 597–601.

Moller, E. (1966). The chewing apparatus: An electromyographic study of the action of the muscles of mastication and its correlation to facial morphology. *Acta Odontologica Scandinavica, 69,* Suppl. No. 280.

Monahan, F. (1941). *Women in crime.* New York: Washburn.

Montepare, J. M., & McArthur, L. Z. (1982, April). *The development of age-discrimination ability and stereotyping of the elderly.* Paper presented at the 53rd meeting of the Eastern Psychological Association, Baltimore, MD.

Montepare, J. M., & McArthur, L. Z. (1986). The impact of age-related variations in facial characteristics on children's age perceptions. *Journal of Experimental Child Psychology, 42,* 303–314.

Montepare, J. M., McArthur, L. Z., & Amgott-Kwan, T. (1984, April). *Variation in gait as a source of age and gender information.* Paper presented at the 55th meeting of the Eastern Psychological Association, Baltimore, MD.

Moore, W. J., & Lavelle, C. L. B. (1974). *Growth of the facial skeleton in the hominoidea.* New York: Academic Press.

Moreland, R. L., & Zajonc, R. B. (1982). Exposure effects in person perception: Familiarity, similarity, and attraction. *Journal of Experimental Social Psychology, 18,* 395–415.

Morris, D. (1967). *The naked ape.* London: Corgi.

Morris, M. G., & Gould, R. W. (1963). *Role reversal: A concept in dealing with the neglected and battered child syndrome.* New York: Child Welfare League of America.

Morrow, P. C., & McElroy, J. C. (1984). The impact of physical attractiveness in evaluative contexts. *Basic and Applied Social Psychology, 5,* 171–182.

Morse, S. J., Reis, H. T., Gruzen, J., & Wolff, E. (1974). The "eye of the beholder": Determinants of physical attractiveness judgments in the U.S. and South Africa. *Journal of Personality, 42,* 528–542.

Mueser, K. T., Grau, B. W., Sussman, S., & Rosen, A. J. (1984). You're only pretty as you feel: Facial expression as a determinant of physical attractiveness. *Journal of Personality and Social Psychology, 46,* 469–478.

Nakdimen, K. A. (1984). The physiognomic basis of sexual stereotyping. *American Journal of Psychiatry, 141,* 499–503.

Napoleon, T., Chassin, L., & Young, R. D. (1980). A replication and extension of "Physical attractiveness and mental illness". *Journal of Abnormal Psychology, 89,* 250–253.

Neisser, U. (1976). *Cognition and reality.* San Francisco: W. H. Freeman.

Nelson, C. A., Morse, P. A., & Leavitt, L. A. (1979). Recognition of facial expression by 7-month-old infants. *Child Development, 56,* 1239–1242.

Newtson, D. (1976). Foundations of attribution: The perception of ongoing behavior. In J. H. Harvey, W. J. Ickes, & R. F. Kidd (Eds.), *New directions in attribution research* (Vol. 1). New York: Wiley.

Nielsen, J. P., & Kernaleguen, A. (1976). Influence of clothing and physical attractiveness in person perception. *Perceptual and Motor Skills, 42,* 775–780.

Nordholm, L. A. (1980). Beautiful patients are good patients: Evidence for the physical attractiveness stereotype in first impressions of patients. *Social Science and Medicine, 14A,* 81–83.

Novak, P. E., & Lerner, M. J. (1968). Rejection as a consequence of perceived similarity. *Journal of Personality and Social Psychology, 9,* 147-152.

Nowak, C. A. (1977). Does youthfulness equal attractiveness? In L. E. Troll, J. Israel, & K. Israel (Eds.), *Looking ahead* (pp. 59-64). Englewood Cliffs, NJ: Prentice-Hall.

Nyman, A. (1978). Personal communication on the archives of the Institut for Undersokning au Svenske Dialekter Och Folkminnen.

Ohman, A., & Dimberg, V. (1978). Facial expressions as conditioned stimuli for electrodermal responses: A case of "preparedness"? *Journal of Personality and Social Psychology, 36,* 1251-1258.

Ohman, A., & Dimberg, V. (1984). An evolutionary perspective on human social behavior. In W. M. Wald (Ed.), *Sociophysiology.* New York: Springer-Verlag.

Olson, R. E., & Laskin, D. M. (1980). Expectations of patients from orthognathic surgery. *Journal of Oral Surgery, 38,* 283-285.

Olweus, D. (1978). *Aggression in the schools.* New York: Wiley.

Ortiz-Monasterio, F., & Serrano, R. A. (1971). Cultural aspects of cleft lip and palate. In W. C. Grabb, S. W. Rosenstein, & K. R. Bzoch (Eds.), *Cleft lip and palate.* Boston: Little Brown & Co.

Ouellette, P. L. (1978). Psychological ramifications of facial change in relation to orthodontic treatment and orthognathic surgery. *Journal of Oral Surgery, 36,* 787-790.

Owens, G., & Ford, J. G. (1978). Further consideration of the "What is good is beautiful" finding. *Social Psychology, 41,* 73-75.

Pallak, S. R. (1983). Salience of a communicator's physical attractiveness and persuasion: A heuristic versus systematic processing interpretation. *Social Cognition, 2,* 158-170.

Pallak, S. R., Murroni, E., & Koch, J. (1983). Communicator attractiveness and expertise, emotional versus rational appeals, and persuasion: A heuristic versus systematic processing interpretation. *Social Cognition, 2,* 122-141.

Panksepp, J. (1981). Hypothalamic integration of behavior. In P. Morgane & J. Panksepp (Eds.), *Handbook of the hypothalmus* (Vol. 3, Pt. B). New York: Marcel Dekker.

Panksepp, J. (1982). Toward a general psychobiological theory of emotions. (with commentaries). *Behavioral and Brain Sciences, 5,* 407-467.

Papousek, H., & Papousek, M. (1983). Biological basis of social interactions: Implications of research for an understanding of behavioral deviance. *Journal of Child Psychology and Psychiatry, 24,* 117-129.

Patterson, K. E., & Baddeley, A. D. (1977). When face recognition fails. *Journal of Experimental Psychology: Human Learning and Memory, 3,* 406-417.

Patzer, G. L. (1985). *The physical attractiveness phenomena.* New York: Plenum.

Peck, H., & Peck, S. (1970). A concept of facial esthetics. *Angle Orthodontist, 40,* 284-317.

Pellegrini, R. J. (1973). Impressions of the male personality as a function of beardedness. *Psychology, 10,* 29-33.

Perrett, D. I., Rolls, E. T., & Caan, W. (1982). Visual neurons responsive to faces in the monkey temporal cortex. *Experimental Brain Research, 47,* 329-342.

Perrin, F. A. C. (1921). Physical attractiveness and repulsiveness. *Journal of Experimental Psychology, 4,* 203-217.

Pertschuk, M. J. (1985). Appearance in psychiatric disorder. In J. A. Graham & A. M. Kligman (Eds.), *The psychology of cosmetic treatments* (pp. 217-226). New York: Praeger.

Peter, J. P., Chinsky, R. R., & Fisher, M. J. (1975). Sociological aspects of cleft palate adults: III. Vocational and economic aspects. *Cleft Palate Journal, 12,* 193-199.

Peterson, L. J., & Topazian, R. G. (1974). The preoperative interview and psychological evaluation of the orthognathic surgery patient. *Journal of Oral Surgery, 32,* 583-588.

Peterson, L. J., & Topazian, R. G. (1976). Psychological considerations in corrective maxillary and midfacial surgery. *Journal of Oral Surgery, 34,* 157-164.

Piers, E. V., & Harris, D. B. (1969). *The Piers-Harris children's self concept scale.* Nashville: Counselor Recordings and Tests.

REFERENCES

Piliavin, I. M., Piliavin, J. A., & Rodin, J. (1975). Costs, diffusion and the stigmatized victim. *Journal of Personality and Social Psychology, 32,* 429–438.
Pitt, E. J., & Korabik, K. (1977). The relationship between self-concept and profile self-perception. *American Journal of Orthodontics, 72,* 459–460.
Pittenger, J. B., & Shaw, R. E. (1975a). Aging faces as viscal-elastic events: Implications for a theory of nonrigid shape perception. *Journal of Experimental Psychology: Human Perception and Performance, 1,* 374–382.
Pittenger, J. B., & Shaw, R. E. (1975b). Perception of relative and absolute age in facial photographs. *Perception and Psychophysics, 18,* 137–143.
Pittenger, J. B., Shaw, R. E., & Mark, L. S. (1979). Perceptual information for the age level of faces as a higher order invariant of growth. *Journal of Experimental Psychology: Human Perception and Performance, 5,* 478–493.
Portjiele, A. F. J. (1921). Zur ethologie Bzw. psychologie von Botanus Stellaris. *Ardea, 15,* 1–15.
Poulton, D. R. (1957). Facial esthetics and angles. *Angle Orthodontist, 27,* 133–137.
Power, T. G., Hildebrandt, K. A., & Fitzgerald, H. E. (1982). Adult responses to infants varying in facial expression and perceived attractiveness. *Infant Behavior and Development, 5,* 33–34.
Prahl-Anderson, B. (1978). The need for orthodontic treatment. *Angle Orthodontist, 48,* 1–9.
Prahl-Anderson, B., Boersma, H., van der Linden, F. P. G. M., & Moore, A. W. (1979). Perceptions of dentofacial morphology by laypersons, general dentists, and orthodontists. *Journal of the American Dental Association, 98,* 209–212.
Pribram, K., & McGuinness, D. (1975). Arousal, attention, and effort in the control of attention. *Psychological Review, 82,* 116–149.
Raymond, G. L. (1909). *The essentials of aesthetics.* New York: G. P. Putnam.
Redican, W. K. (1983). An evolutionary perspective of human facial displays. In P. Ekman (Ed.), *Emotion in the human face* (pp. 212–280). New York: Cambridge University.
Reed, S. C. (1956). *Counselling in medical genetics.* Philadelphia: W. B. Saunders.
Rich, J. (1975). Effects of children's physical attractiveness on teachers' evaluations. *Journal of Educational Psychology, 67,* 599–609.
Richardson, S. A. (1970). Age and sex differences in values toward physical handicaps. *Journal of Health and Social Behavior, 11,* 207–214.
Richardson, S. A. (1971). Children's values and friendships: A study of physical disability. *Journal of Health and Social Behavior, 12,* 253–258.
Richardson, S. A., Goodman, N., Hastorf, A. H., & Dornbusch, S. M. (1961). Cultural uniformity in reaction to physical disabilities. *American Sociological Review, 26,* 241–247.
Richardson, S. A., Koller, H., & Katz, M. (1985). Appearance and mental retardation: Some first steps in the development and application of a measure. *American Journal of Mental Deficiency, 89,* 475–484.
Richman, L. C. (1976). Behavior and achievement of cleft palate children. *Cleft Palate Journal, 13,* 4–10.
Richman, L. C. (1978). Parents and teachers: Differing views of behavior of cleft palate children. *Cleft Palate Journal, 15,* 360–364.
Richman, L. C., & Harper, D. C. (1978). School adjustment of children with observable disabilities. *Journal of Abnormal Child Psychology, 6,* 11–18.
Richman, L. C., & Harper, D. C. (1979). Self identified personality patterns of children with facial or orthopedic disfigurement. *Cleft Palate Journal, 16,* 257–261.
Ricketts, R. M. (1982). The biologic significance of the divine proportion and Fibonacci series. *American Journal of Orthodontics, 81,* 351–370.
Riedel, R. A. (1957). An analysis of dentofacial relationships. *American Journal of Orthodontics, 43,* 103–119.
Ritter, J. M., & Langlois, J. H. (1986, April). *Physical attractiveness: A biasing factor in observing adult-infant interaction?* Paper presented at the fifth International Conference on Infant Studies, Los Angeles.

REFERENCES

Rock, I. (1984). *Perception*. New York: Scientific American Books.
Roll, S., & Verinis, J. S. (1971). Stereotypes of scalp and facial hair as measured by the semantic differential. *Psychological Reports, 28*, 975–980.
Rosenberg, M. (1974, October). *Malocclusion and craniofacial malformation: Self-concept implications*. Paper presented at the workshop on Psychological Aspects of Craniofacial Disfigurement conducted by the Craniofacial Anomalies Branch of the National Institute of Dental Research, Hilton Head, SC.
Rosenberg, M. J., Hovland, C. I., McGuire, W. J., Abelson, R. P., & Brehm, J. W. (1960). *Attitude organization and change: An analysis of consistency among attitude components*. New Haven: Yale University.
Rosenthal, R., Hall, J. A., DiMatteo, M. R., Rogers, P. L., & Archer, D. (1979). *Sensitivity to nonverbal communication: The PONS Test*. Baltimore: Johns Hopkins University.
Rosenthal, R., & Jacobson, C. F. (1968). *Pygmalion in the classroom: Teacher expectations and pupils' intellectual development*. New York: Holt, Rinehart & Winston.
Ross, M. B., & Salvia, J. (1975). Attractiveness as a biasing factor in teacher judgments. *American Journal of Mental Deficiency, 80*, 96–98.
Ross, R. B., & Johnston, M. C. (1972). *Cleft lip and palate*. Baltimore: Williams & Wilkins.
Ross-Kossak, P., & Turkewitz, G. (1984). Relationship between changes in hemispheric advantage during familiarization to faces and proficiency in facial recognition. *Neuropsychologia, 22*, 471–477.
Rubinstein, R. P. (1985). Color, circumcision, tattoos, and scars. In M. R. Solomon (Ed.), *The psychology of fashion* (pp. 243–254). Lexington, MA: D. C. Heath.
Runeson, S., & Frykholm, G. (1981). Visual perception of lifted weight. *Journal of Experimental Psychology: Human Perception and Performance, 7*, 733–740.
Runeson, S., & Frykholm, G. (1983). Kinematic specification of dynamics as an informational basis for person and action perception: Expectation, gender recognition and deceptive intention. *Journal of Experimental Psychology: General, 112*, 585–615.
Rutter, M., Tizard, J., & Whitmore, K. (1970). *Education, health and behaviour*. London: Longmans.
Rutzen, S. R. (1973). The social importance of orthodontic rehabilitation: Report of a five year follow-up study. *Journal of Health and Social Behavior, 14*, 233–240.
Sabatelli, R., Buck, R., & Dreyer, A. (1982). Nonverbal communication accuracy in married couples: Relationships with marital complaints. *Journal of Personality and Social Psychology, 43*, 1088–1097.
Sabatelli, R., Dreyer, A., & Buck, R. (1979). Cognitive styles and the sending and receiving of facial cues. *Perceptual and Motor Skills, 49*, 203–212.
Sabatelli, R. M., & Rubin, M. (1986). Nonverbal expressiveness and physical attractiveness as mediators of interpersonal perceptions. *Journal of Nonverbal Behavior, 10*, 120–133.
Sackett, G. (1966). Monkeys reared in isolation with pictures as visual input: Evidence for an innate releasing mechanism. *Science, 154*, 1468–1473.
Saegert, S., Swap, W., & Zajonc, R. B. (1973). Exposure, context, and interpersonal attraction. *Journal of Personality and Social Psychology, 25*, 234–242.
Safer, M. A. (1984). Individual differences in the metacontrol of lateralization for recognizing facial expression of emotion. *Cortex, 20*, 19–25.
Safier, S. I. (1983). *Beyond the halo effect: Physical attractiveness and impression formation as a function of cue availability*. Unpublished doctoral dissertation, University of Connecticut, Storrs.
Salvia, J., Algozzine, R., & Sheare, J. B. (1977). Attractiveness and school achievement. *Journal of School Psychology, 15*, 60–67.
Salvia, J., Sheare, J. B., & Algozzine, B. (1975). Facial attractiveness and personal-social development. *Journal of Abnormal Child Psychology, 3*, 171–178.
Salzmann, J. A. (1971). Handicapping malocclusion assessment to establish treatment priority. *American Journal of Orthodontics, 59*, 552–567.

Samuels, C. A., & Ewy, R. (1985). Aesthetic perception of faces during infancy. *British Journal of Developmental Psychology, 3,* 221-228.

Samuels, J., & Proshek, J. (1973). The importance of dental appearance in a prestige hierarchy of occupations. *Journal of Dental Research, 52* (Abstract No. 118).

Samuels, M. R. (1939). Judgments of faces. *Character and Personality, 8,* 18-27.

Sanderson, S. F. (1978). Personal communication on the archives of the Institute of Dialect and Folk Life Studies, Leeds.

Sappenfield, B. R., & Balogh, B. (1970). Perceived attractiveness of social stimuli as related to their perceived similarity to self. *Journal of Psychology, 74,* 105-111.

Schaninger, C. M. (1981). Social class versus income revisited: An empirical investigation. *Journal of Marketing Research, 18,* 192-208.

Schlaer, S. (1937). The relation between visual acuity and illumination. *Journal of General Psychology, 21,* 165-188.

Schneider, W., & Shiffrin, R. (1977). Controlled and automatic information processing: I. Detection, search, and attention. *Psychological Review, 84,* 1-66.

Schon, E. (1978). Personal communication on the archives of the Nordiska Museet, Stockholm.

Schour, I., & Massler, M. (1941). The development of the human dentition. *Journal of the American Dental Association, 28,* 1153-1160.

Schumacher, A. (1982). On the significance of stature in human society. *Journal of Human Evolution, 11,* 697-701.

Secord, P. F. (1958). Facial features and inference processes in interpersonal perception. In R. Tagiuri & L. Petrullo (Eds.), *Person perception and interpersonal behavior* (pp. 300-315). Stanford: Stanford University.

Secord, P. F., & Backman, C. W. (1959). Malocclusion and psychological factors. *Journal of the American Dental Association, 59,* 931-938.

Secord, P. F., & Bevan, W. (1956). Personalities in faces: III. A cross-cultural comparison of impressions of physiognomy and personality in faces. *Journal of Social Psychology, 43,* 283-288.

Secord, P. F., Bevan, W., & Dukes, W. F. (1953). Occupational and physiognomic stereotypes in the perception of photographs. *Journal of Social Psychology, 37,* 261-270.

Secord, P. F., Dukes, W. F., & Bevan, W. (1954). Personalities in faces: I. An experiment in social perceiving. *Genetic Psychology Monographs, 49,* 231-279.

Secord, P. F., & Muthard, J. E. (1955). Personalities in faces: IV. A descriptive analysis of the perception of women's faces and the identification of some physiognomic determinants. *Journal of Psychology, 39,* 269-278.

Seligman, C., Paschall, N., & Takata, G. (1974). Effects of physical attractiveness on attribution of responsibility. *Canadian Journal of Behavioral Science, 6,* 290-296.

Seligman, M. E. P. (1970). On the generality of the laws of learning. *Psychological Review, 77,* 406-418.

Sergl, H. G., & Stodt, W. (1970). Experimental investigation of the aesthetic effect of various tooth positions after loss of an incisor tooth. *Transactions of the European Orthodontic Society,* 497-507.

Shalleck, J. (1973). *Masks.* New York: Viking.

Shapiro, B., Eppler, M., Haith, M., & Reis, H. (1987, April). An event analysis of facial attractiveness and expressiveness. In C. A. Samuels (Chair), *Aesthetic Perception During Infancy.* Symposium conducted at the meeting of the Society for Research in Child Development, Baltimore.

Shaw, R., & Bransford, J. (1977). Psychological approaches to the problem of knowledge. In R. Shaw & J. Bransford (Eds.), *Perceiving, acting, and knowing: Toward an ecological psychology* (pp. 1-39). Hillsdale, NJ: Lawrence Erlbaum Associates.

Shaw, R., McIntyre, M., & Mace, W. (1974). The role of symmetry in event perception. In R. B. MacLeod & H. L. Pick, Jr. (Eds.), *Perception: Essays in honor of James J. Gibson* (pp. 276-310). Ithaca, NY: Cornell University.

Shaw, R., & Pittenger, J. (1977). Perceiving the face of change in changing faces: Implications for a theory of object perception. In R. Shaw & J. Bransford (Eds.), *Perceiving, acting, and knowing: Toward an ecological psychology* (pp. 103-132). Hillsdale, NJ: Lawrence Erlbaum Associates.

Shaw, R. E., & Carello, C. (1979). *Are faces special?* Paper presented at the 20th Annual Meeting of the Psychonomic Society, Phoenix, AZ.

Shaw, R. E., Mark, L. S., Jenkins, D. M., & Mingolla, E. (1983). A dynamic geometry for predicting growth of gross craniofacial morphology. In A. Dixon & B. Sarnat (Eds.), *Factors and mechanisms influencing bone growth* (pp. 423-431). New York: Alan R. Liss.

Shaw, R. E., & Pittenger, J. B. (1978). On perceiving change. In H. L. Pick & E. Saltzman (Eds.), *Modes of perceiving and processing information* (pp. 187-204). Hillsdale, NJ: Lawrence Erlbaum Associates.

Shaw, W. C. (1981a). Folklore surrounding facial deformity and the origins of facial prejudice. *British Journal of Plastic Surgery, 34,* 237-246.

Shaw, W. C. (1981b). The influence of children's dentofacial appearance on their social attractiveness as judged by peers and lay adults. *American Journal of Orthodontics, 79,* 399-415.

Shaw, W. C., Addy, M., Dummer, P. M., Ray, C., & Frude, N. (1986). Dental and social effects of malocclusion and effectiveness of orthodontic treatment: A strategy for investigation. *Community Dentistry and Oral Epidemiology, 14,* 60-64.

Shaw, W. C., Addy, M., & Ray, C. (1980). Dental and social effects of malocclusion and effectiveness of orthodontic treatment: A review. *Community Dentistry and Oral Epidemiology, 8,* 36-45.

Shaw, W. C., Gabe, M. J., & Jones, B. M. (1979). The expectations of orthodontics patients in South Wales and St. Louis, Missouri. *British Journal of Orthodontics, 6,* 203-205.

Shaw, W. C., & Humphreys, S. (1982). Influence of children's dentofacial appearance on teacher expectations. *Community Dentistry and Oral Epidemiology, 10,* 313-319.

Shaw, W. C., Humphreys, S., McLoughlin, J. M., & Shimmin, P. C. (1980). The effect of facial deformity on petitioning. *Human Relations, 33,* 659-671.

Shaw, W. C., Lewis, H. G., & Robertson, N. R. E. (1975). Perception of malocclusion. *British Dental Journal, 138,* 211-216.

Shaw, W. C., Meek, S. C., & Jones, D. S. (1980). Nicknames, teasing, harassment and the salience of dental features among school children. *British Journal of Orthodontics, 7,* 75-80.

Shaw, W. C., Rees, G., Dawe, M., & Charles, C. R. (1985). The influence of dentofacial appearance on the social attractiveness of young adults. *American Journal of Orthodontics, 87,* 21-26.

Shea, J. A., & Adams, G. R. (1984). Correlates of romantic attachment: A path analysis study. *Journal of Youth and Adolescence, 13,* 27-44.

Shea, J. A., & Adams, G. R. (unpublished). *Genesis of love: Antecedents of male and female loving relationships.*

Shepherd, J. W., & Ellis, H. D. (1973). The effect of attractiveness on recognition memory for faces. *American Journal of Psychology, 86,* 627-633.

Shepherd, J. W., Ellis, H. D., McMurran, M., & Davies, G. M. (1978). Effect of character attribution on Photofit construction of a face. *European Journal of Social Psychology, 8,* 263-268.

Shoemaker, D. J., South, D. R., & Lowe, J. (1973). Facial stereotypes of deviants and judgments of guilt or innocence. *Social Forces, 51,* 427-433.

Shore, I. L. (1960). A cephalometric study of facial symmetry. *American Journal of Orthodontics, 46,* 789.

Sigall, H., & Ostrove, N. (1975). Beautiful but dangerous: Effects of offender attractiveness and nature of the crime on juridic judgment. *Journal of Personality and Social Psychology, 31,* 410-414.

Sigall, H., Page, R., & Brown, A. (1971). The effects of physical attraction and evaluation on effort expenditure and work output. *Representative Research in Social Psychology, 2,* 19-25.

Simmons, R. G., & Rosenberg, F. (1975). Sex, sex roles, and self-image. *Journal of Youth and Adolescence, 4*, 229–258.

Simms, T. M. (1967). Pupillary response of male and female subjects to pupillary difference in male and female picture stimuli. *Perception and Psychophysics, 2*, 553–555.

Simonds, J. F., & Heimberger, R. E. (1978). Psychiatric evaluation of youth with cleft lip-palate matched with a control group. *Cleft Palate Journal, 15*, 193–201.

Singer, J. E. (1964). The use of manipulative strategies: Machiavellianism and attractiveness. *Sociometry, 27*, 128–150.

Slee, P. T. (1984). The nature of mother-infant gaze patterns during interaction as a function of emotional expression. *Journal of the American Academy of Child Psychiatry, 21*, 385–391.

Smith, A. D., & Winograd, E. (1978). Adult age differences in remembering faces. *Journal of Gerontology, 14*, 443–444.

Smith, D. W. (1978). Growth. In D. W. Smith, E. L. Bierman, & N. M. Robinson (Eds.), *The biologic ages of man: From conception through old age* (2nd ed.). Philadelphia: W. B. Saunders.

Smith, E. D., & Hed, A. (1979). Effects of offenders' age and attractiveness on sentencing by mock juries. *Psychological Reports, 44*, 691–694.

Smith, G. J. (1984, April). *Interpersonal behaviors of preschoolers related to full-length and facial ratings of attractiveness.* Paper presented at the Annual Meeting of the Eastern Psychological Association, Baltimore, MD.

Smith, G. (1985). Facial and full-length ratings of attractiveness related to the social interactions of young children. *Sex Roles, 12*, 287–293.

Smith, L. (1978). Personal communication on the archives of the Ulster Folk and Transport Museum, Holywood, Northern Ireland.

Snyder, M., & Rothbart, M. (1971). Communicator attractiveness and opinion change. *Canadian Journal of Behavioral Science, 3*, 377–387.

Snyder, M. Tanke, E. D., & Berscheid, E. (1977). Social perception and interpersonal behavior: On the self-fulfilling nature of social stereotypes. *Journal of Personality and Social Psychology, 35*, 656–666.

Soble, S. L., & Strickland, L. H. (1974). Physical stigma, interaction and compliance. *Bulletin of the Psychonomic Society, 4*(2b), 130–132.

Solomon, M. R., & Schopler, J. (1978). The relationship of physical attractiveness and punitiveness: Is the linearity assumption out of line? *Personality and Social Psychology Bulletin, 4*, 483–486.

Sontag, S. (1979). The double standard of aging. In J. Williams (Ed.), *The psychology of women: Selected readings.* New York: Academic Press.

Sorce, J. F., Emde, R. N., Campos, J. J., & Klinnert, M. D. (1985). Maternal emotional signalling: Its effects on the visual cliff behavior of 1 year olds. *Developmental Psychology, 21*, 195–200.

Sorell, G. T., & Nowak, C. A. (1981). The role of physical attractiveness as a contributor to individual development. In R. M. Lerner & N. A. Busch-Rossnagel (Eds.), *Individuals as producers of their own development: A life-span perspective* (pp. 389–446). New York: Academic Press.

Sparacino, J., & Hansell, S. (1979). Physical attractiveness and academic performance: Beauty is not always talent. *Journal of Personality, 47*, 441–461.

Spriesterbach, D. C. (1973). *Psychosocial aspects of the cleft palate problem* (Vol. 1). Iowa City: University of Iowa Press.

Squier, R. W., & Mew, J. R. C. (1981). The relationship between facial structure and personality characteristics. *British Journal of Social Psychology, 20*, 151–160.

Starr, P. (1978). Self-esteem and behavioral functioning of teenagers with oral-facial clefts. *Rehabilitation Literature, 39*, 233–235.

Stephan, C. W., & Langlois, J. H. (1984). Baby beautiful: Adult attributions of infant competence

as a function of infant attractiveness. *Child Development, 56,* 576–585.
Stephan, C., & Tully, J. C. (1977). The influence of physical attractiveness of a plaintiff on the decisions of simulated jurors. *Journal of Social Psychology, 101,* 149–150.
Sternglanz, S. H., Gray, J. L., & Murakami, M. (1977). Adult preferences for infantile facial features: An ethological approach. *Animal Behaviour, 25,* 108–115.
Stevens, P. S. (1974). *Patterns in nature.* Boston: Little, Brown & Co.
Stewart, J. E. (1980). Defendant's attractiveness as a factor in the outcome of criminal trials: An observational study. *Journal of Applied Social Psychology, 10,* 348–361.
Strane, K., & Watts, C. (1977). Females judged by attractiveness of partners. *Perceptual and Motor Skills, 45,* 225–226.
Stricker, G., Clifford, E., Cohen, L. K., Giddon, D. B., Meskin, L. H., & Evans, C. A. (1979). Psychosocial aspects of craniofacial disfigurement: A "State of the Art" assessment conducted by the Craniofacial Anomalies Program Branch, National Institute of Dental Research. *American Journal of Orthodontics, 76,* 410–422.
Stritch, T. M., & Secord, P. F. (1956). Interaction effects in the perception of faces. *Journal of Personality, 24,* 270–284.
Stroebe, W., Insko, C. A., Thompson, V. D., & Layton, B. D. (1971). Effects of physical attractiveness, attitude similarity, and sex on various aspects of interpersonal attraction. *Journal of Personality and Social Psychology, 18,* 79–91.
Strong, S. R., Taylor, R. G., Bratton, J. C., & Loper, R. G. (1971). Nonverbal behavior and perceived counselor characteristics. *Journal of Counseling Psychology, 18,* 554–561.
Styczynski, L. E., & Langlois, J. H. (1977). The effects of familiarity on behavior stereotypes associated with physical attractiveness in young children. *Child Development, 48,* 1137–1141.
Subtelny, J. D. (1959). A longitudinal study of soft tissue facial structures and their profile characteristics, defined in relation to underlying skeletal characteristics. *American Journal of Orthodontics, 45,* 481–507.
Suedfeld, P., Bochnepl, S., & Matas, C. (1971). Petitioners' attire and petition signing by peace demonstraters: A field experiment. *Journal of Applied Social Psychology, 1,* 278–283.
Sugarman, D. B., Warner, R. M., & Berg, L. A. (1983, April). *Perceived attractiveness, sex of judge and sex of target: Beyond reliability.* Paper presented at the Annual Meeting of the Eastern Psychological Association, Philadelphia.
Summers, C. J. (1971). The occlusal index: A system for identifying and scoring occlusal disorders. *American Journal of Orthodontics, 59,* 552–567.
Sussman, S., Mueser, K. T., Grau, B. W., & Yarnold, P. R. (1983). Stability of females' facial attractiveness during childhood. *Journal of Personality and Social Psychology, 44,* 1231–1233.
Sutton, P. R. N. (1968). Lateral facial asymmetry: Methods of assessment. *Angle Orthodontist, 38,* 82–92.
Symons, D. (1979). *The evolution of human sexuality.* New York: Oxford University.
Tavris, C. (1977). Men and women report their views on masculinity. *Psychology Today, 10*(8), 34–38, 42, 82.
Taylor, C., & Thompson, G. G. (1955). Age trends in preferences for certain facial proportions. *Child Development, 26,* 97–102.
Tedesco, L. A., Albino, J. E., Cunat, J. J., Green, L. J., Lewis, E. A., & Slakter, M. J. (1983). A dental-facial attractiveness scale: Part I. Reliability and validity. *American Journal of Orthodontics, 83,* 38–43.
Tedesco, L. A., Albino, J. E., Cunat, J. J., Slakter, M. J., & Waltz, K. J. (1983). A dental-facial attractiveness scale: Part II. Consistency of perception. *American Journal of Orthodontics, 83,* 44–46.
Terry, R. L. (1975). Additional evidence for veridicality of perceptions based on physiognomic cues. *Perceptual and Motor Skills, 40,* 780–782.
Terry, R. L. (1977). Further evidence on components of facial attractiveness. *Perceptual and Motor Skills, 45,* 130.

REFERENCES

Terry, R. L., & Brady, C. S. (1976). Effects of framed spectacles and contact lenses on self-ratings of facial attractiveness. *Perceptual and Motor Skills, 42,* 789-790.
Terry, R. L., Davis, J. S. (1976). Components of facial attractiveness. *Perceptual and Motor Skills, 42,* 918.
Terry, R. L., & Kroger, D. L. (1976). Effects of eye correctives on ratings of attractiveness. *Perceptual and Motor Skills, 42,* 562.
Terry, R. L., & Snider, W. G. (1972). Verdicality of interpersonal perceptions based on physiognomic cues. *Journal of Psychology, 81,* 205-208.
Thoman, E. B. (1975). How rejecting a baby affects mother-infant synchrony. In Ciba Foundation Symposium 33: *Parent-infant interactions.* New York: Associated Scientific Publishers.
Thoman, E. B. (1981). Affective communication as the prelude and context for language learning. In R. L. Schiefelbusch & D. Bricker (Eds.), *Early language acquisition and intervention.* Baltimore: University Park Press.
Thomas, R. G. (1979). An evaluation of the soft tissue profile in the North American black woman. *American Journal of Orthodontics, 76,* 84-94.
Thompson, D. W. (1942). *On growth and form.* Cambridge: Cambridge University Press. (Originally published in 1917)
Thompson, G. G. (1946). The effect of chronological age on aesthetic preferences for rectangles of different proportions. *Journal of Experimental Psychology, 36,* 50-58.
Thornton, G. R. (1939). The ability to judge crimes from photographs of criminals: A contribution to technique. *Journal of Abnormal and Social Psychology, 34,* 378-383.
Thornton, G. R. (1943). The effect upon judgments of personality traits of varying a single factor in a photograph. *Journal of Social Psychology, 18,* 127-148.
Thornton, G. R. (1944). The effect of wearing eyeglasses upon judgments of personality traits of persons seen briefly. *Journal of Applied Psychology, 28,* 203-207.
Tinbergen, N. (1951). *The study of instinct.* New York: Oxford University.
Tinbergen, N., & Perdeck, A. C. (1950). On the stimulus situation releasing the begging response in the newly hatched herring gull chick (*Larus a. argentatus* Pont.). *Behaviour, 3,* 1-38.
Tobiasen, J. M. (1984). Psychosocial correlates of congenital facial clefts: A conceptualization and model. *Cleft Palate Journal, 21,* 131-139.
Todd, J. T. (1982). Visual information about rigid and nonrigid motion: A geometric analysis. *Journal of Experimental Psychology: Human Perception and Performance, 8,* 238-252.
Todd, J. T., & Mark, L. S. (1981). Issues related to the prediction of craniofacial growth. *American Journal of Orthodontics, 79,* 63-80.
Todd, J. T., Mark, L. S., Shaw, R. E., & Pittenger, J. B. (1980). The perception of human growth. *Scientific American, 242*(2), 132-144.
Tomkins, S. (1962). *Affect, imagery, and consciousness: The positive affects.* New York: Springer.
Tomkins, S. (1963). *Affect, imagery, and consciousness: The negative affects.* New York: Springer.
Tomkins, S. S., & McCarter, R. (1964). What and where are the primary affects? Some evidence for a theory. *Perceptual and Motor Skills, 18,* 119-158.
Tranel, D., & Damasio, A. R. (1985). Knowledge without awareness: An autonomic index of facial recognition by prosopagnostics. *Science, 228,* 1453-1454.
Trnavsky, P. A., & Bakeman, P. (1976, August). *Stereotype and social behavior in preschool children.* Paper presented at the annual meeting of the American Psychological Association, Washington, DC.
Tronick, E., Als, H., & Adamson, L. (1979). Structure of early face-to-face communicative interaction. In M. Bulliwa (Ed.), *Before speech* (pp. 349-370). New York: Cambridge University.
Tucker, D. M. (1981). Lateral brain function, emotion, and conceptualization. *Psychological Bulletin, 89,* 19-46.
Tucker, D. M. (1986). Neural control of emotion communication. In P. Blanck, R. Buck, & R.

Rosenthal (Eds.), *Nonverbal communication in the clinical context* (pp. 258-307). University Park, PA: Pennsylvania State University.

Tucker, D. M., & Williamson, P. (1984). Asymmetric neural control systems in human self-regulation. *Psychological Review, 91,* 185-215.

Turkat, D., & Dawson, J. (1976). Attributions of responsibility for a chance event as a function of sex and physical attractiveness of target individual. *Psychological Reports, 39,* 275-279.

Turkewitz, G., & Ross-Kossak, P. (1984). Multiple nodes of right-hemisphere information processing: Age and sex differences in facial recognition. *Developmental Psychology, 20,* 95-103.

Turvey, M. T. (1977). Contrasting orientations to the theory of visual information processing. *Psychological Review, 84,* 67-89.

Udry, J. R. (1965). Structural correlates of feminine beauty preferences in Britain and the United States: A comparison. *Sociology and Social Research, 49,* 330-342.

Udry, J. R. (1977). The importance of being beautiful: A reexamination and racial comparison. *American Journal of Sociology, 83,* 154-160.

Udry, J. R., & Eckland, B. K. (1984). Benefits of being attractive: Differential payoffs for men and women. *Psychological Reports, 54,* 47-56.

Unger, R. K., Hilderbrand, M. S., & Madar, T. M. (1982). Physical attractiveness and assumptions about social deviance: Some sex by sex comparisons. *Personality and Social Psychology Bulletin, 8,* 293-301.

Ungerer, J. A., & Sigman, M. (1983). Developmental lags in preterm infants from one to three years of age. *Child Development, 54,* 1217-1228.

Valentine, C. W. (1913). *The experimental psychology of beauty.* London: T. C. & E. C. Jack.

van Lawick-Goodall, J. (1968). The behavior of free-living chimpanzees in the Gombe Stream area. *Animal Behaviour Monographs, 1,* 161-311.

Vaughn, B. E., & Langlois, J. H. (1983). Physical attractiveness as a correlate of peer status and social competence in preschool children. *Developmental Psychology, 19,* 550-560.

Vernikos-Danellis, J., & Wingert, C. M. (1979). The importance of light, postural and social cues in the regulation of the plasma rhythms in man. In A. Reinberg & F. Halbert (Eds.), *Chronopharmacology* (pp. 102-106). New York: Pergamon.

Vinacke, W. E. (1956). Explorations in the dynamic process of stereotyping. *Journal of Social Psychology, 43,* 105-132.

Wagatsuma, E., & Kleinke, C. L. (1979). Ratings of facial beauty by Asian-American and Caucasian females. *Journal of Social Psychology, 109,* 299-300.

Walker-Smith, G. J., Gale, A. G., & Findlay, J. M. (1977). Eye movement strategies involved in face perception. *Perception, 6,* 313-326.

Wallace, R. P. (1941). Apparent personality traits from photographs varied in bodily proportions. *Psychological Bulletin, 38,* 744-745.

Walsh, R. P., & Locke, C. (1980, November). *Perceptions of womens' physical attractiveness across the life cycle.* Paper presented at the 33rd Annual Meeting of the Gerontological Society, San Diego.

Walster, E., Aronson, V., Abrahams, D., & Rottmann, L. (1966). Importance of physical attractiveness in dating behavior. *Journal of Personality and Social Psychology, 4,* 508-516.

Warr, P. B., & Knapper, C. (1968). *The perception of people and events.* London: Wiley.

Warren, W. H., & Shaw, R. E. (1985). Events and encounters as units of analysis for ecological psychology. In W. H. Warren & R. Shaw (Eds.), *Persistence and change* (pp. 1-27). Hillsdale, NJ: Lawrence Erlbaum Associates.

Wegner, D. M., & Vallacher, R. R. (1977). *Implicit psychology.* New York: Oxford University.

Weiser-Aall, L. (1963). Om haren i norsk overlevering. (The hare in Norwegian tradition.) *Norveg, 10,* 55-58.

West, S. G., & Brown, T. J. (1975). Physical attractiveness, the severity of the emergency and helping: A field experiment and interpersonal simulation. *Journal of Experimental Social Psychology, 11,* 531-538.

Weston, J. Y. (1974). The pathology of child abuse. In R. E. Helfer & C. H. Kempe (Eds.), *The battered child*. Chicago: University of Chicago.

Wickler, W. (1973). *The sexual code: The social behavior of animals and men*. New York: Anchor Press.

Wilson, D. W. (1978). Helping behavior and physical attractiveness. *Journal of Social Psychology, 104*, 313-314.

Wilson, E. O. (1975). *Sociobiology: The new synthesis*. Cambridge: Harvard University.

Wilson, P. R. (1968). Perceptual distortion of height as a function of ascribed academic status. *Journal of Social Psychology, 74*, 97-102.

Wilson, W., & Nakajo, H. (1965). Preference for photographs as a function of frequency of presentation. *Psychomic Science, 3*, 577-578.

Wolff, W. (1943). *The expression of personality*. New York: Harper & Row.

Wright, B. A. (1960). *Physical disability: A psychological approach*. New York: Harper & Row.

Yarbus, A. L. (1967). *Eye movements and vision*. New York: Plenum.

Yarmey, A. D. (1979). The effects of attractiveness, feature saliency and liking on memory for faces. In M. Cook & G. Wilson (Eds.), *Love and attraction* (pp. 51-53). London: Pergamon.

Zajonc, R. B. (1980). Feeling and thinking: Preferences need no inferences. *American Psychologist, 35*, 151-175.

Zajonc, R. B. (1984). On the primacy of affect. *American Psychologist, 39*, 117-123.

Zakin, D. F. (1983). Physical attractiveness, sociability, athletic ability, and children's preference for their peers. *Journal of Psychology, 115*, 117-122.

Zivin, G. (Ed.). (1985). *The development of expressive behavior: Biology-environment interactions*. Orlando, FL: Academic Press.

Zuk, M. (1984). A charming resistance to parasites. *Natural History, 93*(4), 28-34.

Author Index

A

Aamot, S., 132, 193
Abel, T. M., 176, 191–192
Abelson, R. P., 210
Abrahams, D., 120, 130, 216, 218
Adams, G. R., 58, 60, 103, 105, 119–124, 127–129, 131–132, 136, 139–140, 156, 197, 218–219, 234
Adamson, L., 151
Addy, M., 189, 213–215
Ainsworth, M. D. S., 152
Albin, M., 151–152
Albino, J. E., 108, 188–189, 198, 220, 223–231, 233–236
Algozzine, R., 128–129, 209
Allen, J. G., 212
Alley, T. R., 7, 17, 54–60, 63–65, 68, 70–72, 75, 81, 87, 90–91, 97–99, 104, 108, 110, 113–114, 129, 132–133, 135, 142, 156, 177–178, 183, 185, 187–188, 196–198, 218–219
Allport, D. A., 159
Allport, G. W., 98–99, 167–169, 181
Als, H., 151
Amgott-Kwan, T., 84
Anderson, L. D., 173, 181
Andrew, R. J., 143
Antonis, B., 159
Apatow, K., 71–72, 76–78, 81, 85, 178

Archer, D., 117, 132, 162
Argyle, M., 184
Aristotle, 63, 168, 197
Aronson, E., 124
Aronson, V., 120, 130, 216, 218
Asch, S. E., 16, 48, 177
Asendorpf, J., 2
Austad, C., 137

B

Babalola, A., 192
Backman, C. W., 198, 222
Baddeley, A. D., 3
Bai, D. L., 178–179, 182–183
Bakeman, R., 104
Baker, S. S., 169, 183
Baldwin, D. C., 235–236
Ballantyne, J. W., 195, 201
Balogh, B., 115
Bandura, A., 153
Barclay, C. D., 20
Barclay, S., 189
Bargh, J. A., 129
Barnes, M., 129–130, 133
Barnes, M. L., 235–236
Barocas, R., 128
Baron, R. M., 6, 54, 65–66, 78, 83, 163
Barrett, K. C., 151

Barrette, D., 163
Barrios, M., 117, 132
Bar-Tal, D., 131
Bartlett, J. C., 3
Basham, R. B., 151
Bassili, J. W., 84
Bateman, G., 194
Bauer, R. M., 144, 159
Baum, M. R., 115
Bayes, M. A., 156
Beach, F. A., 112, 130
Beier, E. G., 52
Bellak, L., 169, 183
Benson, P. L., 125
Benton, J. G., 188
Berg, L. A., 105–106
Bergman, T., 109
Berkowitz, L., 126
Berman, P. W., 52, 61, 106
Bernick, N., 52
Bernstein, I. H., 105–106, 112
Bernstein, N., v
Berry, D. S., 7, 17, 49, 55, 58, 60, 69, 72, 74–76, 79–82, 84–85, 87, 90, 135, 170–171, 174, 178, 181–182, 185–186
Berscheid, E., 58, 64–65, 86, 102–103, 116, 119–121, 128, 130, 137, 139, 172, 188, 197, 204, 218
Bevan, W., 61, 64, 169, 174, 176–179, 181–183, 186, 197
Black, H. K., 128
Blehar, M. C., 152
Block, H., 177
Blumberg, S. L., 52
Bochnepl, S., 210
Boersma, H., 198
Bohrnstedt, G., 204
Boriskin, J. A., 53
Borod, J. C., 144
Boukydis, C., 115
Bovard, E., 150
Bowman, P. C., 64
Brady, C. S., 109, 113
Brandt, A., 168, 174
Bransford, J., 159
Brantley, H. J., 219
Bratton, J. C., 156
Brazelton, T. B., 151
Brehm, J. W., 210
Bretherton, I., 153
Brewer, J. D., 233

Briody, M., 194
Brisman, A., 233
Bromsley, D. B., 63
Brooks, J., 52
Brooks, V., 53
Brophy, J. E., 209
Brown, A., 124
Brown, E. L., 118
Brown, J. H., 121
Brown, J. L., 138
Brown, T. J., 124
Brownlow, S., 80–81
Bruce, V., 3
Bruford, A., 194
Brundage, L. E., 219
Brunswik, E., 6, 53, 110, 176, 181–182, 185, 197
Bryant, N. J., 210
Bryden, M. P., 144
Bryt, A., 176, 191–192
Buchman, H., 2
Buck, P. L., 210
Buck, R., 95, 98, 115, 128, 142–148, 152, 155–156, 158, 161–164, 192
Buckley, M. L., 98
Bugglin, C., 137
Bull, R. H. C., 172, 176, 178, 181, 189
Burns, D. S., 123
Burns, G. L., 137
Burr, C. W., 168
Burstone, C. J., 107
Buss, D. M., 61, 129–130, 133
Byrne, D., 131

C

Caan, W., 143
Campbell, A., 56
Campbell, R., 144
Campos, J. J., 151, 153–154
Camras, L., 143, 153
Cannan, T., 135
Carello, C., 45–46, 77
Carlos, J. P., 225
Carroll, J., 162
Casey, R. J., 138
Cash, T. F., 56, 123, 131, 137, 182, 219
Caul, W. F., 147
Cavior, N., 104, 114, 116, 137
Celhoffer, L., 115
Chance, J. E., 179, 186

Chanowitz, B., 211–212
Charles, C. R., 207–208, 216
Chassin, L., 137
Chinsky, R. R., 219
Christensen, I., 194
Clark, M. E., 61, 82
Cleeton, G. U., 172
Clifford, E., 127, 189, 219–220, 222
Clifford, M. M., 122, 209, 218
Cloonan, H. A., 54, 106
Cobb, S., 150
Cohen, A. S., 127
Cohen, D., 143
Cohen, L. K., 189, 220, 222, 229
Cohen, R., 167, 172–173, 175, 179, 181–183
Cohen, M. M., 121, 193
Coleman, J. S., 130
Comer, R. J., 212
Conny, D. J., 233
Cons, N. C., 220, 227
Converse, P. E., 56
Cook, T. A., 45
Corter, C., 115
Council, J. R., 104
Cox, M. G., 63
Cox, N. H., 102, 107, 110, 198
Crane, P., 127
Crano, W. D., 209
Crnic, K. A., 151
Crofton, C., 116
Cross, J., 57, 102–103, 106–107, 109
Cross, J. F., 57, 102–103, 106–107, 109
Crossman, S. M., 60, 103, 105, 124, 129, 131–132, 139
Crowell, N. T., 232
Culver, C., 151–152
Cunat, J. J., 220, 223–229
Cunningham, M. R., 82, 110, 185
Cutting, J. E., 20, 84
Cysneiros, P. G., 76, 182–183

D

Damasio, A. R., 144–145, 159
Damasio, H., 144–145
Darwin, C. R., 111–112, 119, 143, 168–170, 193
Davidson, R., 152
Davies, G., xiv, 117
Davis, E. L., 225, 235
Davis, J. S., 109
Davis, W. L., 124
Dawe, M., 207–208, 216
Dawkins, R., 193
Dawson, J., 123
Deffenbacher, K., 118
Dell'osso, L. F., 109
Denenberg, V. H., 149
Dennington, R. J., 221
Derlega, V. J., 219
Deri, S., 99
Dermer, M., 111, 124, 216
Deutsch, F. M., 61, 82
Dickstein, S., 154
DiMatteo, M. R., 162
Dimberg, V., 143
Dion, K. K., 102, 104, 116, 126, 128–129
Dipboye, R. L., 123
Divale, W. T., 76, 182–183
Dokecki, P. R., 116
Dongieux, J., 103–104, 110
Doob, A. N., 212
Dornbusch, S. M., 59, 187, 219
Downs, A. C., 57, 129, 131
Draker, H. L., 225
Dreyer, A., 156, 164
Duffield, B. J., 122
Dukes, W. F., 61, 64, 169, 174, 176–179, 181–183, 186, 197
Dummer, P. M., 213–215
Dusek, J. B., 123

E

Eastman, A., 104
Ecker, B. P., 212
Eckland, B. K., 120, 130
Efran, M. G., 125
Eismann, D., 227
Ekman, P., 4, 148, 155, 162, 170, 192, 196
Elder, G. H., Jr., 120
Elder, S. T., 232
Ellis, H. D., xiv, 98, 117, 119
Elman, D., 184
Elovitz, G. P., 122
Emde, R. N., 153–154
Eme, R., 130
Enlow, D. H., 27, 51, 89
Eppler, M., 138
Etcoff, N. I., 144
Evans, C. A., 189, 222

Evans, E. C., 168
Evans, G. E., 194–195
Ewy, R., 138

F

Fafel, J. B., 85
Farina, A., 104, 137, 212
Fatoullah, E., 125
Feinman, S., 110, 114, 117, 153–154
Fernander, L., 52
Ferrera, A., 195
Field, T., 143, 151, 165
Fields, B., 162
Fife, A. E., 196
Findlay, J. M., 109
Fischer, E. H., 104, 137
Fischer, G. H., 197
Fisher, K. W., 71
Fisher, M. J., 219
Fiske, S. T., 63, 211–212
Fitzgerald, H. E., 52–54, 76–77, 105, 133–135
Fleishman, J. J., 98
Fletcher, D., 114, 180
Flores, E. S., 51
Floyd, W., 61, 106
Fogh-Andersen, P., 194
Folkman, S., 159
Ford, C. S., 112, 130
Ford, J. G., 117
Ford, L., 115
Forrest, F. H., 3
Foster, E. J., 57, 110, 117
Foster, T. D., 222
Fox, N. A., 152
Fox, R. N., 223–224, 231
Frazier, P. J., 220, 227
Freedman, D. G., 113–114
Freedman, R., 60–61, 129–132
Freer, T. J., 227
Friedrich, W. N., 53
Friesen, W. V., 4, 148, 155, 162
Frodi, A., 126
Fromkin, H. L., 123
Frude, N., 213–215
Frykholm, G., 20, 84
Fullard, W., 52

G

Gabe, M. J., 192

Gale, A. G., 109
Gale, N. E., 235–236
Gallucci, N. T., 105, 124
Galper, R. E., 175, 186
Gangestad, S., 188
Garcia, J., 159
Garner, W. R., 95
Garrett, C., 131
Geiselman, R. E., 115, 117
Giancoli, D. L., 187
Gibbs, J. E., 142
Gibson, E. J., 12, 142, 159
Gibson, J. J., *v*, 6, 12, 13–16, 18–19, 26–27, 66, 83–84, 142, 148, 159, 184
Giddon, D. B., 189, 222
Gilbert, B., 179, 186
Gill, G. W., 110, 114, 117
Gillen, B., 123–124
Glass, L., 111
Gochman, D. S., 220
Goffman, E., 139, 192
Goldberg, M. J., 188
Goldberg, M. L., 109
Goldberg, S., 52
Goldfield, E., 147–148
Goldin, S. E., 126, 178–179
Goldsmith, H. H., 151
Goldstein, A. G., 2, 104, 139, 179, 186
Goller, W. L., 210
Gonzalez-Ulloa, M., 51
Good, T. L., 209
Goodale, W., 130
Goodenough, F. L., 213
Goodman, N., 59, 187, 219
Goodman, N. R., 163
Goodman, R. M., 121
Goodman, V., 52
Gorlin, R. J., 121, 193
Gould, S. J., 7, 25, 60, 89, 175
Gould, R. W., 91
Graber, L. W., 110, 220–221, 231
Graham, J. A., 113, 115, 180, 183–184, 188
Grainger, R. M., 223, 225, 227
Grant, E. C., 193
Grau, B. W., 59, 115
Gray, H., 83
Gray, J. L., 76
Green, J., 172, 178
Green, L. J., 220, 224, 227–229
Greenberg, M. T., 151
Greenberg, R., 143
Grigoryev, P., 151–152
Groh, T., 137

AUTHOR INDEX 275

Gross, A. E., 116
Gruzen, J., 103, 106, 132
Gurnee, H., 107, 174, 181, 183
Guthrie, R. D., 51, 58, 60, 66-67, 75-76, 81, 87, 110-111, 113, 175, 178, 180-181, 183-184
Gutierres, S. E., 117-118
Gwyndaf, R., 194

H

Hagg, U., 60
Haight, N. A., 115, 117
Haith, M., 109, 138
Hall, J. A., 162
Hallpike, C. R., 180
Hamburg, B. A., 234
Hamid, P. N., 113, 184
Hamm, N. H., 115
Hand, H. H., 71
Hand, W. D., 196
Hansell, S. 103-104, 120, 131
Hansson, R. O., 122
Harlow, H. R., 150
Harper, D. C., 219
Harris, D. B., 213
Harrison, A. A., 115
Harrison, S. K., 129
Hartnett, J. J., 122, 124
Harvey, C. R., 222
Hastorf, A. H., 59, 187, 219
Hatfield, E., *xvii*, 97, 103, 114, 120-121, 129, 131-132, 139, 180
Hatlelid, D., 64, 120
Haviland, J. M., 151
Hebb, D. O., 193
Hed, A., 125
Heider, F., 20, 210-211
Heilman, M. E., 131-132
Heimberger, R. E., 219
Heller, A., 219
Helm, S., 225
Helson, H., 115
Henderson, R., 107, 226
Henker, B. A., 218
Hen-Tov, A., 218
Hernandez, O. A., 106
Hertzman, M., 177
Hess, E. H., 53, 75, 110, 134, 197

Hildebrandt, K. A., 52-56, 60, 65, 76-77, 90, 97-98, 103, 105, 115, 128, 133-135, 156, 177, 183, 185, 187-188, 197-198, 218-219
Hilderbrand, M. S., 177-178
Hill, M. C., 106, 114
Hines, H., 77
Hirsch, B., 233
Hirschenfang, S., 188
Hochberg, J., 53, 175, 186
Hodge, S. E., 111
Hofer, B., 181
Hofer, M. A., 150-151, 154
Hogarth, B., 45
Hohl, T., 232-233
Hole, C., 194
Holmes, D. L., 53-54, 76, 110
Horai, J., 125
Horowitz, H. S., 220, 229
Horton, C. E., 56, 182
Hottes, J., 124
Howard, L. R., 114, 137
Howells, D. T., 213
Howitt, J. W., 107, 226
Hovland, C. I., 210
Huckstedt, B., 54
Hull, C. L., 104, 116, 173, 176
Hulse, F. S., 114
Humphreys, S., 192, 210-211
Hurwitz, D., 185
Hutton, C. E., 232

I

Iliffe, A. H., 102, 104-105
Insko, C. A., 130
Iritani, B., 117, 132
Izard, C. E., 52, 143, 151

J

Jackson, L. A., 125
Jacobson, A., 131, 188-189
Jacobson, C. F., 162
Jago, J. D., 222
Janik, S. W., 109
Jenkins, D. M., 25, 30
Jenkins, V., 138
Jenny, J., 193, 220, 227

AUTHOR INDEX

Jeeves, M. A., xiv
Jensen, S. H., 192
Johansson, G., 20
Johnson, D. F., 57, 104, 122
Johnston, M. C., 107, 176
Jones, B. M., 192
Jones, D. S., 187, 201–204, 221
Jones, G., 76
Jones, L. E., 185
Jones, Q. R., 110, 181
Joseph, G., 123
Jouhar, A. J., 113, 180, 183–184
Justice, B., 91
Justice, R., 91

K

Kagan, J., 218
Kahane, H., 170
Kahn, A., 124, 131
Kaplan, G. A., 18
Kapp, K., 219
Karabenick, S. A., 103, 125
Karaliers, M., 149
Kassin, S. M., 6, 64
Katz, M., 137, 187
Katz, R. V., 225
Keating, C. F., 57–58, 72, 74, 76, 81–82, 110–111, 174, 178–179, 181–185
Kehr, J., 123
Keller, L. E., 105
Kelly, G., 214
Kelly, J. E., 222
Kennedy, C. B., 52
Kennell, J. H., 53
Kenny, C. T., 114, 180
Kenrick, D., 117–118
Kepler, J., 13
Kernaleguen, A., 103, 118
Kerr, N. L., 103–104, 106, 131
Kiener, F., 181
Kilbride, J. E., 76, 182–183
Kimata, L. G., 115, 117
Kimes, D. D., 117, 132
Kirkland, J., 110
Kiyak, H. A., 232–233
Klaiman, S., 162
Klatzky, R. L., 3
Klaus, M. H., 53
Kleck, R. E., 109, 128, 210, 216, 218, 219

Kleinke, C. L., 105, 110
Kligman, A. M., 115, 188
Klima, R. J., 222
Klinnert, M. D., 153–154
Klosinsky, M. J., 98
Knapper, C., 177
Knight, F. B., 172
Knight, J., 111
Koch, J., 125
Kodric-Brown, A., 121
Koff, E., 144
Koffka, K., 66
Kohout, F., 220, 277
Koller, H., 137, 187
Kolodzy, P., 131
Komin, S., 76, 182–183
Korabik, K., 221, 231
Kornhaber, R. C., 212
Korthase, K. M., 56, 106
Koslowski, B., 151
Kozeny, E. D., 172
Kozlowski, L. T., 20
Krate, R., 125
Kravitz, J., 105
Kriger, A., 52
Kroger, D. L., 113
Kuhnel, 181
Kunst-Wilson, W. R., 159
Kurtz, S. T., 103–104, 106, 131

L

LaBarbera, J. D., 143
LaCrosse, M. B., 156
Lamb, C., 151–152
Lamb, M. E., 151
Landy, D., 123
Langer, E. J., 211–212
Langlois, J. H., 58, 103–104, 106, 116, 122, 127–129, 133, 135, 138
Lansdown, R., 187
Lanzetta, J. T., 143
Larrance, D. T., 128
Laskin, D. M., 232
Lauer, E., 176, 191–192
Lavater, J. C., 65, 67, 197
Lavelle, C. L. B., 27
LaVoie, J. C., 123–124, 127
Lawson, E. D., 180
Layard, J., 195

Layton, B. D., 130
Lazarus, R. S., 159–160
Leahy, P., 76, 182–183
Leavitt, L. A., 143
LeBarr, G. H., 71, 74–77
LeDoux, J. E., 158, 160
Lefas, J., 197
Lefebvre, A., 189
Legan, H. L., 107
Lerner, J. V., 116
Lerner, M. J., 210
Lerner, R. M., 103, 116, 125, 128
Leslie, J. E., 3
Leventhal, G., 125
Levin, B., 233
Levine, J., 218
Levine, S., 149
Levitt, L., 212
Levy, J., 145
Lewis, E. A., 220, 223–229, 231, 235–236
Lewis, H. G., 198
Lewis, M., 52, 153
Lewit, D. W., 235
Lewontin, R. C., 175
Ley, R. G., 144
Liebault, J., 167
Liggett, J., 1, 2, 67, 83, 106, 110, 112, 138, 168, 174, 182
Linn, E. L., 110, 221, 235
Lin, T-D., 105–106, 112
Lipnick, J., 74
Livesley, W. J., 63
Livson, N., 59
Locke, C., 56, 104, 115
Lombardi, D. A., 104
London, O., 131
London, R. S., 210
Loper, R. G., 156
Lorenz, K., 52, 66, 74–75, 90, 127, 134–135
Lowe, J., 178
Lowenstein, L. R., 204
Lucker, G. W., xiv, 110, 220–221, 231
Lyman, B., 64, 120

M

Mace, W. M., 16, 18, 28, 30
Macgregor, F. C., 1, 121, 176, 187–188, 191–192, 220, 222
Macurdy, C., 64, 120

Madar, T. M., 177–178
Maier, R. A., 53–54, 76, 110
Main, M., 151
Mainwaring, M., 168
Maisiak, R., 130
Malatesta, C., 151–153, 164
Malpass, R. S., 105
Mar, T. T., 197
Maret, S. M., 105, 109, 133
Mark, L. S., 6, 12, 25, 27–31, 33–40, 42–47, 54, 68, 71, 75, 77, 84, 89, 99
Martin, J. G., 105–106
Maruyama, G., 57–59, 103, 119, 127–128, 137
Marwit, K. L., 126
Marwit, S. J., 126
Massler, M., 60
Matas, C., 210
Mathes, E. W., 120, 131
Maurer, D., 2, 110
Mazur, A., 72, 75–76, 174, 178–179, 183
Mazur, J., 174, 183
McArthur, L. Z., 7, 17, 49, 55, 58, 60, 65–66, 68–87, 90, 97, 119, 135, 170–171, 174, 178, 181–182, 185
McCabe, V., 7, 17, 49, 53, 58, 74, 85, 89–95, 135, 171
McCall, R. B., 52
McCarter, R., 176
McCleary, R. A., 159
McClellan, P., 105–106, 112
McClintock, M. K., 150
McElroy, J. C., 123
McGarry, M. S., 210
McGee, A-M., 170, 179
McGuinness, D., 160
McGuire, W. J., 210
McHenry, R., 184
McIntyre, M., 18, 28, 30
McIver, J. E., 222
McKeachie, W. J., 184
McKelvie, S. J., 133
McLoughlin, J. M., 192, 210–211
McMurran, M., 117
McNamara, J. A., xiv
McNeill, R. W., 232–233
McPherson, J. M., 194
McWilliams, B. J., 219
Mears, C. E., 150
Meek, S. C., 187, 201–204, 221
Melamed, E., 60, 132–133, 188
Melamed, L., 118

Mellon, P. M., 209
Menezes, D. M., 222
Merman, P., 137
Meskin, L. H., 189, 222
Mew, J. R. C., 169, 172
Meyer, R. G., 105, 124
Millard, R., 104
Miller, A. G., 121, 130, 132–133
Miller, H. L., 130
Miller, N., 57–59, 103, 119, 127–128, 137
Miller, R. E., 147
Mills, J., 124
Milord, J. T., 56, 61, 103, 115
Mims, P. R., 122, 124
Minde, K., 115
Mingolla, E., 25, 30
Mirsky, I. A., 147
Mita, T. H., 111
Moller, E., 170
Monahan, F., 125
Montepare, J. M., 70, 72–73, 77, 84
Moore, A. W., 198
Moore, M., 109
Moore, W. J., 27
Moreland, R. L., 115
Morris, D., 192
Morris, M. G., 91
Morrow, P. C., 123
Morse, P. A., 143
Morse, S. J., 103, 106, 132
Moss, M. K., 118
Moyel, I. S., 110, 181
Mueser, K. T., 59, 115
Munro, I. R., 189
Murakami, M., 76
Murroni, E., 125
Muthard, J. E., 64, 111, 167, 170, 182, 184, 186

N

Naccari, N., 125
Nakajo, H., 115
Nakdimen, K. A., 110, 181
Napoleon, T., 137
Nay, W. R., 122, 124
Neisser, U., 148, 159
Neimeyer, G. J., 187
Nelson, C. A., 143
Newcombe, F., *xiv*
Newtson, D., 163

Nielsen, J. P., 103, 118
Nikels, K. W., 115
Nordholm, L. A., 122, 133
Novak, P. E., 210
Nowak, C. A., 56, 60, 103–104
Nyman, A., 194

O

Ohman, A., 143
Olson, R. E., 232
Olweus, D., 213
O'Nan, B. A., 61, 106
Orr, S. P., 143
Ortiz-Monasterio, F., 195
Ortman, L. F., 235
Oster, H., 170
Ostrove, N., 125–126
O'Sullivan, M., 162
Ottinger, D. R., 54, 106
Ouellette, P. L., 233
Owens, G., 117

P

Page, R., 124
Pallak, S. R., 119, 125
Panksepp, J., 149, 151, 154
Papageorge, J., 104, 139–140
Papousek, H., 151
Papousek, M., 151
Parisi, S. A., 143
Paschall, N., 105, 123
Patterson, K. E., 3
Patzer, G. L., 103
Peck, H., 104, 108, 111, 198
Peck, S., 104, 108, 111, 198
Pellegrini, R. J., 114, 180
Perdeck, A. C., 94
Perrett, D. I., 143
Perrin, F. A. C., 112
Pertschuk, M. J., 137
Peter, J. P., 219
Peterson, L. J., 232
Pfeiffer, J. R., 210
Phipps, G. T., 234
Piers, E. V., 213
Pietromonaco, P., 220–221
Piliavin, I. M., 212

AUTHOR INDEX 279

Piliavin, J. A., 212
Pindborg, J. J., 121, 193
Pitt, E. J., 231
Pittenger, J. B., 6, 12, 18, 20, 27, 30-34, 41-46, 54-55, 68-69, 75, 77, 84, 89, 99
Pitts, H., 104
Pless, I. B., 219
Polak, L., 187
Portenoy, B. S., 235
Portjiele, A. F. J., 94
Poulton, D. R., 110
Power, T. G., 134-135
Prahl-Anderson, B., 198, 220
Pribram, K., 160
Proffitt, D. R., 84
Proshek, J., 221
Pythagoras, 197

R

Raymond, G. L., 111, 181
Ragozin, A. S., 151
Ray, C., 189, 213-215
Redican, W. K., 143
Reagan, M. A., 131
Read, D., 119
Reed, S. C., 194
Rees, G., 207-208, 216
Reeves, K., 131
Reich, J. N., 53-54, 76, 110
Reiling, A. M., 52
Reis, H. T., 103, 106, 132, 138
Reiter, L., 53, 110, 176, 181-182, 197
Reynolds, H. N., 18
Reynolds, P., 159
Ribbens, K. A., xiv
Rich, J., 123, 126, 131
Richardson, S. A., 59, 109, 128, 137, 187, 216, 219
Richman, L. C., 219
Ricketts, R. M., 107
Riedel, R. A., 107-108
Ritter, J. M., 122, 138
Rieser-Danner, L. A., 138
Rivenbark, W. H., 130
Robertson, N. R. E., 198
Robinson, N. M., 151
Rock, I., 6
Rodgers, W. L., 56
Rodin, J., 212

Rogers, P. L., 162
Roggman, L., 138
Roll, S., 173, 180
Ronchi, D., 103-104, 131
Rolls, E. T., 143
Ronald, L., 109, 128, 216
Roopnarine, J. L., 128
Rosen, A. J., 115
Rosenberg, F., 130
Rosenberg, M., 222, 234
Rosenberg, M. J., 210
Rosenthal, R., 162, 209
Ross, M. B., 122
Ross, R. B., 107, 176
Ross-Kossak, P., 145
Rothbart, M., 125
Rottmann, L., 120, 130, 216, 218
Rubenstein, C., 218, 219
Rubin, M., 156-157
Rubinstein, R. P., 138
Rudin, D., 74
Runeson, S., 20, 84
Rusiniak, K. W., 159
Rutter, M., 214
Rutzen, S. R., 221

S

Sabatelli, R., 156-157, 164
Sackett, G., 143
Saegert, S., 115
Safer, M. A., 145
Safier, S. I., 104, 119
Salvia, J., 122, 128-129, 209
Salzbach, R. F., 123
Salzmann, J. A., 226
Samuels, C. A., 138
Samuels, J., 221
Samuels, M. R., 53, 176, 182, 197
Sanderson, S. F., 194
Sappenfield, B. R., 115
Saruwatari, L. R., 131-132
Sassouni, V., 103-104, 110
Saul, B. B. B., 212
Sawin, D. B., 127
Saxe, L., 131
Sazima, M. J., 232
Schaninger, C. M., 112
Schlaer, S., 31
Schneider, W., 160

AUTHOR INDEX

Schon, E., 194
Schopler, J., 125
Schour, I., 60
Schumacher, A., 117
Secord, P. F., 61, 64, 111, 167, 169–170, 174–179, 181–184, 186, 196–198, 222, 232
Segall, M. H., 72, 74, 76, 174, 178–179, 182–183
Seiller-Tarbuk, 179
Seligman, C., 123
Seligman, M. E. P., 143
Sergl, H. G., 198
Serrano, R. A., 195
Shalleck, J., 112, 167
Shapiro, B. A., 12, 45–47, 138, 163
Shaw, R., 6, 12, 18, 20–21, 25, 27–38, 41–47, 54–55, 68–69, 75, 77, 84, 89, 99, 159
Shaw, W. C., 99, 110, 123, 176, 187–189, 192, 194, 196–211, 213–216, 220–221, 231
Shea, J. A., 119–120, 140
Sheare, J. B., 128–129, 209
Shepherd, J. W., xiv, 98, 117, 119
Sherman, S., 137
Shiffrin, R., 160
Shimmin, P. C., 192, 210–211
Shoemaker, D. J., 178
Shore, I. L., 111
Sigall, H., 123–126
Sigman, M., 151
Simmel, M., 20
Simmons, R. G., 130
Simms, T. M., 110
Simonds, J. F., 219
Singer, J. E., 113, 117
Skinner, M., 170, 179
Slakter, M. J., 220, 223–225, 227–229, 231, 235–236
Slaymaker, F. L., 53–54, 76, 110
Slee, P. T., 152
Sloan, V. L., 52
Smith, A. D., 3
Smith, D. W., 51
Smith, E. D., 125
Smith, G. J., 102, 118, 129–131
Smith, J., 110
Smith, L., 194
Smith, N., 98
Smith, P. K., 76
Smith, W. T., 137
Smock, C. D., 52

Snider, W. G., 173, 184
Snyder, M., 65, 86, 119, 125, 172
Soble, S. L., 212
Solomon, M. R., 125
Sontag, S., 82
Sorce, J. F., 153–154
Sorell, G. T., 103
South, D. R., 178
Sparacino, J., 103–104, 120, 131
Sprecher, S., xvii, 97, 103, 114, 120–121, 129, 131–132, 139, 180
Spriesterbach, D. C., 219
Squier, R. W, 169, 172
Starr, C. D., 111
Starr, P., 219
Stein, S., 129
Stenberg, C., 151
Stephan, C. W., 58, 103, 106, 122, 126–128, 133, 135
Stern, M., 135
Sternglanz, S. H., 76
Stevens, J., 189
Stevens, P. S., 45
Stewart, J. E., 125
Stewart, R. E., 111
Stodt, W., 198
Strane, K., 139
Stricker, G., 107, 189, 222, 226
Strickland, L. H., 212
Stritch, T. M., 64, 177
Stroebe, W., 130
Strong, S. R., 156
Stuart, J. L., 103, 128
Styczynski, L. E., 104, 116, 128
Subtelny, J. D., 51, 57, 60
Suedfeld, P., 210
Sugarman, D. B., 105–106
Summers, C. J., 226
Sussman, S., 59, 115
Sutton, P. R. N., 51
Svejda, M., 153–154
Swap, W., 115
Symons, D., 55, 61, 120–121, 129–130, 132, 138–139

T

Takata, G., 123
Tanke, E. D., 65, 86, 119, 172
Taranger, J., 60

AUTHOR INDEX 281

Tavris, C., 132
Taylor, C., 105
Taylor, R. G., 156
Taylor, S. E., 211-212
Tedesco, L. A., 108, 188-189, 198, 220, 223-231, 233-236
Tenenbaum, D. R., 85
Terry, R. L., 109, 113, 173, 184
Thiel, D. L., 124, 216
Thoman, E. B., 151
Thomas, R. G., 105
Thompson, D. W., 7, 12, 24-27, 30, 45
Thompson, G. G., 105
Thompson, V. D., 130
Thornton, G. R., 172, 178, 184
Thurman, B., 76, 182-183
Tiber, N., 233
Tidmarsh, W., 219
Tinbergen, N., 94
Tizard, J., 214
Tobiasen, J. M., 220
Todd, J. T., 12, 20, 27-31, 33-40, 45, 54, 68, 71, 77, 87
Topazian, R. G., 232
Tomkins, S., 148, 176
Tougas, R. R., 52
Tranel, D., 144-145, 159
Trehub, S., 115
Trenholme, I., 56, 106
Trevarthen, C., 145
Trimer, C. A., 123, 151
Trnavsky, P. A., 104
Tronick, E., 151
Tuck, B., 98
Tucker, D. M., 144, 148, 160
Tucker, J. L., 71
Tully, J. C., 126
Turkat, D., 123
Turkewitz, G., 145
Turvey, M. T., 159

U

Udry, J. R., 102, 104-106, 120, 130
Unger, R. K., 177-178
Ungerer, J. A., 151

V

Valentine, C. W., 107, 115

Vallacher, R. R., 136
van der Linden, F. P. G. M., 102, 107, 110, 198
Van Hoesen, G. W., 144-145
Van Parys, M. M., 71
van Lawick-Goodall, J., 90
Vaughn, B. E., 128
Verinis, J. S., 173, 180
Vernikos-Danellis, J., 150
Vietz, P., 143
Vinacke, W. E., 171
Virolainen, K., 235
Vukcevic, D. P., 210

W

Wagatsuma, E., 105, 110
Walden, T. A., 143
Walker, E., 126
Walker-Smith, G. J., 109
Wall, S., 152
Wallace, R. P., 174
Walsh, R. P., 56, 104, 115
Walster, E., 58, 64, 103, 119-122, 130, 137, 139, 197, 204, 209, 216, 218
Waltz, K. J., 220, 224, 227-229
Walz, P. J., 57
Warner, R. M., 105-106
Warr, P. B., 177
Warren, W. H., 21
Waters, E., 152
Watson, M. W., 71
Watts, C., 139
Wegner, D. M., 136
Weiser-Aall, L., 192, 194
Weissmann, S., 176, 191-192
Wellens, R., 109
West, R. A., 232-233
West, S. C., 210
West, S. G., 124
Weston, J. Y., 91
Whitmore, K., 214
Wheeler, K., 18
Wiback, K., 123
Wickler, W., 134
Wiggins, N. H., 185
Williamson, P., 160
Wilson, D. W., 124
Wilson, E. O., 142, 147, 193
Wilson, P. R., 117
Wilson, W., 115
Wingert, C. M., 150
Winograd, E., 3

Wirsing, R., 76, 182–183
Wittemann, J. K., 222
Wolff, E., 103, 106, 132
Wolff, W., 174, 177, 182
Woodson, R., 143
Wright, B. A., 193
Wu, T.H., 231

Y

Yarbus, A. L., 109, 177
Yarmey, A. D., 98
Yarnold, P. R., 59

Young, A., *xiv*
Young, R. D., 137

Z

Zajonc, R. B., 115, 159
Zakin, D. F., 128
Zalenski, C. M., 61, 82
Zebrowitz-McArthur, L. (see McArthur, L. Z.)
Zivin, G., 143, 146
Zuckerman, M., 128
Zuk, M., 121

Subject Index

A

Affordances, 66-68, 70-74, 78-79, 83-84, 86-87, 143, 148
Age differences in face perception, 3, 234-235
Aging, *see* Facial growth and aging
Automatic processes, 6, 90, 95, 139-140, 193

B

Beards, *see* Hair
Biomorphicity, 45-47
Birthmarks, 195-196, 199-201, 210-212

C

Child abuse, 74, 85, 91-92, 94, 151
Chin, 66, 71-75, 79, 81-83, 87, 178, 180, 183, 199-201, 232
Cleft lip, *see* Lips
Coordinate transformation systems, 22-25

D, E

Dental development, 60
Ecological psychology, *v-vi*, *xiii-xiv*, 5-6, 13-16, 18-21, 26, 48-49, 65-67, 83-84, 86, 98-99, 136, 142, 147-148, 159-160, 162, 164, 175, 184
Ears, 51, 77, 203
Empathy, 161-164

Eye movements, 109, 177
Eyebrows, 51, 57, 66, 75-76, 79-83, 87, 114, 181-182, 184
Eyeglasses, 109, 113, 173, 181, 183-184, 203
Eyes, 51-53, 57-58, 66-67, 75-76, 78-83, 87, 109-111, 114, 117, 178, 181-182, 197, 203
Event perception, 4, 12, 18-21, 85
 dynamic versus static displays, 3-4, 84-86, 93, 104, 140, 175, 186
 segmentation technique, 163
 slow versus fast events, 20-21

F

Face recognition, *xiv*, 3, 98, 105, 119, *see also* Prosopagnosia
Facial aesthetics, *see* Facial attractiveness, Facial cuteness
Facial anomalies, *xvii*, 112, 121, 127, 187-189, 191-237
 evaluation of, 132, 187, 204-209, 217-232, 234
 facial expressions and, 192-193
 folklore and, 194-196, 200-201
 incidence, 222
 peer relations, 201-204, 214
 physiognomy and, 169, 176, 186, 189, 196-198, 201, 205-210, 221
 self-perceptions of, 217-218, 222-226, 229-232, 235-236

social significance, 17–18, 102, 121, 187–189, 191–222, 237
treatment of, *see* Treatment
Facial attractiveness, *xv–xvii*, 3, 77, 79–83, 98, 101–133, 136–140, 183–184, 218–219
  adverse effects of, 116, 124–126, 131–132, 216
  determinants of, 53, 60, 65, 76, 108–118, 184, 220–236, *see also* Eyes, Facial aging, Sex differences
    dental, 60, 110–111, 197–198, 204–210, 213, 215, 220–233, 235
    genetic, 136–139, 193, 218
  effects of growth and aging, 17, 51–62
  evaluation of, 103–108, 218–220, 226–229, 235, *see also* Facial anomalies
    age differences in, 104–106, 234
    by cephalometric standards, 107–108, 198
    by mathematical standards, 106–108
    Dental Facial Attractiveness Scale, 108, 224–229, 231
  facial expressions and, 108, 115, 128, 156–157
  peer relations and, 116, 118, 128–130, 229, 234, *see also* Facial anomalies
  physiognomy and, 116, 123–124, 177–178, 196–197, 206, 208–210
  self-perception, 109, 113, 116, 214, 224–226, 229, 232, 234–236
  social significance, 64–65, 98, 102, 118–133, 136, 139, 204, 208–210, 214–216, 218–219, 237
  universal standards, 112, 138
  versus bodily attractiveness, 102–103, 118, 132
Facial babyishness, 78–87, 134–135, 174, 178
Facial cosmetics (make-up), 2, 112–115, 131, 182–184, 193, 201
Facial cuteness, 52–55, 76–77, 115, 127, 133–136, *see also* Facial attractiveness, Facial growth and aging
  versus facial attractiveness, 102, 133
Facial growth and aging, 11–12, 17, 19–21, 25–26, 51, 89–90, 183, *see also* Facial attractiveness, Facial cuteness
  perception of, 11–12, 19–20, 30–48
Facial expressions, *xiii*, 73, 97–98, 134–135, 142–144, 147–158, 161–164, 176, 192, *see also* Facial attractiveness, Facial anomalies, Facial feedback hypothesis, Nonverbal sensitivity, Physiognomy
Facial features, 2, 71–74, 77, 133, 177–179, *see also* Eyes, Lips, Nose, Teeth, etc.
Facial feedback hypothesis, 155

Familial influences on face perception, 223, 235–236
Familiarity effects, 104, 111, 115–116, 134–135
Forehead, 51–54, 66–67, 71–74, 92–94, 106, 110, 181

G

Gibsonian theory, *see* Ecological psychology
Golden proportions, 106–107

H

Hair, 60, 67, 106, 109, 113–114, 117, 178–181, 183, 193, 203, 221
Homosexuals, 130

K, I

Kindchenschema, 52–55, 74, 90, 92, 127, 134–135
Identi-Kit, 57, 72, 74, 111, 114, 126, 178
Illusory correlation, 86
Implicit personality theory, 119, 136
Information and specification, 5–6, 41

L, M

Lips, 51, 57, 67, 111, 117, 170, 182–184, 193, 203
Cleft lip, 176, 192, 194–195, 199–201, 219
Mental health, 131, 137, 187–188, 193, 214
Methodological problems, 2–4, 84, 175, 185, 216
Morphogenesis, 12, 24–26

N

Natural constraints, 48
  on events, 12
  on growth, 26–28, 34–35
  on perception, 13–16, 27
Neurological mechanisms, 143–145, 149–150, 160–161
Nonhuman faces, 42–44, 54, 169–170
Nonverbal sensitivity, 143, 147, 158, 161–164
Nose, 51, 67, 77, 83, 106, 109, 176, 182, 203

O

Obesity, 58–59, 219
Occlusion, *see* Facial anomalies, Teeth
Orthodontics, *see* Treatment

P

Parent–offspring relations, 52, 90, 105, 126–127, 150–155, 235–236
Perception of age, *xiii*, 1, 5–8, 41–42, 53–55, 67–80, 84–87, 94–95, 110, 178 *see also* Facial growth
  social effects of, 68–76, 85–87, 79–83, 89–94, *see also* Facial attractiveness, Facial babyishness, Facial cuteness
  transformations and, 30–33, 35–47, 68–69, 71
Perceptual constancy, 98–99
Physiognomy, 63–66, 68–77, 79–81, 83, 99, 117, 167–186, *see also* Facial anomalies, Facial babyishness
  belief in, 63, 168, 171–174, 197
  criminality, 172, 178–179
  facial expression and, 168–171, 174, 176–177, 183, 197
  reliability, 170, 173–186
  theories of, 65–67, 168–171, 185
  validity, 168–173, 176, 185–186, 197–198
Plastic surgery, *see* Treatment
Point-light displays, 20, 84–85
Pre-term infants, 53–54, 115, 151–152, 155
Primacy of affective responses, 98, 144, 158–160
Prosopagnosia, 144–145
Prosthodontics, 233, *see also* Treatment
Puberty, 37, 234

R, S

Racial differences, 105–107, 109, 112, 114, 229
Scale of analysis, 12, 26–30
Self-fulfilling prophecy, 65, 119, 172, 199, 209

Sex differences, 98, 121, 129–133, 145, 147, 157, 162–163, 173, 176, 180, 186, 188, 209–210
  in criteria for facial attractiveness, 61, 81–83, 108, 110–111, 114, 117, 131
  in facial aging effects, 60, 81–83, 129, 132
  in facial appearance, 60, 82–83, 181–182
  in facial attractiveness effects, 126, 129–133
  in judgments of facial attractiveness, 61, 102, 105–107, 117, 229
Sexual attraction, 61, 69–70, 82, 103, 119–121, 130, 192–193
Social referencing, 153–155
Sociobiology, 61, 120–121, 127, 129–130, 132–133, 137–139, 175
Symmetry, 111–112, 170, 177, 199–201, 233
Szondi test, 99

T

Teeth, 107, 138, 202–211, 213, 215, 220–233
Transformations, 27–47, 54, *see also* Perception of age
Treatment, 17, 131, 188, 199–201, 217–218
  evaluation of, 58, 189, 212, 226, 232–234, 236–237
  motivation for, 188–189, 192, 217, 222–225, 229, 231–232, 235–236
  psychological effects, 182, 189, 204, 216, 221–222, 232–234
  Treatment Priority Index, 223–227, 231, 236

U

Upside down faces, 5

W

Wrinkles, 76–77, 114